Heritage, Screen and Literary Tourism

MIX
Paper from
responsible sources
FSC
www.fsc.org
FSC® C014540

ASPECTS OF TOURISM

Series Editors: Chris Cooper, *Oxford Brookes University, UK*, C. Michael Hall, *University of Canterbury, New Zealand* and Dallen J. Timothy, *Arizona State University, USA*

Aspects of Tourism is an innovative, multifaceted series, which comprises authoritative reference handbooks on global tourism regions, research volumes, texts and monographs. It is designed to provide readers with the latest thinking on tourism worldwide and in so doing will push back the frontiers of tourism knowledge. The series also introduces a new generation of international tourism authors writing on leading-edge topics.

The volumes are authoritative, readable and user friendly, providing accessible sources for further research. Books in the series are commissioned to probe the relationship between tourism and cognate subject areas such as strategy, development, retailing, sport and environmental studies. The publisher and series editors welcome proposals from writers with projects on the above topics.

Full details of all the books in this series and of all our other publications can be found on http://www.channelviewpublications.com, or by writing to Channel View Publications, St Nicholas House, 31–34 High Street, Bristol BS1 2AW, UK.

ASPECTS OF TOURISM: 80

Heritage, Screen and Literary Tourism

Sheela Agarwal and Gareth Shaw

CHANNEL VIEW PUBLICATIONS
Bristol • Blue Ridge Summit

DOI 10.21832/AGARWA6249

Library of Congress Cataloging in Publication Data
A catalog record for this book is available from the Library of Congress.
Library of Congress Control Number: 2017046313

British Library Cataloguing in Publication Data
A catalogue entry for this book is available from the British Library.

ISBN-13: 978-1-84541-624-9 (hbk)
ISBN-13: 978-1-84541-623-2 (pbk)

Channel View Publications
UK: St Nicholas House, 31–34 High Street, Bristol BS1 2AW, UK.
USA: NBN, Blue Ridge Summit, PA, USA.

Website: www.channelviewpublications.com
Twitter: Channel_View
Facebook: https://www.facebook.com/channelviewpublications
Blog: www.channelviewpublications.wordpress.com

The policy of Multilingual Matters/Channel View Publications is to use papers that are natural, renewable and recyclable products, made from wood grown in sustainable forests. In the manufacturing process of our books, and to further support our policy, preference is given to printers that have FSC and PEFC Chain of Custody certification. The FSC and/or PEFC logos will appear on those books where full certification has been granted to the printer concerned.

Typeset by Nova Techset Private Limited, Bengaluru and Chennai, India.
Printed and bound in the UK by Short Run Press Ltd.
Printed and bound in the US by Edwards Brothers Malloy, Inc.

Contents

Illustrative Materials

Tables

Figures

Plates

Case Studies

Text Boxes

Preface and Acknowledgements

It is only relatively recently that service-dominant logic (S-DL) and value co-creation have featured in tourism research, and such concepts are serving to re-shape understanding of how contemporary tourist-related interactions, experiences and value are constructed. This book originates from the recognition that such concepts have rarely been used to examine heritage, screen and literary tourism (HSLT), and yet their adoption enables a more critical perspective to be achieved of the demand and supply of HSLT and of how such tourist experiences are created, produced and shaped. In addition, a text which considers heritage, screen and literary tourism together is non-existent, which is surprising given that screen and literary tourism are widely considered to be facets of heritage tourism. The origins of this book consequently stem from such realisations, and in an attempt to inject an alternative critical perspective into the heritage, screen and literary tourism discourses, this text draws on theorisations provided by S-DL and co-creation to consider this global phenomenon.

There are a great many people who helped with the writing and production of the book and to whom we are greatly indebted. We would like to thank Dr Graham Busby, Dr Charlie Mansfield, Dr Steve Butts and Professor Paul Brunt, all of whom provided inspiration in one way or another. Great thanks are due to Sarah Holloway, Graham Busby, Pip Borton, Katy Burton, Jonathan White and Natalie Marchant for providing me with copyright-free photographs to include throughout this book. Lastly, much gratitude must go to Channel View and particularly to Professor Chris Cooper.

Sheela Agarwal
Plymouth University

Gareth Shaw
University of Exeter

The Authors

Sheela Agarwal is a Professor in Tourism Management at Plymouth University's Faculty of Business (School of Tourism and Hospitality, Drakes Circus, Plymouth PL4 8AA, UK; Email: sagarwal@plymouth.ac.uk). Since completing doctoral research on the restructuring of English coastal resorts, in 1995, she has written and co-authored numerous journal articles and book chapters relating to various social and economic aspects of coastal tourism. Her research interests include heritage, screen and literary tourism, disability, migration and social exclusion, crime prevention and persuasion and conceptualisations of place and space.

Gareth Shaw is a Professor of Retail and Tourism Management in the Department of Management at the University of Exeter (Email: g.shaw@ exeter.ac.uk). He has published numerous papers on tourism and co-authored or co-edited the following books including: *The Rise and Fall of British Coastal Resorts* (Cassell, 1997); *Tourism and Economic Development* (3rd edn, Wiley, 1998); *Critical Issues in Tourism* (2nd edn, Blackwell, 2002); and *Tourism and Tourism Spaces* (Sage, 2004). His research interests include tourism and entrepreneurship and small firms, tourism and innovation, and tourism, disability and social exclusion.

1 Heritage Tourism: Exploring the Screen and Literary Nexus

Introduction

> Understanding our past determines actively our ability to understand the present. So, how do we sift the truth from belief? How do we write our own histories, personally or culturally, and thereby define ourselves? How do we penetrate years, centuries of historical distortion, to find original truth? Tonight this will be our quest. (Robert Langdon, *Da Vinci Code*, 2006)

Symbologist, Robert Langdon, lead character of the novel (2003) and later cinematic production (2006) of Dan Brown's *Da Vinci Code*, a detective thriller steeped in history, myth and romance, was referring to the cryptic mystery that lay ahead of him. Accidentally, however, captured by his profane statement, is the essence of the nexus that binds together heritage, literary and screen tourism (HSLT); it contains the existence of a storyline underpinned by the co-creation of memory, history and heritage, conveyed through literary and screen mechanisms, which despite being subject to intense criticism for its inaccurate portrayal of history, has stimulated tourism to Paris and to a range of heritage attractions featured, including the Rosslyn Chapel in Scotland (Martin-Jones, 2014). The *Da Vinci Code*, of course, is not an isolated example of such a nexus; most countries have tapped into such demand and are fully exploiting the selling and retelling of the past, as well as using screen and literary links to attract tourists. For example, tours are offered to the film locations of *Captain Corelli's Mandolin* (Kefalonia) and *The Lord of the Rings* (New Zealand). The 'English Riviera' (southwest England), the birthplace and home of Dame Agatha Christie, and various locations around London including Baker Street and the Docklands which provide the setting for Sir Arthur Conan Doyle's 'Sherlock Holmes' mysteries, are marketed to visitors who are keen to discover the many places featured in these two famous crime writers' books and their subsequent film and TV productions.

Not surprisingly, HSLT is of huge economic, social and political significance to many tourist destinations, reflecting the rapid growth of special interest travel since the 1990s. Indeed, during this decade heritage was one of the most significant and fastest growing components of tourism (Aluza *et al.*, 1998; Herbert, 1995), accounting for almost 40% of all international trips undertaken (UNTWO, 2004). More recently, heritage and culture have become closely integrated with other tourism sectors (UNTWO, 2014a) such as screen and literature, reflecting the diverse ways in which tourism is being produced and consumed by tourists (Richards, 2014). Despite this, few books have been published that focus on heritage tourism per se but that also incorporate detailed analysis of its interconnections between two overlapping but distinctive forms of tourism, namely screen and literary tourism. Such an oversight is remarkable given that HSLT has been an important leisure activity and area of scholarly research since the 1990s (Beeton, 2005; Prentice, 2001; Timothy & Boyd, 2003). Moreover, a multidimensional nexus exists between these three forms of tourism based upon a number of commonalities (Figure 1.1). First, they share many characteristics, such as their cultural relevance and association with cultural tourism, their historical and/or contemporary links, their connection with real and/or fictional events, places or people, and their influence on the negotiation of identities.

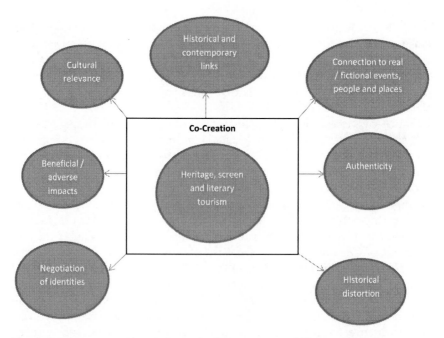

Figure 1.1 Interconnections between heritage, screen and literary tourism
Source: The authors (2017).

Secondly, while experiences now lie firmly at the heart of the tourism industry, because HSLT often requires tourists' involvement in the consumption of reconstructions of aspects of the past and present, fictional and real worlds, arguably service-dominant logic (S-DL) is particularly relevant to all three, as the tourist inevitably plays a critical role in the co-creation of the experience. Thirdly, given the role of the tourist in shaping the experience, HSLT commonly exhibit a host of similar management, marketing and development issues including, for example, authenticity and historical distortion, interpretation, and beneficial and adverse visitor impacts. It is the existence of this nexus which situates screen and literary tourism within the broader context of heritage tourism (Martin-Jones, 2014; Sakellari, 2014), and which necessitates detailed examination within a single text.

Thus, this book addresses the relative lack of publications which examine HSLT together, by providing a comprehensive understanding and evaluation of these three forms of tourism in the context of global tourism development. In particular, it aims to:

(a) enhance knowledge of the relationships between HSLT;
(b) analyse the demand and supply of HSLT;
(c) critically review the development, marketing and management of HSLT in global settings;
(d) comprehensively examine the main issues and concepts relating to HSLT; and
(e) ascertain the future implications of the main issues affecting HSLT.

It begins with this introductory chapter which sets the context for the book, detailing and justifying its theoretical underpinning and the major themes that are discussed. The meaning and nature of HSLT will be examined and their associated products detailed. Then the HSLT nexus will be analysed and the relationships between these three distinct but overlapping forms of tourism will be considered. Arising from this nexus are a number of challenges which relate to the role of the consumer in the co-creation of the tourist experience, and the implications this has for the development, marketing, interpretation, consumption and the planning and management of HSLT.

The Meaning and Nature of Heritage, Screen and Literary Tourism

Defining concepts is never an easy task and providing individual definitions of HSLT is no exception, primarily because their meaning and nature has been widely debated (Garrod & Fyall, 2001; Hewison, 1987; Nuryanti, 1996; Poria *et al.*, 2001; Prentice, 2001; Timothy & Boyd, 2003), as is evident in the following discussion.

Heritage tourism

Much of the difficulty surrounding the definition of heritage tourism stems from controversy linked to exactly what constitutes heritage, and thus a multitude of definitions have been proposed. For example, according to Ashworth and Tunbridge (1996: 105), heritage is 'the contemporary use of the past ... the interpretation of the past in history'. Meanwhile, heritage may be considered to consist of those aspects of the past which people today value; heritage resources may have intrinsic qualities such as age, but the value placed on them depends on the people who use them (Prentice, 1993; Timothy & Boyd, 2003). While it appears that most researchers accept that heritage is linked to the past and that it represents some sort of inheritance which is passed down to current and future generations, both in terms of cultural traditions and physical artefacts (Nuryanti, 1996; Timothy & Boyd, 2003), since not all heritage is kept, it thereby relates to those elements of the past a society wishes to keep. Such a view infers that heritage is selective, as society does not value all heritage and instead it is filtered through a value system which changes over time and space and across societies (Timothy & Boyd, 2003). This changing value attachment to heritage is illustrated by the example of the American Wilderness. Prior to the 18th century this environment was viewed as a dangerous, reviled place, but since the romanticisation of nature in the 18th century, this and other similar landscapes are now appreciated for their intrinsic beauty (Shaw & Williams, 1994).

However, in addition to heritage being subject to selectivity, different views exist about the meaning of heritage as it has been applied to two different types of phenomenon. According to Timothy and Boyd (2003), the first relates to heritage being classified as tangible immovable resources (e.g. buildings, rivers and natural areas), tangible movable resources (e.g. objects in museums or documents in archives), or intangible resources, such as values, customs, ceremonies and lifestyles, including experiences such as festivals, arts and cultural events. Meanwhile, the second phenomenon, in Timothy and Boyd's (2003) view, is associated with heritage being classified according to the type of attraction. They cite some examples, including natural heritage, which is usually associated with protected areas like national parks, living cultural heritage, built heritage, industrial heritage, personal heritage, aspects of regions that have value and significance to individuals or groups of people, and dark heritage (places of atrocity and symbols of death and pain).

Another reason for disagreement about the meaning of heritage is because erroneous associations are often made between history, heritage and culture; in particular, heritage is often equated with history (Timothy & Boyd, 2003). The latter, however, is the recording of the past as precisely as possible in so far as it can be accurate given present-day limitations of knowledge. In contrast, although heritage is part of the past too, it includes a range of past and present aspects of society such as language, culture, identity and locality.

Moreover, history is a scholarly activity which produces knowledge about the past, whereas heritage is a means of consuming that knowledge. Thus, history is what historians regard as worth recording, whereas heritage is what contemporary society chooses to inherit and pass on. In the case of the association between heritage and culture, common misconceptions about their interchangeable use occur because there is an obvious link in that heritage is part of past and present cultural landscapes. The association between culture and heritage is clearly evident in how Tahana and Oppermann (1998: 23) defined cultural attractions as ranging from 'historical monuments to handicrafts or artefacts, from festivals to music and dance presentations, and from the bustling street life of a different culture to the distinct lifestyle of indigenous people'. According to Timothy and Boyd (2003: 5), what has clearly emerged is an expansion of the term 'heritage' to apply not only to historic, natural and built environments, but also to the many dimensions of 'material culture, intellectual inheritances and cultural identities'. In sum, what exists is a heritage spectrum which embraces ancient monuments, the built environment, aspects of the natural environment and many aspects of living culture and the arts (Timothy & Boyd, 2003).

Different views also exist about the meaning and nature of heritage because it is inextricably linked to the context in which it occurs. For instance, according to Timothy and Boyd (2003: 6):

> from a northern European perspective, heritage is not heritage unless it involves a visit to urban places, often the historical cores of old cities. In contrast, in North America, heritage is strongly linked to visiting natural places, particularly national parks but also the cultures of First Peoples, attractions such as museums and galleries in urban environments, festivals in both rural and urban settings, and those special celebrations that highlight national identity. While the natural component of places is important to Australians and New Zealanders, heritage is also linked to the uniqueness of the culture, people (Aborigine, Maori, European settlers) and their identity that coexist within natural places and the built environment.

Given the range of meanings attached to heritage, it therefore comes as no surprise that different views also exist about the meaning of heritage tourism (Ashworth & Larkham, 1994; Garrod & Fyall, 2001; Nuryanti, 1996; Richards, 1996). With this in mind, an alternative approach to clarifying heritage tourism has been offered by Poria et al. (2001), who suggest that heritage tourism is a phenomenon based on tourists' motivation and perceptions rather than on specific site attributes. Poria et al. (2001: 1048) thus identify three types of heritage tourists: '(1) those visiting a site they deem to be part of their heritage; (2) those visiting what they consider as a heritage site although it is unconnected with their own; and (3) those visiting a heritage site specifically classified as a heritage place although unaware of this designation'. On this basis, they define heritage tourism as 'a sub-group of tourism, in which the main motivation for visiting a site is based on the place's heritage characteristics according to the tourists' perception of their own heritage' (Poria *et al.*, 2003: 247–248).

Thus, in an attempt to simplify the complexity of aspects that encompass heritage, a diverse range of definitions of heritage tourism have been proposed. Generally, however, these definitions tend to be polarised around two contrasting approaches, which Apostolakis (2003) describes first as descriptive and second as experiential. With regard to the former, this approach focuses on defining the material components of culture and heritage such as attractions, objects of art, artefacts and relics, as well as more intangible forms of culture and heritage such as traditions, languages and folklore. Often there is also recognition of the difference between primary and secondary elements of heritage tourism activity. In terms of the latter, this approach is based on experiences derived from the consumption of heritage resources and focuses on tourists' decisions to visit a particular destination, on the significance of the individual's experiences and perceptions of the destination (Apostolakis, 2003). By contrast, much neater definitions of screen and literary tourism exist.

Screen tourism

Screen tourism is a generic term that is adopted to describe 'a form of tourism that is generated by TV programmes, video, DVD as well as film that involves big and small screen productions (but not TV programmes designed primarily to promote tourist destinations, such as holiday shows)' (Connell & Meyer, 2009: 194). Film and TV scenes and images have the potential to be long-lasting, creating an enduring and alluring destination product or experience (Beeton, 2005, 2015, 2016), and it is in the specific context of historic screen productions that have generated visits to historic sites where perhaps the closest association between this form of tourism and heritage tourism lies. The novelist and film screenwriter George MacDonald Fraser in his popular Hollywood history of the world (1988) argued that film was a powerful medium for shaping tourists' views of history. Moreover, the historian Rosenstone (1995: 72) argued that well-made historical films can be effective in generating 'new ways of visioning the past', and of increasing the viewers' understanding and appreciation of history.

Frost (2006) cites several examples of period films and screen productions that have induced tourism, including visitation to Rome (particularly the Coliseum) arising from *Gladiator*, visits to battlefield sites stimulated by the film *Gettysburg*, and visits to castles, historic homes and landscapes encouraged by the films *Braveheart* and *A Knight's Tale* and by the film and TV productions of Jane Austen's novel *Pride and Prejudice*. With respect to the latter, Lyme Park, a Palladian mansion surrounded by 1300 acres of deer park, is one of the must-see attractions on any TV/film tour of the north of

England, location for Pemberley in the BBC's 1995 adaptation starring Colin Firth as Mr Darcy and Jennifer Ehle as Miss Elizabeth Bennet. The Pemberley Trail through Lyme Park takes in every scene filmed there for *Pride and Prejudice*, including the bridge where Elizabeth first glimpses Pemberley, the courtyard and garden, and the pool where Darcy dives in to cool off. In 2005 this film was remade for the big screen and featured several Derbyshire historic homes including Belton House, Burghley House, Haddon Hall and Chatsworth House, which now form part of this film tourism trail (Visit Peak District and Derbyshire, 2014). Additionally, several Chinese destinations that have appeared in popular period films and TV shows are now marketed to domestic and international tourists. For instance, tours are offered around Beijing's Forbidden City where *The Last Emperor* was filmed, and to Jiuzhaigou National Park (Sichuan Province), the location of some scenes in *Hero*, a film which tells the story of Jing Ke's assassination attempt on the Emperor of the Qin dynasty in 227 BC (China Highlights, 2015).

However, it is not just period films and dramas that have stimulated tourism. Often it is the interplay between key elements of heritage, such as landscape qualities and features, and the extent to which locations are significant in filming, combined with storylines and characters that induce tourism (Beeton, 2016; Connell & Meyer, 2009). As a result, screen-induced tourism is most likely to occur where locations are conveyed from film to reality, and where there are powerful associations between landscape, place and emotions (Beeton, 2015; Escher & Zimmerman, 2001; Olsberg SPI, 2007). This is particularly well evidenced by J.K. Rowling's *Harry Potter* blockbuster films, in which movie magic transformed Gloucester Cathedral's famous fan-vaulted cloisters into the interior of Hogwarts School of Witchcraft and Wizardry and has worked miracles on Gloucester's tourism industry (BBC, 2005). Other locations in the film to have benefited from increased visitation are Alnwick Castle (Northumberland, UK), which is used as a stand-in for the exterior and interior of Hogwarts in the Harry Potter films (although the wide-angle images are computer generated) and has experienced a 120% increase in visits since the films were released, and the Bodleian Library located at Oxford University. This site doubled as the Hogwarts Library in *Harry Potter and the Philosopher's Stone*, and is especially noteworthy for the scene in which Harry hides under the invisibility cloak as he searches for information on Nicolas Flamel. The films have also encouraged visits to King's Cross Station (Plate 1.1) and the Glenfinnan Viaduct (Scotland). These are the real-life 'sets' used for many scenes featuring the 'Hogwarts Express'; modern-day muggle passengers are able to take a scenic trip on the train that was featured in the Harry Potter films to Goathland station, which became 'Hogsmeade' where eager students arrive at the school on the Hogwarts Express.

This powerful interplay between the significance of heritage locations in film combined with storylines and characters in stimulating visitation is reinforced by Beeton (2016), and is further illustrated by many examples of the use

Plate 1.1 Platform 9¾ at King's Cross Station, London
Source: The authors (2017).

of substitute locations in filming that still resulted in the stimulation of tourism in the places that were intended to be portrayed. One such notable occurrence is the film *Braveheart* (1995), which caused a tourism boom in Scotland due to its depiction of William Wallace and the fight for Scottish Independence, even though it was filmed mostly in Ireland. In this instance, 'a destination is socially constructed by the film-makers' (Connell & Meyer, 2009: 195), and tourists are not attracted to experience the reality of the place but, in Schofield's (1996) view, to co-create personal meaning from the emotions experienced and from the story and setting consumed, even if the boundaries between reality and fantasy are blurred. However, such a phenomenon is not only a central feature of screen tourism as it is also particularly relevant to literary tourism.

Literary tourism

Literary tourism involves travel or movement to a destination due to an interest in some form of literary association with that destination (Robinson & Andersen, 2002). As a consequence, it is closely related to heritage tourism since it results from interest in the personal life histories of writers or in their works of literature which are more often than not set in a historical context. Several such associations may attract tourists, including the connection of a place and/or destination with an author's work. In this instance, the area has become a tourist destination because the author has used it as a background or setting for a novel, and tourists want to visit places or buildings of significance in these novels. This can be illustrated by the examples such as: Verona (Italy), setting of Shakespeare's *Romeo and Juliet*, where tourists can visit Juliet's balcony at Casa di Giulietta or her tomb in the vaults of the San Francesco Monastery; Long Island's north shoreline near New York (USA), which provided the inspiration for Scott Fitzgerald's (1925) novel *The Great Gatsby*; or Brontë country (UK), where many of the buildings and much of the countryside in the novels, most notably *Wuthering Heights*, have strong links with a number of villages and the countryside in the West Yorkshire moors.

The association of a place through the works of an author where a favourable image has been established may attract visitors. Indeed the ability of writers to change prevailing attitudes toward scenery, wilderness and natural beauty by transforming actual landscapes into literary landscapes through imagination and emotion cannot be overstated. Such actions are perhaps best illustrated by the influence of English Romanticism and Wordsworth's works. These drew attention to the intrinsic beauty and spiritual qualities of nature, changing the traditional negative perceptions of nature in the Western world embodied in the writings of Daniel Defoe who, for example, in 1724 described Wales as a country 'full of horror'. In particular, the English Lake District has been noted by several writers to have become a significant destination because of the writings of the Lake poets such as Wordsworth, Coleridge and Southey, all of whom produced more appealing images of the region (Newby, 1981; Squire, 1988). Similarly, Sir Walter Scott created the current image of Scotland and transformed a reviled, distrusted and dangerous land and its people into a romantic scenic playground. Meanwhile, Tennyson, Burns and Dickens all visited parts of the Highlands, and their writings have added further respectability to the area. Moreover, in addition to shaping and changing landscape tastes, romantic literature affected 'tourist styles' by enthusing tourists to visit and experience literary landscapes. Newby (1981) contends that Wordsworth not only helped to create the intellectual climate for a new type of tourism, but also identified the specific locations that tourists should visit through first the descriptions of places in his work and, secondly, by the authorship of one of the most popular 19th century guidebooks.

Furthermore, literary tourism stems not only from the writings of fiction, but also from the desire to see aspects of the author's real life. The visit usually allows contact with places closely associated with the admired individuals, and it allows the sight of and perhaps the chance to touch artefacts or memorabilia. Generally the setting enhances experiential quality (Herbert, 1996). Thus, readers become 'pilgrims who visit a birthplace and imagine an author's childhood, who contemplate the places that inspired poems or books and who pay homage at a graveside or public memorial' (Herbert, 1996: 79). For example, both Chawton House, home to Jane Austen, and Dove Cottage, home to William Wordsworth, have become major tourist attractions. However, they are also attractive to people because they have connections with the works they have created, and visitation is induced in a quest to find the actual place upon which fictional locales are modelled (Herbert, 1996).

There is a merging with the real and the imagined which gives such places a special meaning. For example, in Brontë country and in Catherine Cookson country, visitors are encouraged to encounter the worlds of the writers and of their novels. According to Pocock (1982), a sense of place in a work of literature plays a major part in enhancing the appreciation of novels, can add knowledge about a particular region, and has the power to promote or even initiate a tourist destination.

Another reason for the attractiveness of literary tourist destinations is that these places often evoke distant memories. For example, Squire (1994) studied the reactions of visitors to Hill Top Farm in the Lake District, the home of the writer Beatrix Potter. She found that for many, the visit evoked meanings and emotions which were less concerned with the writer and the content of her *Peter Rabbit* stories, and more with the nostalgic memories of childhood and family bonds, together with Englishness, rurality and former lifestyles. The place acted as a medium through which a range of cultural meanings and values are communicated (Herbert, 1996). Moreover, a final attraction for tourists may be the place itself. Such places are commonly very attractive settings which even without the literary connections might draw visitors; the duality of the general and specific attraction has to be recognised. In short, given the attractiveness of HSLT, it is not surprising that all three have become important niche markets of the modern tourism industry.

The Growth of Heritage, Screen and Literary Tourism

Heritage and literary tourism are not new forms of tourism, having existed for centuries. The Grand Tour is a well-documented form of heritage tourism which flourished throughout the 17th and 18th centuries, and which formed an integral component of the education of young aristocrats. It consisted of visits to cultural centres such as Paris, Venice, Rome and Naples and involved viewing classical antiquities, works of art and architecture, picturesque landscapes, gardens and natural curiosities, as well as mixing with fashionable society on their travels (Towner, 1996). Meanwhile, literary tourism flourished throughout Britain in the late 19th century as dedicated scholars were prepared to travel long distances to experience places linked with writers of prose, drama or poetry (Herbert, 2001). With the rapid growth of printing internationally in the 19th century, British women writers in particular were increasingly defined as literary icons and their homes became popular attractions for an increasing number of British and American visitors. Literary pilgrims from around the world placed a literary significance on the British landscape which publishers, transport operators and the tourism industry exploited. Portable memoirs, guidebooks, periodicals, postcards and maps were printed and disseminated to an increasingly literate and mobile reading public. Both heritage and literary tourists in this sense were well educated, versed in classics and equipped with the cultural capital enabling them to appreciate and understand this form of heritage. For Bourdieu (1984) such people belonged to the 'dominant classes', with tastes and preferences that served as markers of their social position and with patterns of consumption that set them apart.

However, HSLT as we know them today are a more modern global phenomenon, having experienced a transformation in their production and consumption (Apostolakis, 2003), emerging as 'new tourism' (Poon, 1993) niche products in the last 30 years (see Case Study 1.1). These changes reflect the shift from Fordism to post-Fordist forms of production (Ioannides & Debbage, 1997), which created the need to capture the 'increasingly complex and diverse needs of demand' (Fayos-Sola, 1996: 406). Consequently, although there has been a long tradition of the co-existence of heritage activity and tourism (Jolliffe & Smith, 2001), a greater convergence between the two occurred as HSLT attractions were developed in an attempt to satisfy the ensuing 'super-segmentation' (Fayos-Sola, 1996: 406) of demand for unique experiences. According to Apostolakis (2003: 796), 'the unique and at the same time collective nature of heritage [and screen and literary] resources meant that such attractions have developed into a "special" niche in the industry'. They are a contemporary commodity, purposefully created to satisfy contemporary consumption, which has contributed to the development of a diverse landscape of postmodern attractions. According to Urry (1990: 93–94), 'Indeed the way in which all sorts of places have become centres of spectacle and display, and the nostalgic attraction of "heritage", [screen and literary tourism] can both be seen as elements of the postmodern'.

Case Study 1.1 Growth of heritage tourism in Mexico

The tourism industry in Mexico is highly significant. Mexico is the number one destination for foreign tourists within the Latin American region and number two destination in the Americas, ranking worldwide in tenth place in terms of international tourist arrivals, with more than 29.1 million visitors in 2014 (UNTWO, 2014b). Although the appeal for many tourists is traditionally the beach resorts of Cancun, Ixtapa, Playa del Carmen, Cabon San Lucas and Acapulco, for example, Mexico's heritage attractions are attracting increasing attention. This is notably evident in Mexico City which is currently experiencing a marked increase in tourist visitation. Mexico City received 10.4 million tourists in 2009 of which 2.4 million were foreign and the rest were from other parts of Mexico (eTurboNews, 2009) while in 2016, it is expected that it will host approximately

29.6 million domestic and international visitors (Tourism-Review.com, 2017).

Founded in 1325, Mexico City is the oldest city in the Americas and was the capital of the Aztec Empire. It boasts a wealth of heritage attractions and its historic centre is a UNESCO World Heritage Site. Built in the 16th century by the Spanish on the ruins of Tenochtitlan, the old Aztec capital, the city has five Aztec temples, such as the Pyramid of the Sun and the Pyramid of the Moon. The Pyramid of the Sun is the largest building in Teotihuacán, a metropolis built between 150 BC and AD 500, while the Pyramid of the Moon is the second largest. Other attractions of Mexico City include the murals of Diego Rivera, the paintings of Frida Kahlo, the Plaza de Toros México (the world's largest bullring), the Mexican National Palace built on the site of Montezuma's palace, the huge Metropolitan Cathedral, the largest in the western hemisphere, and one of the finest museums in the world, the National Museum of Anthropology and History. Connecting the 21st century to the city's vibrant past are local dancers and drummers who perform at El Zócalo, one of the largest public plazas in the world. Clearly, Mexico City is rich in a diverse range of tangible and intangible heritage resources.

However, there exist many other heritage attractions across Mexico. For example, the central and southern parts of Mexico host several pre-Hispanic civilisations, with the most prominent being the Aztec, Mayan and Olmec. Meanwhile, the Yucatán Peninsula was home to the Mayan people, and many of the indigenous people still speak the language. The area also contains many sites where ruins of the Maya civilization such as Chichen Itza can be visited (see Plate 1.2). The richest of these are located in the eastern half of the peninsula and are collectively known as La Ruta Puuc (or La Ruta Maya). Increasingly, such sites are being promoted by government agencies and departments which have invested money in their development and consolidation as part of the tourism industry (Secretaría De Turismo, 2010). Most notably, the Secretaría De Turismo's (2010) cultural tourism development programme aims to 'coordinate efforts to ensure that this sector develops, strengthening mechanisms and instruments for the long-term benefit of cultural and natural resources, guaranteeing financial and social gains deriving from its projects'. Consequently, actions are being taken to help identify and provide infrastructure and equipment for this sector, creating strategic partnerships to develop and diversify alternative tourism products and helping the economic and social development of the host community and the country in general (Secretaría De Turismo, 2015).

Plate 1.2 El Castillo, Chichen Itza, Mexico
Source: The authors (2017).

In addition, the Cultural Tourism Program included the development of new tourism products at cultural sites, activities that highlight their charms and differentiate cultural destinations. Therefore, a master plan has been devised for identifying and designing cultural tourism products in Mexico's four heritage cities – Guanajuato, Morelia, Querétaro and Zacatecas. This provides a tool to identify existing and potential tourist attractions and heritage resources, including gastronomy, popular art, legends, local fiestas and events. These form part of the range of cultural tourism products on offer, depending on their type, originality, peculiarity or uniqueness, with each city's differentiation and distinctive values (Secretaría De Turismo, 2010). Efforts have also focused on the implementation of the 'pueblos magicos' ('magic towns') initiative led by Mexico's Secretariat of Tourism which promotes selected towns that offer visitors a 'magical' experience – by reason of their natural beauty, cultural riches or historical relevance. The programme was launched in 2001 and by 2014 a total of 87 towns and villages in all 31 states have been awarded the title (Secretaría De Turismo, 2015).

The Significance of Heritage, Screen and Literary Tourism

Given the increasing market segmentation and differentiation of tourism products, HSLT are a phenomenon of global significance, with the market thus becoming highly competitive. This is perhaps because 'capitalising on the positive impacts of HSLT can assist in the strategic development of tourism activity in destinations, by supplementing the product portfolio, increasing tourist awareness and the appeal of the destination, and in turn contributing to the viability of tourism' (Connell & Meyer, 2009: 195). However, precise measurement of all three forms of tourism is problematic, especially when it occurs beyond specific sites such as small settlements or museums, and in the absence of clearly demarcated spatial boundaries as in the case of many cities which tourists are likely to visit for a multitude of different reasons (Busby & Klug, 2001).

In terms of the significance of heritage per se, it is a very important pull and push motivator for tourism. Its effect is perhaps best illustrated by the example of the UK, where it can be argued that virtually all tourism is partly motivated by natural or cultural heritage. For instance, hills, mountains and lakes – which are undoubtedly part of the natural heritage – are an intrinsic part of rural tourism in many locations such as the Cairngorms (Scotland), Snowdonia (Wales) or the Lake District (England). Similarly, the 'club' scenes of cities such as Manchester and Leeds – which attract weekend tourists from London – may be considered to be expressions of the cities' cultural heritage (Nurick, 2000). In general, heritage is important to the success of the UK's tourism, evident from Table 1.1 which demonstrates that a substantial proportion of all holiday visits involved built and living heritage, with activities associated with parks and gardens (54%), pubs (50%), castles and historic houses (48%), museums and art galleries (43%) and religious buildings (35%) being particularly popular (International Passenger Survey, 2011, cited in VisitBritain, 2015).

With regard to visits made in 2014 to visitor attractions in membership with the Association of Leading Visitor Attractions (ALVA), the top ten all have direct relevance to heritage (Table 1.2). This emphasises the pivotal role played by heritage in the UK's tourism trade. VisitBritain (2010) estimated that Britain's heritage attracted approximately £4.5bn worth of spending by inbound visitors annually, equivalent to more than a quarter of all spending by international visitors, and underpins more than 100,000 jobs in Britain. This estimate, however, represents the total amount spent in Britain by visitors who have been drawn to the country by its heritage, and is not an estimate of how much is spent directly on heritage products, such as entrance fees to stately homes. The significance of heritage to the UK's tourism industry is further illustrated by the Anholt Nation Brands Index (GfK Public Affairs and Corporate Communications, 2015), which provides insights into

Table 1.1 Activities undertaken by visitors to Britain

Activities asked about	Visits which involved activity		% of all holiday visits	Nights spent in UK* No. of nights (000)	Amount spent in UK* (£m)
	No. of visits (000)	% of all visits			
Visited museums and art galleries	8,299	27%	43%	86,146	£6,255
Went to theatre/musical/opera/ballet	2,796	9%	14%	33,838	£2,748
Visited castles or historic houses	8,874	29%	48%	91,245	£6,506
Visited religious buildings	6,738	22%	35%	74,920	£4,948
Visited parks or gardens	11,081	36%	54%	114,312	£7,826
Went to countryside or villages	5,336	18%	22%	72,418	£4,205
Went to the coast or beaches	3,582	12%	15%	54,292	£2,853
Went shopping	17,668	58%	71%	162,275	£12,092
Went to the pub	13,886	46%	50%	122,645	£9,393
Went to bars or nightclubs	3,842	13%	14%	42,495	£3,412
Attended a festival	949	3%	4%	16,810	£1,003
Went to a live sport event	1,325	3%	4%	14,673	£1,128
Took part in sports activities	707	2%	3%	10,989	£730

Notes: *Nights and spend are not specifically while undertaking activity but throughout visit to UK.
Source: Adapted from International Passenger Survey (2011, cited in VisitBritain, 2015).

Table 1.2 Visits made in 2014 to the UK's top ten Association of Leading Visitor Attractions

Rank	Visitor attraction	Visitor numbers
1	British Museum, London	6,695,213
2	The National Gallery, London	6,416,724
3	The South Bank Centre, London	6,255,799
4	The Tate Modern, London	5,785,427
5	The Natural History Museum, London	5,388,295
6	The Science Museum, London	3,356,072
7	The Victoria and Albert Museum, London	3,180,450
8	The Tower of London, London	3,075,950
9	Somerset House, London	2,463,201
10	The Library of Birmingham, Birmingham	2,414,860

Source: Adapted from the Association of Leading Visitor Attractions (ALVA, 2015).

the perceptions of the UK's culture and heritage among respondents in 20 countries. In 2014 the UK was ranked third for contemporary culture, fifth for historic buildings and seventh for cultural heritage out of 50 nations; these rankings have remained consistent since 2008 (VisitBritain, 2015). Further research into the role of culture and heritage in the top three inbound UK markets, namely France, Germany and the USA, revealed that it influenced destination choice and that, while shopping was popular across all markets, those from Germany and the USA in particular liked to visit castles, historic buildings and a British pub (VisitBritain, 2014).

Akin to heritage tourism, screen tourism in the UK is also a highly significant activity. Oxford Economic Forecasting (2012) reported that the UK film industry in 2011 had a total economic impact of over £4.6m (approximately €5.4m) on the UK's gross domestic product (GDP), creating the equivalent of 117,400 full-time jobs. Moreover, they estimate that it generates around one-tenth of overseas tourism revenues, contributing around £1bn (€1.2bn) to the UK GDP and prompts about one in every ten overseas visits to the country (Oxford Economic Forecasting, 2012). Research undertaken in 2007 by VisitBritain (2010), however, revealed that going to a TV/film location in the UK was undertaken by only 3.1% of all holiday visitors; 2.5% of those visitors were also visiting friends and relatives, 0.9% were business visitors and 9% were study visitors. These findings suggest that films have only some influence over travellers' destination choices and are not a motivator for everybody.

However, it is not just in the UK where screen tourism attracts visitors as its impact on destinations and communities worldwide has been documented extensively (Beeton, 2001; Chan, 2007; Connell, 2012; Hudson & Ritchie, 2006a, 2006b; Iwashita, 2006; Kim et al., 2007b; Månsson & Eskilsson, 2013; O'Neill et al., 2005; Riley et al., 1998; Tooke & Baker, 1996) (see Table 1.3). For

Table 1.3 Impact of selected screen-induced tourism on tourist destinations

Films and release dates	Impacts
Da Vinci Code (2006)	Visitor numbers to Rosslyn Chapel, near Edinburgh, Scotland – a key location in the film – rose from 38,000 in 2003 to 68,000 in 2004. They peaked in 2007 after the release of the film at 159,000 falling to 138,849 in 2009 but have since risen in 2013 to 144,828 (Månsson & Eskilsson, 2013; Rosslyn Chapel Trust, 2014).
Alice in Wonderland (2010)	Antony House, SW England, the location for the movie, attracted 20,000 visitors in 2008 which has risen to approximately 95,000 after its release (Furness, 2014).
The Hunger Games (2012)	Many scenes from the movie were shot at DuPont State Forest, NC. Before the release of the film in 2011, this destination attracted around 250,000 and rose to over 320,000 after its release (Axtell, 2012).
Harry Potter and the Philosopher's Stone (2001); Harry Potter and the Chamber of Secrets (2002)	Alnwick Castle, Northumberland, UK featured in both films as the backdrop for Hogwarts School of Witchcraft and Wizardry. Before the release of the first film it attracted approximately 60,000 visitors per year. By 2007, 132,000 tourists visited annually (Olsberg SPI, 2007), rising to 280,000 in 2014 (Daniels, 2015), boosted by the release of the final film, The Deathly Hallows (Part 2) in 2011. Day-visit spend from core screen tourists is estimated to be worth £4.3m in 2014 (McVeigh, 2015).

Source: Axtell (2012), Daniels (2015), Furness (2014), Månsson and Eskilsson (2013), McVeigh (2015) and Rosslyn Chapel Trust (2014).

instance, in the Swedish town Ystad, well known for its *Wallander* productions, since filming began in 2004, the town has increased its tourism turnover by 75% to 781m SEK, approximately £9.6m (Månsson & Eskilsson, 2013). The ability of screen tourism to induce visitation is undeniable, and with more people becoming exposed through this media to the wonders of the world and to the excitement of various remote natural environments (Tooke & Baker, 1996), this particular form of tourism is indeed important globally (see Case Study 1.2).

Case Study 1.2 The significance of screen tourism: Bollywood

Bollywood is a major driver influencing and inspiring Indian people to visit destinations which are depicted in Bollywood films. This is because the Indian film industry is one of the largest in the world, producing more than 800 films a year, with an annual turnover of Rs. 60bn, and employing more than 6 million people (VisitBritain, 2010). In addition, this phenomenon has been further fuelled by the creation of India's middle class – numbering about 50 million – who not only have the motivation but also the ability to travel. The sheer scale of the industry is perhaps best illustrated by the 2014 'Bollywood Oscars' held in Florida, which are estimated to have been watched by up to 800 million people around the world (Amrhein, 2014).

Switzerland was one of the first destinations to benefit from Bollywood. It has a long-established association with the Indian film industry with its charming towns, serene lakes and Alpine meadows providing backdrops to many of its cinematic blockbusters (Lander, 2009). As a consequence, it has attracted an increasing number of Indian visitors, with the number of nights spent by Indians (mostly in the summer) doubling in the past decade to 325,000 (Planet Bollywood, 2010). More recently, however, Bollywood has transcended the Indian and Swiss borders with Indian filmmakers now using an array of other destinations in which to shoot their movies, including the Finnish Lapland of Rovaniemi, Poland, Victoria in Australia, Kandahar, Kabul, Brazil, Malaysia, Dubai, New York, Singapore, London, Scotland and Hong Kong. These destinations too are benefiting economically. For instance, Indians spent £24m in Scotland in 2006, in part inspired by the filming of *Kuch Kuch Hota Hai* (1998), *Pyaar Ishq Aur Mohabbat* (2001) and *Kyun! Ho Gaya Na* (2004) around Edinburgh, Glasgow and Stirling (Oswell, 2007). More recently, *Romance Complicated* – an Indian romantic comedy filmed at various locations in Jacksonville and due for release in September 2015 – is expected to generate up to $200,000 in economic impact (Jones, 2015).

Bollywood is hugely significant to destinations worldwide, best evidenced by the fact that nearly every national tourism organisation, including Britain, is attempting to attract the multibillion dollar Bollywood film and entertainment industry to shoot movies, advertise locations and film documentaries at their destinations. Singapore Tourism and the Korean Tourism Board, for example, partially funded the blockbuster *KRRISH*, while the South African Promotion Tourism Board appointed a famous film star, Anil Kapoor, as their board ambassador. Moreover, Bollywood actor Ajay Devgn is participating in a promotional video on Bulgaria advertising the country as a tourist destination, which will be broadcast in India (novinite.com, 2015). Indeed, VisitBritain (2010) state that it is imperative for Britain to realise the financial earning potential of this important segment, as well as the enormous free 'indirect' advertising, publicity and goodwill generated for a destination. With this in mind, in March 2005 the then Culture Secretary of State, Tessa Jowell, struck a deal to develop a co-production treaty between the UK and India which enables filmmakers of both countries to pool their resources to create films which benefit both financially and culturally (VisitBritain, 2010).

Bollywood is particularly important to Britain, as many films are actually shot in London. They are often given names in English as they are seen as catchy, especially for the youth market, such as *Bend it like Beckham, Bride and Prejudice, London Dreams, Bhaji on the Beach* and *Monsoon Wedding*. They also feature well-known London landmarks. For instance, Waterloo Station is a key location in *Jhoom Barabar Jhoom* (2007), around which the story revolves, including a dance sequence. Others include Trafalgar Square, the Natural History Museum, Tower Bridge, the Royal Albert Hall, the Millennium Dome, the Houses of Parliament, Nelson's Column and the London Eye. Moreover, Southall is home to one of the largest Indian communities in London, and was the setting for Simran's home in *Dilwale Dulhania Le Jayenge* (1995). The Albert Memorial features in *Mujhse Dosti Karoge* (2002) and Hyde Park was one of one of the locations for a song, 'Kabhi Khushi Kabhie Gham'.

Visiting such locations is a popular pastime for the thousands of Indian tourists who flock to Britain every year and this, combined with the large number of Indian films being shot in the UK, has prompted VisitBritain, Britain's national tourism organisation, to bring out a 'Bollywood map' depicting the locations where popular films have been shot . More recently, Scotland, a popular destination with Bollywood producers, has followed suit, creating their first ever Bollywood map with Bollytrails highlighting some of the locations that have featured in over 20 Indian movies (VisitScotland, 2015). The Indian market has shown fairly consistent growth in visits to the UK since 1993. However, the biggest increases in the number of Indian visitors to the UK have been since 2003. Nearly a quarter of Indian visitors are visiting friends and relatives (VFR). VFR is an very important market for Britain, and makes up a significant proportion of all visits, staying for an average of 40 nights at a time (VisitBritain, 2010).

In comparison with heritage and screen tourism, it is widely acknowledged that literary tourism is of significance to destinations (Beeton, 2015, 2016; Frost, 2006a, 2006b; Herbert, 1996, 2001), and it is considered lucrative by many tourist boards and government organisations around the world, many of whom have developed specific strategies designed to exploit the economic potential of this niche tourism market. For example, Belfast City Council approved its first literary tourism strategy in 2009 and pledged £158,000 to bring the city's literary heritage to life and to promote characters, writers, poets and playwrights on the world stage. This involved the development of literary tours and trails, a literary guide, the implementation of a literary app for mobile devices, increasing literary events and programming, and effective e-marketing of literary tourism (Belfast City Council, 2017). The Belfast Literary Guide and iphone app now guides visitors through the city where its finest writers lived, walked and worked. Such writers include Seamus Heaney, known across the world as one of the finest poets, while illustrious visitors from John Keats to E.M. Forster, Anthony Trollope to Kate O'Brien, have written about the city (Belfast City Council, 2017). However, despite recognition of the economic benefits literary tourism may bring destinations, there are scant data documenting its volume and value. Nevertheless, the importance of literary tourism to the UK is demonstrated, albeit crudely, by a list of the top five literary cities compiled by the *National Geographic* (2015; see Table 1.4), in which the UK features strongly, taking the top three places. Thus, despite data deficiencies, it is clear to see that HSLT are highly significant activities in destinations across the world, and their importance is likely to remain as existing and new products associated with these three forms of tourism continue to be offered and developed.

Heritage, Screen and Literary Tourism Products

Given the complexity of consumer demand in a post-Fordist era, it is of no great surprise that the range of HSLT products is vast and, as Table 1.5 demonstrates, it is clearly not homogeneous. Aside from the array of product types that exist, they differ greatly in terms of the geographical scale of their significance which varies from being perceived as having global notoriety to being of national, local or personal importance (see Table 1.6 for examples). Of course, classifications of this nature are somewhat simplistic, arbitrary and highly subjective, with perceptions of significance varying from one individual to another. Categorising the significance of HSLT at national and local levels is also particularly problematic. This is due to the global pervasiveness of the media, resulting in the wide-scale release of even locally produced films, combined with the interpretation of most literary works into screen productions, together with the increasing practice of using HSLT landmarks and associations in international destination marketing and branding campaigns. Thus, it is impossible to provide examples of HSLT that are of solely national and local significance since they are likely to attract some foreign visitors as well as domestic tourists. However, despite these limitations, viewing HSLT in this way is valuable as it provides a useful

Table 1.4 Top five literary cities

Destination	Description
(1) Edinburgh, Scotland	Famous authors who lived or wrote about this city include Sir Arthur Conan Doyle, J.K. Rowling, Robbie Burns, Sir Walter Scott, Robert Louis Stevenson, Ian Rankin and Alexander McCall Smith.
(2) Dublin, Ireland	Authors who drew inspiration from this city include Yeats, Heaney, James Joyce and Jonathan Swift. Key attractions include the James Joyce Tower and House, the Dublin Writers' Museum and the National Library of Ireland. The Dublin Literary Pub Crawl features actors and writers who guide tourists through some of the city's most famous literary haunts.
(3) London, England	London was the birthplace or home of many of the greatest authors of all time, including Charles Dickens, Geoffrey Chaucer, John Milton, John Keats and H.G. Wells.
(4) Paris, France	This city has a rich and diverse literary history, frequented by French authors like Victor Hugo, Voltaire and Alexander Dumas, as well as American writers such as Gertrude Stein, Ernest Hemingway and F. Scott Fitzgerald. It boasts famous bookstalls ('Les Bouquinistes') lining the Seine, and famed literary cafés like Les Deux Magots, once frequented by greats like Hemingway and Albert Camus.
(5) St Petersburg, Russia	This city's remarkable literary history is celebrated through the works of Leo Tolstoy, Anton Chekhov, Alexander Pushkin and Fyodor Dostoyevsky. Dostoyevsky inhabited a number of apartments throughout the city, and in his last, where he wrote *The Brothers Karamazov*, there is now a museum dedicated to his life.

Source: Adapted from National Geographic (2015).

framework for summarising the impact of the vast array of products available.

In terms of heritage, world-famous natural landscapes such as the Great Barrier Reef (Australia) or built heritage attractions including the Great Pyramid of Giza (Egypt) or the Colosseum in Rome attract large numbers of tourists from many countries; with respect to the latter, visits to ancient monuments, for example, are largely motivated by the belief that such objects really are linked to the remote past. Indeed, according to Timothy and Boyd (2003), for many tourists, visiting international heritage attractions is a way of appreciating universal civilisation and achieving some degree of human unity. On a national scale, historical monuments often represent national ideals and pride, and such sentiment can be an

Table 1.5 Heritage, screen and literary tourism products

Natural history attractions	Nature reserves, nature trails, aquatic displays, wildlife parks, zoos, caves, gorges, cliffs, waterfalls
Scientific attractions	Science museums, technology centres
Primary production attractions	Farms, dairies, agricultural museums, vineyards, fishing, metal shops, glass makers, silk workers, lacemaking, craft villages
Manufacturing centres	Pottery, porcelain factories, breweries, cider factories, distilleries, industrial history museums
Transport attractions	Transport museums, railways, canals, shipping and docks, civil aviation, motor vehicles
Sociocultural attractions	Prehistoric and historic sites, domestic houses, history, costume, furniture museums, museums of childhood
Attractions associated with historic people	Sites, areas and buildings associated with famous writers, painters and politicians
Attractions associated with significant historical events	Sites, areas and buildings associated with significant events in history
Performing arts attractions	Theatres, performing arts, circuses
Pleasure gardens	Ornamental gardens, period gardens, arboreta, model villages
Theme parks	Nostalgia parks, historic adventure parks, fairy tale parks
Galleries	Art and sculpture
Festivals and pageants	Historic fairs, festivals, reconstructions, festivals
Stately and ancestral homes	Palaces, castles, country houses, manor houses
Religious attractions	Cathedrals, churches, abbeys, mosques, shrines, temples, springs, wells
Military attractions	Battlefields, military airfields, naval dockyards, prisoner of war camps, military museums
Genocide museums	Sites associated with the extermination of other races or other mass killings of population
Towns and streetscapes	Historic urban centres, buildings, shops, urban settings
Locations associated with film, TV and literary settings	Built and natural sites which provide the backdrop or key locations for films, TV programmes and literature
Villages and hamlets	Rural settlements, architecture, pastures
Countryside and treasured landscape	National parks, rural landscapes
Seaside resorts and seascapes	Seaside towns, marine landscapes, coastal areas
Regions	Counties and other historic regions identified as distinctive by residents and visitors
Living culture	Less tangible objects and activities such as traditions, ways of life, ceremonies and rituals, dances, agricultural practices, culinary habits

Source: Adapted from Timothy and Boyd (2003) and Prentice (1993).

Table 1.6 Heritage, screen and literary tourism products: Examples of scales of significance

Scale of significance	Heritage tourism examples	Screen tourism examples	Literary tourism examples
Global	The Great Pyramid of Giza (Cairo, Egypt)	*The Lord of the Rings* trilogy (New Zealand)	*Diary of a Young Girl* (Amsterdam)
	The Great Barrier Reef (Cairns, Australia)	*Australia* (Western Australia)	*The Da Vinci Code* (Paris, France)
	The Colosseum (Rome, Italy)	*Slumdog Millionaire* (Mumbai)	*The Millennium Trilogy* (Stockholm)
National	Cradle Mountain (Tasmania)	*Jumong* (Samhanji, South Korea)	*Don Quixote* (Madrid and Alcalá de Henares, Spain)
	The Arc de Triomphe (Paris, France)	*Miracle in Milan* (Milan, Italy)	*Dream of the Red Chamber* (Beijing, China)
	The Millennium Monument (Putrajaya, Malaysia)	*Ned Kelly* (Victoria, Australia)	*Anne of Green Gables* (Canada)
Local	Hunan Provincial Museum (Changsha, China)	*Blackball* (Torquay, UK)	*L'Assommoir* (Paris, France)
	Fremantle Prison (Fremantle, Australia)	*Krrish* (Singapore)	*Maigret and the Yellow Dog* (Concarneau, France)
	The Gaslamp Quarter (San Diego, CA)	*Monga* (Wanhua, Taipei)	Yueyang Louji (Hunan, China)
Personal	Arlington National Cemetery (Arlington, TX)	*Bridge over the River Kwai* (Western Thailand)	The Tales of Beatrix Potter (Lake District, UK)
	Auschwitz (near Krakow, Poland	*Saving Private Ryan* (Normandy, France)	Hans Christian Andersen fairy tales (Copenhagen Denmark)
	The Mormon Church (Salt Lake City, UT)	*The Boy in the Striped Pyjamas* (implied to be Auschwitz, Poland	

Source: The authors (2017).

important stimulus for preserving the built environment in Western societies. Examples of such include Paris' Arc de Triomphe which honours those who fought for France, particularly during the Napoleonic Wars, and the Millennium Monument at Putrajaya which marks important periods and milestones in Malaysia's history. However, natural attractions may also be considered of national significance. For example, in 2009 children of Tasmania nominated Cradle Mountain as their favourite national heritage icon (The Examiner, 2009).

Heritage of local significance is that which is valued by, and has meaning for local communities. Examples of local landmarks include China's Hunan Province Museum boasting an abundant collection of relics excavated from the Mawangdui Han Tombs and bronzeware belonging to the Shang and Zhou dynasties, and Fremantle Prison (Fremantle, Australia), once one of the most notorious prisons in the British Empire, housing British convicts, local prisoners, military prisoners, enemy aliens and prisoners of war. In addition, Timothy and Boyd (2003) argue that communities need familiar landscapes so that they can remain in touch with their own collective pasts in a changing world. Thus, an example of such includes the Gaslamp Quarter of San Diego, CA – an area of great architectural charm, its streets lined with original 19th century buildings.

Meanwhile, personal heritage relates to people's emotional connections to particular places, and illustrations of such include the Arlington National Cemetery, spanning an area of 624 acres (2.53 km^2), in which veterans and military casualties from each of the nation's wars are interred, ranging from the American Civil War through to the military actions in Afghanistan and Iraq. Another illustration is Auschwitz, located near Krakow (Poland), the largest of the German concentration camps where millions of Jews were exterminated. Moreover, many visitors are attracted to the Mormon Church (formerly known as the Church of Jesus Christ of Latter-Day Saints) situated in Salt Lake City, UT, in order to trace their family history as it maintains the largest collection of genealogical data in the world (McCain & Ray, 2003).

With respect to screen tourism, many Hollywood blockbuster movies have had a global impact on tourism, encouraging visitors from around the world to travel to specific locations featured in the films. One such case in point includes The Lord of the Rings (LOTR) trilogy based on the novels by J.R.R. Tolkien. The three films (The Lord of the Rings: The Fellowship of the Ring, The Lord of the Rings: The Two Towers and The Lord of the Rings: The Return of the King) were shot entirely in various locations throughout New Zealand: the rolling hills of Matamata became Hobbiton, while the volcanic region of Mount Ruapehu was transformed into the fiery Mount Doom where Sauron forged the One Ring, and Queenstown was the setting for numerous scenes including the Eregion Hills and the Gates of Argonath (New Zealand Tourism Guide, 2017). The popularity of LOTR has seen New Zealand tourism companies offer a range of tours which expose the breathtaking scenery captured in the films. According to Gilsdorf (2006), the annual tourist influx to New Zealand jumped from 1.7 million in 2000 to 2.4 million in 2006 to approximately 3.3 million in 2016 (Statistics New Zealand, 2016); undoubtedly some of this increase can be attributed to the LOTR phenomenon.

Another example is the epic romantic movie *Australia*, released in 2008 and starring Nicole Kidman and Hugh Jackman. This was filmed primarily in the Kimberley region of Western Australia and is credited with helping to maintain visitor numbers to Australia despite the recession (The Age, 2010). The impact of this film on tourism was aided by the linking of an aggressive AU$1m publicity campaign entitled 'See the Movie, See the Country', promoted by Tourism Western Australia, to its release in the United States, Canada, Japan, Europe and South Korea. In addition, the director, Baz Luhrmann, made a AU$50m series of commercials promoting the country. Meanwhile, *Slumdog Millionaire* has created a flourishing slum tourism industry which promises fee-paying outsiders a glimpse of life inside Mumbai's shantytowns (Blakely, 2009).

There are many examples of films and television programmes which engender national or anti-national pride and sentiment or which deal with issues that have shaped a nation, and as a consequence locations of such screenings are of interest, particularly but not exclusively to domestic tourists. Examples include: *Jumong*, the very first Korean historical drama, filmed mainly in Samhanjii, a theme park in Naju, which attracts more than 5000 tourists daily (Korea Tourism Organisation, 2016); *Miracle in Milan*, an Italian anti-nationalist classic created by the neo-realist filmmaker Vittorio di Sica and set around the city's already popular tourist attraction, the Piazza del Duomo; and *Ned Kelly*, set and filmed in and around Victoria, Australia. The latter is a particularly interesting example, since although there were expectations that the film would attract international tourists given the parallels between Kelly and other outlaws such as Robin Hood, Billy the Kid and Jesse James, it did not achieve box office success. According to Frost (2006a: 252), 'in just over a year since its release *Ned Kelly* took just US$6.4m (which equals an audience of perhaps 1 million), of which 85% was from Australian cinemas'. Its direct impact, Frost (2006a) contends, was therefore more on the domestic rather than the international tourism market, which is not surprising given that Ned Kelly is a cultural heritage phenomenon in Australia, with his story being debated and disputed for 120 years.

Meanwhile, despite the global release of most films and television programmes, there are also many examples of lesser known movies and television programmes which are likely to have stimulated mainly local interest. For instance, *Blackball* (2003), a British comedy film, featured locations around Torquay, Devon (UK), including the opening aerial shot and most significantly Kings Bowling Club renamed in the film 'Royal Torquay Bowling Club'. Other examples are *Krrish*, filmed extensively in Singapore and released in 2006, which has attracted domestic tourists who are interested in viewing the 30 locations used in the film (Yue, 2009), and *Monga*. This was filmed in Taipei's Wanhua district, which in the first four days following the film's release grossed approximately NT$75m (US$2.43m), and stimulated crowds of local tourists, keen to visit the locations featured in the film. Liang-hsi-hao, a food stand shown in the film, reported a quantum leap in sales of its specialty squid broth (Taiwan Today, 2010).

Furthermore, there are instances of films and television programmes generating tourism to specific places because the featured locations have some kind of personal significance. In this context, emotional attachment to such places often occurs because they are associated with particular historic events involving war, violence, death, depravity and human suffering. For example, *The Bridge over the River Kwai*, a 1957 fictitious British WWII film borrowing the building of the Burma Railway in 1942–1943 for its historical setting, has stimulated tourism, with visits primarily motivated by the desire to pay homage to the 13,000 prisoners of war who died and were buried along the railway during its construction (Tunbridge & Ashworth, 2017). Other examples of screen productions which are likely to have stimulated visits to featured places born out of personal interest include *The Boy in the Striped Pyjamas* (2008), which explores the horror of a WWII extermination camp, implied to be Auschwitz (Poland), already Poland's most popular tourist attraction, and *Saving Private Ryan*, which drew graphic attention in its opening scene to the enormous loss of life during the D-Day landings in Normandy (France), particularly Omaha Beach, and resulted in a 40% increase in American visitors to Normandy after its release (Keeble, 1999).

In terms of literary tourism, again it is possible to distinguish several scales of significance, although the extent of significance of some literary works alone has become somewhat blurred by the release of screen adaptations. Nevertheless, at a global level, *The Da Vinci Code* (featuring Paris, London and Edinburgh) is credited with increasing tourism to locations featured in the plot, interest in which heightened after the release of the film in 2006. Eurostar, the high-speed train service linking the UK with France and Belgium, led the largest ever international campaign to boost tourism to London, Paris and Edinburgh on the back of the release of the blockbuster movie, promoting it worldwide through a series of marketing and promotional initiatives, especially in the USA, France, Belgium and the UK, including TV, online and in-terminal exposure. Eurostar also worked with VisitBritain, VisitLondon and VisitScotland, as well as with Maison de la France, to encourage tourists to take their own Da Vinci Code trail and follow in the footsteps of the book's hero, Robert Langdon (Eurostar, 2006). Other examples of globally significant literary works which have attracted thousands of tourists from all around the world to featured key locations include Dan Brown's *Angels & Demons* (Vatican City and Rome, Italy) (Faust, 2009; Gordon, 2009) and the *Diary of a Young Girl* by Anne Frank (Anne Frank House, 2015).

On a national level, there are many instances of novels written by authors famous in specific countries which have generated national interest and pride, and consequently domestic tourism. For example, Cervantes, the Spanish novelist, poet and playwright best known for *Don Quixote*, is celebrated across Madrid through statues and commemorative plaques

Plate 1.3 Statues of Don Quixote and Sancho Panza at the Plaza de España, Madrid, Spain
Source: The authors (2017).

(Plates 1.3 and 1.4), while his birthplace, Alcalá de Henares, a quaint university town situated 35 km northeast of Madrid, attracts hordes of domestic tourists keen to pay homage to the man largely credited with writing the first modern text. Moreover, *Dream of the Red Chamber*, written for the most

Plate 1.4 Commemorative plaque marking the location of Juan de la Cuesta's shop where Don Quixote was first printed, Calle Atocha, Madrid, Spain
Source: The authors (2017).

part by Tsao-Hsueh-Chin, is considered by many to be the greatest master-piece of Chinese classical novels of the Ming and Qing dynasties (China Highlights, 2016). The novel is set against the backdrop of the Grand View Garden, a replica of which has been constructed in southwest Beijing and now attracts many domestic tourists. Further, literary tourism may be stimulated by a nation's interest in the homes of their most famous authors such as L.M. Montgomery's *Anne of Green Gables*, set on Prince Edward Island in Canada (Squire, 1996).

Some literary works are of primarily local significance, having importance and holding value to mainly local communities; this is not to say that they do not attract international visitors, just not that many of them. For example, Zola's *L'Assommoir* (*The Grog Shop*), a 19th century classic French naturalism novel set in Paris, specifically featuring the Place de l'Assommoir, attracts specialist local visitors. Simenon's *Maigret and the Yellow Dog* is another example, celebrated by an annual festival held in Concarneau, the setting of the novel, organised and sponsored primarily by local people (Mansfield, 2015). Moreover, the 'Yueyang Lou ji', Chinese prose written during the Song dynasty (960–1297), attracts local tourists to the Yueyang Tower in Hunan Province, one of the oldest in China, since it was written to commemorate its renovation. In fact those who are able to recite the prose are granted free entry and during the Spring Festival holiday 6000 locally drawn tourists were given free admission (China Daily, 2013).

There are also literary works which have great personal significance for their readers. Squire (1994) and Busby and George (2004), for example, note that key locations associated with Beatrix Potter, such as her home, Hill Top Farm, or *The Tailor of Gloucester* shop (College Court, Gloucester) often evoke feelings of nostalgia, childhood memories and emotions among visitors. Meanwhile, numerous reviews on TripAdvisor from tourists who have visited various attractions in and around Odense and Copenhagen, Denmark, associated with Hans Christian Andersen, author of fairy tales including 'The Ugly Duckling', 'The Princess and the Pea' and 'The Little Mermaid', note the childhood memories that were evoked by their experience. For example, one tourist wrote about the Little Mermaid statue located in Copenhagen, '... seeing her encouraged me to re-read H.C. Anderson after many years. What a treat to be reminded of the wonderful tales that Anderson wove for us' (TripAdvisor, 2013a). Another who visited the museum located in Odense wrote: 'I am not a child by far, but I enjoyed this attraction. It is not very modern, a bit outdated and not very large ... But in my case it brought back memories. I used to love fairy tales, and the fairy tales from Hans Christian Andersen were very special to me as a child' (TripAdvisor, 2015). Similarly, others stated: 'This was interesting and brought back memories of the stories we all heard during childhood' (TripAdvisor, 2013b); and 'Relive childhood memories of your favourite books and stories' (TripAdvisor, 2014a).

Despite there being some blurring between global, national, local and personal boundaries, when taken together, these varying levels of scales of significance suggest that HSLT experiences are all linked by the notion of being shared (Timothy & Boyd, 2003), thereby creating an individual and collective sense of belonging. Shared experiences are made more meaningful through the power of the narrative which emotionally and cognitively connects the resource with the tourist. Often they weave the impact of the past on the present and visually and/or performatively convey stories of change which involve struggle, disruption, celebration and progress. In doing so, several interrelationships emerge underpinned by co-creation, which together produce an HSLT nexus.

The Heritage, Screen and Literary Tourism Nexus

The HSLT nexus revolves around co-creation and comprises three inter-relationships, which inextricably bind these three niche tourism products together (Figure 1.2).

Co-creation

The term co-creation, introduced by Prahalad and Ramaswamy (2000) and developed further in a series of subsequent publications (2001, 2004), was used to describe the emergence of a new relationship between producers and consumers (Azevedo, 2009), from passive audiences to active players, in light of an increasing demand for more participative and interactive experiences (Scott *et al.*, 2009). According to Prahalad and Ramaswamy (2004: 6), 'armed with new tools and dissatisfaction with available choices, consumers want to interact with firms and thereby co-create value'. Thus, co-creation was defined as 'The joint creation of value by the company and the customer; allowing the customer to co-construct the service experience to suit their context' (Prahalad & Ramaswamy, 2004: 8). This is achieved by being 'networked, active, informed and involved in consumer communities' (Prahalad & Ramaswamy, 2004: 5). Co-created value thereby arises from customised, unique and personal experiences, and is fundamental to high-quality interactions which, according to Prahalad and Ramaswamy (2004), are crucial to competitive advantage.

Since Prahalad and Ramaswamy's seminal work in 2000, there has been growing discussion among academics about how consumers engage with producers to co-create experiences through consumption. Many consumers, it is argued, are co-creators and co-producers of value through service experiences and relationships (Vargo & Lusch, 2004), with such experiences, based on engaging customers by providing a memorable and personal product, appealing to their sensations. For Holbrook (2006: 213),

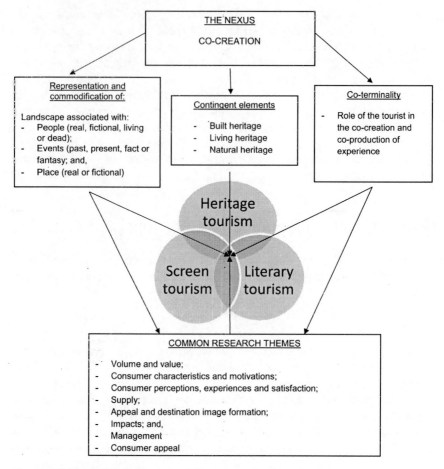

Figure 1.2 The heritage, screen and literary tourism nexus
Source: The authors (2017).

'value resides not in an object, a product or a possession but rather in and only in a consumption experience'. Such thinking led Vargo and Lusch (2004) to challenge the traditional goods-dominant logic of marketing and to instead present the service-dominant logic which placed customers as the co-creators of value. Underpinned by eight foundational premises, these were subsequently amended and developed to include a further two premises in 2008 (Table 1.7).

The foundational premises provide insights into these new tendencies that characterise firm–customer interactions. The first premise (FP1) places service at the heart of value creation as service is exchanged for service. Customers are viewed as operant resources. They apply their skills, knowledge and expertise to create the service which is the essence of the exchange

Table 1.7 Foundational premises of service-dominant logic

Premise number	Foundational premise
FP1	Service is the fundamental basis of exchange
FP2	Indirect exchange masks the fundamental basis of exchange
FP3	Goods are a distribution mechanism for service provision
FP4	Operant resources are the fundamental source of competitive advantage
FP5	All economies are service economies
FP6	The customer is always a co-creator of value
FP7	The enterprise cannot deliver value but only offer value propositions
FP8	A service-centred view is inherently customer oriented and relational
FP9	All social and economic actors are resource integrators
FP10	Value is always uniquely and phenomenologically determined by the beneficiary

Source: Adapted from Vargo and Lusch (2008).

(Vargo & Lusch, 2008). FP2, the second foundational premise, acknowledges the fact that, because there are many products, processes, money and institutions involved in service provision, the service basis of exchange is not always obvious. Meanwhile, FP3 indicates that durable and non-durable goods derive their value through use or, in other words, via the service that they provide. The fourth foundational premise (FP4) highlights that it is the comparative ability of actors which causes desired change and which may result in competitive advantage, while FP5 recognises that, although service has been central to the economy for many years, its importance is becoming more apparent as specialisation and outsourcing increase (Vargo & Lusch, 2008). FP6 asserts that value creation is based on the interaction of operant resources and their contribution to the co-creation of value, and FP7 stipulates that firms cannot create and deliver value alone; instead, they are facilitators of value as they can only offer value propositions which create the service following the end-user's acceptance, participation and consumption (Cesaroni & Duque, 2013). The eighth foundational premise (FP8) emphasises that service is customer centric and interactional, whereas FP9 places value creation within the context of networks, reflecting the fact that often organisations and individuals motivate and constitute the service exchange. Finally, FP10, the tenth foundational premise, indicates that value is always judged by the end-user depending on the specific situation (time, place and network relationships) the actor is in. Value is perceived and determined by the consumer and is thus idiosyncratic, experiential, contextual and value laden (Vargo & Lusch, 2008).

Co-creation therefore comprises a number of dimensions – co-constructed personalised experiences, joint value creation, dialogue, involvement, engagement and co-production – which enables value to be created and extracted (Figure 1.3). Although, by implication, there is some overlap between co-creation and co-production in value creation, both are viewed as different concepts (Ballantyne & Varey, 2008: 5). This is because co-production occurs when the customer actively participates in the creation of the service experience itself. Thus, co-creation of an experience can take place without co-production, particularly if the customer does not want to actively participate and produce any part of the service because they prefer to take a more passive role (Minkiewicz et al., 2009). Indeed, consumers producing goods and services for their own consumption has led to the term 'prosumption' being coined, an acronym for the combined activities of production and consumption. Xie et al. (2008: 110) define prosumption as 'value creation activities undertaken by the consumer that result in the production of products they eventually consume and become their consumption experiences'.

Since its conception and subsequent amendment, S-DL has evolved as a result of the contributions of several academics including Lusch and Vargo (2014, 2016). Indeed, in an attempt to provide a more precise delineation of its conceptual underpinnings, Lusch and Vargo (2014) reduce the ten foundational principles to six, which are aligned along four axioms (Table 1.8). More recently, in order to provide a clearer articulation of the mechanisms of

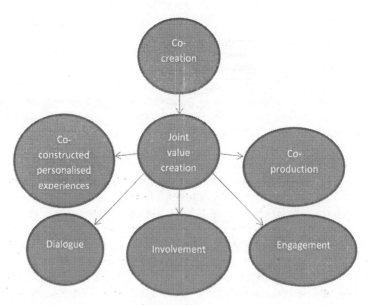

Figure 1.3 Dimensions of co-creation
Source: The authors (2017).

Table 1.8 The axioms of service-dominant logic

Axiom	Description
Axiom 1/FP1	Service is the fundamental basis of exchange
Axiom 2/FP6	Value is co-created by multiple actors, always including the beneficiary
Axiom 3/FP9	All social and economic actors are resource integrators
Axiom 4/FP10	Value is always uniquely and phenomenologically determined by the beneficiary
Axiom 5/FP11	Value co-creation is coordinated through actor-generated institutions and institutional arrangements

Source: Adapted from Vargo and Lusch (2016).

coordination and cooperation involved in value creation, Vargo and Lusch (2016) introduce an 11th foundational principle and a fifth axiom which focuses on institutions and institutional arrangements in systems of value creation. In addition, co-creation has been applied to many different perspectives and contexts (Vargo & Lusch, 2016) including tourism, and many have acknowledged its importance since it is an industry that sells experiences (Kim, 2010; Scott et al., 2009; Volo, 2009). Such developments, according to Richards (2014), have been linked to the rise of the experience economy (Pine & Gilmore, 1999), marked by experience production and by tourists' desires for self-actualisation and creative expression. This trend, in turn, is leading to more co-creation of experiences between consumers and producers as they no longer charge for goods and services but for the experience (Richards, 2014), which should therefore be made as real, memorable, stimulating, compelling, personal and satisfying as possible (Andrades & Dimanche, 2014; Pine & Gilmore, 1999). In such experiences, tourists are co-creators of their experiences (Bertella, 2014; Campos et al., 2015; Prebensen et al., 2013; Tan et al., 2013) and of value (Rihova et al., 2013) through the meanings they derive from consumption that they have created, directed, produced and consumed.

Co-creation is particularly relevant to HSLT. For example, Ashworth and Larkham (1994: 16) state that 'heritage is a contemporary commodity purposefully created to satisfy contemporary consumption', while Poria et al. (2003) argue that those visitors who view a place as bound up with their own heritage are likely to behave significantly different from others. Moreover, all three forms of tourism are experience centric, and offer cognitive and emotional stimuli and facilitate service experience and consumption (Chan, 2009). As McIntosh (2009) contends, valued dimensions of the experience are produced in part by visitors through their personal thoughts, feelings, emotions, imaginations and backgrounds which tourists bring to the setting. According to Minkiewicz et al. (2009: 3) 'by encouraging visitors to co-create their service experience, the aspects that they individually value are likely to be incorporated into the experience, making it unique and personal to each individual visitor'. According to Binkhorst (2005), co-creation of the tourism experience results from the interaction of an individual at a specific place and time and within the context of a specific act. Prahalad and Ramaswamy (2004: 10) speak of an 'experience environment', referring to a space where dialogue can take place between producer and consumer. Within the context of HSLT, it is within this space or nexus that a number of inter-relationships occur.

Nexus interrelationships

Perhaps the first and most obvious relationship between HSLT is that all three represent and commodify elements of an area's heritage and cultural traditions, associations and links for tourism purposes. In essence, this aspect of the nexus encompasses the consumption and production of a tourism landscape that is associated with people (real or fictional, living or dead), events (past or present, fact or fantasy) and/or place (real or fictional). Such aspects have been represented and commodified to a range of tourist audiences, and have been used extensively worldwide to create hugely significant market segments of the tourism industry.

Related to this representation and commodification of landscape is the second interrelationship that constitutes the HSLT nexus, this being the contingency of all three forms of tourism on aspects of an area's built, natural and living heritage. Indeed, many HSLT locations acquire specific meaning only because of a person, event, movie and/or literary association featured there. Without that, the place such as a castle or a stately home may be indistinguishable from any other. According to Busby and Klug (2001), in the case of *Notting Hill* in which the stately home of Kenwood House was featured, the heritage site experienced a 10% increase in visitors in August 1999 alone after the launch of the film. Tobermory, a tiny town located on the Isle of Mull (Scotland), which provides the setting for the children's TV programme *Balamory*, also provides an illustration of this contingency. The programme is filmed in the town using the exteriors of several painted houses which feature prominently throughout the show (Connell & Meyer, 2009). Moreover, another illustration of this interrelationship is that of a tourism landscape that juxtaposes centuries of heritage with popular culture, via the 1981 television adaptation of Evelyn Waugh's novel *Brideshead Revisited* and a two-hour remake for cinema – Castle Howard, located in North Yorkshire. From another perspective, it is the medium of the movie which has magnified the living heritage of Kefalonia in the form of *Captain Corelli's Mandolin*. Both movies are escapist, if partially factual, and have created a tourism landscape to be consumed.

The third element of the HSLT nexus involves the co-terminality of consumption and production (Hall *et al.*, 2008), and the ensuing interrelationship between the tourist in the co-creation of all three forms of tourism. While tourism, in a postmodern society, has traditionally been conceptualised as a highly complex series of production-related activities (Richards, 1996), all tourist experiences in fact involve meaning and similarly form part of wider processes of cultural production and consumption (Busby & Klug, 2001). Such a notion has been captured by both Burgess (1990) and Squire (1994), who adopt Johnson's (1986) 'circuits of culture' model (Figure 1.4) to theorise ways in which meanings are encoded by the producers or promoters of visitor attractions and which are then decoded by visitors. Postmodern tourists use the power of their intellect and imagination to receive and communicate messages, constructing their own sense of place (Nuryanti, 1996), be it historic, screen or literary related, to create their individual journey of self-discovery. In doing so, physical space is replaced through sensibilities by an image of place which is no less real, while the phenomenon of sense or spirit of place highlights the experiential nature of the individual's engagement (Busby & Klug, 2001). Thus, the role of the tourist and the product in co-creating the experience is now commonly accepted to lie at the heart of HSLT. For example, Moscardo (2001: 5) believes heritage tourism to be 'an experience which is produced by the interaction of the visitor with the resource', and argues that the linkages between the site, the potential tourists' motives and their perceptions can be conceived as an interactive process. People embark on HSLT motivated by their intrinsic feelings of nostalgia (Hewison, 1987: 45; Pretes, 1995), social distinction (Bourdieu, 1984) and the need for an authentic experience (Cohen, 1988). The drive to satisfy their original motivation triggers the demand for heritage displays and such manifestations, capable of satisfying tourists' desires, transforming heritage, screen and literary associations into a product.

There are many examples that illustrate the HSLT nexus. One such case is the story of Anne Frank, a young Jewish girl who hid for more than two years with her family in an annexe of a house on Prinsengracht, Amsterdam in order to escape persecution during the WWII Nazi occupation of The Netherlands. During this period and up until the point when the family were

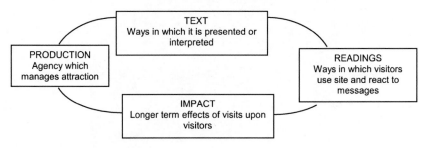

Figure 1.4 Circuits of culture
Source: Adapted from Johnson (1986, cited in Herbert, 1996: 78).

betrayed, captured and sent to concentration camps, Anne kept a diary in which she described her daily life in the annexe, the isolation and the fear of discovery, Although she died of typhus in Bergen-Belsen in March 1945, only a few weeks before this concentration camp was liberated, her diary survived and was published in 1947. The first interrelationship of the HSLT nexus is evident as the author (Anne Frank), her story (of being hidden for over two years), and the place (the house and its annexe), has subsequently been represented and commodified in a variety of ways for tourism purposes. This has occurred through the sale of her diary which is available in 55 languages and through the many movie, play and TV dramatisations. In addition, the house is now a museum dedicated to the retelling of the life and times of Anne Frank and also acts as an exhibition space to highlight all forms of persecution and discrimination (Plate 1.5). Over 9000 visitors came to view the house in the first year after the diary was published. Between the years 1960 and 1970, there were twice as many visitors, and currently it attracts over 1 million people each year (Anne Frank House, 2015).

The second interrelationship of the nexus is also identifiable as this example is highly contingent on aspects of heritage, these being the historical

Plate 1.5 Anne Frank's House, Prinsengracht, Amsterdam, The Netherlands
Source: The authors (2017).

backdrop of WWII and the Holocaust, and the house itself which has acquired meaning simply because Anne and her family secretly lived there. Furthermore, this example demonstrates the nexus's third interrelationship, the co-terminality of HSLT. This occurred as a result of the opening of the Anne Frank Museum, the screen dramatisation of Anne's story and the publication of her diary. Together, these actions have involved the tourist in the co-creation of the experience by stimulating the imagination and by drawing on the spirit of the person, event and place in order to convey a story of courage, goodness, hope, desperation and tragedy.

As well as there being examples which demonstrate the three interrelationships which form the core of the HSLT nexus, there are a number of identifiable research themes that are common to all three forms of tourism (Table 1.9). However, despite there being much commonality between HSLT, studies have tended to treat each of these forms of tourism as separate entities, and few explore the links between them. Moreover, when taken together, these common research themes demonstrate that although much attention has been paid to establishing the supply and demand components of HSLT, less interest, particularly within the realms of screen and literary tourism, has been paid to exploring the relationship between demand and supply, and notably of the role of the consumer – the tourist – in co-creating the visitor experience. For instance, Connell and Meyer (2009) note a gap in the literature with regard to the on-site experience of screen tourists, and consequently there is little understanding of how screen tourists perceive, interact and relate to the destination.

Indeed, according to Shaw et al. (2011), there has been a relative failure of tourism research to incorporate research paradigms like S-DL. This lack of research is surprising given the increased pervasiveness of S-DL and value creation in light of the co-terminality of consumption and production (Hall & Williams, 2008). Moreover, the lack of research relating to HSLT in the context of S-DL and value creation is remarkable, particularly since the development, marketing, interpretation, planning and management of attractions and destinations are all in danger of losing their way if they fail to focus on engaging customers and promoting what Shaw et al. (2011) term tourism centricity. According to Richards (2014), producers are now dream makers, creating value through stories and narratives. These enable destinations to stand out in a globally competitive marketplace and facilitate tourists in playing an active and integral role in creating their own experiences. The exchange of knowledge and skills between the tourist and the producer can produce a more locally driven authentic experience. However, the tourist often has intrinsic universal standards against which the authenticity of any aspect of HSLT is considered and judged. Therefore, authenticity is likely to be a negotiated construct (Apostolakis, 2003) and, combined with the tourists' interaction with the resource visited, the resulting experience may be somewhat removed from what was initially envisaged. Given the occurrence

Table 1.9 Common research themes

Theme	Examples of heritage tourism studies	Examples of screen tourism studies	Examples of literary tourism studies
Volume and value of activity	Kim *et al.* (2007a); Ma *et al.* (2015); Su and Lin (2014)	Busby and Klug (2001); Connor and Kim (2013); Kim *et al.* (2007b); Riley *et al.* (1998); Tooke and Barker (1996)	Connor and Kim (2013); Herbert (1996); Robinson and Andersen (2002)
Consumer characteristics and motivations	Goh (2010); Poria *et al.* (2003, 2006); Teo *et al.* (2014); Yankholmes and McKercher (2015)	Busby and O'Neil (2006); Chan (2007); Macionis and Sparks (2009); Singh and Best (2004)	Busby and Devereux (2015); Herbert (1996, 2001); Smith (2003)
Consumer perceptions, experiences and satisfaction	Biran *et al.* (2011); Chen and Chen (2010); de Rojas and Camarero (2008); Laing *et al.* (2014); Masberg and Silverman (1996)	Carl *et al.* (2007); Connell (2012); Connell and Meyer (2009); Kim (2010); Singh and Best (2004)	Earl (2008); Herbert (2001); Smith (2003)
Supply	Leask and Yeoman (1999); Prentice (1996); Richards (1996); Timothy and Boyd (2003)	Beeton (2005); Buchmann (2010); Connell (2012)	Herbert (1995, 1996); Robinson and Anderson (2002); Steibel (2004)
Product appeal and image formation	Dahles (1998); Leask and Yeoman (1999); Pearce and Tan (2004); Yale (1991)	Busby and Haines (2013); Connell (2005); Frost (2006b); Hudson and Ritchie (2006a, 2006b); O'Connor *et al.* (2010)	Hoppen *et al.* (2014); Robinson and Andersen (2002)
Impacts and management	Goulding and Domic (2009); Hampton (2005); Poria *et al.* (2006); Ruiz Ballesteros and Hernández Ramirez (2007)	Busby and Klug (2001); Im and Chon (2008); Riley *et al.* (1998); Young and Young (2008)	Herbert (2001); O'Connor and Kim (2013); Squire (1996)

Source: The authors (2017).

of co-creation in HSLT, perhaps it is best therefore to view all three forms of tourism within the framework suggested by Poria *et al.* (2003) who, writing in the context of heritage tourism, argued that it is a social phenomenon. More importantly for some, it is an emotional experience, that people come to 'feel' rather than simply to gaze, to be educated or to enjoy themselves (Urry, 1990).

Conclusion and Book Structure

Overall, this first chapter has introduced HSLT. It has discussed their growth and significance, highlighted the relevance and importance of S-DL and co-creation to HSLT, and detailed three interrelationships – representation and commodification, contingent elements, and co-terminality – which together form the HSLT nexus. Some common research themes have also been identified and, in so doing, the limited use of co-creation as a framework in which to critically evaluate the development, interpretation, marketing and management of HSLT has been highlighted.

This book attempts to further explore HSLT within the broad context of S-DL and co- and value creation. In Chapter 2 the demand for HSLT and their associated key market segments including school groups and the local community is discussed. This is followed by an in-depth examination of visitor motivations and typologies. In Chapter 3 the use and re-representation of various aspects of history by the HSLT industry is detailed. This is because the growth of such forms of tourism during the 1980s and 1990s stimulated huge debates about how the past is viewed and used, and its impact on the health of society. Consequently, this chapter revisits this debate and applies some of the relevant arguments to an examination of the use of HSLT for political purposes.

This chapter has already acknowledged that HSLT is of huge value and significance, but developing, operating and managing sites, whether museums, galleries and/or national parks, is a costly undertaking. Chapter 4 considers some of the issues that are important to HSLT attraction development, focusing in particular on the fundamental tensions that exist between desires for conservation and commercial success, between the need to provide an authentic and yet entertaining experience, and on funding and quality issues.

Chapter 5 focuses on interpretation, which is an extremely important issue to HSLT. This is because often the central challenge in linking these three forms of tourism lies in the reconstruction and retelling of events through interpretation. This chapter thus examines the meaning of interpretation and ascertains its importance. It then documents Tilden's guiding principles of interpretation and introduces the interpretive planning process. Some interpretive approaches, techniques and media are discussed in relation to specific sites, attractions, towns and regions. Moreover, cross-cultural and special needs issues are considered, and the relevance and application of semi-ology to the study of HSLT is analysed.

Given the economic and social significance of HSLT to many destina-tions around the world, it is vital that it is commercially viable and success-ful. Chapter 6 moves on to consider in detail consumption and experience processes, and it analyses the factors which influence such processes. In addi-tion, the various vehicles for consumption, such as literary and screen festi-vals and societies, are discussed, followed by detailed consideration of visitor satisfaction.

Marketing obviously plays a key role in attracting visitors and this issue is the focus of Chapter 7. While some of the general principles of marketing are applicable, it is not the intention of this chapter to discuss marketing in general but rather to focus on those aspects of marketing that are affected by the special character of these niche sectors. Chapter 8 then discusses the meaning and importance of visitor management and examines the utility of existing visitor management procedures and frameworks. This is because the HSLT market sector is no different from other forms of tourism in that it brings positive and negative impacts to destination economies, societies and environments. The key challenge for destination managers is to maximise the benefits of this market sector and minimise the negative impacts; in other words it is vital to promulgate sustainable forms of tourism, and this is primarily achieved through visitor management. Specific management tools and techniques are detailed and, in particular, the challenges facing World Heritage Sites are considered. The discussion concludes with Chapter 9 which summarises the main issues discussed throughout the book, and examines these in the context of the present and future prospects of HSLT. Some future study perspectives and avenues are also highlighted.

2 Demand and Heritage, Screen and Literary Tourism Markets

Introduction

Over the past three decades, the importance of and demand for HSLT to localities, regions and nation's economies has grown (see Chapter 1). Globally, these forms of tourism are a well-established phenomenon as the search for experiences in destinations has created a thriving industry. In Australia, for example, cultural and historical attractions at destinations are popular, accounting for 13.5 million domestic day trips in 2015 (Tourism and Transport Forum, 2016). Literary tourism is particularly lucrative in Britain, as evidenced by the value of tourism to Stratford-Upon-Avon, Shakespeare's birth town. In 2013 it was estimated that tourists spent approximately £152m in the town, with about £13m spent in the local economy each month (Stratford-Upon-Avon District Council, 2013). Oxford Economic Forecasting (2012) estimate that film tourism contributed around £1.9bn in visitor spending with about 10% of tourism trips to the UK being attributable in some way to film associations in 2011, while Ernst and Young (2009) estimate that in New Mexico film tourism is estimated to be worth US$124m. Few places exist today in the world that have not been affected in some way or another by heritage, literature or screen coverage gained from novels, films, documentaries and TV productions.

Despite such growth, there is still a distinct lack of understanding about aspects of the demand for HSLT. For example, Poria *et al.* (2006) state that very little research considers the relationships between tourism and the heritage space visited. This contention reiterates earlier observations by Tunbridge and Ashworth (1996: 69), who noted that the study of heritage settings 'must shift from the uses of heritage to the users themselves and thus from the producers (whether cultural institutions, governments or enterprises) to the consumers'. Meanwhile, Connell and Meyer (2009) and Kim (2010) highlight the fact that there is scant research into film tourism experiences associated with TV programmes. According to Kim (2012), there is also a general lack of understanding of how film tourism experiences are influenced by audiences' TV viewing experiences, associated with audience responses to and engagement with a TV programme's output (Kim *et al.*, 2009). Such a lacuna is surprising given that the core product of tourism is arguably the beneficial experiences gained (Goodall, 1993) and that co-creation is widely recognised to be fundamental in creating value and value extraction (Prahalad & Ramaswamy, 2004). Thus, studies of tourist experiences, according to Prentice *et al.* (1998b: 2), 'need to be "grounded" in the realities that tourists themselves describe'.

Demand for HSLT provides the focus for this chapter and is analysed within the contexts of the HSLT nexus, drawing on theorisations provided by S-DL and co-creation. The chapter begins by discussing in general the reasons for the growth of these forms of tourism, and examines the nature of the demand. It then moves on to consider the tourist per se, their motivations and the benefits obtained from visits to associated sites and areas. It also discusses some typologies that have been devised which seek to portray similarities and difference in the nature of tourism demand. Following this, the chapter evaluates experiences. Such a consideration is important as, according to Prentice *et al.* (1998b: 3), 'without an understanding of the touristic experiential dimensions, product development lacks a scientific basis, a weakness of particular concern for experiential attractions' including heritage, literary and screen attractions offering interpretations of real and imagined pasts and place. The discussion then concludes with a brief summary and some final thoughts.

Demand for Heritage, Screen and Literary Tourism

Demand for HSLT increased rapidly from the 1980s onwards, with growth being influenced by factors which were also responsible for the expansion of tourism more generally; these include an increase in leisure time, rising disposable incomes, the growth of international travel and an increase in mobility due to car ownership (Timothy & Boyd, 2003). Additionally, however, specific reasons account for increasing demand such as higher levels of education, an ageing population, a greater interest in nostalgia (see Chapter 3 for more in-depth discussion), the decline of the manufacturing industry in many Western countries resulting in the desire to re-use redundant buildings thereby generating opportunities for consumption, and the pervasiveness of media, especially the growth of the entertainment industry (Hudson & Ritchie, 2006b). High-profile movies have created demand for specific destinations, such as *Rob Roy* (Scotland), *Crocodile Dundee* (Australia) and *Gorillas in the Mist* (Rwanda) (Grihault, 2003). While the significance and importance of these forms of tourism to local, regional and national economies is recognised, thus suggesting that all economies are service economies, as Vargo and Lusch (2008) suggest in their fifth foundational premise, their global volume and value is not known as such data tend not to be widely available.

Table 2.1 Forms of literary tourism

Form	Observations
(1) Elements of homage to specific locations	To view the background against which a work was produced in order to gain insights into the work and the author. The emergence of the literary pilgrim (Butler, 1996) occurs.
(2) Significant locations in the work of fiction	The novel *Tarka the Otter* by Henry Williamson brings tourists to its setting in North Devon (Wreyford, 1996)
(3) Appeal of areas because they were appealing to literary and other figures	Connected with literary figures (Squire, 1996), where the setting enhances the quality of contact, sights and memorabilia (Herbert, 1996). Also relevant to public sector promotion, for example, the Daphne du Maurier Festival (Busby & Hambly, 2000).
(4) Literature so popular that the area becomes a tourist destination in its own right	This form is illustrated by Charles Kingsley's *Westward Ho!*, resulting in the creation of the eponymously named seaside resort in Devon (Busby & Hambly, 2000).

Source: Adapted from Butler (1996).

As Chapter 1 established, the pursuit of unique experiences has resulted in the 'super-segmentation' (Fayos-Sola, 1996: 406) of demand. Consequently, there is no one single HSLT product as different forms have been created for the variety of markets that exist. This diversity is captured by Butler (1996), who identifies four forms of literary tourism (Table 2.1), while Busby and Klug (2001) add a fifth to include travel writing as it is a vehicle through which places and people have been re-interpreted and communicated to wider audiences. Bill Bryson's books such as *Notes from a Small Island*, *The Lost Continent* and *Down Under* are good examples of this. Additionally, Busby and Klug (2001) highlight several types of movie tourism (Table 2.2) which, together with Butler's (1996) contribution, serve to highlight the complexity of demand. Given these, who then are the heritage, screen and literary tourists? Do they have particular characteristics? What are their motivations for engaging in these types of tourism and is it possible to identify distinct types? It is these matters that this chapter next turns its attention to.

The Heritage, Screen and Literary Tourist

Well-educated scholars and/or the wealthy are generally understood to comprise the first heritage and literary pilgrims. Both were usually well versed in the classics, possessed sufficient cultural capital to appreciate visitation of this nature and were prepared to travel long distances. According to Bourdieu (1984), they belonged to the dominant classes, and their tastes, preferences and consumption patterns served as markers of their social

Table 2.2 Forms and characteristics of movie tourism

Form	Characteristic
Film location as attraction in own right (Evans, 1997; Riley, 1994; Tooke & Barker, 1996)	Some destinations not perceived as tourism worthy prior to film success, whereas others already receiving tourists (Riley et al., 1998)
Movie tourism as part of a main holiday (Evans, 1997)	Tourists visit TV or movie sites or book-related tours while on holiday, despite no previous location knowledge (Evans, 1997)
Movie tourism as main purpose of special interest visit (Evans, 1997)	Visiting a given destination, as a direct results of its screen profile (Evans, 1997)
Movie tourism packages created by the private sector (Evans, 1997)	Coach and tour operators providing themed excursions and holidays
Movie icons for tourists to gaze on as focus of visit (Riley et al., 1998)	Scenery, history, themes, symbols and relationships as icons and 'hallmark events' for movie tourism (Riley et al., 1998)
Movie tourism to places where filming only believed to have taken place (Tooke & Barker, 1996)	Visits occur to places represented, even where filming occurred elsewhere, raising questions of illusions, reality and authenticity in context of what tourists are expected to see and why (Busby & Hambly, 2000; Herbert, 1996; Tooke & Baker, 1996)
Movie tourism as part of romantic gaze (adapted from Urry, 1990)	The romantic movie tourist gazes on images constructed and reinforced through film, establishing a semi-spiritual relationship with the place gazed upon (Urry, 1990)
Movie tourism as pilgrimage, nostalgia, escape (Riley & Van Doren, 1992)	Films becoming pilgrimage points in their own right
Travel programmes (adapted from Squire, 1996)	A vehicle through which places and people have been reinterpreted and communicated to wider audiences (Squire, 1996)

Source: Adapted from Busby and Klug (2001).

position that set them apart (Herbert, 2001). However, with the growth and segmentation of these forms of tourism, along with the emergence of screen tourism, a reappraisal of the nature of demand has been necessary.

Today it is widely accepted that, while heritage, screen and literary pilgrims still exist, consumers are overwhelmingly drawn from the service class, made up of affluent, educated, professional and business people in white-collar occupations (Prentice, 1993; Thrift, 1989; Urry, 1995). Indeed, Herbert's (2001) study confirmed an association between social class and heritage visitation including literary places, as does Yan et al.'s (2007) examination of international heritage tourists to Taiwan. Similarly, a study undertaken of Canadian heritage tourists found that they were more affluent than the 'typical' domestic traveller, with an average household income of $60,000 compared to $54,900 for the latter. Higher household incomes were also found to be consistent with higher levels of formal education: over a quarter of those surveyed had at least one university degree (28%), and a further 42% had post-secondary education (Research Resolutions and Consulting, 2003). Vargo and Lusch's (2016) foundation premises one (service is the fundamental basis of exchange), four (operant resources are the fundamental source of competitive advantage) and six (the customer is always a co-creator of value) are clearly relevant here, as the design and creation of the service experience will be influenced by the availability of such operant resources combined with the ability of the tourist to use their knowledge, skills and experience to co-create the experience they wish to consume.

Heritage, literature, movies, documentaries and TV programmes create destinations that have a dual attraction to both general and special interest tourists (Andersen & Robinson, 2002). Macionis (2004), for example, distinguishes between the serendipitous film tourist (who just happens to be in a destination portrayed in a film), the general film tourist (who while not specifically drawn to a film location participates in film tourism activities), and the specific film tourist (whose activity seeks out places that feature in films). Thus, it is the meaning and value derived that tourists attach to such resources that inspires actual visits, thereby reinforcing Vargo and Lusch's (2016) tenth foundation premise that value is always uniquely and phenomenologically determined by the beneficiary. This notion also features within both Butler's (1986) forms of literary tourism and Busby and Klug's (2001) forms of movie tourism. Consequently, motivations play an important role in influencing demand.

Motivations of heritage, screen and literary tourists

Understanding motivations is an important avenue of research for all three forms of tourism. In attempting to draw a distinction between leisure and recreation motivations, studies within this context stress the need to understand the ways in which tourists interact with spaces and resources (Poria et al., 2006), and have identified a wide range of reasons for visitation (Davies & Prentice, 1995; Herbert, 2001; Prentice et al., 1998b; Richards, 2002; Timothy & Boyd, 2003). Shackley (2001: 1), for instance, notes that in addition to worship, 'sacred historic spaces are visited because they represent great works of art, have architectural merit, provide attractive settings and atmosphere, and are "part of a great day out"'. While investigating the link between perceptions and motivations, Poria et al. (2006) meanwhile identified three categories, these being: (1) willingness to feel connected to the history presented; (2) willingness to learn; and (3) motivations not linked with the historic attributes of the destination. Just as there are general and special interest tourists, there are general and specific motivations for visiting HSLT destinations. Exactly which type of motivation is more dominant is, however, open to debate. Herbert (1995: 34) suggests that 'visitors to literary places are more purposeful and have specific reasons for making their visits'. In contrast, Macionis and Sparks (2009) found that the majority of film tourists were incidental, casual or serendipitous (Croy & Heitmann, 2011).

In relation to general motivations, Herbert (2001) notes that geographical convenience can provide a general motivation for visitation, particularly when a literary destination is a stopping point en route to another destination, and is situated within a scenic environment and/or range of facilities such as restaurants or coffee and souvenir shops. With reference to the latter, there are a host of very specific internal motivations for visitation, with perhaps the primary reasons being the existence of an inherent interest and a desire to learn. According to Ousby (1990: 8), 'tourists don't visit country houses or ruins or nature just for fun but out of the belief that the experience will in some way educate or uplift them'; clearly, perceptions of value extraction as outlined by Vargo and Lusch's (2016) tenth foundational premise (see Table 1.7) are relevant here. Pocock (1992) meanwhile identified a modern version of the literary pilgrim who was seeking to learn and be educated.

Another motivation is a willingness to feel an emotional connection with the resource being experienced. McCain and Ray (2003) and Poria *et al.* (2006) found this motivation present, particularly in relation to heritage tourists. Squire's (1994) research on Beatrix Potter's Hill Top House indicated that for many tourists it was the desire to evoke emotions and memories of their childhood, notions of Englishness and rural nostalgia for the countryside that provided the main reasons for visitation. An array of studies have also addressed this phenomenon within screen tourism, notably in relation to *The Lord of the Rings* (LOTR) in New Zealand (Beeton, 2005, 2015; Tzanelli, 2004), *The Da Vinci Code* in Paris, London and Rosslyn, Scotland (Karakurum, 2006), *Blade Runner* in Los Angeles, CA (Brooker, 2005), *The X-Files* in Vancouver (Brooker, 2007), *Braveheart* in Scotland (Edensor, 2005), Harry Potter in the UK (Iwashita, 2006), *The Beach* in Thailand (Tzanelli, 2007) and James Bond (Reijnders, 2010a). They reveal that it is the emotional connection that motivates tourists. This may be stimulated by the level of empathetic involvement with the character or storyline (Kim & Richardson, 2003), the desire to be in the actual places where the scenes were shot (Carl *et al.*, 2007; Macionis & Sparks, 2009), or by a combination of contingent elements. Such occurs in the case of the 1980s' Australian films in which the natural environment provided the backdrop to the film and, together with the portrayal of uncomplicated indigenous lifestyles and the struggle of man with the environment, stimulated a surge in American tourists (Riley & van Doren, 1992).

Other internal motivators might include: ego enhancement, status and prestige (Macionis & Sparks, 2009); fantasy (Beeton, 2005, 2010, 2015; Riejnders, 2010a); the desire for a vicarious experience or, in other words, living someone else's life (Macionis & Sparks, 2009); novelty (Chan, 2007; Macionis & Sparks, 2009; Singh & Best, 2004); authenticity (Bolan & Williams, 2008; Buchmann, 2010; Frost, 2006a); and social obligation which, it is argued, explains many tourists' reasons for visiting sites associated with death and disaster such as Auschwitz in Poland (Poria et al., 2006). What is clear here is that heritage, screen and literary tourists are a heterogeneous group in terms of their motivations for visiting a site or destination. They are likely to exhibit many different motivations and just because a motivation may be to relax does not mean that there is not also a desire to be informed or educated. This is reinforced by Herbert (2001: 326) in his analysis of Jane Austen literary tourists, many of whom he states 'were able to combine interest and relaxation in ways they found to be acceptable and pleasurable and these were not mutually exclusive features of the visit'. Additionally, different sites may induce different motivational profiles, especially since, according to Uzzell (1996), the same historic location such as a battlefield may be visited for different reasons at various points in time. Tourists from one generation may come to pay homage and remember, while younger ones may view the visit as a day trip or excursion. Despite the heterogeneity in demand together with the complexity of HSLT motivations, the characteristics of visitors are of great interest to academics and practitioners.

Typologies of heritage, screen and literary tourists

Some typologies have been put forward that seek to categorise tourists based on their characteristics. Petersen (1994) developed one of the earliest, identifying four different types of heritage tourism visitors. The first he labels *aficionados*, who are preservationists and professional in their study of history. The second comprise *event visitors*, who visit sites on special occasions (e.g. festivals), the third consist of tourists who are away from home and are visiting historic sites, and the fourth include casual visitors who visit the site because it is a convenient green place. In a later study, Prentice et al. (1993) divided heritage tourists and visitors into five dominant groups, these being: (1) educated visitors; (2) professionals; (3) families or groups; (4) school children; and (5) nostalgia seekers.

Visitors have also been differentiated by their motivations and experiences gained. In a study of visitor experiences of product design (setting) and visitor perceptions in Rhondda Heritage Park, an experiential attraction developed to enhance a former colliery, Prentice et al. (1998b) discovered five types of visitors. The first were those visiting out of personal interest in local history, comprising 32.1% of the park's market. These were often without children, were of a lower social class and had a strong sense of identity with industrial Wales. The second were labelled as those from a higher social class and comprised 12% of the market. They learnt something useful about the past and were generally impressed by the dangers faced by the miners. The third type of visitor came from white-collar households, accounting for 25.2% of the market, the fourth were those with children (15.8%), and the fifth were young professional households (constituting 13.2% of the attraction's market). Other attempts at developing visitor typologies have focused less on distinguishing between visitor characteristics and instead emphasised motivations, particularly the degree of affinity with the heritage resource/site being viewed. Poria *et al.* (2001), for example, identified three new types of heritage tourists on this basis, with these being: (i) those visiting a site they deem to be part of their heritage; (ii) those visiting what they consider to be a heritage site although it is unconnected with their own; and (iii) those visiting a heritage site specifically classified as a heritage place although unaware of this designation.

Given the diversity in HSLT demand, it is not surprising that there seems little to distinguish heritage from screen and literary tourists. After all, the majority of literary and screen attractions entail heritage and therefore can be regarded as a particular kind of heritage tourism (Martin-Jones, 2014). Indeed, a number of studies appear to support this contention. One such one is Squire's (1994) study of Beatrix Potter's Hill Top House in the Lake District, where the writer's house museum is located and which served as the setting for her children's tales. Another is Herbert's studies (1996, 2001) of Jane Austen's residence, Chawton House in Hampshire, which is now a museum, and Laugharne in South Wales, believed to be the setting of Dylan Thomas's *Under Milk Wood* (1954) and where the Boathouse is located in which Thomas lived, now a museum about the artist. These studies found that the majority of literary tourists were of a mature age – 35 years or older, mostly drawn from the service class, engaged in managerial, professional or white-collar occupations.

Having an understanding of demand for HSLT is essential as it enables appropriate and relevant products to be developed and marketed (see Chapters 4 and 7) and visitors to be effectively managed (Chapter 8). However, knowledge of the experiences of these tourists is also immensely important as it is this that lies at the heart of the nexus (p. 2; Figure 1.1), and provides the motivations to visit prior to consumption. Thus, it is this issue that the remainder of this chapter focuses upon.

Experiences of Heritage, Screen and Literary Tourists

Early research into heritage experiences occurred within the context of museums and other similar attractions. Emphasis was placed on the setting through which experiences are facilitated which was largely achieved through the presentation of artefacts (Prentice *et al.*, 1998b). In this context, understanding the experience essentially involved an examination of the link between the individual (the tourist) and the displayed object or site

(Prentice *et al.*, 1998b). Today, the way in which spaces are communicated to tourists continues to be critically important to the tourists' experience of a setting (Poria *et al.*, 2006), which in turn may also affect how the experience is co-created together with the satisfaction or value derived from the visit (see Chapter 6; Ashworth, 1998; Garrod & Fyall, 2000; Goulding, 1999; Moscardo, 1996; Timothy & Boyd, 2003). This is particularly the case in screen and literary tourism since the media act as 'pull' factors (Riley & Van Doren, 1992), by generating awareness, interest and appeal in the geographical locations and imaginations in which they feature, and framing tourists' anticipation and perceptions of and experience in the portrayed locations.

However, according to Poria *et al.* (2006), attention should not be given only to the physical attributes of the site. It is therefore also important to carefully consider the interaction between the tourist and the place visited, the event experienced and/or the object viewed (Case Study 2.1), a contention reinforced by S-DL and co-creation. Focusing on the heritage context, Poria *et al.* (2006) go on to explain that this should be done both with reference to the spaces in which heritage artefacts are presented and in other spaces as well, which will lead to a better understanding of the subject. Indeed, Prentice *et al.*'s (1998b) earlier study of tourist experience at the Rhondda Heritage Park in Wales revealed dimensions of experience which comprised feelings and cognitive manipulation and centred on learning goals. Thus, these studies suggest that the determinants of experience are multi-attribute in quality, as the same product can be experienced in many different ways because tourists employ different processes to give meaning to an experience. They also serve to emphasise Vargo and Lusch's (2016) first and fourth foundational premises, which both focus on the tourist who is responsible for co-creating the resulting service experience through the interaction of their operant resources.

Case Study 2.1 Visitor experiences of *The Lord of the Rings* tours, New Zealand

New Zealand is known as 'Middle Earth' to fans of the LOTR trilogy as all three films (*The Fellowship of the Ring, The Two Towers* and *The Return of the King*) were shot at 350 purpose-built sets and in more than 150 locations all over New Zealand. The hills of Matamata became Hobbiton (Plates 2.1 and 2.2), while the volcanic region of Mount Ruapehu was transformed into the fiery Mount Doom where Sauron forged The Ring (Plate 2.3). Queenstown was the setting for numerous scenes including the Eregion Hills and the Gates of Argonath.

Various scenes were also shot in numerous conservation sites and national parks. Thus, plants which were uprooted to make room for the

Plate 2.1 Matamata, New Zealand became the location of 'Hobbiton'
Source: The authors (2017).

film sets were temporarily housed in big custom-made nurseries and then replanted. In Queenstown, the site of heavy battle scenes during which up to 1100 people were on set each day, plants were protected by laying red carpet. Costing more than NZ$640m, it is the first time an entire feature film trilogy has been filmed all at once, over a two-year period, with the same director and cast (New Zealand Tourism Guide, 2016).

The popularity of the LOTR trilogy has given rise to the development of a number of New Zealand tourism companies offering a wide range of location site tours, many of which are personalised. Flat Earth

Plate 2.2 The picturesque location of 'Hobbiton' at Matamata, New Zealand
Source: The authors (2017).

Plate 2.3 The imposing Mount Ruapehu, New Zealand
Source: The authors (2017).

New Zealand Experiences (TripAdvisor, 2014b), for example, offer three types of tours. The first is a tour of Middle Earth film locations which comprises a half-day experience visiting the following film locations: Rivendell where Frodo recovered from his knife attack; the Anduin River where the Fellowship voyaged to Amon Hen; the river where Aragorn was washed ashore after the attack of the wargs; the Gardens of Isengard, the site of the orcs felling the trees and where Gandalf rode to see Saruman; Mount Victoria lookout and Buckland Forest where the hobbits hid from the Nazgûl and where they found the mushrooms on the road; Dunharrow Rohirrim encampment; and the quarry used for the filming of Helm's Deep in Rohan and Minas Tirith in Gondor.

The second tour is an extension of the first, providing a full-day experience. In addition to the previously mentioned locations, this tour also visits Fernside Lodge which was transformed into part of Lothlórien and Gladden Fields where Sméagol and Déagol fought for The Ring at the lakeside. Also visited is Miramar, production headquarters and home to the director, Peter Jackson and many of the cast and crew, and Weta Cave, a mini museum dedicated to the LOTR trilogy in Wellington. A third Deluxe Middle Earth tour extends Tour Two with a helicopter trip over the limestone formations that formed The Dimholt road (the Paths of the Dead).

A cursory examination of customer feedback and TripAdvisor reviews of these tours reveals several insights into the visitors, their motivations for visiting and their experiences. It appears that general and special interest tourists participate in the tours and are motivated primarily by the desire to learn more about the film, its production and about the director, cast and crew, and to experience the scenery in which filming took place. These motivations are evidenced by the following statements:

'I just wanted to let you know that we had a wonderful time on our quick tour of the Lord of the Rings filming locations with Garth on the weekend. You guys have a great set up and Garth was just great – totally passionate about his job and he really knew his stuff re. Lord of the Rings. He must have done a great job as my partner had not seen any of the films (I discovered this on the morning of the tour) but he has remembered everything about all the locations we went to and has been able to describe it all to our friends and family while showing them our photos.' (Therese, Australia, New Zealand Tourism Guide, 2016)

'I think the thing that makes the Flat Earth tour so good is the intimacy of a small group. It's not just the movie locations, but meeting other fans of the movies and books, and also getting that different perspective from someone who was actually a part of the movies, without being overwhelmed by 29 other supposed fans. Although those three crazy women were pretty overwhelming by themselves hahaha!!!' (Leigh USA, New Zealand Tourism Guide, 2016)

'... Now when I look back & go through my photographs I wonder if the trip really took place or was it just a dream? I would love to be in Wellington for the Return of the King Premier, but would I be able to see Viggo in person & survive after that, I am not sure! Thank you! Thanks indeed for that absolutely fabulous guided tour that you provided us (along with hot coffee at Rivendale & lovely lunch). I shall remember it all my life.' (Rashmi, India, New Zealand Tourism Guide, 2016)

'We did the extended tour, and boy was it worth it. Our guide Jack, who also happens to be a founder of the NZ chapter of the Tolkien Society, was chock full of knowledge about the different sites and even managed to impress a self-professed fanatic on the subject. Through nine hours of touring we were thoroughly satisfied with our Lord of the Rings experience. Would recommend to all fans of the films, and the books as well. Worth every penny!' (Asbojn T, TripAdvisor, 2014b)

The visitor experience was heavily influenced by the desire to emotionally connect more closely with the films. This was achieved by either interacting directly with members of the cast or crew or by re-enacting scenes from the films, and is clearly demonstrated by the following statements:

'My sister and I had an amazing time! Our guide, Nathan, was really fun and very knowledgeable. It was just the three of us, but I felt like he went above

and beyond to make sure we had an amazing time. He could tell I was a big fan and I really loved that he gave me the chance to recreate some of my favorite scenes from the movie. A great tour!!' (Reine S May, TripAdvisor, 2014b)

'We had a fantastic day. Jack Machiela, our tour guide for the day, picked us up bang on time in a luxurious new Toyota minibus for a wonderful tour of various LOTR locations. What he didn't know about LOTR wasn't worth know-ing and his enthusiasm and energy were infectious. He was an extra in some of the scenes and a founder member of the New Zealand Tolkien society. I suspect he can speak at least one of the Elvish languages. He illustrated many of the sites with photos and clips on his iPad and was a mine of information about how some of the scenes were composed. We also had fun re-enacting some of the scenes using simple props – for example when Aragorn is rescued from the river bank by his horse Brego.' (Paulofpleshy, TripAdvisor, 2014b)

'The whole family really enjoyed the experience. Dawn made us all welcome and her tales from the movies really brought the locations alive. Great fun with the masks and swords!' (LlamaSyd, TripAdvisor, 2014b)

Co-creation is clearly important here, as the extent to which a tourist becomes emotionally involved with an object, person, event, film, TV pro-duction, literary work or site can greatly influence the experience. Voase (2003: 260) claims that tourists to historic settings bring with them 'a set of memories … and a set of anticipations based on those memories'. Couldry (1998) suggested that becoming a film tourist requires considerable amounts of emotional investment. Carl *et al.*'s (2007) investigation of on-site experi-ences of film tourists visiting Hobbiton (Matamata) and Wellington, two main locations of LOTR in New Zealand, found that tourists with a high degree of involvement were willing to re-enact actions or scenes from the film in order to experience the filmed landscapes from the perspectives of the film's characters. Such contentions serve to illustrate the applicability of Vargo and Lusch's (2016) sixth foundational premise, this being that the tourist is always the co-creator of value.

Indeed, Roesch (2009) claims that most LOTR film tourists attached intrinsically deeper meanings to the filmed locations involving emotional and empathetic spatial involvement. Moreover, he notes that for film tour-ists, especially purposeful rather than incidental film tourists, the film loca-tions were experienced as 'sacred places rather than as sites of spectacle' (Roesch, 2009: 134). This contention reinforces Couldry's (1998) labelling of film tourism locations as ritual sites and reiterates the notion that the viewing and subsequent actual experience with the locations depicted are highly personalised, subjective and unique to each individual. Moreover, as Kim (2012: 389) argues, it is based on the tourists' 'own pleasure, emotion, imagination, interpretation and memory'. Similarly, Kim's (2010) work on

Winter Sonata, a Korean TV drama series, revealed that previous viewing experiences of a TV series, or in other words the tourists' operant resource (Vargo & Lusch, 2004), not only co-creates 'personalised memories and attachment with its filmed locations, but also inspires film tourists to enhance their touristic experiences by re-enacting cinematic scenes' (Kim 2012: 389).

Meanwhile, Reijnders (2011a) found that some tourists attempting to connect with Stoker's novel *Dracula* (1897) and screen adaptations wished to gain an emotional experience which he terms the 'lieux d'imagination' (Reijnders, 2011a: 15). This occurs when the Dracula tourist wishes to come 'closer to the story' and to make a connection through a symbiosis between reality and imagination. This is sometimes achieved by the re-enactment of certain scenes by fans, or they sleep in the same hotels as the characters and eat the same meals as the characters in the book (Reijnders, 2011a). Kim (2010) labels such involvement 'emotionally oriented interaction' which includes not only identification with and liking for individual characters, but also accounts for emotional reactions to the story, dialogues, situations and title music. Clearly, with high levels of emotional interaction, the blurring of reality and fiction becomes a distinct possibility (see Chapter 1).

A desire for audience involvement and engagement (Kim & Rubin, 1997; Perse, 1990; Rubin & Perse, 1987) has also been found to influence the co-created experience. Reijnders (2011b) revealed that it was stimulated by the existence of an inner experience among *Dracula* tourists. This was characterised by the desire to make a concrete comparison between the portrayed landscape and the 'truth' behind the story (Reijnders, 2011b). They achieved this by comparing the spatial descriptions that Stoker made and the visual representations from the films with the physical reality of the actual environment. Perse (1990), however, discovered that repeated face-to-face interaction with media personalities in particular through long-running soap operas or TV dramas could lead to an audience member developing feelings of intimacy with the character. Moreover, it was found that audiences often completely immerse themselves in the situation, albeit artificially, and react to the actors as if they were real persons in their immediate environment. Such involvement has been termed para-social interaction, originally defined by Horton and Wohl (1956) as an imaginary sense of intimacy by an individual audience member with a media figure. More recently, it has been used to encompass cognitive and affective reactions, interpersonal involvement and affective bonds that comprise audience involvement.

Other studies of audience involvement and engagement have revealed it to be multidimensional. Kim (2012) investigated the extent to which it occurs with a serialised TV drama and affects actual on-site film experiences at its former filmed locations, this being Daejanggeum Theme Park, the main filmed location of *Jewel in the Palace*, in Yangjoo, South Korea. This study indicated that the audience's cognitive-oriented interaction and their behaviour-oriented involvement were the main drivers that positively affected their on-site film experiences. In terms of the former, Kim (2012) states that this refers to the degree to which audiences cognitively pay attention to particular characteristics or to other distinctive characteristics of the programme and go on to think about its educational and/or informational content once the programme is over. With respect to the latter, behaviour-oriented interaction relates to the degree to which individuals talk to or about media characters during and after consumption, and rearrange daily activities to make time for viewing (Kim, 2012). Sood (2002) also revealed audience involvement and engagement to be multidimensional, comprising two main elements: (i) reflection (referential and critical); and (ii) para-social interaction with the media. In this study he defined referential reflection as the degree to which an individual relates a media programme to personal experience. More specifically, the referential 'connects the programme and real life in terms of the viewers' own lives and problems as if they were relating to the characters as real people and in turn relating these real people to their own real worlds' (Kim, 2012: 390). Meanwhile, 'critical reflection is defined as the degree to which audience members distance themselves from and engage in production values of a media programme' (Kim, 2012: 390).

Another factor which influences experience is the intermingling of destination and screen images (Frost, 2010). Co-creation, co-production and co-terminality are inevitably crucial to this process as tourists are drawn to destinations through the consumption of images of places used as backgrounds and foregrounds in the popular media productions (Urry, 1990). Emotional bonds are also created as 'destinations and experiences are enhanced in the viewer's memory by special technological effects, an association with famous actors and highly attractive settings' (Tooke & Barker, 1996: 88). The significance of such bonds between tourists as audiences and filmed locations in terms of film tourism experiences is well documented through the work of Riley et al. (1998) in particular. This study contends that 'if some part of a movie is extraordinary or captivating, it serves as an icon which viewers attach to a location shown in the movie. This icon could be a single event, a favourite performer, or a location's physical features' (Riley et al., 1998: 924). According to Urry (1990), non-tourism related cultural and social practices are playing an increasingly important role in constructing tourism spaces and tourist experiences in contemporary tourism, so much so that people's initial experiences with any locations are primarily through popular media consumption; consequently, reality is the secondary comparison.

When taken together, this discussion demonstrates the importance of co-creation, a key feature of the HSLT nexus (p. 2) in underpinning demand for HSLT, the dimensions of which are summarised in Figure 2.1. It is the tourists' anticipation of co-creative participation in the experience prior to consumption, sometimes referred to as co-invention or co-design (Binkhorst

Figure 2.1 Dimensions of the co-creation of heritage, screen and literary tourism demand
Source: The authors (2017).

& Den Dekker, 2009; Ek *et al.*, 2012) which acts as a powerful draw to engage in these forms of tourism. Most notably this discussion also highlights the applicability of S-DL to HSLT as it demonstrates, as Vargo and Lusch (2004) profess in their fifth foundational premise, that most if not all economies are service economies. Additionally, given the operant resources (memories, knowledge, education, experience, money and skills) associated with heritage, screen and literary tourists, they have become the producers and actors as opposed to passive audiences that enable value co-creation to be created and extracted. While in some instances, the motivations driving the demand for HSLT may be easily identified by an individual, others such as the desire for para-social interaction may be unrecognised or suppressed. Consequently, Vargo and Lusch's (2004) third foundational premise (goods are a distribution mechanism for service provision) is of notable relevance here since it recognises that intangibles may also contribute to the co-creation of the service experience. This, combined with their first, fourth, sixth and tenth foundational premises, go some way toward explaining exactly how the tourist is able to co-create the experience prior to consumption.

So far this chapter has focused on detailing aspects relating to demand that occurs or, in other words, that relates to those tourists who participate in HSLT. However, another important type of demand that is worthy of attention is that which is unmet or latent. This is because, although non-visitors are extremely problematic to research or quantify, potentially they are a valuable segment of demand to understand if sites and destinations are to attract new visitors and encourage back those who seldom or no longer visit.

Latent Demand

According to Timothy and Boyd (2003: 73), latent demand refers to the 'difference between the potential participation in tourism within the population and the current level of participation'. Within the context of HSLT, it can therefore be understood to relate to people who have never visited a related site or destination, who never think about visiting, who used to visit but no longer do so and/or who infrequently visit. While research of latent demand for these three forms of tourism is virtually non-existent, insights can be gained from studies that have investigated non-visitation among young adults (18–26 years old) to museums and art galleries (Bartlett & Kelly, 2000; Beeho et al., 1997; Kelly & Bartlett, 2009; Korn, 2008; McCarthy & Mason, 2008; Mokhtar & Kasim, 2012; Shrapnel, 2012), and a variety of reasons have been identified.

The perception that museums lack interest and relevance to the needs and wants of young adults has been cited by a number of academics as a reason for non-visitation (McCarthy & Mason, 2008; Mohktar & Kasim, 2012; Shrapnel, 2012). Kelly et al. (2002) note that young adults' perspectives of museums are that they are preoccupied with the past instead of being more forward looking and representing the present and future. Moreover, Korn (2008) states that young adults view museums as dictating, uninviting and firmly structured – a finding reinforced by Kelly and Bartlett (2009) whose research suggests that they see museum exhibitions as boring, unapproachable and protective. According to Korn (2008) and Shrapnel (2012), young adults desire an environment which enables them to be social, feel comfortable and to learn and share ideas. Kelly and Bartlett (2009) state that young people prefer social venues where they have the opportunity to meet and learn from like-minded people, while Kelly et al. (2002) note that young adults desire exhibitions which cater for group engagement and allow them to share and compare, not just simply read and review. Social media has certainly played an important role in this perception as it has inevitably altered the way in which information is obtained, exchanged and assimilated. Thus, young adults now desire interaction which enables them to engage with the content matter (Kelly & Bartlett, 2009; Korn, 2008), thereby co-creating and co-producing the experience.

Childhood experiences of museum visitation have also been identified as a contributing reason for latent demand among young adults. According to Anderson *et al.* (2000) and Kelly and Bartlett (2009), memories of enforced school visits to museums have significantly influenced young adults' decisions to visit museums later in life as such visits are associated with education as opposed to entertainment. Indeed, Bradburne (1998) and Falk and Dierking (2012) agree that museums need to move away from being educational venues to those that encourage casual learning. This view is supported by Leinhardt *et al.* (1998), who argue that museums should encompass a multifaceted, outward-looking role as hosts who invite visitors to their venue to wonder, encounter and learn as they choose.

In addition, perceptions of the high cost of visiting museums are a barrier that is preventing young adults' museum attendance (Mokhtar & Kasim, 2012; Shrapnel, 2012). Most young adults are students, or are just starting their career in the workforce and consequently have very limited disposable income (Kelly & Bartlett, 2009). Mohktar and Kasim (2012) and Shrapnel (2012) also found that lack of time during the day was an obstacle. Meanwhile, the sterile environment that is often found at museums has been found to influence visitation. McCarthy and Mason (2008) state that young adults do not feel as if they are a part of museums and they do not feel at home and Korn (2008) claims that young adults do not view museums as being comfortable, inviting or relaxing venues. This view is shared by Beeho *et al.* (1997), who state that young adults feel they are out of their comfort zone. Such a perception is, as Fleming (1999) suggests, a psychological barrier caused by the notion of threshold fear which dissuades people from entering spaces where they feel uncomfortable.

Latent demand, however, is not just caused by the conscious decisions of tourists to not visit, as disability acts as a major barrier to non-participation in tourism. Smith's (1987) seminal study of the barriers and obstacles to participation facing the disabled identified three main types. The first labelled 'environmental' includes attitudinal, architectural and ecological barriers. Smith (1987) notes that the living environment and the attitude of others, particularly negative attitudes of non-disabled tourists toward disabled individuals, is often cited by disabled people as a barrier to participation in tourism. This contention is supported by Daruwalla and Darcy (2005). Moreover, despite the implementation of disability discrimination legislation in many Western countries, architectural barriers still exist and there are many sites and destinations that are still inaccessible to disabled tourists (Israeli, 2002). Meanwhile, some natural obstacles or ecological barriers are difficult to overcome by an unassisted person who has a disability. The second types of barrier to disabled person participation in tourism identified by Smith (1987) are those that relate to the 'interactive' skills of the individual, most notably their ability to communicate, while the third are 'intrinsic', associated with the participants' physical, psychological and/or cognitive functioning.

In addition, other types of barriers have been identified such as perceptual accessibility (Daruwalla & Darcy, 2005; Smith, 1987; Yau et al., 2004). This relates to people's awareness of the existence of supporting facilities and organisations and to an individual's assessment of their own capabilities in relation to the ability to undertake tourist activities. According to Smith (1987), lack of previous experience often translates into low assessment and avoidance due to the fear of failure. Some disabled people do not have sufficient financial resources for tourism at their disposal and therefore face financial barriers; others are prevented from participating in tourism due to a lack of information about tourism opportunities for the disabled. Without reliable, accurate and comprehensive information about where to go, what activities are available and what challenges will be met en route, a disabled person is unable to plan adequately and for some this barrier may too difficult to overcome. Furthermore, disabled tourists may be prevented from participating in tourism due to the existence of transport barriers (Abeyraine, 1995; Cavinato & Cuckovich, 1992) with air travel noted as being a particularly stressful experience (Darcy, 2012; Poria et al., 2010). Of all of these barriers, intrinsic barriers are argued to be the greatest obstacle to tourism participation. This is because feelings of incompetence may over time lead to feelings of generalised helplessness resulting in reduced future participation (Lee et al., 2012; Yau et al., 2004).

Conclusion

This chapter has focused on the demand for HSLT and has discussed in depth motivations, tourist types and typologies in addition to experiences within the context of the HSLT nexus and theorisations provided by S-DL and co-creation. It is argued that the co-creation of demand is a key part of the HSLT nexus which binds these three forms of tourism together. This is because value co-creation and extraction is inevitably influenced by the nature and extent of tourists' interaction with the resource, thereby illustrating the relevance of Vargo and Lusch's (2016) first, third, fourth, sixth and tenth foundational premises to examinations of HSLT demand (see Table 1.7).

Arguably, tourists are now seeking more than ever before more creative experiences (Richards, 2013) that are contingent upon interaction with built and natural resources. Their motivations for doing so and the resulting experiences are complex but essentially reflect the outcome of the desire to co-create (see Figure 2.1). This is not least because, in the words of Kim

(2012: 387), 'tourists' anticipations, expectations and experiences are constructed and contextualised by television and cinematic narratives and mediated representations of other lands or even periods with embedded signs, myths and symbolic meanings'. Despite existing research, there is still much to be learnt about the motivations, types and experiences of heritage, screen and literary tourists. Such understanding is immensely important as it is precisely the co-creation of the inner experience of tourists which lies at the heart of all three forms of tourism. Indeed it is precisely where an imaginary world coincides with reality and where the boundaries between fact and fiction become blurred – an issue that is discussed in more detail in the next chapter.

3 The Heritage, Screen and Literary Tourism Debate

Introduction

HSLT has grown in significance worldwide (see Chapter 1). While the economic importance of these three forms of tourism has been widely documented (Busby & Klug, 2001; Herbert, 2001; Timothy & Boyd, 2003), the benefits of heritage tourism to society in particular have been intensely contested. Drawing on the earlier work of Lowenthal (1985) and Wright (1985), Hewison (1987) has most notably been vociferous in the 'heritage tourism debate'. He argues that in its quest to entertain rather than educate, this form of tourism has distorted the past, has fuelled an obsession with a sanitised, rose-tinted version of history, has encouraged nostalgia, and as a consequence has stifled innovation thereby creating a climate of decline. Moreover, the inaccurate presentation of the past has been manipulated and exploited for political purposes, either to create and strengthen national identities or to politically legitimise existing or new regimes.

Although this debate primarily concerns heritage tourism and at first glance may appear to be rather outdated, it is equally relevant to screen and literary tourism since they also involve the portrayal of the past and, in doing so, promulgate nostalgia and backward-looking thinking. Indeed, arguably such a debate lies at the heart of the HSLT nexus. This is because it is the outcome of the consumption and production of all three forms of tourism, occurring as a result of co-creation, the (re)representation and commodification of people, places and events, the use of contingent elements and co-terminality. In addition, it serves to highlight the limited attention to date within S-DL and co-creation discourses that has been directed at resources that are not necessarily value adding; instead, by resulting in historical distortion and the blurring of fact and fiction, they may be value destroying, thereby leading to poorer quality experiences and lesser value (Neuhofer, 2016).

It is within the context of the HSLT nexus, and couched in the frameworks provided by S-DL and co-creation, that this chapter revisits the heritage tourism debate. Thus, in the first part of the chapter the key arguments underpinning this debate are detailed. In particular, there is in-depth consideration of the extent to which HSLT results in historical distortion and its implications for the health of society. In the second part of the chapter the politics of HSLT are discussed and the politicisation of these three forms of tourism is considered. More specifically, the use of HSLT in diaspora and to reaffirm contested and dissonant heritage is analysed, and the role in this process of organisations and agencies, such as UNESCO and the Heritage Lottery Fund within the UK, are assessed. Following this, some conclusions are posed.

The Heritage Tourism Debate

The heritage tourism debate, initiated by Hewison (1987), encompasses a robust exchange of opinions concerning the benefits for society of this niche market sector. Its origins are rooted in an earlier, broader debate concerning the role of heritage within society and England's alleged obsession with the past. Wright (1985), for example, in his book *On Living in an Old Country*, drew a connection between decline and the contemporary obsession with heritage. Meanwhile, Lowenthal (1985: xviii) stated that 'English attitudes towards locale seem permeated with antiquarianism – a settled bent in favour of the old or the traditional, even if less useful or beautiful than the new'. In short, both argued that because the English were unable to cope with social and cultural upheaval which characterised the 1970s and 1980s, turning to the past for consolation, heritage became a key word in a wider debate about the nation's identity. According to Lumley (1994), it stood as a metaphor for a post-Imperial Britain that was steadily losing out to other countries in the struggle for industrial and commercial competitiveness.

Commenting specifically in relation to the prolific growth of the heritage tourism industry during the 1970s and 1980s, Hewison reiterated the notions of Wright (1985) and Lowenthal (1985), stating that England had indeed become obsessed with the past, citing the demand for historical re-enactment as 'evidence of the persistent fantasy that it is possible to step back into the past' (Hewison, 1987: 83). Arguably, these early observations highlight an emergent trend involving consumer co-creation and S-DL, centring on participation and interaction with the resources consumed (Vargo & Lusch, 2004). Such growth, Hewison contended, is creating a climate of decline, through the promotion of a culture that is backward looking, anti-industrial and anti-technological, fearful of the present, escapist and incapable of innovation.

Moreover, in its quest to make a profit by entertaining rather than educating, heritage tourism is preserving and commodifying a 'bogus history' based on a 'collective myth' comprised of rose-tinted memories. Such recollections are heavily steeped in nostalgia, which in itself consists of a selective, idealised and inaccurate version of the past, usually just within living memory. Indeed, it is the historical distortion of the past which Hewison (1987) argues is unhealthy for society. This is because it may in some instances preserve unjust social values of an earlier age of privilege or exploitation which may be continued into the present. In addition, Hewison (1987) argues that heritage tourism is not an appropriate substitute for industrial enterprises since the jobs available have no bearing on the future skills of society. By implication, it therefore appears that in this context heritage resources are not value adding but value destroying (Neuhofer, 2016).

Many commentators, however, including Lowenthal (1985) and Walsh (1990), have been highly critical of Hewison's propositions, arguing instead that the heritage boom was a sign of change and innovation rather than decline. Indeed, both contend that the growth of heritage tourism should be seen less as an inability to come to terms with change and more as a strategy for enabling change; it thus may be considered to be a value-adding resource (Neuhofer, 2016). This is because it has become a variant of development, used to economically regenerate declining inner-city areas worldwide. It is, after all, an economic resource that can be utilised to offset employment losses occurring in declining primary and secondary industries (Case Study 3.1). Thus, according to Lumley (1987, 1988), heritage should be reinterpreted as a sign of postmodernity rather than as the downside of modernity with its failures and disappointments. Moreover, Walsh (1990) and Lumley (1994) argue that heritage tourism is of great value to society as lessons may be learned from the past. Additionally, it shows concern for the past and in conserving resources for future generations. Furthermore, Lowenthal (1985), Walsh (1990) and Lumley (1994) criticise Hewison's arguments, stating that it is impossible to have an accurate view of the past. As Hewison (1987) states, heritage is a kind of bogus history, based on myth which draws on history. Importantly, however, heritage is not historically accurate as even scholarly historical research reinterprets the past. It is irrecoverable and in this sense it is always going to be distorted and present a standardised past.

Case Study 3.1 Heritage conservation and urban redevelopment in Kaohsiung, Taiwan

Kaohsiung, Taiwan's second largest city, is situated on its southwest coast, and is home to more than 1.5 million people. It grew from a small village established by the Dutch in the 17th century to become not only Taiwan's leading harbour city, but also the island's key industrial area. However, due to global shifts in production, Kaohsiung City has more recently experienced a decline of its primary and manufacturing industries, and the downgrading of the once-thriving seaport, resulting in dilapidated urban fabric, high unemployment and a loss of a sense of place.

Kaohsiung is in urgent need of regeneration, and consequently the city government has initiated plans for redevelopment through the integration of heritage conservation with urban regeneration. Such an approach has been adopted in order to bring back a sense of life and to help secure the social coherence, economic efficiency and environmental sustainability of the city. Moreover, it was indeed an appropriate approach as the city has a long and varied history spanning three centuries and possesses a diverse and rich heritage. It is home to many ancient temples such as the Queen of Heaven (Plate 3.1), one of the oldest structures remaining in Kaohsiung, the city walls dating back to the Qing dynasty, the Old British Consulate (Plate 3.2), the Qitiou Fortress and the Lighthouse (Plate 3.3). Meanwhile, many historic buildings and monuments have already been conserved, including the Old Gate at Fengshan and Confucius's Temple (Plate 3.4).

In addition, other historic buildings have been redeveloped and converted into other uses. For instance, the Municipal Office is now a history museum (Plate 3.5), while the old Kaohsiung Train Station built in 1940 in typical Imperial style and faced with demolition was conserved and relocated to an adjacent site in 2002 (Plate 3.6); it currently functions as an exhibition centre displaying ideas for the integration of heritage with urban development, creating a space for reflection and observation as well as transforming anxieties about change and uncertainty into positive anticipation of the future.

Plate 3.1 Queen of Heaven Temple (Tianhou Temple), Kaohsiung, Taiwan
Source: The authors (2017).

Plate 3.2 The Old British Consulate, Kaohsiung, Taiwan
Source: The authors (2017).

Plate 3.3 The Lighthouse, Kaohsiung, Taiwan
Source: The authors (2017).

Plate 3.4 Confucius Temple, Kaohsiung, Taiwan
Source: The authors (2017).

Besides historic landmarks, elements of the city's industrial heritage have also been conserved, perhaps best illustrated by the example of the reconstruction of the former Tangrong brick kiln in 2004, one of Taiwan's earliest factories (Plate 3.7). The production of the Tangrong

Plate 3.5 Municipal History Museum, Kaohsiung, Taiwan
Source: The authors (2017).

Plate 3.6 The old Kaohsiung Train Station, Kaohsiung, Taiwan
Source: The authors (2017).

Brick Kiln played an important role in Taiwan's economic boom in the 1960s and 1970s. However, as construction methods changed drastically, it was forced to close in 1985, and plans are afoot to reopen this building as a museum.

Plate 3.7 Tangrong Brick Kiln, Kaohsiung, Taiwan
Source: The authors (2017).

Although originally conducted in the context of heritage tourism, this debate is equally relevant to screen and literary tourism as history is ripe for the mining of ready-made stories of adventure and romance but in the process may also distort the past and provide an inaccurate presentation of history. The extent to which screen and literary tourism value co-creates or co-destroys is debatable, though, and very much depends on the operant resources and expectations of those reading or watching the material. This contention therefore suggests that Vargo and Lusch's (2004) foundational premises one (service is the fundamental basis of exchange), four (operant resources are the fundamental source of competitive advantage) and 10 (value is always uniquely and phenomenologically determined by the beneficiary) are important here in influencing the service exchange process (see Table 1.7).

Historical subjects, both people or events, have always attracted filmmakers and novelists (Tables 3.1 and 3.2), both of which have produced historical dramas based on past events or famous persons in history. Some historical dramas attempt to portray a historical event or biography accurately, to the degree that historical research will allow. Other historical dramas are fictionalised tales of an actual event, or a person and their deeds. Table 3.1 demonstrates some examples of historical movies set within different eras, ranging from prehistory, Ancient History (up to the fall of the Roman Empire), the Middle Ages (5th–15th centuries), Early Modern times (16th–17th centuries), the 18th and 19th centuries, the 20th century and the late 20th century, each varying in terms of their historical accuracy.

The Alamo, for example – the 1960 movie starring John Wayne – is based on the actual events and characters surrounding the creation of Texas. It dramatises the Battle of the Alamo, a siege which lasted 13 days in 1836, constituting the most celebrated military engagement in Texan history. With respect to historical accuracy, this film provides a reasonably accurate factual account of the historical situation as far as it is known. However, while the lead characters, Jim Bowie and Crockett, are not presented as paragons of virtue, various less palatable aspects of their lives are ignored. No mention is made of Jim Bowie's slave-running days or the fact that he allegedly married his wife for her money. Crockett is also much less heroic in the movie than he was purported to be in real life, as historical records show that he came to Texas in the hope of restarting his political career.

Sink the Bismarck! is another good example of a historical movie based on an actual event. It is a 1960s film based on the novel by C.S. Forester (*The Last Nine Days of the Bismarck*), and is about the German battleship Bismarck which boasted cannon that were 19 yards long and which was sent to strangle Britain into submission by striking at the vulnerable convoys in the Atlantic. In terms of its historical accuracy, it gives an accurate portrayal of the long-distance nature of combat between battleships, which was essentially an artillery duel at sea where binoculars were needed to see the enemy

Table 3.1 Examples of historical movies

Era	Historical movies
Set in prehistoric times	*10,000 BC* is set in the prehistoric era and tells the story of a tribe of hunter-gatherers called the Yagahl.
	Bharat Ek Khoj is a 53-episode TV series which dramatises the 5000-year history of India from its beginnings to the coming of Independence in 1947.
	The Clan of the Cave Bear is about a Cro-Magnon woman who gets separated from her family during an earthquake and is found by a group of Neanderthals.
	Quest for Fire is a science fantasy adventure set in Palaeolithic Europe.
Set in Ancient History	*Clash of the Titans* is based on the legendary adventures of the Greek hero, Perseus.
	Troy is set in the Bronze Age (c. 1190 BC) and is based on Homer's *Iliad*, an epic poem which tells of the battles and events during the weeks of a quarrel between King Agamemnon and the Warrior Achilles.
	Cleopatra is a fictitious drama based on the Egyptian Queen during the first years of the Roman Empire (1st century BC).
	Alexander is based on the life of Alexander the Great (4th century BC).
Set in the Middle Ages (3rd–15th centuries)	*King Arthur* is set in the last years of the Roman occupation and tells the story of King Arthur, depicting him as a Roman warrior as opposed to a medieval king as he is more commonly believed to have been.
	The Castilian is a romanticised Spanish film about Ferdinand Gonzalez, a significant 10th century figure of the Reconquista.
	The Viking Sagas is a fictitious film based loosely on the Icelandic sagas, prose histories describing events which took place on the island during the 10th and early 11th centuries.
	Pope Joan dramatises the life of a woman, possibly fictitious, who may or may not have disguised herself as a man and rose to the status of Pope in the 9th century.
Set in Early Modern times (16th–17th centuries)	*Princes in the Tower*, set in England in the 1490s, dramatises the trial of Perkin Warbeck who claimed to be Prince Richard, rightful heir to the throne.
	The Other Boleyn Girl is a dramatisation about Anne Boleyn, Queen of England.
	Elizabeth is a dramatisation about Elizabeth I, Queen of England.
	Cromwell is a dramatisation about Oliver Cromwell, 1st Lord Protector of the Commonwealth of England, Scotland, and Ireland 1653–1658.

(Continued)

Table 3.1 (Continued)

Era	Historical movies
Set in the 18th and 19th centuries	Amadeus is a dramatisation about the life and death of Mozart.
	The Alamo is based on the creation of Texas, USA and dramatises the Battle of the Alamo, a siege which lasted 13 days in 1836 and which constitutes the most celebrated military engagement in Texan history.
	Amistad is a dramatisation of the 1839 mutiny aboard a ship carrying African slaves bound for the USA.
	Gone with the Wind is an epic romance-drama film set in the Old South in and around the American Civil War.
Set in the 20th century	Evita is based on the life of Eva Perón, who became First Lady and spiritual leader of Argentina during the years 1946–1952.
	Ghandi is a biographical film based on the life of Mahatma Ghandi, who led the non-violent resistance movement against British colonial rule during the first half of the 20th century.
	Sink the Bismarck! is based on a fictionalised account of the sinking of a German battleship, the Bismarck.
	Titanic is a fictionalised account of the sinking of the Titanic, the largest passenger steamship in the world, on 10 April 1912.
Late 20th century	The Good Shepherd is a fictional film loosely based around real events surrounding the rise of the CIA's Counter Intelligence Unit.
	Hotel Rwanda is based on the Rwandan genocide which occurred in 1994, during which an estimated 800,000 people were murdered.
	JFK dramatises the events leading up to the assassination of President John F. Kennedy and alleged subsequent cover-up, through the eyes of the former New Orleans District Attorney, Jim Garrison.
	Cry Freedom is set in the late 1970s, during the apartheid era of South Africa, and centres around the real-life events involving the black activists Steve Biko and his friend Donald Woods.

Source: The authors (2017).

clearly. Furthermore, the movie shows the agonising guesswork involved in searching for a tiny speck in the vast ocean; the scenes of carnage that followed each battle are chilling, especially when men are left inside a flooded compartment. However, while it is entertaining, the movie's greatest weakness is that the story is mainly presented from the British viewpoint, primarily that of the Operations Division. Moreover, although the majority of characters are based on real people, the story is told mainly from the point of view of Shepherd, who is a fictional character. In addition, in the film, Admiral Günther Lütjens, commander of the Bismarck, is filled with confidence even though the Bismarck was sent to sea with only one heavy cruiser as escort instead of several battleships and heavy cruisers as was originally planned. However, the real Lutjens had protested strongly, wanting to wait until other ships such as the Scharnhorst, Guiseneau or the Tirpitz, the Bismarck's sister ship, were ready. Furthermore, the movie also fails to show that, despite the lengthy search, the British would never have found the Bismarck if Lütjens' fixation on promoting the cause of the surface navy had not driven him to repeatedly send really long messages to Germany which enabled HF/DF receivers to triangulate his rough position. Since the film was made with the active support and assistance of the Admiralty, the top leaders are seen through rose-tinted glasses.

There are also many examples of historical fiction novels, some of which are listed in Table 3.2. An early example of historical fiction is Luó Guànzhōng's 14th century *Romance of Three Kingdoms* which covers one of the most important periods of Chinese history. In England, Daniel Defoe was one of the first successful writers in this genre, with works such as *Robinson Crusoe* using historical settings. The historical novel was further popularised in the 19th century by writers classified as Romantics. Many regard Sir Walter Scott as the first to have used this technique in his novels of Scottish history such as *Waverley* (1814). Victor Hugo's *The Hunchback of Notre Dame* (1831) furnishes another 19th century example of the romantic-historical novel, as does Leo Tolstoy's *War and Peace*.

Dealing with history creates a host of dilemmas for the filmmaker and the novelist, as much of our view of what we know is shaped by what is seen on the screen and by what we read. For example, whose viewpoint is represented and to what extent are the real facts presented? It is also important to note that movies and novels must have audience appeal and the circumstances of and events leading up to certain events may be too shocking or too complicated to be presented easily. It is not surprising, therefore, that movies and literary works can result in an inaccurate portrayal of the past. Perhaps more importantly, however, such historical distortion occurs because there is a blurring of fact and fiction (Table 3.3), often associated with heroes and heroines and well-known characters of literary works, films and TV programmes, or with places which feature significantly in both book and screen versions.

Table 3.2 Examples of historical novels

Era	Books
Set in prehistoric times	*The Earth's Children* series (Jean M. Auel): five novels about a Cro-Magnon woman.
	The Gift of Stones (Jim Crace): about a boy from the Stone Age who explores the world beyond the village and discovers people who know how to make and use bronze.
	The Inheritors (William Golding): about conflict between the Neanderthals and Homo Sapiens.
	Pillar of the Sky (Cecilia Holland): about the building of Stonehenge, UK.
Set in Ancient History	*I, Claudius* (Robert Graves): set in Ancient Rome and based on the Roman Emperor Claudius.
	The Last of the Wine (Mary Renault): set in Ancient Greece and based on the life of Alexias, a young aristocrat during the Peloponnesian War.
	The Silver Chalice (Thomas B. Costain): about a silversmith who is commissioned to make a cover for the Holy Grail during the years following the crucifixion.
	Death Comes as the End (Agatha Christie): about a young widow in Thebes in 2000 BC who returns to her father's house shortly before he brings home a concubine who falls or is pushed to her death from a cliff.
Set in the Middle Ages (3rd–15th centuries)	*The Name of the Rose* (Umberto Eco): a historical murder mystery set in an Italian monastery in 1327.
	Romance of Three Kingdoms (Luó Guànzhōng): the epic tale of the Han Dynasty during the 3rd and 4th centuries.
	The Hunchback of Notre Dame (Victor Hugo): set in 15th century France, a gypsy girl is framed for murder by the infatuated Chief Justice and only the deformed bell ringer of Notre Dame Cathedral can save her.
	The Pillars of the Earth (Ken Follett): set in the middle of the 12th century, about the building of a cathedral in the fictional town of Kingsbridge, England.
Set in Early Modern times (16th–17th centuries)	*Robinson Crusoe* (Daniel Defoe): about a castaway called Robinson Crusoe who spends 28 years on a remote tropical island near Venezuela.
	The Three Musketeers (Alexandre Dumas): set in the 17th century, recounting the adventures of a young man, d'Artagnan, after he leaves home to become a guard of the musketeers.
	Waverley (Sir Walter Scott): set during the Jacobite Rebellion of 1745, the story of a young dreamer and English soldier, Edward Waverley, who was sent to Scotland in 1745.

	Anne of Austria (Evelyn Anthony): a biographical novel about Anne of Austria, the wife of the French king Louis XIII and mother of Louis XIV.
Set in the 18th and 19th centuries	*War and Peace* (Leo Tolstoy): detailing events leading up to Napoleon's invasion of Russia, and the impact of the Napoleonic era on Tsarist society, as seen through the eyes of five Russian aristocratic families.
	A Tale of Two Cities (Charles Dickens): set in London and Paris before and during the French Revolution, depicting the events which took place involving the peasantry and the aristocracy.
	The Quincunx (Charles Palliser): set in 19th century England, concerning the varying fortunes of John Huffam and his mother.
	The Painter (Will Davenport): about a modern woman who discovers a diary written 300 years ago that describes the rivalry of the painter Rembrandt van Rijn and the poet Andrew Marvell for a woman's love.
Set in the 20th century	*All Quiet on the Western Front* (Erich Maria Remarque): describing a German soldier's extreme mental and physical stress during WWI, and the detachment from civilian life felt by many of these soldiers upon returning home from the front.
	The Road to Welville (T.C. Boyle): set in 1907, the story of John Harvey Kellogg, inventor of Kellogg's cornflakes and his Battle Creek Sanatorium.
	Birdsong (Sebastian Faulkes): the experiences of soldier Stephen Wraysford while serving on the Western Front in WWI.
	Empire of the Sun (J.G. Ballard): set during the WWII, the story of a young British boy, Jim Graham, who lives with his parents in Shanghai which becomes occupied by the Japanese.
Late 20th century	*The Historian* (Elizabeth Kostova): set in the 1970s, interweaving the history and folklore of Vlad Țepeș, a 15th-century prince of Wallachia known as 'Vlad the Impaler', and his fictional equivalent Count Dracula together with the story of Paul, a professor, his 16-year-old daughter and their quest for Vlad's tomb.
	Sepulchre (Kate Mosse): based in two time periods, 1891 and the present day, following two heroines who are separated by more than 100 years.
	Diana: In Pursuit of Love (Andrew Morton): based on tapes made by Diana for Morton, along with interviews with friends, advisors and colleagues.
	Ronnie Biggs: The Inside Story (Mark Gray and Ted Currie): written by two of Ronnie Biggs's closest friends, providing insight into the mind and subsequent treatment by the judicial and penal systems of the man who became a legendary household name for his role in one of Britain's most notorious crimes, the Great Train Robbery of 1963, and his subsequent life on the run upon his escape from prison in 1965.

Source: The authors (2017).

Table 3.3   Fact or fiction: Examples from screen and literary tourism

Fiction	Fact
Sherlock Holmes and his faithful assistant are fictional detectives created by Sir Arthur Conan Doyle. According to the stories, between 1881 and 1904, Holmes and Watson lodged at 221B Baker Street, London NW1 6XE, a first floor flat.	Up until 1936, 221B Baker Street was an actual lodging house. In 1990 it opened as a museum dedicated to Sherlock Holmes in which the famous first floor study is maintained as it is featured in the novels. The existence of the museum suggests and reinforces the idea in the minds of many that Holmes and Watson were real people, a notion that is strengthened by the presence of a commemorative plaque on the house's exterior that states the years of Holmes's supposed residency.
Dracula is a novel written by Bram Stoker featuring the fictional character of Count Dracula, partly set in the Carpathian Mountains on the borders of Transylvania, Bukovina and Moldavia.	There is some confusion concerning whether the fictional character of Count Dracula and the real Transylvanian-born Vlad III Dracula of Wallachia, otherwise known as 'Vlad the Impaler' are one and the same person, due to some historical references within the novel. Moreover, Bran Castle (Romania) is marketed as the home of Count Dracula even though Stoker locates his Castle Dracula in the Borgo Pass in northeast Transylvania – a long way from the Wallachia border.
Neighbours is an Australian soap opera set around Ramsay Street, a fictional cul-de-sac in the fictional Melbourne suburb of Erinsborough.	Pin Oak Court in Vermont South, Melbourne doubles for Ramsay Street and is a real cul-de-sac, the residents of which allow the filming of external scenes. It is a popular tourist attraction and tours run to the cul-de-sac throughout the year.
King Arthur is a legend about a great King, his knights of the round table and Merlin the wizard and it is set in the fictitious kingdom of Camelot. This legend has been the subject of a wealth of literary works by great classical authors such as Tennyson, Wordsworth, Mark Twain and T.S. Eliot. In addition, many screen productions around the legend have been made including *The Mists of Avalon*, *Prince Valiant*, *Excalibur*, *Merlin* and *Quest for Camelot*.	The fictitious character of King Arthur is often mistaken for Arthur, a British leader of the late 5th and 6th centuries who, according to Medieval history, led the defence of Britain against Saxon invaders in the early 6th century. In fact Tintagel, Cornwall (UK) is marketed as being the location of Camelot's infamous castle and as a result has become a popular tourist attraction.

Baantjer was a Dutch novelist of detective fiction and a former police officer. He is well known for a series of detective novels set in Amsterdam, featuring Police Inspector DeKok and his side-kick Sergeant Vledder. These novels have been dramatised into a film and a long-running TV series.	The lead characters are fictional, as are the storylines. Although tourists are able to visit various locations featured in the novels and the screen dramatisations, many of these locations either do not actually exist or are situated differently from where they are portrayed. For example, Café Louis where DeKok spends much of his time propped up on a bar stool exists; however, it cannot be found in the Red Light District as the series suggests, but on a side street just on its outskirts.
The Adventures of Tom Sawyer is a novel written by Mark Twain, featuring the fictional characters of Tom Sawyer and his friend Huckleberry Finn, and is set in Hannibal, Missouri, a growing port city which lies along the banks of the Mississippi River. Tourists are able to visit the fictitious places which feature in the novel and subsequent screen dramatisations, such as Tom Sawyer's Fence and Mark Twain Cave on Route 79, which was made famous as the site where Tom and Becky got lost.	Samuel Clemons, or Mark Twain as he later became known, grew up in Hannibal, MO. Tourists are able to visit locations directly associated with the author, such as his boyhood home at 208 Hill Street, and those of his family friends such as Garth Woodside Mansion, home to Colonel J.H. Garth, and Plaster House at Hill and Main Street, home of Dr Orville Grant.
Madame Bovary, written by Gustave Flaubert, is a novel set in provincial northern France, in a fictitious town, Yonville. It is about a doctor's wife, Emma Bovary, who has adulterous affairs and lives beyond her means in order to escape the banalities and emptiness of provincial life.	Yonville is entirely fictional but is based on several small towns in Normandy, particularly Forge-les-Eaux and Ry. After the novel became a modern classic, the citizens of Ry erected a monument to Flaubert, claiming the dubious honour of having been the model for Yonville. Today the connection with *Madame Bovary* has come to dominate Ry, as tourists can visit restored homes from the era, and take an extensive 'Bovary' tour.

Source: The authors (2017).

This is particularly the case with historical fiction which tells a story that is set in the past, unlike historical drama movies and novels which have as their setting a period of history and which attempt to portray the spirit, manners and conditions of a gone-by age. The setting therefore is usually real and based on historical facts and contains a mixture of historical persons and fictional principal characters. In addition, famous events are often portrayed from perspectives that have not been recorded in history, in which fictional characters either observe or actively participate. Moreover, such historical characters are also often portrayed to deal with these events but not in a manner which has been previously recorded. In other examples, a historical event is used to enhance a story's narrative; it provides the background context in which the story's characters deal with situations (personal or otherwise) unrelated to the historical event. In such a case usually names of people and places are fictitious. Historical distortion of the past clearly occurs in the contexts of HSLT and it may not always be value adding, particularly if the tourist distinguishes the untruths and this recognition diminishes the experience and value extracted (Neuhofer, 2016). As a result, historical distortion is argued to be an integral component of the nexus, which is value destroying and which inextricably binds these three forms of tourism together.

Historical Distortion and the Nexus

The inaccurate portrayal of the past lies at the core of the HSLT nexus since its occurrence results from the influence of the four key interrelationships: co-creation, re-representation and commodification, contingency and co-terminality – which underpin these three forms of tourism (see Chapter 1, Figure 1.1). This contention is hardly surprising given that the past, whether it is that which involves people, places and/or events, is re-represented and commodified, with varying degrees of historical accuracy. Moreover, the past is also contingent on aspects of the built, living and natural environment or, as Reijnders (2009: 165) states, 'couleur locale', all of which have been inevitably altered and modified through human-induced change. Thus, that which existed in bygone eras can never be fully recaptured and any attempts to do so will be historically inaccurate. Furthermore, the historical distortion of the past may also result from co-terminality, occurring during the co-creation of a 'real' visitor experience which is based on a perishable and/or fictitious product (Case Study 3.2).

The relevance of the historical distortion of the past to the HSLT nexus is perhaps most neatly illustrated through the example of Sir Walter Scott's literary works, and in particular *Rob Roy* and its subsequent screen dramatisations which together have had a major influence on the creation and reinforcement of the modern image of Scotland. The novel re-represents and commodifies stories surrounding an actual person, Rob Roy MacGregor, who was a soldier, businessman, cattle rustler, outlaw and hero. Set in the 18th century, it is contingent on the living and natural heritage, as Scott wrote about a way of life that had been destroyed by the English and which glorified the Highland way of life. Through his descriptions of the Scottish landscape and Scottish culture and by attempting to capture a way of life which had largely disappeared, however, Scott's re-representation of Scotland was not entirely historically accurate, being far more romantic than was the case. Indeed, he presented a sanitised rose-tinted version of history which ignored the fact that *Rob Roy* was set in a period of great political turmoil, at the time of the Jacobite Rebellion in 1745 which resulted in many thousands of deaths at the infamous Battle of Culloden. In fact, Samuel Johnson's (1775) *A Journey to the Western Islands of Scotland*, a travel narrative about an 83-day journey, depicted Scotland as a wild and primitive place. Such romantic notions of Scotland, though, have been further entrenched by the screen dramatisations of *Rob Roy*, most notably the 1995 movie production starring Liam Neeson. In a quest for co-terminality, the Trossachs have become Rob Roy country, and in 2002 a new unofficial long-distance footpath called 'Rob Roy Way' was developed to link up many places that featured in his life. This, however, provides visitors with another opportunity to consume a historically distorted view of the past and to confuse reality with fantasy.

Case Study 3.2 Historical distortion and the nexus: The case of *Sepulchre*

Sepulchre, written by Kate Mosse, is essentially a ghost story which is based in two time periods, 1891 and 2007, and is inspired in part by Charles Baudelaire's poem 'Sépulture'. It employs a dual-narrative structure in which a contemporary female protagonist, Meredith, retraces the steps taken by an earlier character, Leonie. This piece of historical fiction is largely set in southwest France, more specifically the Languedoc region, and draws heavily on folklore relating to the supernatural associated with this area. Indeed, according to Housham (2007), the French intelligentsia at the end of the 19th century were intoxicated with symbolism, theosophy (a doctrine of religious philosophy and mysticism) and the occult. Moreover, Housham goes on to state that authors such as Edgar Allan Poe, best known for his tales of the macabre and mystery, were adored among French society during the late 19th century, and to be a *poète maudit* was the height of fashion.

Throughout the novel, Mosse re-represents various aspects of history, drawing on a great period of turmoil affecting France during this era to add context to her fictional tale. Thus, there are many references to key events in 19th century French history such as the commune, the French Revolution and Emperor Napoleon I. *Sepulchre*, though, is also contingent on the built, living and natural environments, influenced by the spirit of places captured in the notions of *couleur locale* and *genus loci,* best illustrated through her descriptions of landscapes and places featured in the novel. Moreover, much of the action in this novel is based around Carcassonne, Rennes-les-Bains and the estate of the Domaine de la Cade. Carcassonne is a fortified, medieval city, Rennes-les-Bains is a small isolated spa town, while Domaine de la Cade is an imagined place.

As well as re-representation and contingency, *Sepulchre* also encourages co-terminality; featured at the end of the novel is 'The Sepulchre Tour' which details key locations featured, whether real or fictitious, which readers may visit. For example, writing of Carcassonne, Mosse (2008: 9) states: 'Find the lock on the Canal du Midi, round the railway station and up the steep hill to the Cimetière Saint-Vincent.' Specific places within Rennes-les-Bains that are mentioned in the novel and also featured in this tour include:

- The River Salz (Plate 3.8), where readers can trace Meredith's footsteps as she walked down the Allee des Bains de la Reine to the banks of the River Salz past the open air swimming pool filled with hot mineral-rich spa water; over 100 years previously, Leonie came this way too and saw the rich, ailing visitors, pampered with servants and towels;
- The Far Bank, where you can make your way toward a low concrete bridge and a storm drain where Meredith saw a face in the water;
- The bridge, where there is a steep stone staircase that climbs up out of the river gorge to the cluster of intertwined streets that make up the heart of Rennes-les-Bains. These are the roads and alleyways that Leonie explored, virtually unchanged in layout. A plaque near the corner of the rue de la Poste, close by where Mosse imagined another character, Audric Baillard's house to be, shows the depth reached by the flood waters in the terrible rains of 25 October 1891, at eye-level on the wall (Plate 3.9); and
- La Place des Deux Rennes (Plate 3.10). At the heart of the town is the Place des Deux Rennes – the place known by Leonie as the Place du Peron. Here Meredith witnessed a funeral cortege.

Plate 3.8 The River Salz at Rennes-les-Bains, France
Source: The authors (2017).

Plate 3.9 Bridge at Rennes-les-Bains, France
Source: The authors (2017).

Plate 3.10 La Place des Deux Rennes, France
Source: The authors (2017).

Indeed, the blurring of fact and fiction as a result of HSLT may be more broadly linked to the postmodern concepts of hyper-reality and simulacra. In terms of hyper-reality, this describes the hypothetical inability of consciousness to distinguish reality from fantasy, especially in technologically advanced postmodern cultures. One of its early theorists, Eco (1975), described how contemporary culture is full of re-creations and themed environments, stating that these fabrications are created in an effort to come up with something that is better than real, more exciting, more inspiring, more terrifying and generally more interesting than what we encounter in everyday life. Meanwhile, with respect to simulacra, Baudrillard (1983) argues that a simulacrum is not a copy of the real, but becomes truth in its own right or in other words the hyper-real. Recreational simulacra include re-enactments of historical events or replicas of landmarks, such as Colonial Williamsburg and the Eiffel Tower, and constructions of fictional or cultural ideas, such as Disney's fantasy land. Indeed, the various Disney parks have by some philosophers been regarded as the ultimate recreational simulacra, with Baudrillard (1983: 83) noting that Walt Disney World Resort is a copy of a copy, 'a simulacrum to the second power'.

As well as heritage attractions, hyper-reality and simulacra may also be associated with screen and literary tourism. For example, *The Lord of the Rings* (LOTR) film trilogy has exposed New Zealand to a global audience of potential travellers. It is packaged and promoted as the 'Home of Middle-Earth', and thus the destination and the sites within it have become iconic landscapes. But, similar to other film tourism destinations, the screen locations encompass a combination of real places, film sets and digital enhancements; as a result, the tourists will not necessarily be able to experience the landscapes conveyed by the films (Carl *et al.*, 2007).

Connell and Meyer (2009) note a similar occurrence in relation to the children's television programme *Balamory*. While *Balamory* is artificially constructed, the portrayed screen attributes, such as the exterior of the coloured houses and the landscape setting, are based on reality and directly contribute to the tourist experience. However, not readily available for consumption are the characters and social setting created by the programme. This is because Tobermory is a real community which bears only a visual resemblance to the screen production. In essence, the tourist experience consists of the opportunity to consume the coloured houses used in filming, while experiencing the ambience of the real community. According to Connell and Meyer (2009), supporting Eco's (1975) analysis that the consumption of hyper-reality is important in its own right, conceptions of reality and pretence appear to be mixed for *Balamory* tourists. Thus, Carl *et al.* (2007) conclude that the more accurate that hyper-reality representations are, the greater the satisfaction and the more enhanced the tourist experience. Perhaps then, the ultimate expression of hyper-reality occurring within the HSLT nexus is 'The Wizarding World of Harry Potter' created by the Disney Corporation (Case Study 3.3), as 'within its magic enclose, is fantasy that is absolutely reproduced' (Eco, 1975).

Case Study 3.3 Harry Potter, hyper-reality and simulacra

'The Wizarding World of Harry Potter' is a theme park which opened in Orlando, Florida on 18 June 2010 at a cost of approximately US$200m, based on the concept of J.K. Rowling's wizard kid Harry Potter and his magician friends who go to Hogwarts School of Witchcraft and Wizardry. The *Harry Potter* series of books has been translated into 65 languages and sold more than 325 million copies globally. The films, produced by Warner Brothers, have grossed more than US$3.5bn (£1.7bn) at the box office worldwide. According to Bill Davis, president of Universal Orlando Resort, 'we have brought to life a cultural phenomenon that has captured the hearts and minds of millions of people around the world'.

The 20-acre site includes reproductions of the fictitious village of Hogsmeade (Plate 3.11), the Hogwarts School of Witchcraft and Wizardry (Plate 3.12), the Hogwarts Express train, Ollivanders wand shop, headmaster Albus Dumbledore's office, the Gryffindor common room, and the Defence against the Dark Arts classroom. Great effort has

Plate 3.11 The fictitious village of Hogsmeade
Source: The authors (2017).

Plate 3.12 Hogwarts Castle
Source: The authors (2017).

been made to ensure that the theme park remains faithful to the accurate portrayal of the various locations featured in the book and screen versions. Indeed, Oscar-winning production designer, Stuart Craig, who worked on the Harry Potter films, led the creative design for the park. According to Craig, 'our primary goal is to make sure this experience is an authentic extension of Harry Potter's world as it is portrayed in the books and films'.

Thus, the park is a miniature recreation of Harry Potter's world. At its entrance, visitors are welcomed through a stone arch into Hogsmeade village by a steam-blowing Hogwarts Express train. Before them stretches a scene straight out of the novel and movies: crooked chimneyed Olde English shops crowd along a winding street, their snow-capped roofs glistening in the Florida sunshine. On the right is Zonko's Joke Shop selling sneakoscopes and extendable ears, and next door is Honeydukes sweet shop. Only food authentic to Harry's world is provided such as Cornish pasties and Scotch eggs, pumpkin juice and Butterbeer served up in The Three Broomsticks.

The park also hosts a number of rides, again based on adventures featured in the novels and movies, including the Dragon Challenge, Flight of the Hippogriff, and the Forbidden Journey. The Dragon Challenge ride is a combination of two roller coasters zooming at super-fast speed along loopy tracks almost colliding against each other, and racing past realistic models of the dangerous dragons found in the Triwizard Tournament of *Harry Potter and the Goblet of Fire*. Meanwhile, the Flight of the Hippogriff and Harry Potter and the Forbidden Journey involve audiovisual techniques to stimulate the high-speed broomstick ride and encounters with the Dementors, serpents and spiders.

However, it is not just hyper-reality and simulacrum that is of relevance to the historical distortion of the past, as more recently, particularly within the context of heritage tourism, the heritage debate has incorporated a political dimension. Many argue (e.g. Ashworth, 1994; Johnson, 1995; O'Connor, 1993; Palmer, 1999; Peleggi, 1996; Pretes, 2003) that heritage tourism been used and manipulated for political purposes in creating, reinforcing, reinventing and excluding national identities, and for justifying contentious decisions such as wars, revolutions and/or coups d'état. Likewise, screen and literary tourism are powerful and persuasive vehicles of political messages and, as a result, have been used for similar purposes.

It therefore appears that, contrary to conceptualisations of S-DL and co-creation, instead of value creation clearly there is much value-destroying (Neuhofer, 2016) potential attached to the use of these resources in these ways. The political nature of HSLT is perhaps because 'tourism [itself] is not just an aggregate of merely commercial activities; it is also an ideological framing of history, nature and tradition; a framing that has the power to reshape culture and nature to its own needs' (MacCannell, 1992: 1). Indeed, the debate surrounding the role of tourism in the renegotiation and dissemination of history has gained much importance recently due to the fact that contested identities underpin many of the world's most savage political conflicts (Timothy & Boyd, 2003). Moreover, more recently there has been a boom in genealogical research, most notably in the area of diaspora, stimulated by screen and literary tourism (Martin-Jones, 2014). Thus, the remainder of this chapter focuses on the politics of HSLT, and examines its relevance to the four elements that constitute the nexus, these being co-creation, re-representation and commodification, contingency, and co-terminality.

The Politics of Heritage, Screen and Literary Tourism

Heritage is a powerful political weapon as it entails the representation of values and is commonly used (intentionally or otherwise) to manipulate, exclude and reinvent history through the selective use of a vast array of pasts. Such use has been termed by Poria and Ashworth (2009: 523) as 'heritagization'. This describes the process in which heritage is used as a resource to achieve certain social and political goals, and largely occurs because it is rare for a country to have an equal balance of ethnic groups in terms of numbers, wealth or political influence (Byrne, 1991). According to Poria and Ashworth (2009: 522), 'one of its main goals is establishing solidarity among members of a group by highlighting the differences between them and others so that this differentiation will legitimise a certain social order'. In this context, heritagization is not about the past, but about the use (and abuse) of the past to educate and to influence public perceptions and viewpoints. It is on occasion intentionally based on invented, hidden, and purposely selected pasts.

While a wealth of research exists concerning the politicisation of heritage tourism, it is only relatively recently that attention has been paid to the politics of screen and literary tourism in relation to diaspora (Basu, 2007; Martin-Jones, 2014; Rains, 2003; Wobst, 2010). This is hardly surprising since heritage can be viewed as 'a symbolic embodiment of the past, reconstructed and reconstituted in the collective memories and traditions of contemporary societies, rather than being perceived as a mere apotheosis of bygone times' (Park, 2010: 119). It is part of a symbolic system which creates and recreates shared values in society. Moreover, the tourist gaze is not politically neutral, for the representation of history in HSLT can act to legitimise existing social and political values and structures. Consequently, heritage is 'a unifying sign (Bessiere, 1998) which preserves and reconstructs the collective memory of a social group, thereby enhancing the group's social and cultural identities' (Park, 2010: 119).

Creation and affirmation of national identity

Re-representation and commodification are intertwined in the affirmation, maintenance and reinforcement of national identities both for tourists and citizens. Societies, ethnic groups and governments subjectively interpret the past to meet their own ideological goals, and it is not uncommon for governments to utilise heritage, literature and screen productions in one form or another to shape opinion, to build nationalism and to create images that reinforce their political ideals (Palmer, 1998). Indeed, several scholars (Johnson, 1995; Light, 2001; Palmer, 1999; Pretes, 2003) note the promotion of heritage sites as being important in the construction of a national identity as the viewing of heritage sites offers domestic tourists a lens into a nation's past. It therefore enables people of that nation to understand 'who they are and where they have come from' (Palmer, 1999: 315). However, the creation and reinforcement of national identities through re-representation and commodification is highly contingent on tangible and intangible elements of a nation's past as they have the potential to constantly remind nationals of the symbolic foundations upon which a sense of belonging is based (Park, 2010) and to legitimise 'a specific social reality which divides people into "we" and "they"' (Poria & Ashworth, 2009: 552). Particular ideologies are thus conserved and re-represented and commodified for tourists and citizens through a variety of heritage sites, and it is the networks of organisations, institutions and individuals, referred to by Vargo and Lusch (2004) in their ninth foundational premise, which are intricately involved in the service experience.

In the context of heritage tourism, such sites include museums, historic houses, monuments and markers, tours, heritage districts, heritage attractions, tourism landscapes and other public spaces. These spaces aim to highlight and entrench differences and social boundaries, set apart people's identity and provide up-to-date reasons for that segregation (Tunbridge & Ashworth, 1996). In addition, though, a sense of national belonging may be evoked through collective memories and myths and symbols of a nation and its people. Therefore, intangible aspects of heritage like superstitions, crafts, folk songs and folklore are also part of the underlying elements of national identity that are often tapped. Some states establish folk museums in an effort to preserve national culture and identity precisely for this purpose, as in the case of the Welsh Folk Museum which aimed to re-represent rural Wales for the Welsh population (Timothy & Boyd, 2003). But it is war in particular which arouses powerful nationalist emotions (Ashworth, 1990). This is why so many countries emphasise war heritage including battlefields, national cemeteries and tombs of unknown soldiers to engender a sense of collective patriotism. Heritage can also be used to 'build supra-nationalist identity/unity as in the case of the European Union (EU) where the European Commission and other bodies (for example the Council of Europe) are attempting to solidify and promote a common European heritage to build unity among member nations' (Timothy & Boyd, 2003: 270).

The use of heritage for the creation and affirmation of national identity is also dependent upon co-terminality. Heritage tourism plays a crucial role 'in providing certain "ritualised circumstances" through which shared social memory can be effectively inscribed and collectively communicated within specific heritage settings. People's experience of heritage tourism can be considered as an important medium in facilitating the maintenance of national imagination' (Park, 2010: 119). Palmer (2005) notes that heritage tourism enables people to conceive, imagine and confirm their belonging to a nation. Meanwhile, Park (2010: 134), in a study of Changdeok Palace, South Korea, notes that the experience 'potentially facilitates individuals to either rediscover or reaffirm innate cultural connections to the nation', and emphasises the importance of individual interpretation and unofficial narratives in articulating and affirming national identity especially in relation to the emotive and subjective nature of heritage consumptions and experiences. Moreover and perhaps most importantly, he concludes his study by stating that Changdeok serves as a symbolic agent encouraging the nation's felt history to be articulated and consumed, thus enabling South Korean nationals to maintain and entrench their sense of national identity. Meanwhile, Chronis (2005: 386), drawing on the co-construction of heritage at Gettysburg, demonstrates how a landscape is being 'symbolically transformed and used by service providers and tourists alike to negotiate, define and strengthen social values of patriotism and national unity'.

In a similar way to heritage tourism, film and novels may be used to create and affirm national identities and thus, as Vargo and Lusch (2004) state in their seventh foundational premise, they are facilitators of value as of course it is up to the individual to derive and extract value. In terms of screen tourism, one such example is *Gandhi*, a 1982 biographical film based on the life of Mahatma Gandhi who led the non-violent resistance movement against British colonial rule in India during the first half of the 20th century. Another illustration of a movie which reinforces national identity is *Invictus*, which tells the story of Nelson Mandela, a world-renowned political activist who fought to end racial prejudice and apartheid in South Africa. It is based on John Carlin's book *Playing the Enemy*, and tells the story of Mandela's first term as South African president, during which he initiates a venture to unite the apartheid-torn land by enlisting the national rugby team, the Springboks, itself a symbol of the old regime, to win the 1995 World Cup. With regard to literary tourism, Jawaharlal Nehru's autobiography *Toward Freedom*, written during his imprisonment for campaigning for Indian independence, promoted India's national identity and its right to sovereignty. Meanwhile, the book *The Great Escape* by Paul Brickhill and the subsequent film released in 1963 stirs national sentiment through a true story of an escape by Allied prisoners of war from a German POW camp (Stalag Luft III in Żagań) during WWII.

All, therefore, draw on a historically determined sense of national heritage which (re)represents history and depicts negotiated images of a country; these are then promulgated by institutions, films and books. It is these complex constructions of memory, history and heritage, often steeped in myth and romance (Martin-Jones, 2014; Rains, 2003), which are promoted to internal audiences and identified target markets and which create diasporic heritage, screen and literary tourists. In consuming these resources, the tourist almost inherits a fictional memory which is designed to stimulate a sense of return and belonging. But it is the co-creation of such images which inevitably leads to tensions between national identity, memory and heritage, since most countries have multiple pasts (Wobst, 2010). This is noted by Rains (2003), who examined the portrayal of Ireland in the film *The Quiet Man* (1952), and revealed how these conceptions were used to construct an image of belonging that appealed to the Irish-American diaspora. In particular, she revealed that the memory of the home nation among the American-Irish diaspora was collective and cross-generational rather than being individual as might be expected. Diasporas, therefore, have different notions of national pasts compared to those located in a nation since they are likely to be based on historically collective memory as opposed to the lived reality (Martin-Jones, 2014).

From this discussion it should be apparent that HSLT plays a fundamental role in communicating a sense of social and/or cultural identity, consequently creating sites for people to come together and reflect on inherited collective pasts (Prentice & Andersen, 2007) and/or to draw on constructed memories and images of belonging and homecoming (Rains, 2003). However, it is also important to remember that HSLT does not always emphasise one dominant reconstruction and reinterpretation of collective memory and it is often assisted by state-based and hegemonic forms of national sovereignty. Thus, as Vargo and Lusch (2004) state in their seventh (the enterprise cannot deliver value but only offer value propositions) and ninth (all social and economic actors are resource integrators) foundational premises, they facilitate 'ways in which individuals variably position themselves in a broader context of cultural construction and symbolic embodiment of the nation and national identity' (Park, 2010: 120). Such positioning is enhanced by state actions, designed to create nationalist fervour and attachment to a national identity in order to legitimise and consolidate a new or existing political regime, in the face of potentially competing heritages of sociocultural groups or regions. In doing so, legitimisation of these regimes may also be achieved.

Political legitimisation

As ethnically diverse societies have the tendency for fragmentation, and as traditional tools of sociopolitical socialisation (e.g. education, ethnic policy) are increasingly ineffective (Bandyopadhyay *et al.*, 2008), heritage tourism in particular has emerged as a tool for states to disseminate a shared identity (Graburn, 1997). Such a practice has long been used by newly independent countries, where governments have attempted to unify their citizens by manufacturing nationhood, national identity and engendering patriotism. Moreover, HSLT are often used to create a nationalist fervour and image that is intended to transcend the world and manipulate or alter people's perceptions. Positive images are therefore created abroad which attempt to provide credence to newly independent nations or to nations that desire a heightened global image (Timothy & Boyd, 2003), and there are many examples of countries that have used heritage tourism in this way. For example, Bossen (2000) reported that governments of newly independent nations like Singapore and Malaysia have used touristic representations to foster nationalism. Meanwhile, Chronis (2005) and Goulding and Domic (2009) cite the example of Croatia, a country that has experienced enormous political and social change over the last century.

Thus, the use of HSLT for political legitimisation purposes involves re-representation and commodification, contingency and co-terminality in much the same way as the creation of a national identity, drawing on networks of organisations, institutions and individuals akin to Vargo and Lusch's (2004) ninth foundational premise. In terms of re-representation and commodification and contingency, festivals, special events and re-creations of culture are used to develop and represent national identity and patriotism, and may in some cases attempt to achieve this by stimulating xenophobia and public disdain toward other ethnicities and previous ruling groups (Timothy & Boyd, 2003). However, as Chronis (2005) notes, representations of the past in the present inevitably involve the imposition of current values and ideologies which in turn result in the rewriting, purification and sanitisation of history.

For example, according to Goulding and Domic (2009: 88), 'nothing appears to be more ancient than the Croatian language which on closer examination is revealed to be a hybrid engineered version, reintroduced and reshaped to strengthen feelings of national identity and belonging after the liberation of 1992'. Hobsbawn and Ranger (1983) term the rewriting of the past as the 'invention of tradition', whereby traditions and customs have an older appearance and character, but actually originate recently and are sometimes invented. These inventories or recent additions may take the form of symbolic rituals which repeatedly include certain values and norms of behaviours, which in turn engenders continuity with a historical past. Thus, in this context, museums and heritage are often cultural carriers of ideology, or facilitators of value as described in Vargo and Lusch's (2004) ninth foundational premise, embedded in selective versions of history.

In terms of co-terminality, however, while museums and heritage offer a connection with the past and reinforce a sense of pride and belonging, according to Chronis (2005) history and heritage can be consumed in a variety of other forms which may hold greater cultural significance. For example, in a study of Croatia, Chronis (2005) found that it was the heritage of the 'everyday' – the heritage that resonates in the very fabric of the culture – that provided a deep sense of meaning. Moreover, he revealed that heritage was more than just a means of cultural or national identification. Although the overall experience was linked in part to the confirmation of identity as 'Croat', more importantly it was also associated with highlighting difference or, in other words, emphasising the division between the 'other', namely Serbia. Thus, it is clear that the very essence of politics is power, and heritage by its very nature is a political phenomenon since history is always told from the perspective of the winners of wars and people in positions of power (Timothy & Boyd, 2003). Indeed, 'little attention has been paid to the 'remaking' of history in societies that have undergone radical political and cultural change in recent years' (Goulding & Domic, 2009: 88). However, it is not just in the context of newly independent countries that a sanitised, purified version of the past may be presented, as such a practice may also occur when heritage is dissonant or contested.

Dissonant and contested heritage

Dissonant and contested heritage occurs when there 'is discordance or a lack of agreement and consistency' in understanding and representing heritage (Tunbridge & Ashworth, 1996: 20). A good example of this is the Eureka Stockade in Ballarat, Australia, an organised rebellion by gold miners which took place in 1854, and was named so for the stockade structure erected by miners during the conflict. The event was the culmination of disorder in the Ballarat region during the Victorian gold rush, with miners objecting to expensive mining items, the high cost of a miner's licence, taxation, and the actions of the government and the police. It is the only armed rebellion in the history of Australia, and while there is some dispute over its exact location, its basic details are not contested. As shown in Table 3.4, there are five main schools of historical thought as to what Eureka signifies. Which school of thought has been adopted affects the interpretation provided at heritage attractions and events and the entire visitor experience (Frost, 2006b).

Generally though, dissonant and contested heritage is usually associated with complex multidimensional communities in ethnic and social terms (Timothy & Boyd, 2003), as conflicting interests within and between communities may arise concerning the portrayal of specific aspects of heritage, particularly if the content and the means of communication are contested

Table 3.4 Schools of historical thought as to the meaning of Eureka

Liberal	Birthplace of Australian democracy. A fight for freedom against oppressive government
Radical Nationalist	Fight for Australian nationalism and independence from Britain
Sceptical Left	Pessimistic view. Limited long-term benefit for workers
Conservative Revisionist	Democratic reforms were not caused by Eureka. They would have happened anyway
Capitalist Triumph	The miners were independent small capitalists protesting against bureaucratic government interference

Source: Goodman (1998, cited in Frost, 1997: 4).

(Bandyopadhyay *et al.*, 2008). Olsen (2000) identified three situations that are likely to lead to contested heritage, these being when:

(i) There are two or more groups claiming the same or overlapping heritage. The same places have different meanings for different groups and each group believes that their view is correct, while that of the other group(s) is not. For example, different versions of India's history aggravate Hindu–Muslim relations. While both groups share similar colonial and indigenous heritages, their views and interpretations of those heritages have led to contestation between the two groups;

(ii) There are divisions within a group over what aspects of their heritage to emphasise and share with the public. Tunbridge and Ashworth (1996) term this division as 'undesirable transmission' when there are messages that society or sections of it would rather not hear themselves or permit others to hear; and

(iii) There are two different groups with parallel heritages, often leading to questions about which, or whose, heritage should be preserved. This area of contestation primarily involves conflict between indigenous and colonial communities, and has been a focus of postcolonial studies concerned with the interpretation and use of colonial heritage in areas where the indigenous population has begun to rediscover and assert its own collective identities. This has subsequently led to the development of an atmosphere where cultural and racial diversity and multicultural sensitivities are high.

As this chapter has demonstrated, it is not uncommon for presiding governments to utilise HSLT to shape opinion, to build national identity and to create images that reinforce their political ideals. This is undertaken by destroying or excluding heritage, creating fictitious pasts, and manipulating the truths underpinning history and heritage (Timothy & Boyd, 2003).

Although dissonance, whether it is obvious or hidden, is inherent in all heritage sites, the degree to which this occurs varies greatly (Tunbridge & Ashworth, 1996).

However, perhaps the best example of its occurrence relates to the representation of slavery at plantations. They are sites of death, disaster and depravity on which the enslaved and slavers once resided and wherein chattel bondage and racial oppression took place in America (Buzinde & Santos, 2008; Roushanzamir & Kershel, 2001). Recently rearticulated as heritage products, former slave plantations have come to dominate public toured spaces in the 21st century in the American South (Dann & Seaton, 2001). The commodification of these spaces has resulted in representational incongruities and discrepancies (Dann & Seaton, 2001), most notably through 'the social construction of master narratives that selectively and seductively shape the past into embraceable and restorative national legacies' (Buzinde, 2007: 470).

Indeed, previous research has played an important role in illustrating the various forms of dissonance evident within plantation representations, with examples including the omission of contentious historical periods (Roushanzamir & Kershel, 2001), the spectacularisation and trivialisation of contentious pasts (Dann & Potter, 2001), and the elimination of terms such as slave and slavery (Butler, 2001). In addition, according to Buzinde and Osagie (2011: 44), 'given that slavery is one of the most unsettling chapters in the nation's history, such constructions are often underpinned by articulations of collective memory that actively negotiate contemporary politics of race and the nation's contentious past'. The end result, they argue, 'is an engineering of collective memory that discursively manifests within master commemorative narratives, celebrating dominant value systems while concurrently marginalising subaltern histories' (Buzinde & Osagie, 2011: 44). Consequently, Buzinde and Santos (2008: 470) conclude that 'the plantation is not a neutral locale, but rather a political space operating as an historical system of meaning in which collective memory obliges the present and the social construction of the past as heritage'.

Other places around the world that experience problems relating to a dissonant and contested heritage do so as they host ethnic pluralism. Kyrgyzstan is a good example of one such country as it is made of up diverse ethnic and religious groups. Although ethnic Kyrgyz represent less than 53% of the population, they comprise around 40 tribes. The ethnic Kyrgyz are Turkic in origin and are believed to have originated from the Yenesei region of Siberia and whose language belongs to the Ural-Altaic family. Other major ethnic groups in Kyrgyzstan are Russian (18%), Uzbeks (12.9%), Ukrainian (2.5%) and Germans (2.4%). Thus, because of the ethnic diversity, there is a need to balance the reassertion of ethnic Kyrgyz identity with the desire to develop a fully inclusive state (Thompson, 2004). In addition, 'the culture of the ethnic Kyrgyz majority has been most heavily influenced by their nomadic and tribal past and in particular the epic poems. It is therefore the intangible elements of their heritage with which the Kyrgyz identify most closely' (Thompson, 2004: 371). People, perhaps through their communities, decided on what heritage to preserve, value and incorporate into their identity but while heritage benefits someone, it also disadvantages someone else. Moreover, while it makes 'some feel better, more rooted and more secure … [it] simultaneously makes another group feel less important, less welcome and less secure' (Howard, 2003: 147), or in other words is value co-destructive (Neuhofer, 2016).

Given that the meaning of a nation is often contained in the stories that are told about it, it is hardly surprising that dissonance is intrinsic to the nature of heritage. Such a view is presented by Ashworth and Tunbridge (1996: 21), who state that 'it is not an unforeseen and unfortunate by-product of the heritage assembly process'. These narratives or cultural texts are constructed in the present as 'life comes to us in the form of stories' (Gubrium & Holstein, 1998: 163). Thus, people acting as story builders do not simply record the world, but instead create (Olson, 1990). Moreover, since storytelling is not 'the act of an autonomous and independent actor' (Gergen & Gergen, 1988: 40), the narrator becomes an agent who relates the story in a particular medium (Bal, 1997), and who presents a personalised expression of the storyteller's own idiosyncratic reading and poetic aptitude (Chronis, 2005). This approach 'is especially true when stories refer to real-life events or historical accounts where an individual "writer" cannot be identified' (Chronis, 2005: 388). Consequently, within any story there are multiple narratives that can be constructed, and the public is often faced with the challenge of navigating numerous competing stories (Cronon, 1992). The nature of value, whether positive or negative, therefore created and extracted will inevitably depend on the operant resources deployed, i.e. Vargo and Lusch's (2004) first premise, on their ability to influence the service experience captured by Vargo and Lusch's (2004) fourth premise, on the interaction of the operant resources, their sixth and eighth premises, and on their perceptions of value, their tenth foundational premise.

However, according to Chronis (2005), co-creation and co-terminality also plays a key role in heritage dissonance. This is because narratives are conversations and the active role of the listener should be also considered (Robinson, 1981). At the very least, the listener participates in story telling by assigning his or her meaning. But the listener's involvement extends beyond mere interpretation. According to Braid (1996: 6), significant meaning is generated in the ongoing, active process of following a narrative during which 'the listener repeatedly tries to integrate the unfolding narrative and the dynamics of performance into a coherent and meaningful interpretation of what happened'. Moreover Chronis (2005: 389) states that 'during the experience of following, listeners constantly fill narrative gaps, recontextualise the narrative events in terms of their own experiences, and actively engage their imagination'. Thus it is the interaction of the tourist, encompassed within Vargo and Lusch's (2004) fourth, sixth and eighth foundational premises, which is integrally involved in value creation and value extraction (Table 1.7).

Collective amnesia

Just as HSLT may be used for political purposes to canonise certain beliefs over time, they may also facilitate collective amnesia among a nation. This requires the manipulation of the collective memory of a nation by overlooking and erasing aspects of heritage which a nation chooses to forget or suppress (Buzinde & Santos, 2008). It occurs because certain aspects of history are uncomfortable, embarrassing or because, by doing so, the society or its leaders can achieve some political/ideological objectives often with a racist slant (Timothy & Boyd, 2003). Ashworth (1995) terms the deliberate erasing of the dominant past as 'dis-heritage' where some social and ethnic groups are written out of the script of history. Indeed, societal memory loss has resulted in many diverse heritages throughout the world being excluded from conservation and interpretation and being hidden from the tourist gaze (Case Study 3.4). Such collective amnesiac representational strategies not only annihilate the histories of marginalised groups from the official heritage narrative but also foster feelings of disinheritance and exacerbate historical and contemporary issues of racism (Lowenthal, 1985).

According to Timothy and Boyd (2003: 259), 'One of the primary methods used to exclude certain pasts is through education and official curricula'. They draw on MacKenzie and Stone's (1990: 3–4) work which describes four reasons why an 'excluded past' exists in education:

  (i) 'Schools' curricula are already overcrowded and education leaders argue that time cannot be used on new subjects when the survival of many long established (e.g. mathematics and social studies) disciplines is in question;
 (ii) Teachers' own ignorance has allowed some important aspects of the past to be excluded. Many textbooks for example ignore contemporary understandings of the past;
(iii) Studying some parts is commonly seen as an extravagant luxury that has little direct relevance to today's society; and
(iv) Aspects of the past are sometimes excluded intentionally for political or ideological reasons.'

Thus, through education and based on their own ideologies, dominant institutions can reveal only what is palatable and what they want the public to know, thus demonstrating, as Vargo and Lusch (2004) suggest in their ninth foundational premise, that networks of networks constitute the service experience and can be co-destructive (Neuhofer, 2016). The dominant production process traditionally conceals conflicting histories, favouring instead a bias toward more picturesque, less controversial accounts of the past that 'exclude what is most pedagogically productive in critical history – that which provokes discomfort, disquiet and critical questioning' (Handler & Gabler, 1997: 226). This form of silencing shameful pasts is in fact allegedly essential to the preservation of state power and hegemonic knowledge formation; silences are inscribed by those who view certain aspects of the past as 'unattractive, unacceptable and/or dangerous for … whatever reason' (Cohen, 1994: 46). These practices of omission and/or deletion are also evident within the processes of destination image manipulation undertaken in order to renew, recreate and reposition tarnished images (Timothy & Boyd, 2003). Illustrative of this phenomenon is the practice implemented by Alabama (USA). Given its association with numerous widely-known racial controversies, Alabama repositioned its marketing slogan 'From Civil War to Civil Rights' (Chronis, 2005).

Case Study 3.4 Celebrating Black heritage in America

The disgraceful and inhumane treatment of Africans at the hands of white Americans and Europeans did not end with the abolition of slavery but continued well into the 20th century in many places. The suppression of Black heritage in both nations until quite recently is indicative of this. For centuries, Black heritage has been hidden from public view in both the US and the UK, since slavery is an issue that is an embarrassment for both nations.

However, African and white Americans have finally begun to realise the need to resurrect this forgotten element of history, resulting in increasing attention to preserving and interpreting elements of the heritage of slavery and subsequently African-American/Black legacies. Such a realisation is evidenced by the rapid development of Black heritage attractions in the US in recent years. The National Great Blacks in Wax Museum is the first wax museum of African-American history in the nation and in Baltimore, MD to be developed (Plate 3.13). Established in 1983, its prime objectives are to stimulate an interest in African-American history by revealing little known and often neglected historical facts, to use great leaders as role models to motivate the young to achieve, and to improve perceptions of identity by dispelling myths of racial inferiority and superiority. In 1984 it received just over 2000 visitors, with this figure rising to 43,000 in 1989 to nearly 300,000 today (National Great Blacks in Wax Museum, 2016).

Plate 3.13 The National Great Blacks in Wax Museum, Baltimore, MD
Source: The authors (2017).

In addition to heritage attractions, heritage trails have also been created in many American cities. Perhaps the best illustration is the Black Heritage Trail in Boston, MA, which links more than 15 sites that are important to American Black history. The state itself played an important role in the history of Black slavery, being the first to declare it illegal in 1783. Subsequently, a sizeable community of free Blacks and escaped slaves developed in Boston, settling on the north face of Beacon Hill and in the North End. The trail begins at the Museum of African-American History, which houses interactive exhibits that tell the story of the American Civil Rights Movement and Boston's Black history. Next is the African Meeting House (Plate 3.14), the first African-American church in the US, built in 1806, which hosted many key players in the Anti-Abolitionist movement. Responding to pressure from black and white abolitionists, President Lincoln created the first Black military regiment, the 54th Regiment of Massachusetts Volunteer Infantry, whose contributions are commemorated by a monument depicting their farewell march down Beacon Street (Plate 3.15). Other sites featured on the trail include Fort Wagner (site of military action involving the 54th Regiment led by Colonel Shaw who was killed in action), significant schools, institutions and houses, ending at the Lewis and Hayden House, which provided shelter to many runaway slaves from bounty hunters.

Interest in Black heritage and slavery generally, however, has also been stimulated by screen and literary dramatisations. For example, the

Plate 3.14 African Meeting House, Boston, MA: The oldest Black church in the USA
Source: The authors (2017).

film *Amistad* is a historical drama directed by Stephen Spielberg which is based on a true story of a slave mutiny that took place aboard a ship of the same name in 1839 and the legal battle that followed it. Meanwhile, another example is *Uncle Tom's Cabin* (1852), an anti-slavery novel written by American author Harriet Beecher Stowe. It depicts the reality of slavery, drawing on a fictitious central character, Uncle Tom, a long-suffering Black slave. This particular novel was hugely influential during the 19th century in helping to fuel the Abolitionist cause in the 1850s, which culminated in the American Civil War.

Plate 3.15 Monument commemorating the Massachusetts 54th Regiment, Boston, MA
Source: The authors (2017).

Moreover, visitation to specific black heritage sites has inevitably been stimulated by the generation of screen and literary tourism. A particularly good illustration of this is the 1989 American war drama film, *Glory*, based on the 54th Massachusetts Volunteer Infantry as told from the viewpoint of Colonel Robert Gould Shaw, its commanding officer during the American Civil War. The storyline is based on the personal letters of Colonel Shaw and from a pair of novels, *Lay This Laurel* by Lincoln Kirstein and *One Gallant Rush* by Peter Burchard. It features Fort Wagner, a key site included within the Boston Black Heritage Trail.

There are many countries which must deal with racially excluded pasts, including South Africa, Canada and Germany (Case Study 3.5). According to Buzinde (2008: 484), 'all societies must have the capacity to moderate debates over their contentious pasts, especially considering that heritage sites form an increasingly crucial role in the unofficial education process'. Such sites often represent national identities to both the domestic and international public and, much like the mass media, serve as a means through which the national and international public learn about themselves and others. Thus, rather than manipulating the collective memory into imagined shared heritage experiences and communal history, Levy and Sznaider (2002) suggest a more socially sensitive alternative method. They call upon the use of cosmopolitan memory, which assumes 'the mutual recognition of the history of the "Other"' or in other words suggest that 'the act of reconciliation' within atrocity heritage 'becomes the central mnemonic event' (Levy & Sznaider, 2002: 103). Moreover, the acknowledgement of the other 'diffuses the distinction between memories of victims and perpetrators. What remains is the memory of a shared past. It is not shared due to some mythical desire and the belonging to some continuing community of fate, but as a product of a reflexive choice to incorporate the suffering of the "Other"' (Levy & Sznaider, 2002: 103).

Case Study 3.5 Holocaust education in Nazi Germany

Education in Germany is the responsibility of the Federal States (*Lander*). Education policy is coordinated on a national level by a standing conference of state (*Land*) ministers of education and cultural affairs. It is this body that has issued specific guidelines for teaching about the Holocaust which have been in force in the West German states since 1960 and within the whole of Germany since reunification in 1990.

What is taught in classrooms in Germany is determined by: (a) state government syllabus directives issued in accordance with the national guidelines mentioned above; and (b) by state government approved textbooks that are produced by independent textbook publishers. The syllabus directives do not establish lesson plans. Instead, they determine the topics to be covered for every given grade and subject, and the teaching objectives to be achieved.

Postwar political education in Germany has been largely determined by a serious effort to try to understand the horrors of the Nazi dictatorship and to put in place safeguards in order to prevent history from repeating itself. Thus, in each *Lander*, the Education Ministry recommends that that teaching must seek to counter obliviousness to the past and critically examine tendencies toward a 'normalisation' of German historical awareness. With this in mind, examination of the causes of the success of National Socialism in Germany must be a focal point in teaching (Grimm, 2010). In addition, each *Lander* recommends that teaching should be devised in such a way that students realise the present and future significance of remembering National Socialism. Therefore, the teaching of these topics must address the questions associated with the responsibility of later generations, as well as increasing awareness of present manifestations of neo-Fascism and neo-Anti-Semitism. Above all, teaching must convey the perspective of the victims and give students the opportunity to learn about everyday life under National Socialism in a vivid and tangible way (Grimm, 2010).

Consequently, teaching about Nazi dictatorship and the Holocaust is compulsory at all types of schools in Germany and at all levels of education, and is not limited to a niche in the history syllabus. Instead, it is discussed in different ways, in a number of subjects and at different points in time. For example, in history classes, the Nazi period is dealt with in the context of 20th century Germany or world history. Students who pass the *Abitur* exam, the prerequisite for university study at the age of 18 or 19, receive a formal historical presentation of German history in the 20th century twice – once during the ninth or tenth grade and once during their final two years before graduation. Moreover, in religion or ethics classes, the Holocaust is discussed with reference to the guilt and responsibility of those Germans who did not risk their lives to fight National Socialism or to protect Jews. Whatever the subject being covered, a visit to a Holocaust memorial or to a Holocaust museum at the site of a former concentration camp is a standard feature of school excursions. In fact, the largest category of visitors at former concentration camps is often German high school students led by their teachers.

It is an uncomfortable past to remember. Since WWII, Germany has been grappling with how best to educate its people on all aspects of their Nazi past. Such a struggle is captured in the novel and film *The Reader* by Bernhard Schlink, published in Germany in 1995 and in the US in 1997; it is set post-WWII and tells the story of law student Michael Berg, who re-encounters a former love nearly a decade after the relationship ended as she defends herself at a war crime trial. The story is a parable which deals with the difficulties experienced by postwar generations of comprehending the Holocaust. *The Reader* explores how these postwar generations should approach their forefathers who took part in or witnessed the atrocities. This issue lies at the heart of the Holocaust literature in the late 20th and 21st centuries and of course Holocaust education in Germany, particularly as the victims and witnesses die and living memory fades.

Historical cleansing and heritage genocide

Collective amnesia clearly demonstrates how HSLT may be used for political propaganda. Given that these forms of tourism are powerful political tools, during wars, civil unrest and political instability heritage is sometimes targeted and destroyed as this is symbolic of crushing national patriotism and solidarity (Smith, 1998). Indeed, of the 31 countries that the World Heritage Centre lists as containing World Heritage in Danger, 21 have associations with war, civil unrest or political instability (Table 3.5). Such extreme use of heritage has been termed 'heritage genocide' by Talley (1995) or 'historical cleansing' by Timothy and Boyd (2003), to describe the destruction of heritage through violent means.

Unfortunately, there are many examples of cultural absolutism, most notably occurring in countries such as the former Yugoslavia, Armenia and Sri Lanka which have experienced and/or are experiencing conflict. In the case of the former, concerns are being expressed at the destruction of Azerbaijani cultural heritage in Armenia, particularly in the occupied Nagorno-Karabakh area and in several adjacent regions undertaken by the Armenians, motivated by the desire to remove all signs that these lands belonged to Azerbaijanis (*The Guardian*, 2015). Meanwhile, with respect to the latter, there are ongoing Tamil protests at the alleged destruction of their heritage in the north and east of the island, the former heart of the Tamil heartland and the focus of intense political conflict between Tamils and the Sinhala-Buddhist regime governing Sri Lanka. It is claimed that Sinhala-Buddhist nationals are seeking to re-establish their national identity and occupation in what was once Tamil-held territory by renovating Buddhist heritage and neglecting the Tamil's Hindu heritage (Sands, 2014). Such

Table 3.5 List of World Heritage in Danger and political instability

Country	World Heritage in Danger	Political situation
Afghanistan	• Cultural landscape and archaeological remains of the Bamiyan Valley (2003) • Minaret and archaeological remains of Jam (2005)	War began on 7 October 2001 as the USA launched Operation Enduring Freedom along with the British Armed Forces and the Afghan United Front following the 11 September 2001 attacks. Despite movement toward the formation of a stable central government, the Taliban remains a serious threat to the stability of the country.
Belize	• Belize barrier reef system (2009)	There are ongoing border disputes between Belize and Guatemala. Current concerns include the country's heavy foreign debt burden, high unemployment and growing involvement in the South American drug trade resulting in increasing lawlessness throughout the country.
Central African Republic	• Manova-Gounda St Floris National Park (1997)	A series of financial crises during the 1990s has rendered this country politically unstable, evidenced by a series of military mutinies and civil unrest. This situation is ongoing as the economy remains fragile with government authority outside the capital being minimal.
Cote d'Ivoire	• Comoe National Park (2003) • Mount Nimba Strict Nature Reserve (1992)	Despite being one of the most prosperous West African States, the country has been plagued by political turmoil since 1999, culminating in civil war in 2002. Although a fragile ceasefire has been in place since 2003, there are still incidents of widespread fighting requiring the presence of UN and French peacekeeping forces to help stabilise the country.
Democratic Republic of Congo	• Garamba National Park (1996) • Kahuzi-Biega National Park (1997) • Okapi Wildlife Reserve (1997) • Salonga National Park (1999) • Virunga National Park (1994)	Dogged by political instability since the 1960s and a war (1998–2003) marked by mass genocide, this country continues to be affected by violence and insecurity, creating an ongoing humanitarian disaster.
Egypt	• Abu Mena (2001)	After years of relative stability, political unrest began in 2010, resulting in the overthrow of the longstanding president Mubarak and the military assuming leadership. After a number of years of violent protests and unrest, stability has now returned with the election of a new president.
Ethiopia	• Simen National Park (1996)	Has been racked by civil war since 1977, including a secessionist war in the northern province of Eritrea, an irredentist war with Somalia, and regional rebellions, notably in Tigray and Oromia. The population experienced massive human rights abuse and intense economic hardship including acute famine in 1984–1985. Strained cross-border tensions with Eritrea and Somalia continue as do inter-tribal clashes.

Georgia • Bagrati Cathedral and Gelati Monastery (2010) • Historical monuments of Mt Skheta (2009)	Since gaining independence in 1991 with the breakup of the Soviet Union, Georgia has been beset with ongoing civil unrest in the breakaway regions of Abkhazia and South Ossetia. However, since the previously divided opposition has been united in 2013, the country is enjoying a period of relatively stability.
Guinea • Mount Nimba Strict Nature Reserve (1992)	Has experienced a series of coups since the mid-1980s, and the subsequent imposition of an authoritarian regime. The political situation continues to be fragile, following a bloodless coup in 2009 and reports of mass rapes and other human rights atrocities.
Iraq • Ashur (Qal'at Sherqat (2003) • Samarra Archaeological City (2007)	Since the Gulf War, tensions between Iraq and the Western world have been tense. On 23 March 2003 a coalition of forces led by the UK and UK took military action and there is ongoing violence.
Jerusalem • Old City of Jerusalem and its City Walls	Violent clashes between Israel and Palestinian self-rule in the West Bank have been ongoing since the 1990s.
Madagascar • Rainforests of the Atsinanana (2010)	Following weeks of political turmoil and protests, a military coup overthrew the president, creating a transitional government in 2009. Political instability is ongoing.
Mali • Timbuktu (2012) • Tomb of Askia (2012)	Mali has experienced political instability since 2011 but has recently signed an internationally mediated peace accord in 2015.
Niger • Air and Tenere Natural Reserve (1992)	The Niger Government has long been plagued with political instability and chaos having experienced a succession of military coups d'état since the 1990s.
The Occupied Palestinian Territories • Birth-place of Jesus: Church of the Nativity and pilgrimage route (2012) • Land of Olives and Vines – cultural landscape of Southern Jerusalem, Battir (2014)	Violence and political instability continue to beset this territory with frequent incidences of fighting, demonstrations and bomb attacks.
Peru • Chan Chan Archaeological Zone (1986)	During the 1980s Peru faced considerable external debt, ever-growing inflation, a surge in drug trafficking and massive political violence between the Shining Path, the Tupac Amaru Revolutionary Movement and the Government of Peru, which has resulted in an estimated 70,000 civilian deaths; there is ongoing political instability.

(Continued)

Table 3.5 *(Continued)*

Country	World Heritage in Danger	Political situation
Solomon Islands	• East Rennell (2013)	Ethnic violence and endemic corruption have been prevalent since the 1970s and political instability continues to undermine civil society.
Syria Arab Republic	• Ancient city of Aleppo (2013) • Ancient city of Bosra (2013) • Ancient city of Damascus (2013) • Site of Palmyra (2013) • Crac des Chevaliers and Qal' at Salah Eh-Din (2013)	Anti-government protests broke out in 2011 and the country is currently blighted by civil war, compounded by indiscriminate aerial bombardment since 2013. According to a January 2015 UN estimate, the death toll has reached 220,000. As of January 2016, approximately 13.5 million people were in need of humanitarian assistance in Syria, with 6.5 million people displaced internally and an additional 4.4 million Syrian refugees, making the Syrian situation the largest humanitarian crisis worldwide.
Venezuela	• Coro and its port (2005)	Like many Latin American countries, Venezuela has experienced a succession of coups d'états since the 1990s, with political turmoil heightening in the mid-2000s. There is an uneasy calm at present.
Yemen	• Historic town of Zabid (2000)	There is ongoing political conflict between the Government of Yemen and a minority religious group (Shi'a) in North Yemen. There is also continued civil unrest in the south.

Source: Adapted from CIA (2016), Foreign and Commonwealth Office (2016) and UNESCO (2016).

actions reaffirm conquered territory and effectively reduce Tamil claims on the territory, reducing them to historically inferior intruders.

There are many ways in which HSLT may be used for political purposes which result in historical distortion of varying extents. However, it is not governments alone that are guilty of such practices. Some organisations that involve government participation have also become embroiled in issues relating to contested or dissonant heritage. Thus the ninth foundational premise of S-DL is relevant here since it stipulates that networks, organisations and individuals construct the service experience (Vargo & Lusch, 2004). In this context, however, instead of creating value, given the existence of historical distortion, value co-destruction is occurring. An example is the United Nations Education, Scientific and Cultural Organisation (UNESCO). It operates at an international level, and seeks to contribute to peace and security by promoting collaboration through education, science and culture. In the context of heritage, this is pursued through the facilitation and maintenance of collaborative agreements to secure the world's cultural and natural heritage primarily through World Heritage Site designation by proxy of its special cultural or physical significance.

However, in some circumstances, World Heritage Status designation can bring about much conflict as the heritage UNESCO is seeking to protect may or may not reflect the interest of all nationals. Such a case in point is illustrated by Levuka, Fiji, where the main impetus driving the pursuit of World Heritage Status originates from outside the island. Indeed, of those involved few are Fijians, and if Levuka were to stand any change of being successfully nominated for inclusion on the World Heritage list, supporters of its nomination must obtain widespread support within Fiji (Harrison, 2004). But this was easier said than done as Levuka's residents were divided on the benefits that World Heritage Status would bring, and on Fiji's main island, Ovalau, there was little consideration of the town's historical importance. Most indigenous Fijians consider it at best an irrelevance to modern Fiji as it is not clear whose heritage Levuka represents; however, the historical port town finally obtained World Heritage list inscription in 2013.

Another pertinent example of an organisation related to a national government is the Heritage Lottery Fund (HLF) that operates across Britain. It uses money raised through the National Lottery, and gives grants to sustain and transform the UK's heritage. It is the largest dedicated funder of Britain's heritage, having a budget of around £205m a year which is administered through a range of grant schemes (Table 3.6). Since the fund began in 1994 it has supported more than 30,000 projects, allocating £4.5bn across the UK. Since its inception, however, the HLF has attracted much debate, primarily concerning the public value of the heritage that receives funding and how to measure it. Value remains at the heart of all heritage practice; it is what justifies legal protection, funding or regulation. Indeed in public value terms something is only of value 'if citizens either individually or collectively are

Table 3.6 Heritage Lottery Fund grant schemes

Scheme	Scheme description
Heritage Grants (above £100,000)	Main programme for grants over £50,000 for all kinds of heritage that relate to the national, regional and local heritage in the UK.
Sharing Heritage (£3000–£10,000)	A grant that enables the exploration and sharing of a community's heritage and can encompass anything from the recording of personal memories to the conservation of wildlife.
Young Roots (£10,000–£50,000)	Applicable to projects led by young people, it aims to involve 13–25 year olds in finding out about their heritage, developing skills, building confidence and promoting community involvement.
Our Heritage (£10,000–£100,000)	This initiative enables heritage to be protected and shared and encompasses anything from personal memories and cultural traditions to museum collections, archaeological sites and rare wildlife.
Townscape Heritage (£100,000–£2m)	Helps communities regenerate conservation areas, displaying social and economic need.
Parks for People (£100,000–£5m)	Supports the regeneration of existing designated urban or rural green spaces, the main purpose of which is informal recreation and enjoyment.
Landscape Partnerships (£100,000–£3m)	Led by partnerships of local, regional and national interests which aim to conserve areas of distinctive landscape character throughout the UK.
Heritage Enterprise (£100,000–£5m)	Supports the repair of neglected historic buildings, giving them productive new uses.
Start-Up Grants (£3000–£10,000)	To pump-prime the creation of a new organisation to look after heritage or to engage people with it. Also supports existing groups, taking on new responsibilities for heritage.
Transition Funding (£10,000–£100,000)	Supports strategic change which enables organisations responsible for managing heritage to become more resilient or more effective in their management. Supports the acquisition of new skills or knowledge, or new models of governance, leadership, business and income generation.
First World War: Then and Now (£10,000–£100,000)	Supports the exploration of heritage of the First World War.
Grants for Places of Worship (£10,000–£250,000)	Supports high-level work to listed places of worship.

Source: Heritage Lottery Fund (HLF, 2016a).

willing to give something up in return for it' (Kelly *et al.*, 2002: 4). The stewardship role of heritage organisations is about looking after those assets that people value, whether through protecting buildings, funding projects or opening sites to the public.

Thus, inherent in this concept is the public's role in the co-creation of heritage. Instead of funding what an organisation deems important, in contrast it asks the public which buildings and open spaces they value in their local area and then allocates funds accordingly. With this approach in mind, the HLF undertook a series of Citizen Juries exploring public values on heritage, and in particular sought to ascertain their views on a series of projects funded by the HLF. This work is ongoing and seeks to ensure that 'if heritage is to embrace public value, it will require a radically different mind-set ... it means taking genuine interest in what our citizens think, and not just consulting in a ritualistic and formulaic way because we have to' (Jowell, 2006). Such decision making relating to what is protected and conserved is consequently moving away from something that is exclusive and is determined by experts on behalf of society, toward something that recognises the importance of widespread public participation in identifying and caring for what is valued collectively.

Conclusion

The past is a powerful resource and is susceptible to a host of ideological interpretations. This chapter focuses on revisiting and re-examining the heritage debate in the context of the HSLT nexus, drawing on theorisations provided by S-DL and co-creation. More specifically, it considers the extent to which all three forms of tourism result in the historical distortion of the past and examines the implications of such sanitisation for the health of society. Given the ease to which heritage, screen dramatisations and novels lend themselves to propaganda, this chapter moves on to discuss the way in which their commodification, through tourism, is being used for a variety of political purposes, a practice that is most commonly associated with countries experiencing war, civil unrest, instability and racial prejudice.

While the heritage debate may seem at first glance to be outdated, overall this chapter highlights the relevance of S-DL and co-creation and the role played by other elements of the HSLT nexus, these being (re)representation and commodification, contingency and co-terminality, in the politicisation of HSLT. Arguably, early observation of an obsession with the past and the demand for historical re-enactments highlights an emergent trend involving consumer co-creation and S-DL, centring on participation and interaction with the resources consumed (Vargo & Lusch, 2004). S-DL and co-creation have traditionally been associated with value co-creation and value extraction. Indeed, the conservation and preservation of the past for future generations via participative mechanisms, the use of HSLT resources for urban redevelopment and regeneration, the generation of diasporic audiences fuelling a boom in genealogical tourism, and the reaffirmation of national identities all result in value co-creation (see Figure 3.1).

However, what the heritage debate also clearly draws attention to is the contextual co-destruction of value evidenced by historical distortion and the blurring of fact and fiction through the creation of collective memories drawing on sanitised and rose-tinted versions of the past, which are backward thinking and drenched in nostalgia and which are based on *couleur locale* (Reijnders, 2009: 165). Such an outcome may result from a variety of different uses of heritage, screen and literary resources (see Figure 3.2), which include hyper-reality and simulacra, the political legitimisation of new or existing regimes, particularly if they are oppressive or non-democratically elected, the reaffirmation of contested and dissonant heritages, collective amnesia and heritage genocide. Value co-destruction may therefore occur if the untruths are identified or when truths are destroyed. However, in the case of the former for many tourists, it may be beyond their operant resources

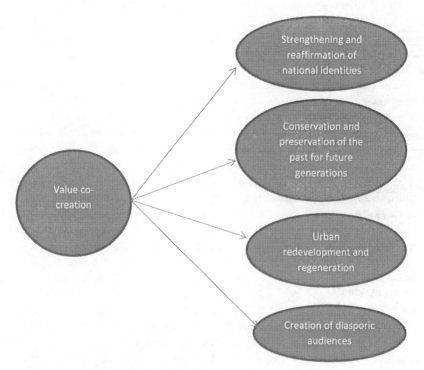

Figure 3.1 Examples of value co-creation within the heritage, screen and literary tourism debate
Source: The authors (2017).

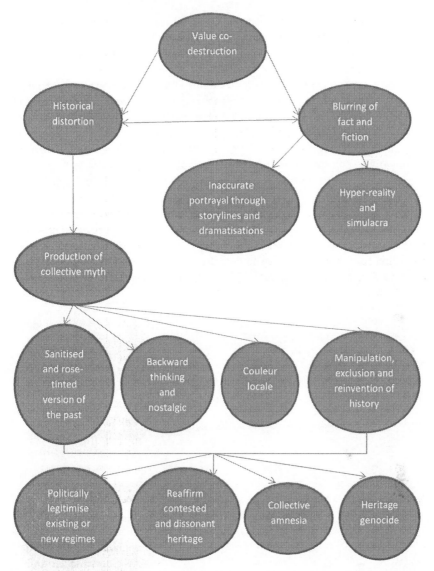

Figure 3.2 Examples of value co-destruction within the heritage, screen and literary tourism debate
Source: The authors (2017).

to be able to distinguish between reality and fantasy, fact and fiction. This might particularly be the case where hyper-reality and simulacra are concerned in the creation of near-perfect representations or where distorted versions of the past are presented through national museums or through established educational systems.

The extent to which HSLT value co-creates or co-destroys therefore very much depends on those consuming the material, thereby suggesting that Vargo and Lusch's (2004) foundational premise one (service is the fundamental basis of exchange), four (operant resources are the fundamental source of competitive advantage), six (the customer is always a co-creator of value), eight (a service-centred view is inherently customer oriented and relational) and ten (value is always uniquely and phenomenologically determined by the beneficiary) are important here in influencing the service exchange process (see Table 1.7). Additionally, though, Vargo and Lusch's seventh (the enterprise cannot deliver value but only offer value propositions) and ninth (all social and economic actors are resource integrators) foundational premises are also important, since value cannot be co-created or co-destroyed without an array of networks of institutions, organisations and individuals which facilitate value and which constitute the service experience. The accurate portrayal of the past is a key consideration for many HSLT destinations and sites and thus this line of examination is continued in the following chapter which concentrates on examining HSLT development in a variety of contexts.

4 Heritage, Screen and Literary Tourism Development

Introduction

Although HSLT has been fuelled by rising income and education levels (see Chapter 2), Richards (1996) states that there has also been a significant supply-induced element of demand, as associations with the past and with screen and literary links have been exploited by those engaged in destination development (see Chapter 7 for a fuller discussion). Given the economic significance of HSLT, it is perhaps not surprising that many destinations are avidly developing one if not all of these forms of tourism so as to capture additional promotion, visitor awareness and visitor numbers. Indeed, as Chapter 1 has demonstrated, many places have successfully developed these niche products, are attracting thousands of visitors per annum, and are reaping the many economic and sociocultural benefits associated with HSLT.

Developing these three forms of tourism, however, is a costly business and while the benefits they induce are desirable, it rarely occurs without the need to overcome many challenges to such development. Framed once again within the context of the HSLT nexus and drawing on S-DL and co-creation, this chapter focuses on its development and discusses some of the issues which arise. In the first part of this chapter, the different scales – destination and site specific – at which HSLT have been developed are considered. The costs of financing and operating HSLT attractions are also examined. This is followed in the second part by consideration of selected key difficulties which have arisen from such developments, relating primarily to the scarcity of funding and the tensions that exist between conservation and business.

Heritage, Screen and Literary Tourism Development

HSLT are now important pillars of many national, regional and local tourism strategies. For example, HSLT have all featured in the UK's national tourism strategy for many years (VisitBritain, 2012), whereas in the Republic of South Africa, screen tourism in particular was identified as a potential new niche product in the country's national tourism strategy (Department of Tourism, 2011). There are also many illustrations of regional and local strategies which voice ambitions of developing HSLT. The Sapphire Coast Heritage Strategy (2011–2015), for instance, forming a significant part of Australia's coastline wilderness, aims to provide 'a new range of heritage experiences that can encourage visitors to stay longer and spend more in the region' (Evaluate Communicate Evolve, 2010: 2). In Red Cloud, NE, home to the novelist Willa Cather, strategies are being developed to attract more heritage and literary tourists (Yost, 2014).

Many destinations are transforming the links associated with the past or with real or fictional events, people and places into symbolic capital, which in turn is being used to create new attractions, events and spectacles. For some authors, the use of these resources heralds the collapse of boundaries between the 'cultural' and the 'economic', and represents a key feature of postmodernity (Harvey, 1989; Jameson, 1985; MacCannell, 1976). HSLT development involves all elements of the nexus (see Chapter 1 for explanation; Figure 1.1). Destination development is reliant, as Vargo and Lusch (2008) state, on networks of organisations and institutions (FP9) who collaborate and coordinate their activities (FP11) in order to facilitate value (FP7), and is contingent on aspects of the natural, built and living heritage which are represented and commodified to create notions of place. Often this is achieved by bringing together, in clusters or themes, aspects of HSLT to tell a specific story or to present a particular narrative. It is in this context that co-terminality is also important as visitors are highly involved in its co-creation. This is because meaning is derived from visitor encounters and from the social construction of place (Connell, 2012; Pocock, 1981; see Chapter 2 for a fuller discussion) and emphasises the fact that consumers and their operant resources co-create the service experience (FP1, FP4, FP6, FP8), and that the value extracted is judged by the end-user (FP10). Indeed, this sentiment is captured by Tuan (1974) in what he terms 'topophilia', which describes how notions of place are generated through a viewer's attachment, whether personal or emotional, to a theme or story, to characters and a setting, resulting in the development of an affective bond between people and place (Connell, 2012). Moreover, in a bid to use HSLT as a tool for diversification and economic regeneration, such provision is consumption driven (Britton, 1991; Richards, 1996). As Chapter 2 demonstrates, the consumer now exerts an important influence over the production, form and location of the development of these niche forms of tourism (Vargo & Lusch, 2008).

This form of development, however, has similar requirements to tourism development more generally. On the one hand, appropriate infra- and super-structure must be in place in order to cater for the demands of domestic and international tourists, while on the other, there is a need for stable political conditions as travellers search for safe and interesting places to visit. The absence of safety within a destination often overrides the quality of experiences and attractions that destinations can offer visitors, effectively stunting the development of tourism until a time when much calmer, peaceful conditions prevail (Boyd, 2000; Buckley & Klemm, 1993; Wall, 1996). Indeed, the impact of political instability on the development of tourism generally and of HSLT more specifically is clearly evident in Northern Ireland (Case Study 4.1), where the presence of terrorism since 1969 has contributed to delayed development of the province's HSLT potential. Where suitable conditions exist for HSLT, it may be developed on a macro and/or micro scale, with the latter relating to a particular site (e.g. a specific attraction), and the former pertaining to a destination, whether a region or a geographically defined place (e.g. town, city, village).

Case Study 4.1 The development of HSLT in Northern Ireland

In Northern Ireland, due to the presence of terrorism, the period 1969–1993 has been described by writers such as Baum (1995) as 'lost years' in terms of tourism growth and development when compared to the phenomenal 100% growth enjoyed by the rest of northern Europe over the same period. Indeed it was not until the Good Friday Agreement in 1998 and the operation of the devolved government that attention began to be focused on the enhancement of the tourism infrastructure. In 1998 the Northern Ireland Tourist Board, the Arts Council of Northern Ireland and their partners published Northern Ireland's first Cultural Tourism Strategy. It acknowledged the province's international standing in literature, the visual arts and the traditional arts, the role of the heritage sector as the tourist's primary point of cultural reference, and the extent of visitor interest in Northern Ireland's recent history. In order to create a world-class, unique visitor experience, the further need to develop Northern Ireland's product portfolio through investment in iconic attractions was identified in the Tourism Strategic Framework for Action 2004–2007 document (Northern Ireland Tourist Board, 2004).

Five signature projects were identified and recognised as being capital intensive and included the following:

– *The Giant's Causeway, Antrim and Causeway Coast* is unique in Ireland, incorporating a globally recognised geological phenomenon and attracting visitors for centuries because of the outstanding natural environment and its associated myths and legends. Launched in April 2003, this project focused on the development of a signed 'world-class' tourist trail – The Causeway Coastal Route. The installation of brown directional signage was one of the key recommendations within the Causeway Coast and was launched in 2007 aimed at encouraging the dispersal of visitors throughout the region. The route navigates over 80 miles of stunning scenery including nine scenic inland routes and three Areas of Outstanding Natural Beauty, namely the Antrim Coast & Glens, Causeway Coast and Binevenagh. In addition, it facilitated the development of a visitor centre and facilities at the Giant's Causeway site (Plate 4.1), at a cost of approximately £18.5m (Northern Ireland Audit Office, 2011).

– *Titanic.* This embraces the development of a premium 'must see' visitor destination for the people of Belfast and visitors to Northern

Plate 4.1 The Giant's Causeway, Co. Antrim, Northern Ireland
Source: The authors (2017).

Plate 4.2 The Titanic Signature Building, Belfast, Northern Ireland
Source: The authors (2017).

Ireland (Plate 4.2). Costing £97m, this iconic building is located in the heart of the Titanic Quarter and was opened in 2012. It showcases the story of the Titanic and the wider theme of shipbuilding and seafaring in Belfast, including the engineering, industrial, social, cultural and economic origins and connections. The Titanic Signature Project forms part of a major regeneration project of the former Harland and Wolff shipbuilding yards at Belfast's Titanic Quarter. Titanic Quarter Limited is behind the £7bn largest waterfront development in Europe and it has transformed the 185 acre brownfield site into a new maritime quarter. It includes over 7500 new apartments as well as business, leisure, tourism and education facilities. The development is expected to create at least 25,000 new jobs over the next 15 years (Northern Ireland Audit Office, 2011).

– *The Walled City of Londonderry,* also known as Derry, has a history stretching back to the 6th century AD when a monastery was founded there by the Irish Saint Columba/Colmcille (AD 521–597). The Walled City is one of the most complete within the British Isles and the only complete walled city in Ireland. The aim of this signature project is to enhance the quality of the Walled City as a place to live, work, visit and invest. To date, work has been undertaken in two phases. Phase 1, which is complete, included a number of elements such as: the conservation and preservation of key buildings (The Playhouse Theatre, First Derry Presbyterian Church and Saint Columb's Cathedral), visitor signage and orientation, and the regeneration of tourist attractions such as the Tower Museum refurbishment and development of the Museum of Free Derry; new signage and interpretation around the city walls; and city centre environmental improvements in Guildhall Square and Waterloo Place. Phase 2 is currently ongoing and includes: a built heritage programme; a lighting strategy; a business and cultural animation programme; and environmental improvements all aimed at enhancing the tourism offer of Londonderry. To date over £10m has been invested in this project (Northern Ireland Audit Office, 2011).

– *St Patrick's Christian Heritage*. This project is primarily based on the urban centres of Armagh and Downpatrick, with Bangor and Newry as secondary clusters, although the project does have an affinity and resonance with all of Northern Ireland and, indeed, the island of Ireland. A three-year action plan was launched in March 2005, developed around six priority themes, namely: working in partnership, developing a Saint Patrick's Trail, creating a memorable experience, developing a coordinated events and festival programme, strong marketing and branding, and developing cross-border activities. The plan, which is 80% complete, is currently being reviewed with local stakeholders and a revised updated plan will be produced for the next three years. The project has also been awarded a capital allocation of £5m through the Comprehensive Spending Review. Through NITB's Tourism Development Scheme (PfG), £3.5m of this money will be administered to develop projects which NITB believe will enhance the St Patrick/Christian Heritage Signature Project area (Northern Ireland Audit Office, 2011).

– *The Mournes*. This is an Area of Outstanding Natural Beauty which is seeking National Park status. Tourism in the Mournes currently contributes some £72m to the local economies of Banbridge, Down and Newry and Mourne. Under the Programme for Government (PfG), the Mournes Signature Project has received £4m and the Northern Ireland Tourist Board continues to work with local authorities, private sector organisations and the Mourne Heritage Trust in recognising and developing key projects which will further enhance the visitor experience. The Mourne Signature Project Action Plan identifies key priorities such as tourism infrastructure, responsible access, natural and cultural heritage, capacity building and quality assurance and quality (Northern Ireland Audit Office, 2011).

Each of these five projects offers characteristics that are unique and drive the brand through presenting what is distinctive and iconic about

Northern Ireland. They provide core attractions for the wider destination and opportunities for the private sector to develop services and products for the visitor. Fully realized, they have the potential to achieve a step change for Northern Ireland, driving the local economy and making a key contribution to growing visitor numbers and spend.

The development work on these projects is now coming to fruition and the Signature Projects are open and have started attracting new visitors to Northern Ireland. Titanic Belfast has been particularly successful, welcoming more than 2.5 million visitors since opening in March 2012; in 2015 it was named Europe's best visitor attraction in the European Group Travel Awards (Titanic Belfast, 2015). However, despite the development of these signature attractions, overall progress has been slow as the Northern Ireland tourism industry has some way to go before it reaches its full potential. This unfulfilled potential reflects the fact that it lost some three-quarters of its global market share of incoming visitors at the start of the Troubles. It currently gains barely one-fifth of the out-of-state visitors to the island of Ireland, whereas before the Troubles it reached almost two-fifths of all island-inbound tourism (Department of Enterprise, Trade and Investment, 2010).

Heritage, Screen and Literary Destination Development

Destinations provide an important arena for the development of HSLT, not least because many authors stress the salience of place (e.g. Pred, 1984; Tuan, 1974, 1991; Kong et al., 1997). Agnew and Duncan (1989: Preface), for instance, stated that 'place provides both the real, concrete settings from which cultures emanate to enmesh people in webs of activities and meanings and the physical expression of those cultures in the form of landscapes'. Tuan (1991) meanwhile acknowledged the importance of understanding place, particularly the paired features, localities, regions and landscapes that make up the earth's surface. Since places are best thought of as a process of 'becoming' (Pred, 1984), they embody multiple levels of sedimented history. Indeed, according to Kong et al. (1997: 55), they 'have depth which goes beyond the visible landscape: they contain layers of meaning derived from different biographies and histories'. In effect, therefore, places are recorders of the passage of time in which memorable events have occurred or in which prominent personalities have lived. An association of a place with its past and present, however, is complex as Chapter 3 demonstrates; it is constructed and reconstructed as each generation emphasises particular historical truths and erases other versions of the past.

Given the significance of the past and the present, and of events and people to place, constructing a notion of place is extremely relevant to HSLT (Connell, 2012; Herbert, 2001; Teo & Yeoh, 1997). Additionally, Kong *et al.* (1997) argue that such constructions should include those experiences that reside in the imagination or even those that exist in simulations and iconographies (Kong *et al.*, 1997; see Chapter 3). Consequently, notions of place have resonance with the fictional nature on which HSLT is sometimes based (see Chapter 1 for a fuller discussion). In the context of screen tourism, for example, Shiel (2001) states that space in film should be understood in terms of the space of the shot, the setting and the geographical relationship between settings and sequencing. Moreover, Lukinbeal and Zimmermann (2006) contend that screen productions are packed with cultural additions that transform a real place into a fictitious environment. Indeed, a number of high-profile tourism destinations such as the UK, Korea, USA and Australia utilise film-related aspects in inbound marketing campaigns (Case Study 4.2). In particular, the New Zealand Tourism Ministry has harnessed the images portrayed in films like *The Piano*, *Whale Rider* and *The Lord of the Rings* trilogy to construct notions of place which are then re-represented in marketing initiatives. Due to the power of films and TV productions in constructing notions of place, destination management organisations (DMOs) and specific film production/promotion units currently operate across the world to encourage filmmakers to use destinations and specific sites for on-location sets (Connell, 2012).

Case Study 4.2 *The No. 1 Ladies' Detective Agency*: The HSLT nexus epitomised

The No.1 Ladies Detective Agency is a TV series based on the novels written by Scottish author, Alexander McCall Smith. They focus on a detective agency opened by Mma Ramotswe and her courtship with Mr J.L.B. Matekoni. It was filmed on location in Gaborone, the capital and largest city of Botswana, situated between Kgale and Oodi Hills, close to the South African border, and was the first film or TV production to be undertaken in Botswana. The government spent $5m to make sure the film was made in Botswana. This investment has been instrumental in Gaborone's construction of notion of place and in diversifying the tourism industry which is based almost entirely on the country's unique natural and cultural heritage. Not surprisingly, since 17% of the country comprises national parks or game reserves, wildlife and to a lesser extent the wilderness are Botswana's primary attractions, attracting approximately 170,000 visitors annually (Siyabona Africa, 2016).

Gaborone and the community within it is described in some depth in the novels and, given their significant role combined with the production of screen dramatisation on location, has inevitably created a notion of place, thereby attracting enthralled visitors. In response to such demand, Africa Insight and other specialist tour operators such as African Excursions offer tours to the places that feature in the novels such as the film set of the detective agency (Plate 4.3) and Mma Ramotswe and Mr J.L.B. Matekoni's house on the fictitious Zebra Drive (Plate 4.4). Visitors are also able to enjoy a cup of red bush tea on the veranda of the President's Hotel (Plate 4.5).

On a general level, *The No.1 Ladies' Detective Agency* tours therefore combine content alluded to in the books and the screen production – highlighted by appropriate readings – with points of local interest. Gaborone thus provides the real, concrete setting, the experience of which reveals the essence of Alexander McCall Smith's observations on Botswana. However, in this instance, the construction of notions of place is more complex due to McCall Smith's habit of including real as well as imaginary characters and places in his novels. For example, with respect to the latter, while Mma Ramotswe and Mr Matekoni are fictitious, Dr Moffat, their doctor and Bishop Mwamba who presided over their marriage are real-life characters who tourists may encounter during their tour. Meanwhile, in terms of the former, tourists can shop in the

Plate 4.3 The No.1 Ladies' Detective Agency, Gaborone, Botswana
Source: The authors (2017).

Plate 4.4 Mma Ramotswe's house on Zebra Drive, Gaborone, Botswana
Source: The authors (2017).

Riverwalk Mall, where Mma Ramotswe and her side-kick, Mma Grace Makutsi, often shop (Plate 4.6), and Zebra Drive does not exist and is based on Zebra Way (Plate 4.7). Thus, by enmeshing fictional and real characters and places, by linking the hyper-real with the real and by blurring fact with fiction, *The No.1 Ladies Detective Agency* reinforces

Plate 4.5 The President's Hotel, Gaborone, Botswana
Source: The authors (2017).

Plate 4.6 The Riverwalk Mall, Gaborone, Botswana
Source: The authors (2017).

Kong *et al.* (1997: 55) contention that 'place is often constructed by a nesting of different but overlapping images and interpretations'. Additionally, the fantasy of an African oasis that McCall Smith creates is situated outside the flow of history of a troubled Africa, plagued by AIDS/HIV, violent warlords, child soldiers and genocide. In doing so, it provides an excellent example of the HSLT nexus and of the issues which may arise as a result.

Plate 4.7 Zebra Way – inspiration for Zebra Drive, Gaborone, Botswana
Source: The authors (2017).

Thus, within destinations, HSLT construct notions of place by linking individual assets and creating an overall product which encourages longer stays by visitors and a critical mass of points of interest that can motivate visitation to a region or a place (Jones *et al.*, 2007). This activity inevitably involves some degree of specialisation, involving networks of organisations and institutions collaborating in order for co-creation to occur, and reinforces the relevance of Vargo and Lusch's (2016) fifth, ninth and 11th foundational premises to the examination of HSLT development. Such linking is largely achieved within a destination through the development of specific places such as book towns, or through the creation of trails, festivals and distinct clusters in the form of districts or quarters.

Book towns

The concept of the book town relates to a town, usually small and usually rural, which has brought together a number of bookshops, events such as book fairs and festivals, and other businesses based on writing, reading, and publishing. In practice, many of the shops focus on the selling of second-hand, antiquarian or specialised books and associated items, as well as businesses promoting the practice of traditional book arts that include calligraphy, binding, papermaking and printing. Additionally, books are often combined with arts and crafts or a café (Seaton, 1996). Writers associated with film, travel, gardening, cooking, photography and artists are drawn to these towns. Book towns have evolving identities as they have become magnets for new forms of heritage tourism and sites for preserving the memory of traditional print culture and also for embracing new technologies.

The first book town was established in Wales in 1961 in Hay-on-Wye, and from humble beginnings it is now visited by millions of people, serving to economically regenerate a once small dying-out village (Case Study 4.3). The book town is a further development from the traditional antiquarian bookshops, offering a wider variety of books in a smaller area. Bookshops themselves have turned into an international attraction as book towns have spread around the world. As recently as 1990 there were only four book towns globally: Hay-on-Wye (Wales), Redu (Belgium), Becherel (Brittany, France) and Montolieu (Aude, France).

There are now over 20 towns throughout the world describing themselves as Book Towns or Book Villages, although the International Organisation of Book Towns (IOB) currently lists 16 in Europe and one in Malaysia, one in South Korea and one in Australia (IOB, 2016; Table 4.1). There are several reasons for the recent increase in the second-hand book trade. First, never have so many books been written and edited, and never has space in bookshops been more valuable, and so their supply of books changes quickly. Secondly, increased leisure time for reading has prompted a search for books that are out of print, and thirdly, books are rather cumbersome, particularly when moving house for instance, and thus some find their way into second-hand bookshops, waiting there for new, grateful owners.

Case Study 4.3 Book town development in Hay-on-Wye, Wigtown and Sedbergh, UK

Richard Booth, an entrepreneur, first developed the concept of the book town when he began filling up an abandoned cinema in his small home town, Hay-on-Wye, with second-hand books in the early 1960s. Hay lies on the Welsh side of the Welsh/English border. It was originally conceived of as a specialist retail outlet rather than a tourist development (Seaton, 1996). Booth bought stocks of defunct or underutilised property and turned them into bookshops. This concentration of second-hand books within Hay-on-Wye began attracting visitors, and today there are over 30 bookshops but one in particular is huge (Cinema Bookshop), holding over 2,000,000 volumes (Plate 4.8).

By 1995, the book town of Hay-on-Wye was attracting 1 million tourists a year, with a third estimated to be international (TIC estimate 1996 reported in Seaton, 1996). Hay's association with books precipitated a brand extension in 1998 – the annual Hay Literary Festival – which has become one of the most important festivals in the English speaking world, attracting around 100,000 visitors over the two weeks of the festival in

Plate 4.8 The Hay Cinema bookshop, Hay-on-Wye, UK
Source: The authors (2017).

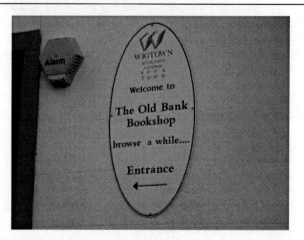

Plate 4.9 Wigtown's Old Bank Bookshop, UK
Source: The authors (2017).

May and June (Baker, 2014). Hay has become one of the most successful new British tourism developments since the war, out-performing comparable towns elsewhere and making a major contribution to tourist numbers in Wales, particularly those from overseas (Seaton, 1996). It is estimated the Literary Festival generates about £3.6 million (VisitWales, 2016) and it attracts key British figures and the likes of Bill Clinton.

Wigtown, situated in the southwest of Scotland, was officially designated as Scotland's national Book Town in 1998, and is now home to over 20 book-related businesses (Plates 4.9 and 4.10). Its origins differ from those

Plate 4.10 Scotland's largest and oldest second-hand bookshop
Source: The authors (2017).

of Hay-on-Wye in that it was planned as a book town in order to regenerate a very depressed town; the main employers – a creamery and a distillery – closed in the 1990s, although the Bladnoch Distillery has now reopened and is distilling its own whisky (Wigtown Festival Company, 2016). Modelled on Hay-on-Wye, it attracts over 50,000 visitors annually (Wigtown Festival Company, 2016). Wigtown also hosts an annual book festival which showcases the works of authors. Its 17th anniversary was marked in Wigtown Festival Company (2016) with over 300 events over a ten-day period, and in doing so, it contributed to the economies of Dumfries and Galloway.

Sedbergh, located in Cumbria, northwest England, has become another well-known book town (Plate 4.11). It began as a book town project which started after the 2001 Foot and Mouth Disease outbreak in order to encourage an increase in tourism as a means through which to diversify a flagging economy. A printers' finisher (book maker), writers and several bookselling businesses were already based in the town, and the company Sedbergh Book Town was set up in 2003, charged with the responsibility of developing a community of businesses involved in selling, writing, publishing and designing books and other publications. Since then more bookshops have opened and in May 2006 Sedbergh was officially recognized as England's Book Town when it was elected into the IOB (IOB, 2016). The Sedbergh Book Town Literary Trust was created as a charity in 2007 and it aims to make Sedbergh 'the very best Book Town it can be, worthy of national status, and a centre of excellence for literature and the written word' (Sedbergh Book Town Literary Trust, 2016).

Plate 4.11 Sedbergh's book centre, UK
Source: The authors (2017).

Table 4.1 Examples of the International Organisation of Book Towns

Book town	Description
Bredevoort Boekenstad, The Netherlands	A fortified town in the municipality of Aalten in the area of Gelderland is known as the Dutch Hay-on-Wye on account of its antiquarian and second-hand booksellers. The book town was officially opened on 27 August 1993 by Dr J.C. Terlouw, Royal Commissioner of Guelderland, who is also a writer of children's books and patron of the Bredevoort Book Town Foundation. Twelve booksellers were by then established in seven shops in Bredevoort. The launch included a large book fair at which 160 booksellers were represented, attracting 12,000–15,000 people. The launch featured an events programme which included a Reynard the Fox exhibition, book valuations, and exhibitions of bookbinding and literary etchings. There was also a poetry reading night on the 17th century moat, and evening lectures, theatre performances and literary readings. Every third Saturday of the month a specialised book market takes place (Bredevoort, 2016).
Fjaerland, Norway	The book town, six hours north of Oslo and about five hours from Bergen, is a small 300-inhabitant rural village in Western Norway. It was established as a deliberate tourism venture rather than a retail development. The book town was launched in June 1996 with considerable publicity and the participation of the Norwegian Minister of Culture, Richard Booth of Hay-on-Wye, and Jostein Gaarder, author of the best-selling novel *Sophie's World*. Starting out very modestly in 1995, it now stocks about 2.5 miles of shelving, filled with books, in a variety of abandoned buildings – from ferry waiting rooms, stables and local banks to a post office and a grocery shop. Besides taking care of books, the idea here was also to preserve the old buildings (Den Norske Bokbyen, 2016).
Kampung Buku, Malaysia Melaka	Book Village Malaysia Melaka was officially launched by the Rt Hon. Datuk Seri Hj. Mohd Ali bin Mohd Rustam, Chief Minister of Melaka on 17 April 2007. Currently, it is the only book village in operation in Malaysia. There are approximately 15,000 books in this book village that are available for reading, reference and purchase which are supplied by eight resident publishers with additional support from the Melaka State Government. In addition, this book village aims to carve a niche for itself as a reference and resource centre for books and reading materials concerning the State of Melaka. This also includes books written by writers originating from Melaka (Angkawi Insight, 2016).

Montereggio, Italy	Set in Tuscany, this town has an established heritage of book selling and printing, and is the origin of one of Italy's most prestigious literary prizes, the Premio Bancarella, whereby booksellers across Italy vote on the bestseller (Wandering Italy, 2016).
Redu, Belgium	Redu, founded in 1984, is one of the major European book towns and the first in Belgium and the continent. It is a small historic village with a population of 450, in the Belgian Ardennes, one hour from both Luxemburg and Brussels. There are now 24 bookshops, five galleries, 11 restaurants, a paper manufacturer and a bookbinder. In Redu, the development of bookshops has been accompanied by the development of an ancillary retail sector related to books including two antique shops and a number of galleries. The village has achieved massive coverage and claims to be the most successful village in Belgium and the leading tourist attraction in the Luxemburg/Ardennes region. Redu has developed a programme of cultural events to support the book town's appeal and complement its cultural character. One of the big annual events is the Nuit du Livre, when the book town is open all night and a diverse programme of entertainments is staged (Redu Village du Livre, 2013).
Sedbergh, UK	The Sedbergh Book Town project was started after the 2001 Foot and Mouth Disease outbreak in order to encourage an increase in the number of visitors, whose enjoyment of the beautiful countryside around Sedbergh supports the functioning of vital town centre amenities. The company, Sedbergh Book Town, was set up in 2003 to develop a community of businesses involved in selling, writing, publishing and designing books and other publications. Sedbergh started with an excellent base to build upon as a book town, with a printer's finisher (book maker), writers and several bookselling businesses already based in the town. Since then more bookshops have opened and, in May 2006, Sedbergh was officially recognised as England's book town when it was elected into the IOB (Sedbergh Information Centre, 2016).
Tvedestrand, Norway	Located on Norway's south coast, Tvedestrand is one of two book towns in Norway, the other being Fjaerland, offering a selection of fiction and non-fiction books, several cafes and restaurants and an events programme (VisitNorway, 2016).

(Continued)

Table 4.1 (*Continued*)

Book town	Description
Wünsdorf-Waldstadt, Germany	Established in 1997 as a book town, Wünsdorf-Waldstadt is located in Brandenburg, Germany and is home to thousands of books housed in three large antiquarian bookshops (Büecherstadt Tourismus, 2016).
Urueña, Spain	Located in the province of Valladolid, this medieval town is the first 'villa del libro' (book village) in Spain. It hosts 12 bookshops selling old or out-of-print books, including El Rincón Escrito, Alejandría Bookshop, the 'Wine Museum' cellar bookshop (specialising in literature about wine), Alcuino Caligrafía, El 7 Bookshop (specialising in the world of bullfighting), and the Artisan Book Binding Workshop of Urueña. It also has an e-learning centre with a specialised library, workshops, garden, exhibition hall, assembly room and permanent exhibition 'Between the lines. A history of books'. In addition, this village also holds public readings, and organises calligraphy, illustration and book binding courses. On special dates such as World Book Day or on the village's anniversary in March, this place becomes a real celebration with conferences, round tables, story telling, origami workshops, extraordinary concerts and dinners (Schellhase, 2016).

Source: Compiled by the authors (2017).

The surge in interest in books and in book towns has consequently created a host of unique niche destinations based around literary tourism, and has spawned a new related form of tourism – bookstore tourism.

Bookstore tourism

Originating from a grass-roots effort to support locally owned and operated bookshops, many of which have struggled to compete with large bookstore chains and online retailers, bookstore tourism primarily promotes independent bookshops. This initiative was begun in 2003 by Larry Portzline, a writer and college instructor in Harrisburg, PA who led 'bookstore road trips' to other cities and recognised its potential as a group travel niche and marketing tool. He promoted the concept with a how-to book and website, and groups around the USA soon began offering similar excursions, usually via a chartered bus and often incorporating book signings, author home tours and historical sites (Larry Portzline, 2016). In 2005–2006 two regional booksellers' associations – the Southern California Booksellers Association and the Northern California Independent Booksellers Association – embraced bookstore tourism, offering trips to independent bookstores in Los Angeles, San Diego and San Francisco, CA. The bookstore tourism movement encourages schools, libraries, reading groups and organisations of all sizes to create day trips and literary outings to cities and towns with a concentration of independent bookstores. It also encourages local booksellers to attract bibliophiles to their communities by employing bookstore tourism as an economic development tool. Others benefiting include local retailers, restaurants, bus companies and travel professionals.

Heritage, screen and literary tourist trails

As mentioned earlier, HSLT development may also take place within a destination and involve the creation of trails. There are numerous examples of trails worldwide which connect points of local and/or regional interest and significance. For example, Hong Kong's Lung Yeuk Tau ('Mountain of the Leaping Dragon') heritage trail takes visitors on a scenic journey into the history of the Tang clan, one of the five largest clans in the New Territories. It is said that a dragon could once be seen leaping in the mountains here, which is how the area got its name. It begins at the magnificent Taoist temple complex Fung Ying Seen Koon, and passes the walled villages of Ma Wat Wai and Lo Wai, before ending at the 18th century Tang Chung Ling Ancestral Hall (Hong Kong Tourism Board, 2016). Meanwhile, the Texas Heritage Trails Program (THTP) is a regional initiative, based around ten scenic driving trails, and includes heritage tourism attractions and communities both on and off the trail. The programme began with the establishment of the Texas Forts Trail Region in 1998. The THTP received national recognition with the Preserve America Presidential Award in 2005. This award was given for exemplary accomplishment in the preservation and sustainable use of America's heritage assets, which has enhanced community life while honouring the nation's history (Texas Historical Commission, 2016).

In terms of screen tourism, commercially operated tours of film locations such as *The Lord of the Rings* in New Zealand are commonplace, as are tours of film celebrity homes, haunts and associated film sites. A good example of the latter is the bus tour of Beverly Hills which stops outside the homes of past and present celebrities (Connell, 2012). With respect to literary trails, often these connect places which inspired and/or feature in the works of famous writers or which have some association with their lives. The Southern Literary Trail is an example of a regional initiative linking towns and cities across America's southern states of Alabama, Georgia and Mississippi which provided the tapestry of stories, characters and settings for great American writers such as Tennessee Williams, Richard Wright, William Faulkner and Eudora Welty (Southern Literary Trail, 2016). Of course, rarely are such trails separate entities as often they encompass aspects of historical, screen and literary significance organised into a distinct cluster.

Heritage, screen and literary clusters

Clusters also provide an arena for HSLT development. These may be quarters or districts comprising an area with a group or complex of buildings, or a large area with many buildings and properties. It may also comprise an entire administrative area with a concentration of resources with heritage, screen and literary associations that distinguishes it from its surroundings. Clusters may be found in urban or rural environments. Moreover, according to the Ontario Ministry of Tourism, Culture and Sport (2016: 5), 'they may include residential, commercial and industrial areas, rural landscapes or entire villages and hamlets with features or land patterns that contribute to a cohesive sense of time or place'.

Often the development of heritage tourism clusters equates with the creation of heritage conservation districts (HCDs), the significance of which extends beyond its built heritage, structures, streets, landscapes and other physical and spatial elements to include important vistas and views between and toward buildings and spaces within the district (Case Study 4.4). Although HDCs are unique, many share a common set of characteristics. These may include:

- a concentration of heritage buildings, sites, structures, designated landscapes and natural landscapes that are linked by aesthetic, historical and sociocultural contexts or use;
- a framework of structured elements including major natural features such as topography, land form, landscapes, water courses and built form such as pathways and street patterns;

- a sense of visual coherence through the use of such elements as building, scale, mass, height, material proportion and colour that convey a sense of time and place; and
- a distinctiveness which enables districts to be recognised and distinguishable from their surroundings or from neighbouring areas. (Ontario Ministry of Tourism, Culture and Sport, 2016: 9–10)

In terms of designating a district, different places will have very different rules and regulations. Most, though, will involve the production of a plan that must contain a statement of objectives, detail of a district's cultural heritage value or interest, a description of the district's heritage attributes and

---

Case Study 4.4 Heritage Conservation Districts in Ontario, Canada

Part V of the Ontario Heritage Act provides for the designation of HCDs, seeking to protect heritage that extends beyond individual buildings – because of its special character and the distinctive architectural quality of individual buildings (Ontario Ministry of Tourism, Culture and Sport, 2016). The first was designated in 1980 – Meadowvale Village, established in Mississauga. In April 2005 the Ontario Heritage Act was strengthened to provide municipalities and the province with enhanced powers to preserve and promote Ontario's cultural heritage. Today there are 123 HCDs across Ontario.

HCDs vary in size and character. In terms of the latter, the majority of Ontario's designated HCDs comprise residential or commercial districts and they often incorporate natural heritage features such as green open spaces, trees, parkland and waterways. Each HCD is distinct and is defined by the varied qualities of the natural and cultural resources within its boundary. In terms of the former, HCDs also vary in size. Although most are defined by a number of properties that form a character area, a single property – usually of a complex nature – may also be a HCD. The largest HCD in Ontario is the combined north and south Rosedale HCDs with a total of 1800 properties, mostly residential. It displays a Victorian character – relatively unchanged streetscapes, row housing and single residences displaying 19th century architectural style and an integrity in form.

Selected examples of HCDs in Ontario include: Galt Downtown, a late 19th century commercial block in the city of Cambridge; Fort York in Toronto which includes over 40 acres, original earthen fortification, block houses, a cemetery, magazines and garrison buildings (Plate 4.12); the square in Goderich, a 19th century urban square with a unique layout based on classic design principles; Kleinburg-Nashville in the city

Plate 4.12 Fort York, Toronto
Source: The authors (2017).

Plate 4.13 Downtown Collingwood, Toronto
Source: The authors (2017).

of Vaughan, a discontinuous district which links two scattered former mill villages within their natural settings; and Downtown Collingwood which encompasses the downtown core and waterfront that was once an industrial centre and now has housing and natural elements (Plate 4.13).

District designation enables the council of a municipality to manage and guide future change in the district through the adoption of a district plan with policies and guidelines for conservation, protection and enhancement of the area's special character. In addition, designation ensures that the community's heritage conservation objectives and stewardship will be respected during the decision-making process. It commemorates what it values and contributes to its sense of place. HDC designation allows resources and relationships to be identified and protected (Ontario Ministry of Tourism, Culture and Sport, 2016).

Source: Adapted from Ontario Ministry of Tourism, Culture and Sport (2016).

those of properties within the district, policy statements, guidelines and procedures for achieving the stated objectives, and a description of external alterations. Following the production of a plan, most will follow an iterative process similar to that outlined in Figure 4.1.

As well as the existence of heritage districts or quarters, there are also examples of screen and literary quarters worldwide, although the presence of the former is less abundant due to the fact that movies or TV programmes are rarely filmed in one location. However, some destinations have provided the location for numerous movies and screen adaptations. A good example of one such destination is New Orleans, and in particular its French quarter, which has provided the backdrop to some of the most memorable moments in film history and is one of the most frequently filmed areas in the world over the last 30 years, appearing in *The Big Easy, A Streetcar Named Desire, Live and Let Die, The Expendables* and *Interview with a Vampire*, among others. Indeed, more than 30 locations that featured in movies around this historic neighbourhood can be visited.

An illustration of a literary cluster is the Barrio de las Letras, Madrid (Spain), with the latter literally translated as 'letters'. It was inhabited by illustrious masters such as Gongora, Tirso de Molina, Calderon de la Barca and Lope de Vega, and contains many sites of literary significance. These include the Church of San Sebastian, for instance, where Lope de Vega is buried and where many renowned writers such as Larra and Zorilla were married. Another important site is the Iglesia de San Sebastian Church where José Cadalso is alleged to have frequently visited his sweetheart's tomb at the cemetery and was arrested one night by the police when he attempted to dig

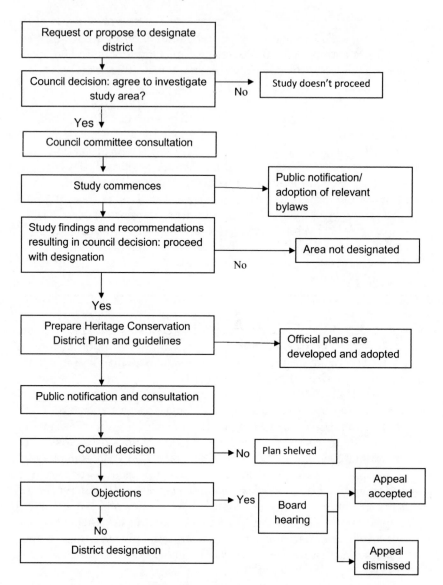

Figure 4.1 The process in designating a heritage conservation district
Source: Adapted from Ontario Ministry of Culture (2006).

up her body. This story provided the inspiration behind his novel *Noches lúgubres*, which is considered to be one of the key works of Spanish Romanticism.

In addition, within the Plaza de Santa Ana is the Teatro Español which stands on the site once occupied by the Corral del Principe playhouse which staged the works of Lope de Vega and Tirso de Molina. Also within this literary quarter is Calle de las Huertas, on which next to No. 45 is the Convento de las Trinitanarias Descalzas where Lope de Vega's daughter, Sister Marcela de San Felix (playwright and poet) lived. Other places of interest are the house where Cervantes died in 1616, the house where Cervantes' *Don Quixote* was first published, the Casa Museo de Lope de Vega, the house of Lope Vega for 24 years and now a museum dedicated to his life, and the Ateneo, once a refuge for literal ideas, now a cultural institution boasting the largest newspaper libraries in Europe with publications from all over the continent. Moreover, the Barrio de las Letras' literary heritage is captured in the pavements, as literary quotes can be found in gold lettering scattered throughout the streets (see Plate 4.14).

There are clearly many examples of HSLT development that have occurred throughout the world. Often, such developments are linked to festivals which celebrate aspects of a destination's heritage or its screen or literary associations. Heritage, film and literature can be used to diversify an event's existing product portfolio, to showcase a destination's resources, to market a destination's appeal, to strengthen a destination's image, and to contribute to the rejuvenation of tourism spaces, while at the same time creating significant economic impacts.

Heritage, screen and literary festivals

HSLT festivals have been increasing in number throughout the 1990s and the new millennium, and are now an established part of the cultural

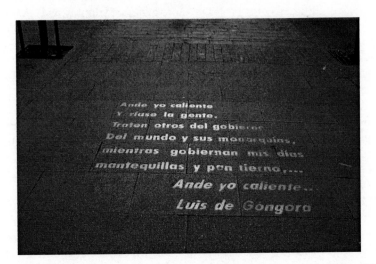

Plate 4.14 Quotes by famous Spanish writers adorn the pavements of Madrid's Barrios de las Letras
Source: The authors (2017).

economy. These are usually annual events, lasting between one and three days, although some may last between one and two weeks. Heritage festivals reaffirm national identities, particularly of perhaps marginalised groups (see Chapter 2 for a fuller discussion of the politics of HSLT). One such example is the Memphis Music and Heritage Festival, hosted by the Centre for Southern Folklore. It takes place on Main Street in Downtown Memphis, TN. For two days, all Memphis cultures are represented by a wide variety of performances and demonstrations. Local bands of every kind take to several street stages, as do local chefs and other experts on regional novelties. Art lines the streets, and this colourful festival is packed with rock, rap, gospel, blues, marching bands, folk, jug bands and workshops throughout the day. Another illustration is the National Asian Heritage Festival held in Washington, DC, in celebration of the Asian Pacific American Heritage Month. The event showcases Asian art and culture with a wide array of activities including live performances by musicians, vocalists and performance artists, Pan-Asian cuisine, martial arts and lion dance demonstrations, a multicultural marketplace, cultural displays and interactive activities.

There are thousands of film festivals around the world, stimulating the development of a film festival economy in a range of cities (Connell, 2012). A film festival is an organised, extended presentation of films in one or more screening venues, usually in a single location. More recently, film festivals hold outdoor movie screenings. They may be old films or new releases, and depending upon the focus of the individual festival can include domestic and international films. In addition, there may be a focus on a specific filmmaker or genre (e.g. film noir) or subject matter (e.g. horror film festival). A number of film festivals specialise in short films, each with its defined maximum length. The first major film festival was held in Venice in 1932; the other major and oldest film festivals of the world are: Cannes Film Festival (1946), Festival del film Locarno (1946), Karlovy Vary International Film Festival (1946), Edinburgh International Film Festival (1947), Melbourne International Film Festival (1951), Berlin International Film Festival (1951) and Toronto International Film Festival (1976). The Edinburgh International Film Festival in the UK was established in 1947 and is the longest continually running film festival in the world. The Raindance Film Festival is the UK's largest celebration of independent film making and takes place in London in October each year.

Likewise, there are many instances of literary festivals, also known as book festivals or writers' festivals, featuring a variety of presentations and readings by authors, as well as other events, delivered over a period of several days, with the primary objectives of promoting the authors' books and fostering a love of literature and writing. Writers' conferences are sometimes designed to provide an intellectual and academic focus for groups of writers without the involvement of the general public. The Hay Festival is perhaps the best known and oldest literary festival (Case Study 4.3) in the English-speaking world and, 25 years after this annual event first began, it has evolved into a not-for profit institution running 15 festivals across five continents (Hay Festival, 2016).

So far, this chapter has focused on HSLT development at the destination level. In doing so, it has highlighted a number of different ways in which these three niche forms of tourism have been developed and are developing. Moreover, it highlights their contingency on selected environmental resources, the importance of the (re)representation of such resources and of co-terminality, all of which are key elements of the HSLT nexus. Moreover, it demonstrates how HSLT destinations facilitate value, Vargo and Lusch's (2008) seventh premise, how specialisation (e.g. book towns and film festivals) can create value, their fifth premise, and how networks of organisations and institutions collaborate and coordinate their activities to co-create value, their ninth and 11th foundational premises. In addition to the wealth of destinations now attracting heritage, screen and literary tourists, there has been a boom in the development of specific visitor attractions, particularly during the last 30 years. It is the development of HSLT at the site level toward which this chapter now turns its attention.

Heritage, Screen and Literary Tourism Attraction Development

As discussed in Chapter 1, there has been much growth of HSLT fuelled by a production boom in the development of attractions worldwide. For instance, the increase in specialised museums alongside the general collections enshrined in the national museums and galleries has been one of the major forces behind museum growth throughout the 1990s (Richards, 1996). The number of museums in The Netherlands grew by 30% between 1985 and 1990, and in Germany by 33% between 1986 and 1990 (Richards, 1996). A second driving force of this boom in recent years has been the development of attractions related to regional and local culture and history (Richards, 1996). Just as the rise of nationalism was an important stimulus for heritage development in the 19th century, so regionalism and localism is proving an important spur to heritage, screen and literary production today.

Developing HSLT attractions, however, is an expensive undertaking. The cost of restoring a property, maintaining it, installing the necessary facilities required by tourists (i.e. toilets, café, souvenir shops), establishing and running an interpretive programme, site conservation and visitor management is enormous. The example of Tissington Hall (Derbyshire, UK) perhaps demonstrates the sheer expense. Built in 1609, it has 12 bedrooms, seven bathrooms (three functioning), 48 chimneys, 4032 panes of glass and an estate comprising 1900 acres, eight farmhouses and 40 rented cottages and annually costs £150,000 a year to run (Goldhill, 2014). According to the Historic Houses Association (2016), the combined backlog of repairs to privately owned historic houses stands at roughly £390m.

Just as development costs vary greatly from attraction to attraction, so do their operating costs. Basic costs usually include:

- staff costs;
- purchase of goods for resale;
- food and beverages;
- marketing;
- overheads (e.g. rent and rates, electricity and heating, accountancy fees, insurance, bank charges, security and maintenance);
- taxes (if the business qualifies as a VATable activity, PAYE/NI wages and salaries, corporation tax);
- capital expenditure (e.g. interactive audiovisual display or artefacts); and
- loan repayments (e.g. loans, mortgages, lease or hire purchase contracts).

Some of these costs, such as full-time staff pay, rent and rates, lease of equipment, bank repayments, insurance and accounting fees, are fixed on a weekly, monthly or annual basis and there is little scope to avoid them although it may be possible to reduce them. In addition, though, seasonal costs may be incurred, for example costs for additional staff, such as guides and actors, during the summer months. Other costs may be driven by sales, including purchases of food and beverages and goods for resale, for example. These vary depending on levels of business activity, as the more sales that occur, the more variable costs may be incurred. Meanwhile, there may be costs driven by business decisions to improve performance, enhance visitor expenditure or increase capacity, e.g. by adding new displays. These will give rise to one-off costs which often require significant outlay. Finance usually needs to be arranged from lenders to fund one-off costs including set-up costs, new buildings or equipment and health and safety compliance. Other discretionary costs (e.g. marketing and promotion spend and staff development) are often incurred when the objective is to increase capacity by improving performance or by enhancing the customer experience (Timothy & Boyd, 2003).

Overall, for an attraction to remain viable it must have enough sales to cover all fixed and variable costs; however, one of the greatest pressures facing HSLT attractions is the lack of availability of both capital and revenue funding streams. The current economic climate and competing financial pressures of other capital projects has led to a reduction in available funding streams, and consequently an increase in competition between organisations to secure this funding.

Funding Heritage, Screen and Literary Attraction Development

The funding of HSLT attractions may derive from direct sources such as the EU's Convergence Fund, and from national, regional and local governments. Often public agencies that have an interest in conservation and education may have a limited budget for providing one-time gifts to private and non-profit sector projects. This is normally done on a highly competitive basis and justification has to be made as to why the individual site is deserving of the money. Most national governments in the developed world have programmes of this nature. In the UK, for example, the National Lottery has become a very important source of funding for museums and galleries and their collections, libraries and archives, historic buildings and sites, and industrial, maritime and transport heritage. Museums in the UK in particular have been major beneficiaries, having received over £750m in funding from the Heritage Lottery Fund (HLF), the organisation established to distribute lottery funds, since its initiation in 1994. According to the HLF (2016b), its philosophy focuses on conservation and access, and it strongly seeks wider benefits from the projects it supports: education, regeneration, social inclusion and local employment are among the most obvious of these.

Most of the HLF grants are given through the main capital grants programme, in recognition of the considerable capital needs of the UK's physical heritage. A revenue grants programme is designed to help communities use and enjoy their heritage, to develop new audiences for the heritage (either as visitors, volunteers or through other forms of participation), and to further people's knowledge of why their heritage is important and relevant (HLF, 2016b). HLF's portfolio of grant programmes also includes theme-based or sector-specific streams which target areas of particular importance. These can be relevant to tourism, either very specifically (major paintings, such as Botticelli's 'The Virgin Adoring the Sleeping Christ Child' bought with HLF support, have boosted visitor numbers at galleries where they have been displayed) or generally, for example through improvements to townscapes in areas such as resort towns, which have a high tourism profile.

In the current era of austerity resulting in government cutbacks to funding across Europe, sponsorship has become one of the most important generators of direct and indirect income for HSLT attractions. This entails a form of 'in-kind' exchange, whereby some sort of service is provided in exchange for another service or money. One example would be an airline offering monetary gifts or plane tickets to a trust property in exchange for using its name and logo on trust brochures and signage. Donations are also important income generators but, unlike sponsorship, do not have any in-kind intentions attached to them. To elicit small-scale and personal donations, managers at public, private and non-profit attractions place dona-tion boxes near entrances and exits as a way of motivating people to put spare change or more into the site's conservation fund. Perhaps the most sought-after form of donation entails gifts from estates, corporations and philanthropic individuals. The advantage of non-profit heritage sites is that they are usually considered to be trusts or foundations – in essence, charities – that can offer tax benefits to contributors.

The formation of partnerships is another way of funding HSLT attrac-tions and again demonstrates the need, as Vargo and Lusch (2016) state, for networks of organisations and institutions to collaborate and cooperate in order to enable tourists to co-create value (foundational premises nine and 11). Despite being niche elements of tourism activity, a marked uptake of HSLT initiatives by destination marketing organisations (DMOs) and eco-nomic development organisations is notable within an increasingly global context. Private and public sector based destination tourism partnerships, known as destination management and/or marketing partnerships (DMPs), have been a growing trend for the past several years. In these times of tight budgets and growing demands, tourist destinations have looked for more and more ways to share costs, skills and resources for mutual benefit, and such partnerships have many benefits including:

- cost sharing for construction projects, exhibit projects, marketing ser-vices, staff training and development;
- providing 'credibility' by having the right 'names' associated with spe-cific development;
- providing expertise that may not be available 'in house';
- cutting costs in marketing and advertising sites or attractions; and
- help in grant writing or other revenue generation.

There are various kinds of tourism partnerships between different organisa-tions and agencies and how these partnerships function varies greatly (HDC International, 2016a).

Given the scarcity of financial resources, site managers have become fis-cally responsible for increasing revenue and controlling operating costs. As a result, HSLT attraction managers have begun offering a variety of services to visitors in an attempt to keep them longer and to encourage them to spend more. Aside from direct funding, the most widespread and most traditional means of earning money has been user fees, the most common being entrance and admission fees. Entrance fees are monies paid to enter larger open areas like parks, zoos and gardens, while admission fees are more related to entrance into buildings and other structures like museums, galleries, castles, historic houses or attractions (Timothy & Boyd, 2003). Rental costs may also be considered a user fee when visitors purchase the right to utilise some part of a historic house or artefact. Letting out rooms for wedding receptions, professional meetings and family reunions are common examples of this. Some HSLT attractions have begun offering membership. Individual members and families, by being members, often have almost unlimited admission to the attraction. According to Timothy and Boyd (2003: 145) 'car parking and participation costs for special events and additional activities are also becoming more common fee-based sources of revenue'. Supporting special events and extracurricular activities, particularly during the off-season, can also offset operating costs. In addition to the participation fees, event organisers can be 'charged rental utility and other service fees or they might be required to pay a percentage of their proceeds to the hosting attraction. Theatrical performances, concerts and sporting events are particularly suitable for many heritage attractions' (Timothy & Boyd, 2003: 145).

Retailing is another important source of revenue for HSLT sites, particularly since there is evidence to suggest that these tourists spend more while on vacation. Several different retail items at attractions are very popular including: miniature replicas, guidebooks, photo albums, camera film and batteries, postcards, sweets, t-shirts, calendars, coffee mugs, pens and pencils (Timothy & Boyd, 2003). Lodging and catering are other sources of income that might be considered. Accommodation facilities and food services have the potential to lengthen visits and increase additional spending. Interpretation can be used to increase visitor expenditure. The most common way is through audiotape rentals, selling maps and guidebooks, and offering expensive group tours.

Remaining commercially viable is a challenge for most HSLT attractions, and government funding of these sites, particularly those that lie within the heritage domain, has sparked a great deal of debate, specifically concerning public value. Such controversy is perhaps not surprising given that heritage is of course selective, based on what people value and want to hand on to future generations (see Chapter 1 for a fuller discussion). The impact of the UK's National Lottery specifically on heritage and tourism has come under close scrutiny, partly due to the national media's attention on the financial difficulties experienced by a small cluster of high-profile lottery-funded schemes such as the ill-fated National Centre for Popular Music, Sheffield. Costing in excess of £15m and largely funded by the National Lottery, it closed down after only just over a year in operation (Plate 4.15). In addition, the extent to which the existing pattern of lottery awards represents a fair and equitable investment in the quality of life across UK society has been questioned, as has the biased distribution of money to sites in and around London, leaving regional and local attractions extremely cash strapped. Thus, evidence from the evaluation of completed projects is essential to enable policy makers and opinion formers in the heritage and tourism sectors to make substantive judgements about the real changes that have been delivered through Lottery funding. Perhaps one of the main reasons why there are no clear-cut answers lies in the dichotomy which exists between conservation

Plate 4.15 The former National Centre for Popular Music, Sheffield, UK
Source: The authors (2017).

and business, particularly in the case of HSLT development, which is contingent upon finite natural, built and cultural resources, involving re-representation and commodification and co-terminality.

Conservation and Business: Opportunity or Threat?

The conservation of natural, built and cultural resources is wide ranging and, according to Timothy and Boyd (2003: 94–96), three main approaches exist, these being:

  (i) *Preservation*, which refers to a situation where a choice is made to maintain the site in its existing state; a great deal of effort and expenditure is involved in this work to maintain the property and impede deterioration;
 (ii) *Restoration*, which is sometimes also known as reconstruction and involves putting displaced pieces of a building or site back together and/or removing pieces and amendments that have been added through time; and
(iii) *Renovation*, which is also known as adaptation and entails making changes to a site while still maintaining a proportion of its historic character.

Invariably, the goals of HSLT sites shape the strategies embraced by management which are in turn heavily influenced by visitor expectations (Timothy

& Boyd, 2003). The four sectors that tend to own different types of HSLT attractions – public, private, non-governmental and voluntary/non-profit – all have different aims and goals. In the case of public sector ownership, a site is owned and possibly operated by a government department or agency, and in most countries it assumes a major role in heritage conservation. In Moscow, for instance, the homes of the great Russian writers such as Tolstoy, Chekhov and Dostoyevsky have been perfectly preserved by the state. Perhaps the best example in the UK is English Heritage which is a government agency that operates a large number of the most visited heritage attractions in England.

Within the private sector, conservation and business do not necessarily sit alongside each other comfortably. These are profit-driven sites and so they must be commercially viable and successful; the primary goal is profit. However, HSLT attraction managers must also consider conservation and education as a long-term strategy which is necessary in order to sustainably manage their resources. Universal Film Studios, Los Angeles, CA, for instance, owned by MBC Universal, one of the world's leading media and entertainment companies in the development, production and marketing of news and information to global audiences, despite being a working movie studio and major visitor attraction offering studio tours, also conserves old sets of famous films. One particular set that has been conserved is the legendary 'Bates Motel' from the film *Psycho*, constructed in the back lot in 1959 (Plate 4.16). It became an iconic symbol of eeriness and has appeared in countless films.

Plate 4.16 The infamous Bates Motel featuring in the film *Psycho*, Universal Studios, Los Angeles, CA
Source: The authors (2017).

There are many examples of non-profit, voluntary and charitable organisations responsible for the conservation of HSLT sites. Internationally, the United Nations Educational, Scientific and Cultural Organisation (UNESCO) is of course the most well-known. Comprising representations from most nation states, it seeks to encourage the identification, protection and preservation of cultural and natural heritage around the world considered to be of outstanding value to humanity. The Durrell Wildlife Conservation Trust is another example of an international charity which is working toward saving species from extinction. It was founded by Gerald Durrell, who in addition to being a zookeeper, conservationist, TV presenter and naturalist is perhaps best remembered as an author, particularly for his book *My Family and Other Animals* (1956) which tells of his idyllic childhood on Corfu. Committed to conserving the diversity and integrity of natural heritage, Durrell has developed a worldwide reputation for pioneering conservation techniques. On a more national, regional or local basis, voluntary, non-profit and/or charitable organisations generally tend to operate museums, cemeteries, heritage trails and historic buildings. As their primary goal is to earn enough revenue to continue to exist, they usually charge entrance fees, a large proportion of which should be expended directly back into site maintenance. Perhaps the best known and most widespread non-profit heritage body in Britain is the National Trust. Its purpose is to raise enough money every year to continue to maintain its conservation activities.

In some circumstances, conservation may be an unintended consequence of HSLT. For example, four buildings on Wing Lee Street, Hong Kong, whose demolition became highlighted after they were featured in an award-winning film, *Echoes of the Rainbow*, were subsequently renovated and preserved after a public outcry (Pan & Ryan, 2013; Plate 4.17). The quest for conservation is onerous, though. In addition to the need to operate on a sound financial basis, there are a number of broad challenges to HSLT development across the developed and developing worlds. These relate to threats imposed by modernisation, visitor pressure, criminal damage, local residents' perceptions, environmental pressures, colonial legacy and loss of authenticity, and unless they are tackled, value co-destruction may taint the tourist experience.

Modernisation

Economic transformation is a driving force of many developed and developing economies and more often than not, particularly in the latter context, development and modernisation are more highly prioritised than heritage preservation. Indeed the Global Heritage Fund (2012) claims that the long-term global benefits of cultural heritage are often discounted against opportunities for short-term domestic economic development. This results in the demolition of ancient cities and buildings to make way for modern infrastructure and the neglect of archaeological sites which are often surrounded

Plate 4.17 Wing Lee Street, Hong Kong
Source: The authors (2017).

by poorly planned commercial development. According to Timothy and Boyd (2003), while recent history shows that people and societies in the Western developed world have an increasing desire to conserve the past, residents of developing countries commonly associate preservation with backwardness which often results in a lack of desire to conserve.

Visitor pressure

Serious damage caused by wear and tear, litter and vandalism occurs mainly at heritage sites, particularly those that have gained UNESCO World Heritage status, as a result of excessive visitor pressure (Garrod & Fyall, 2000; Li et al., 2008; Wager, 1995). Clambering tourists at ancient monuments such as the Egyptian Pyramids, Skellig Michael (County Kerry, Ireland) and Hadrian's Wall (UK) have played a major role in the deterioration of the sites themselves, including the erosion of stairs and paving stones as a result of thousands of tourists' feet. Decorative motifs and carvings are also at risk due to thousands of hands touching delicate artwork. Some sites are visited so intensely during high seasons that managers have limited access as a means of preventing wear and tear. For example, after experiencing years of clambering tourists often numbering more than 2000 an hour during the summer, Stonehenge began suffering visible degradation. Many of the stones were being worn away and earthworks around them were being heavily trampled. In response, the Department of the Environment erected a perimeter fence in 1978 to protect the site. Although not allowed inside the fence, visitors to Stonehenge are permitted to wander freely outside the barrier for a fairly close-up view of the stones. Wear and tear is also caused by the moisture and condensation created by breathing, sweating and touching which can affect delicate surfaces and paintings. The Ajanta caves (Maharashtra, India), for instance, house numerous early Buddhist paintings dating back to the 1st and 2nd centuries. Many of these artworks are crumbling due to an excessive number of tourists visiting the site and disrupting the delicate microclimate of the caves.

Criminal damage

Criminal damage at HSLT sites in developed and developing countries also poses certain challenges for conservation. According to a report commissioned by English Heritage and undertaken by Bradley *et al.* (2012), more than 200 crimes a day are being committed against Britain's historic sites, with 75,000 being recorded in 2011. Criminals have targeted World Heritage Sites, listed buildings, churches, parks and gardens, battlefields, conservation areas and a shipwreck site. The damage suffered included metal theft, looting, vandalism, graffiti and arson (Plate 4.18). In particular, the most precious buildings were worst affected with nearly a quarter of Grade I and II listed structures subject to some type of criminal damage. The report

Plate 4.18 Clifford Tower, York (UK) is an unusual 13th century keep on top of William the Conqueror's fortress and is a principal feature of York's medieval castle; it was vandalised with graffiti in 2010
Source: The authors (2017).

concluded that metal theft was the biggest single threat to the country's landmarks, as official figures reveal more than 1000 metal theft offences are occurring every week in Britain. In recent months high-profile targets of criminals have included York Minster and the Bishop's Palace in Lincoln (UK), while the problem of metal theft was highlighted by the theft of a £500,000 Dame Barbara Hepworth bronze sculpture from Dulwich Park, London.

Albania is another example of a country that is experiencing the destruction and theft of its heritage since the 1990s, as the country struggled through a period of anarchy and lawlessness following the collapse of the Communist regime. A fresco painted by the country's widely considered greatest icon painter Onufri was damaged after thieves with axes and knives twice cut through the painting in late December and early January 2012–2013 in an attempt to steal it. Following public uproar, the Albanian Institute of Monuments has installed 88 new security cameras in dozens of churches. The financial cost of such action is burdensome (Andoni, 2013) but considered necessary to protect these sites from looters. Much of what is stolen from historic locations is sold illegally on the international collectors' market. Weak security, impoverished or unstable nations and those with corrupt governments have created conditions where such illicit activity has flourished.

However, it is not just the issue of the protection and physical rectification of the damage at heritage sites that is of interest here, as the treatment of vandalism within heritage management in particular poses some philosophical difficulties as well. Given that current heritage best practice aims to avoid strategies which focus solely on single often arbitrary periods or narratives in a site's history in favour of those which recognise all of the site's layers of significance (see Chapter 3 for a fuller discussion of the politics of HSLT), it is debatable whether contemporary vandalism and/or graffiti represents conservation sacrilege or just another archaeological feature (Merrill, 2011). After all, such acts were not uncommon practice in Ancient Egypt as a means of rewriting history, and remain visible today. This is most notably evidenced by attempts to delete the existence of Queen Hatshepsut, Pharaoh of Egypt, through the destruction and defacement of her monuments, statues and images after her death in 1458 BC.

Local residents' perceptions

Heritage conservation is a relatively new notion in many third world countries, and in the daily struggle for survival it is not surprising that few people appreciate the need for it or value it. Numerous examples exist of residents in developing countries establishing their homes and villages inside historic sites/ancient ruins or immediately adjacent to them. As a consequence, conflicts arise between residents and organisations involved in the restoration and conservation of such sites. The development of a tourism industry that utilises religious relics of the past may cause further friction with locals who use the site for religious purposes, and tourism at HSLT sites can have the effect of not allowing local people access to their own sacred sites and to places associated with their own heritage. Moreover, conflict occurs when traditional people and original owners are removed from their own land. This type of action was all too common in the creation of natural heritage landscapes, particularly in the establishment of national parks in Africa where this draconian action was taken to shape pleasure grounds for elite societies of the past as well as for modern safari tourists. It has only been through the use of partnership arrangements that local people have started to reclaim and share in the benefits of presenting their natural heritage to visitors (Timothy & Boyd, 2003). By contrast, in most of the developed world, people have a tendency to grow more interested in their personal heritage as they age (see Chapter 3 for discussion on the heritage debate and nostalgia). However, local residents' perceptions in developed countries may also be negatively affected, particularly if they live in historic communities and at heritage places which attract mass numbers of tourists, thereby creating anxiety and discord (see more detailed discussion in Chapter 8) as noted by Hailey (1999) in York (UK), Simpson (1999) in Prague (Czech Republic), and Hailey et al. (2005) in Bath (UK).

Environmental pressures

A variety of environmental pressures pose challenges for conservation. Unless historic buildings and structures are regularly maintained, the effects of wind, rain and intense heat will cause deterioration. Moreover, pollution caused by heavy industry, high volumes of traffic and inadequate waste disposal systems are other broad challenges to the conservation of HSLT sites (Timothy & Boyd, 2003). At the Taj Mahal, for example, factories and other elements of heavy industry have for many years created conditions wherein chemicals and other pollutants released into the air have begun to damage the monument. Similar problems exist with the Pyramids of Giza, Egypt. Litter is another problem at HSLT sites: fast-food containers, cigarette butts, broken bottles and cans not only ruin the ambience of an attraction, but also are expensive to clean up.

Colonial legacy

Legacies of colonialism pose a number of complex difficulties for the conservation of colonial and local heritage. In terms of the former, for some, the heritage stemming from a former foreign powers rule may represent a period of oppression and thus, in attempt to cast off these shackles, there may be little will or desire for the conservation of colonial heritage which represents contested and/or dissonant heritage (see discussion in Chapter 3 on dissonant and contested heritage). With respect to the former, very often the rule of foreign powers delayed independence and sometimes forced local people to abandon their indigenous religious beliefs and cultural values. Indeed, it was not uncommon for colonial powers to use extreme measures to control independent thinking and to muffle emotions of national pride on the part of native residents. Following decolonialisation, alienation from such values has hampered efforts to restore pride and traditions resulting in long-term implications as countries like Indonesia, India and Rwanda are today facing great difficulties in trying to create a spirit of nationalism and common heritage (Timothy & Boyd, 2003).

Loss of authenticity

Given that HSLT development inevitably involves the (re)presentation and commodification of various aspects of a destination's built and natural resources, and co-terminality, it is not surprising that such developments can result in a loss of authenticity (see Chapter 6 for an in-depth discussion of authenticity). With respect to the development of heritage tourism, the staging, re-creation, reconstruction, commodification and marketing of products in such ways that they are no longer primitive, preindustrial, untouched and original, or in other words historically inaccurate, has been widely criticised (Carnegie & McCabe, 2008; Chhabra et al., 2003; Hewison, 1987). Hewison (1987) argues that information is largely taken out of context, is presented in a superficial way and is displayed primarily for the purposes of 'edutainment' as means of attracting visitor interest and revenue.

But it is not just heritage tourism that is associated with a loss of authenticity, as much has been written about the misrepresentation of place, people and culture through screen and literature (Beeton, 2015, 2016; Connell, 2012). Landscapes featured in screen productions are often associated with meaning and symbolism (Bordwell & Thompson, 1993), elements that are heightened by the use of *mise-en-scène* (design aspects of film production and arrangement of scenes in front of the camera), cinematography and editing processes (Connell, 2012). It is these features that create an imagined geography of places, settings and landscapes in the minds of the viewers (Moran, 2006). In turn, the 'reel' exists simultaneously as a 'real' environment (Cresswell & Dixon, 2002). Moreover, inauthenticity and the existence of blurred boundaries between reality and fantasy among tourists may also be fuelled by place substitution which occurs in screen adaptations and literature. Indeed, there are many examples of screen tourism occurring in places that were intended to be portrayed rather than in an actual location where the story is based (Beeton, 2015; Butler, 2011).

As a consequence, real places are sometimes confused with imagined ones and, as demonstrated by Chapters 2 and 7, due to co-terminality of the visitor experience, imagined locations are sought by tourists of a particular place or space. As Butler (2011) observes in the title of a recent paper, 'It's only make believe', the appeal of a real location shown in a film may be greater than the actual place. Furthermore, screen adaptations and literature may also result in the appropriation and commodification of place and culture that serves to diminish authenticity. Gibson (2006: 160), for example, identifies how costume dramas and films based on heritage and nostalgia act as the 'visual economy of tourism', particularly in relation to American audiences. Moreover, Connell (2012: 1023) cites the example of Rains (2003) who 'explores this notion in the cinematic representations of the Irish diaspora and the return home, depicted in *The Quiet Man*, which was a film criticised for its romantic and nostalgic idealisation of Ireland, but one much treasured by American audiences seeking to negotiate collective cultural memories and identity'.

In addition, Connell (2012) cites the examples of Laffont and Prigent (2011) and Durham (2008) who both discuss the misrepresentation of destinations in films. In the case of Laffont and Prigent's study, only the most representative parts of cities were selected as film sets, with Paris being the most prominently used city to portray 'Frenchness'. Durham examines the representation of France and French culture in three films: *Amelie*, *Chocolat* and *Le Divorce*, all of which were created by American filmmakers. In doing so, he argues that although Paris is one of Hollywood's favourite locations, the film misrepresents France, and the real locations included in the film would not in reality be attractive to tourists. Of course, the appeal and extent to which tourists are satisfied with their experience depends on the availability and deployment of their operant resources (Vargo & Lusch, 2004) since images merely strengthen clichés and stereotypes. But films do not need to set out to accurately represent a destination because they are intended as works of fiction in any case. Where care must be shown is where marketing campaigns are launched on the back of such films, when DMOs use destination imagery from films to promote place qualities (see Chapter 7 for a fuller discussion). In such cases, the mismatch between perceptions and reality potentially creates disappointing tourist experiences, a theme considered by Busby and O'Neill (2006) and Connell and Myer (2009) (see Chapters 3 and 6 for further discussion) and emphasised by Vargo and Lusch (2016) in their tenth foundational premise which states that the value co-created and extracted is always judged by the end-user.

Conclusion

HSLT has been widely used as a tool for development worldwide and the focus of this chapter has been to consider its development at a site and destination level within the context of the HSLT nexus (Figure 1.1), while at the same time drawing on insights provided by S-DL and co-creation. With

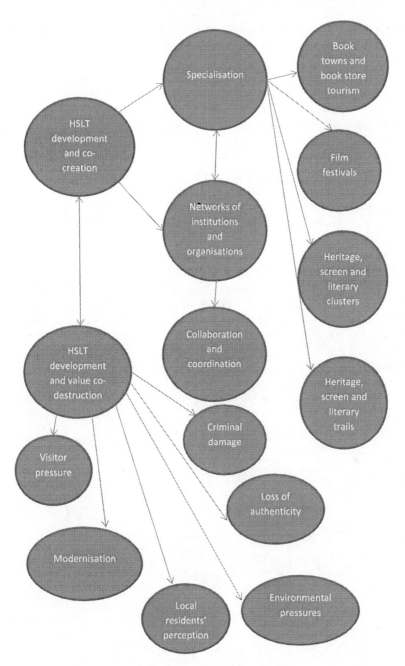

Figure 4.2 Dimensions of heritage, screen and literary tourism development and co-creation
Source: The authors (2017).

regard to the latter, these three forms of tourism are commonly employed to diversify and regenerate flagging economies, usually through the creation of themed towns, as in the case of book town or bookstore tourism, districts and clusters. In this context and as Vargo and Lusch (2016) suggest in their fifth, seventh, ninth and 11th foundational premises (see Table 1.7), the service experience is comprised of specialisation and of networks of organisations and institutions which collaborate and coordinate activities to co-create value (Figure 4.2).

But as has been discussed, development is contingent on a variety of factors, not least political stability. In terms of the former, issues influencing development are detailed and, in particular, attention is drawn to the variety of funding sources that are now exploited in order to ensure commercial viability. This chapter ends with a discussion of the many challenges to the development of HSLT at destination and site levels, including modernisation, visitor pressure, local residents' perceptions, criminal damage, environmental pressures, colonial legacy and loss of authenticity. These issues have serious implications for the cost of developing, maintaining and operating HSLT developments and highlight the potential for value co-destruction (see Figure 4.2). Additionally, these challenges draw attention to the existence of an uneasy relationship between the need for these to be commercially viable, while ensuring the conservation of resources on which they are contingent. This consideration of the challenges to the development of HSLT is extended further in the next chapter which focuses on interpretation. More specifically, its aims, goals and problems encountered at destination and site levels are examined.

5 Interpretation for Heritage, Screen and Literary Tourism

Introduction

Interpretation for HSLT is the communication of information about, and the reconstruction and explanation of, people, events, objects, place and phenomena using personal and/or non-personal methods. It is a central feature of the HSLT nexus associated with co-creation, (re)representation and commodification of related contingent elements of the built, living and natural heritage, and involves co-terminality since the tourist plays a key role in the co-creation of the experience (see Chapter 1). While there is a significant body of knowledge about interpretation in a heritage and literary tourism context (Howard, 2003; Moscardo, 1996; Poria *et al.*, 2009; Uzzell, 1989; Yeoman & Drummond, 2001), much less research has been undertaken in relation to screen tourism, particularly in relation to its impact on people's interaction with place (Beeton, 2015, 2016; Buzinde & Santos, 2009).

In the contexts of HSLT and S-DL and co-creation, this chapter explores the meaning and guiding principles of interpretation and its aims and, in doing so, establishes some of the benefits that it may bring to sites, destinations and regions. The interpretive planning process is then introduced and some interpretive approaches, techniques and media are outlined. Given that interpretation is deeply rooted in co-creation which is constructed through communication and the visitor experience, the end product, namely education and/or entertainment (or edutainment, as it has been termed) is considered, followed by discussion of some challenges to interpretation posed by the heterogeneity of tourist motivations and experiences and by cross-cultural and special needs. Next, issues related to the evaluation of interpretation are explored. The chapter ends with a summary and some concluding thoughts.

Interpretation: Meaning and Principles

Tilden, one of the early pioneers of interpretation defined interpretation as an 'educational activity which aims to reveal meanings and relationships through the use of original objects, by first-hand experience, and by illustrative media, rather than simply to communicate factual information' (Tilden, 1977: 7). Walsh-Heron and Stevens (1990: 101) define interpretation as 'the basic art of telling a story of the place, an object or an event', while Light (1995: 34) proposes that 'in its widest sense then, interpretation is a means, indeed almost an art, of communicating ... which enables a visitor to develop a better understanding of the resource'. In a heritage tourism context, it is primarily concerned with the use of information about the past to display a destination or a specific site to visitors and locals in order to enhance their experience (Howard, 2003). Meanwhile, in relation to literary and screen tourism, it is used to explain places associated with literary and screen authors, characters and celebrities regardless of whether such places are linked with their life or associated with their fictional creations. Interpretation is a professional activity which requires creativity, imagination and innovation as it must encourage visitors to create their own mental space to complete the reconstruction. As a consequence, it is a significant aspect of value co-creation during the visitor's experience (Moscardo & Ballantyne, 2008) and forms a key part of the product offered to the visitor.

Although focused on the countryside and national parks, the guiding principles of interpretation were conceptualised by Tilden in his book *Interpreting Our Heritage* (1957), in which he defined six principles that formed the basis of the visitor engagement strategy used by the United States National Park Service. The first states that 'Any interpretation which does not somehow relate to what is being displayed or described or to something within the personality or experience of the visitor will be sterile' (Tilden, 1977: 9). Implicit within this principle is that a visitor will comprehend the interpretation in their own way which is influenced by personal knowledge and experience. According to Herbert (1989: 194), 'Interpretation must therefore be meaningful and capable of being understood in various frames of reference'. Tilden's second principle is concerned with information: 'Information as such, is not interpretation. Interpretation is revelation based upon information. They are different things but not all interpretation includes information' (Tilden, 1977: 9). Herbert (1989: 194) elaborates upon this by stating that: 'Interpretation is the art of conveying information; it has a teaching and an illuminating role which reaches out to the visitor. It conveys not simply facts but also meanings and values.'

Tilden's third principle states that 'Interpretation is an art which combines many arts whether the materials presented are scientific, historical or architectural' (Tilden, 1977: 9). The messages that interpretation seeks to convey are often subjective and qualitative; they reach out to the emotions and affective properties. Those who interpret should rely on the arts of creativity and imagination. This leads onto the fourth principle, which states that 'The chief aim of interpretation is not instruction, but provocation' (Tilden, 1977: 9). Rather than presenting factual, sterile subject matter, it is concerned with stimulation and with increasing visitor awareness of what is being seen or experienced (Herbert, 1989). Meanwhile, Tilden's fifth principle states that 'Interpretation should aim to present a whole rather than a part and must address itself to the whole man rather than any phase'. Finally, the sixth principle says that 'Interpretation addressed to children (up to the age of 12 years) should not be a dilution of the presentation to adults, but should follow a fundamentally different path' (Tilden, 1977: 9). Taking these principles together, interpretation may be used to achieve a variety of different aims (Herbert, 1989; Light, 1995).

Aims of interpretation

First, interpretation involves co-production and is employed to enhance the visitor experience, whether this is through education and/or entertainment by making learning fun while at the same time provoking a deeper understanding. Often it is a key part of the product offered to the visitor; however, in some instances it may be an add-on feature to generate a feeling among visitors that they have experienced real value for money. For instance, a series of nature trails were created in Thorpe Park as an additional facet to the rides and entertainments already provided. Secondly, interpretation may be used to encourage visitors to stay longer and thereby potentially increase expenditure in accompanying facilities. Thirdly, it may be used to attract more visitors to an area, a locality or a region in order to promote economic development, most notably to create jobs and income or to encourage regeneration and provide alternative sources of employment. Fourthly, by interpreting a site through its real or fictitious linkages, whether to place, person or event, it is possible to maintain the differences between tourist destinations. By doing so, the production of identical destinations is avoided and the promotion of uniqueness and individuality is facilitated, thereby helping to preserve visitor appeal.

Fifthly, interpretation is not just used to communicate factual information but to also invoke a response and perhaps to change attitudes and opinions (Herbert, 1989). Thus, according to Alderson and Low (1976: 61), 'in the interpretation of a documentary historic site, a visitor should learn not only what events occurred in this place at a specific time in history, but why they occurred in just this place and nowhere else'. Additionally, as Chapter 3 demonstrates, often it is used therefore for propaganda purposes as a means to change or influence visitor attitudes to support the purposes of a specific organisation. For example, large landowning organisations may use interpretative techniques to put forward the land management policies of their organisation which may not be conservation oriented.

Sixthly, interpretation has been widely used as a soft and hard visitor management tool. With regard to the former, the problems and pressures facing the area are explained to the visitor in order to make them aware of its value and highlight potential consequences if the area is not managed appropriately. Here the aim is to generate greater understanding, appreciation and protection (Tilden, 1977: 37) and to change visitor attitudes so that it induces more thoughtful and considerate behaviour. In terms of the latter, interpretation is used to lead visitors away from fragile areas (Herbert, 1989), and employs techniques such as guided walks and waymarked trails to shepherd the public away from heavily eroded or fragile environments toward areas that are more able to withstand visitor pressure (Beckmann, 1988; Hooper & Weiss, 1991). Seventhly, an aim of interpretation may be to enhance tourism provision and promotion through the linking of products with marketing using theming and branding techniques. Thus, an attraction with a strong theme may be linked to the wider marketing activities of a tourist destination by promoting a similar theme.

However, interpretation does not just aim to generate benefits for the tourism industry but can also be used advantageously for and by host communities. Indeed, Ballantyne and Uzzell (1998) argue that interpretation may reinforce sociocultural values, helping local people understand their locality and its significance, thereby boosting self-confidence, community self-interest and pride. By involving local people in the narration of their own stories, interpretation may also encourage development at a community level and generate a strong local identity. Moreover, their involvement with visitors has the potential to facilitate intercultural communication and interaction and create local recreational opportunities.

In short, interpretation is provided at a destination, be it a specific site, locality or region. It fulfils a multifunctional role as it may serve as an education, entertainment, management and business tool. At the very heart of interpretation is co-creation, without which value would not be experienced or extracted. As such, Vargo and Lusch's (2016) second, third, seventh, ninth and 11th foundational premises are particularly relevant here as these may be related to the role and aims of interpretation in creating the experience environment. FP2 (indirect exchange masks the fundamental basis of exchange), for instance, highlights the interdependency of products and processes in co-creation, and certainly it is only the most iconic or self-explanatory products from which visitors are able to derive and extract value without any accompanying interpretation. FP3 (goods are a distribution mechanism for service provision) points to the importance of interpretation, a non-durable good, in the exchange process, while FP7 (the enterprise cannot deliver value but only offer value propositions) emphasises the fact that it is up to the tourists themselves to derive and extract value, the extent to which is in part dependent on the success of interpretation. Meanwhile, FP9 (all social and economic actors are resource integrators) and FP11 (value co-creation is coordinated through actor-generated institutions and institutional arrangements) draw attention to the use of interpretation and the processes involved in product and destination branding.

Ultimately, value co-creation requires that interpretation focuses on the visitor and their needs. In HSLT, as Chapter 2 demonstrates, these may be diverse and include the schools market (this group varies in itself due to different levels) and long-stay domestic and international visitors, business tourists and day trippers, all of whom may or may not visit in order to be formally educated. Thus it is imperative that a region, local area or site is quite clear as to who their visitors and what their needs are. In addition, it is critical to know what might be interpreted, how it might be interpreted, when, where and how the resource(s) should be interpreted, and how the effectiveness of interpretation can be monitored. This necessitates the existence of a coherent and coordinated approach to interpretive planning.

Interpretative Planning

Interpretation is a sensitive and demanding task and the extent to which it is applied in practice depends very much on the aims and objectives of the organisation responsible for the resources that require explanation, and on their characteristics. Even before the interpretive planning process begins, it is important to recognise the existence of a general set of influences that affect it. Perhaps the most crucial point to take into consideration is the number of visitors that is expected, simply because there is an obvious need to maintain a balance between the needs of the resource and the visitor. As mentioned earlier, interpretation can be a positive management tool that helps to ameliorate the potential impacts of increased tourist contact. By controlling the information content and positioning of interpretation, visitors can be hurried through pressure points, distributed more evenly around places (sites, localities or regions), or steered away from sensitive areas.

Additionally, the appropriateness of the scale of interpretation is another influence that must be taken into account since it is important that it does not impair, reduce the significance of, or detract from the quality of that which the visitor came to see. Attention must also be given to understanding the visitors and their needs. Interpretation addressed to different visitor segments should follow fundamentally different approaches but should also be able to co-exist. Furthermore, since tourism by its very nature is attracted to the most fragile and unique places of the world, the nature of the site and/or destination, notably its fragility or robustness and capacity, is a key consideration that will exert an influence on the interpretive planning process. Thus, it is necessary to consider the number of visitors a destination already receives and whether any potential increase in visitor numbers will destroy the quality of the resource and/or reduce the quality of the visitor experience. Finally, the budget available, including initial set-up, maintenance and operational costs, must be taken into account as it influences the nature and extent of interpretation.

Interpretation must follow a clearly defined planning process that is cyclical and iterative (Figure 5.1). It begins with the 'setting of the objectives'. These might be quite general, e.g. visitors will leave the destination having enjoyed their time, or they may be quite specific, e.g. the visitor will have a better understanding. At this stage of the process, it is vitally important to be clear about the desired achievements. The setting of objectives in turn provides a measurable standard against which interpretation can be monitored and evaluated. This stage is then followed by an 'audit of resources' and

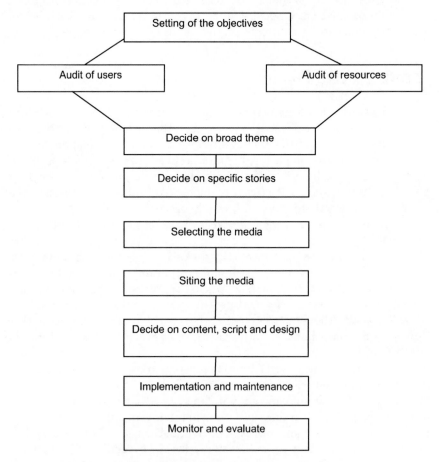

Figure 5.1 The interpretive planning process
Source: The authors (2017).

an 'audit of visitors'. With respect to the latter, knowledge of the visitor is critical as this inevitably influences the objectives of the interpretive planning process in addition to the broad themes presented. In terms of the latter, an inventory or stocktaking exercise should be undertaken where available resources are closely scrutinised and decisions taken as to which should be interpreted. Other sites in the catchment area and existing interpretation should also be examined at this juncture to prevent duplication.

Once both audits have been completed and the results analysed, the third stage of the process is to 'decide on the broad themes' that will provide the overarching framework of interpretation and the unifying thread with which to link specific stories. Any exhibits or information discordant to the themes identified must be rejected. Indeed, one of the common failings of interpretation is to include too many themes, thereby confusing the message and the visitor. Once this has been achieved, the fourth stage involves 'deciding on specific stories', which must fit into the broad theme previously decided upon. 'Selecting the media' and 'siting the media' are the fifth and sixth stages of the process. These stages are important as they can influence visitor flow and the pace of movement and thus help to avoid potential points of congestion or over-pressure. It is also during these stages that planners and managers need to exercise sensitivity and consider its visual or aural intrusion or even the potential for damage which may reduce the overall quality of the visitor experience. Additionally, media selection involves choosing the stories and media most appropriate to the theme as well as considering the most appropriate ways through which the stories can be imparted. Taking a rather extreme example, for instance, of concentration camps, the suffering of the Jews would not be appropriately conveyed through live interpretation. The ability and speed at which costs may be recouped is another important consideration when selecting and siting the media, particularly if the site or destination is not expected to attract many visitors in the short term. Ensuring that the visitor is involved as much as possible is an additional imperative to bear in mind.

Once these decisions have been made, it is possible to 'decide on the specific content, script and design', the eighth stage of the interpretive planning process. Writing interpretive text is a skill that requires thought and practice. The best text tells a story and uses a range of creative techniques to bring a site or object to life and there are a number of writing techniques that help relate the text to the audience (Text Box 5.1). In general, a 'reading age' of 9–12 is a good level at which to write interpretive text as it uses very few technical or scientific terms and is easily understood by the great majority of older children and adults (HDC International, 2016b). 'Implementation and maintenance', the ninth stage, can then occur, followed by the tenth, 'Monitoring and evaluation', driven by the need to assess objectively if the interpretation is functioning as originally planned and meeting the objectives.

Text Box 5.1 Interpretation writing techniques

Address the reader in the first person. This means referring to them as 'you', for example: 'You can see the lichen clinging to the trees, taking in water and nutrients from the air'.

Use active rather than passive verbs. This makes the text sound more natural and lively, for example: 'we manage' is far better than 'this site is managed by'.

Use metaphors, analogies and comparisons. These help people relate what you're telling them to something else they know about, for example: 'Loch Ness is so deep it could fit in 100 Nelson's Columns, one on top of the other' and 'Jays are a bit like us. When we're hungry, we pop to the fridge for some food we bought earlier. When Jays are hungry, they dig up an acorn they buried earlier'.

Use humour. It can be a very effective way of relating to and engaging your audience, but be careful; not everyone finds the same things funny.

Ask questions and engage your audience's imagination. The text can ask specific questions and get your audience to imagine things, for example: 'What famous drink comes from this innocent-looking bush?'.

Use first-person narrative. It can be very effective to adopt a character to narrate your story. This means your interpretive text is written in the first person.

Write in short sentences and paragraphs. Long sentences and paragraphs are very off-putting. Most people won't even bother to begin reading them or will be so bored halfway through they will find something more interesting to do instead.

Avoid jargon and technical terms. They will confuse or alienate the reader. Write in plain English and use pictures as they are often far better at communicating than words.

Only use one idea per sentence. Vary the length of a sentence for better rhythm.

Look out for potentially loaded words. These show bias and can make the reader take a contrary stance on principle, for example: 'people' and 'we' are far better than 'man', 'woman', 'him' or 'her'; remember clichés make people switch off.

Rewrite, edit ruthlessly and rewrite again. Always end up with fewer words than you started with.

Always keep your audience in mind. Write in simple and clear conversational language. Above all, don't just communicate facts and figures – let the writing tell a story.

Source: HDC International (2016b).

In order to obtain the many benefits associated with interpreting resources for HSLT, a destination – be it town, city, village or region – can also be interpreted in much the same way as a site, following a flexible and iterative interpretive planning process. However, producing these strategies is infinitely more difficult, primarily because of the costs and time involved in collating and analysing the necessary information across a wider geographical area. Figure 5.2 demonstrates the type of detail that is required to

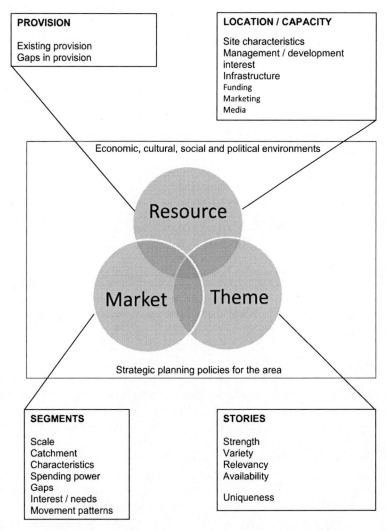

Figure 5.2 Design of city, town, village or regional interpretive strategies
Source: The authors (2017).

produce a town, city, village or regional strategy and is comprised of three key elements, these being resources, market and theme, located within broader influences imposed by the economic, social, cultural and political environments and the planning context. In terms of resources, existing provision must be established so that duplication may be avoided and potential gaps identified. Location and capacity issues also inform the audit of resources and include site characteristics, developer, management or media interest, existing infrastructure, the availability of funding, current marketing initiatives and good practice. With respect to the market, this involves undertaking detailed market segmentation analysis whereby information regarding the scale, catchment, characteristics, spending power, visitor interests and needs and movement patterns is collected and gaps in existing visitor markets are highlighted. In relation to theme, existing and potential stories, their variety, strength, relevancy, uniqueness, availability and any interrelationships must be established in an attempt to create a *genus loci* (sense of place) for individual quarters or areas within a town, city, village or region and across the destination itself. Case Study 5.1 provides an example of a regional interpretive strategy that has recently been produced for Anglesey in Wales.

Case Study 5.1 A regional interpretive strategy for Anglesey, Wales

Anglesey or Ynys Môn is a 276 square mile island situated approximately 200 metres off the northwest coast of Wales (Plate 5.1). The County of Anglesey also covers Holy Island and other small surrounding islands and is rich in heritage, screen and literary associations. Approximately three-quarters of its population are Welsh speaking and it is separated from the mainland by the Menai Strait which is spanned by the Menai Suspension and Britannia bridges. Historically, Anglesey has been associated with the Druids, an educated and professional class which existed in the Iron Age among the Celts. But the island has also been home at various points in history to the Romans, the Vikings, the Saxons and the Normans, before being acquired by Edward I of England in the 13th century after the defeat of Llewelyn ap Gruffydd, the last Prince of Wales. From the 18th century onward, Anglesey became important for copper mining and serviced demands for metal to produce funds, metal plating for ships and coinage. Parys Mountain, located in the northwest of the island, became the largest copper mine in the world, employing 1500 people at its peak in the 1760s, but declined soon after the end of the Napoleonic Wars.

Plate 5.1 The Island of Anglesey, Wales
Source: The authors (2017).

Today Anglesey has several thriving towns. Holyhead on Holy Island is Anglesey's biggest town and has a busy ferry port, with routes to Dublin (Ireland) and Dun Laoghaire, a seaside town about 7.5 miles south of Dublin. The historic town of Beaumaris to the east of the Island boasts Beaumaris Castle, a World Heritage Site, built by Edward I after his defeat of the Welsh princes, as well as the historic mansion Henllys Hall, which is now a hotel. The island also has the village with the longest place name in Britain: 'Llanfairpwllgwyngyllgogery chwyrndrobwllllantysiliogogogoch', which translated means 'The church of St Mary in a hollow of white hazel near a rapid whirlpool and near St Tysilio's church by the red cave'.

Having almost 100 miles of coastline and varied inland habitats, Anglesey also has rich and varied natural heritage, providing homes for a wide variety of animals and flora. Notable sites include the cliffs at South Stack which provide home to thousands of seabirds such as guillemots, razorbills, kittiwakes, puffins and peregrine falcons (Plate 5.2). The vegetation is mainly heather and in the summer there is a stunning display of maritime wildflowers. Another example is Newborough Warren, a sand dune complex colonised by thousands of rabbits, marram grass, dune pansies, sea cattails and sea spurge. Between the dunes, in the marshy hollows called the slacks, a rich flora can be found composed of creeping willow and varieties of orchid including the marsh orchid along with butterwort, grass of parnassus and yellow bird's-nest. Birds common to the dunes include herring gulls, oystercatchers, lapwings,

Plate 5.2 South Stack, Anglesey, Wales
Source: The authors (2017).

curlew, skylarks and meadow pipits. The dunes are also home to an abundance of toads and lizards as well as insects.

As well as being rich in heritage, Anglesey has many screen and literary associations. In terms of the former, South Stack Island and its lighthouse is the location of the film *Take Down*, a thriller about a group of rich young people taken hostage on the island. The Pinewood Pictures production is the first feature film to receive money through the Welsh Government's new £30m media investment budget which provides funding to films shooting at least 50% of their principal photography in Wales. Anglesey also provided the main location to the 2006 film *Half Light*, starring Demi Moore and Hans Matheson. Particular sites used include Ynys Llanddwyn (Plate 5.3), Llanddwyn Beach, Newborough Beach, Maltreath Beach and Llanbadrig Church (Cemaes Bay). A number of famous screen celebrities were also born on Anglesey, including Dawn French (actress, writer and comedienne) and Huw Garmon and Hugh Emrys Griffith (actors).

In terms of literary associations, some notable writers were born on Anglesey such as Henry Austin Dobson, poet and essayist, and John Morris-Jones and Goronmy Owen, two Welsh poets. The famous author of 19th century literary classics including *Oliver Twist* and *Great Expectations*, Charles Dickens, visited Anglesey after the sinking of the ship *The Royal Charter* in an exceptional storm that hit the island on

Plate 5.3 Ynys Llanddwyn, Anglesey, Wales
Source: The authors (2017).

25–26 October 1859. The ship was infamous as it was carrying passengers from the Australian gold mines, each carrying boxes laden with this precious metal. Only 40 of the 490 passengers and crew survived despite the heroic efforts of the islanders to save them. Charles Dickens writes movingly of the wreckage aftermath, published in Issue 11 of his journal, *All Year Round*; it was later included in his book *The Uncommercial Traveller*. As well as inspiring many Welsh literary works, Anglesey is the setting for John Wheatley's three novels, *A Golden Mist*, *Flowers of Vitriol* and *The Weeping Sands*. The series includes an account of the sinking of *The Royal Charter*, featuring fictional accounts from the viewpoints of a passenger and a Moelfre resident, combined with the story about a South African woman with Moelfre ancestors who returns there and discovers the history of the wreck.

Given Anglesey's varied heritage, screen and literary connections, a regional strategic plan for the interpretation of the natural and cultural heritage of Anglesey was commissioned by Cadw, the Welsh government's historic service, as part of a wider initiative to create an integrated pan-Wales heritage interpretation plan (Cadw, 2012; Touchstone Heritage Management Consultants *et al.*, 2011). Production of Anglesey's interpretive plan followed a process similar to that outlined in Figure 5.2. It began with the establishment of interpretive aims and objectives, followed by collating an inventory of the available interpretive resources, identifying the key interpretive topics, themes and stories, defining the resources available, identifying the most appropriate places at which to tell the stories, identifying the most appropriate, effective, imaginative and interactive media to use, developing a hierarchy of interpretive provision, identifying the operational and revenue implications, and establishing an effective mechanism for delivery. It is anticipated that the plan will help maximise the economic value of heritage by increasing the number, length and value of visits to Wales. The project will also help open up Wales's outstanding heritage to a wider audience by making it more enjoyable both for visitors and for people who live in Wales.

Much attention has been placed on improving the visitor experience by providing a more integrated range of heritage tourism activities. Through the development of heritage trails and packages, for example, the intention is to connect individual heritage sites with other heritage attractions, the local community and with the surrounding area, as well as to link to broader interpretive stories and themes. More specifically, the project focuses on: improving physical and intellectual access to heritage sites to attract a wider range of visitor; marketing, promotion, referrals and product packages; using iconic sites as gateways to other 'hub' attractions for regional heritage attraction development; undertaking access and safety improvements at sites; and developing and implementing pan-Wales heritage interpretation themes and stories. The main themes that have been identified are:

- Prehistoric origins and Roman invasion of settlement;
- Spiritual and inspirational landscapes;
- The castles and princes of Wales (Princes of Gwynedd, Princes of Deheubarth, Owain Glyndwr, Edwardian castles and Marcher Lords);
- Wales: the first industrial nation; and
- Defence of the realm.

The island's heritage will be promoted from several hubs based on four quadrants which relate to the northeast, northwest, southeast and southwest of the island and iconic sites will act as gateways to other attractions. A website entitled 'Anglesey: A Bridge Through Time' has also been developed, with functions that will apply digital technology to signpost visitors to the tours and trails (Anglesey Tourism, 2016).

So far, the meaning and principles of interpretation have been discussed, followed by consideration of the interpretive planning process at site, local, regional and national levels. At the centre of this process is the tourist and his or her needs. By implication, therefore, interpretation must be as Vargo and Lusch (2008) suggest in their eighth premise, customer centric and interactional. Moreover, co-creation is dependent on the extent to which interpretation enables customers to derive value, Vargo and Lusch's (2008) seventh foundational premise, and encourages interaction with the tourists' operant resources (premises one, four and six) (see Table 1.7). Another key part of the process involves decisions surrounding the types of techniques and media that are used to present the broad themes and stories to the intended audiences. As discussed earlier in this chapter, such decisions need to take into account the nature of the resource being interpreted so as not to comprise quality or cause damage. Inevitably, interpretive techniques and the media used are heavily influenced by the available budget which must be factored into initial set-up costs as well as maintenance expenses.

Interpretive Techniques and Media

There are a variety of different interpretive techniques and media used. Perhaps the most simplistic involves letting the objects speak for themselves and basically equates to the provision of no interpretation. It usually occurs when the objects have an inherently 'romantic' quality or provide concrete irrefutable evidence of the past. Indeed, some resources have intrinsic beauty and special atmosphere which for many visitors can be more powerful than any explanation. Many 19th century museums have collections with very little accompanying information (Plate 5.4). Visitors

Plate 5.4 Tutankhamun's death mask is exhibited at Cairo Museum, Egypt with no accompanying interpretation
Source: The authors (2017).

thus bring their own ideas and perceptions with them and they are uncon-strained in their interpretation. However, the value of this approach to the visitor experience is debatable as interpretation is necessary for visitors to see the importance of the objects and have a quality experience. This is because, according to Herbert (1995), only a small segment of the popula-tion has the cultural capacity or, in Vargo and Lusch's words, the 'operant resources' to appreciate objects and to place them in their broad historical context.

Publications – for example leaflets, pamphlets and guidebooks – are another technique and form of media. In their simplest form they serve to direct the visitor around the site and/or destination as most guidebooks are designed to act as souvenirs rather than as instant information givers. This is because they provide more detailed information than it is possible to give or to absorb during the visit. Guidebooks are used extensively by screen and literary tourists but they are not always included on heritage trails. According to Beeton (2005, 2015) their styles can vary; some focus on the sites if there are a sufficient number that are located in relatively close proximity; others concentrate on the story and the background of the book, film or TV production or on the history associated with its subject matter. A particularly successful example of such is *The Lord of the Rings Location Guidebook* written by Brodie in 2003, which contains details and images of the trilogy. Talks and commentaries are another very effec-tive form of interpretation as they allow direct contact and interaction with a person, particularly if that person is someone who provides recol-lections of past experiences. At the 'Big Pit' in Gwent, for example, former miners are employed as guides. The passage of time will eventually hinder the use of this technique and interpretation must resort to other forms of media such as recorded reminisces of old tin miners to give a flavour of past conditions.

Walks with or without a guide are a popular technique used by many HSLT attractions and destinations (Plate 5.5). Guided walks require the guide to be well versed and trained to encourage personal interaction and two-way communication. Unguided walks lack personal contact and rely on the visitors providing their own interpretation and understanding. Trails with signposts and/or leaflets are a popular interpretive method used by many HSLT sites and destinations. They can help the visitors see and appre-ciate things of interest, persuade them to visit neglected areas and prevent them from visiting sensitive areas. Meanwhile, interpretive panels are per-haps the most widely used interpretive technique, usually used to convey a message about the site or resource and generally to provide the main medium through which the story of a site can be told (Plate 5.6).

A more costly but effective interpretive technique is the use of recon-structions to provide a backcloth and more meaningful context in which to place the objects on display or to tell a story. One of the earliest applications

Plate 5.5 Guided walk around the former extermination camp, Auschwitz, Poland
Source: The authors (2017).

Plate 5.6 An interpretive panel at Auschwitz, Poland
Source: The authors (2017).

of this technique occurred at Jorvik Viking Centre in York, England. Here, they used three reconstructed scenes, these being:

(i) *The Viking Street*: motivated by the discovery of closely packed 10th century timber buildings and based on very careful archaeological evidence that emerged from the excavation. Each building is fully researched as is all aspects of life – smells, dyed wool hanging ready to be woven;

(ii) *Reconstructed archaeological dig*: visitors are able to see more closely the actual timbers of the buildings featured in the Viking Street; and

(iii) *Reconstructed finds*: a hut and a reconstructed laboratory have been erected where finds are conserved and soil analysed.

Within such reconstructions and as a standalone technique, sound is also used. Jorvik, for example, recreates sounds of the Viking Street, conveying a babble of voices, the sound of a baby crying, and men sighing as they load ships. This method has a number of advantages as it is cheap, it stimulates people's imagination and the actors' voices add a human dimension.

Audiovisual media is increasingly being used at many HSLT sites as it is an effective way of orientating visitors and providing them with introductory information. Live interpretation is also particularly effective since it provides an opportunity for personalized presentations which are tailored to the needs and interests of the audience. A personal interpretation enables the interpreter to tailor presentations to the needs and interests of the audience. Each interpreter is carefully trained and given a handbook for each location which contains lots of information. It also sets out what are identified as the six key 'take home' messages for them to impart. However, it is labour intensive and needs careful management. Another technique is the use of interactive exhibits. They allow visitors to touch objects from the past to help them explore the work. In particular such exhibits may use 3D computer graphics.

More recently, augmented reality is an innovative and exciting interpretive technique and media have been developed using smartphone technology to interact with the past and create added value. It allows the visitor to see and explore 3D reconstructions of lost or fictional structures and/or landscapes. The images can be supported by audio and the images can be linked to make a tour. Augmented reality has been applied to HSLT. With regard to heritage, it has huge potential to actively involve tourists in learning about and experiencing various museum settings and artefacts as never before. According to the Digital Tourism Think Tank (2015), interactive digital story-telling techniques have recently been applied to museum settings to enhance the visitor experience. For example, the Digital Binocular Station (DBS) makes the static contents of a museum come to life, leading to an interactive, dynamic and interesting adventure which increases visitor retention time and return visits (Digital Tourism Think Tank, 2015).

The application of augmented reality in museums can also simulate otherwise impossible experiences, as they are able to revive extinct animal species, worn-out frescos, broken artefacts or formerly existing ancient temples and historic buildings. For example, the first cultural heritage site that benefited from an augmented virtual reconstruction of an ancient temple was Olympia in Greece, where researchers developed the ArcheoGuide AR system. And a team at the Beijing Institute of Technology has produced a virtual reconstruction of the Yuanmingyuan Gardens in Beijing, created in the 18th century, which was destroyed due to armed conflict and looting in 1860 during the Second Opium War. Without high-resolution photography, China's current citizens had to rely on paintings and sketches to see how the beautiful gardens once appeared (Saenz, 2009). Cluny Abbey in France has a simpler AR system for tourist time travel – just a giant screen that acts as a 'window to the past'. Millions of visitors come to the abbey each year, so this system may be the single most used augmented reality device in the world (Saenz, 2009).

Furthermore, by using Layar, virtually any tourist can point their phone now toward the original location of the Berlin Wall and see its virtual representation as a realistic 3D model. Recently, The Netherlands Architecture Institute announced the launch of the free Urban Augmented Reality (UAR) app, available in eight cities in The Netherlands, which enables residents and tourists to experience the urban environment as 'it once was', 'how it might have been' and as 'it would be in the future' (Digital Tourism Think Tank, 2015). In Paris, visitors can download the Then and Now app for iOS and Android, allowing them to see historical images layered onto physical surroundings. Users can travel back in time and view more than 2000 places of interest as they were 100 years ago (Han *et al.*, 2014). In addition, screen tourism is benefiting from this technology. A new smartphone app called AR Cinema can actually bring a screen tourist into their favourite films, as it is able to show the scene(s) that were shot at particular locations. At present this facility is available for films set in London, but the developers want to add additional cities. Clearly this innovative idea has the potential to add a whole new layer to the tourism trade in cities like London, New York, Toronto and other frequently used shooting locations.

As this discussion demonstrates, there are a variety of interpretive techniques and forms of media that may be used to co-create value. However, those with the greatest visitor appeal use stories which relate to and/or come out of the visitor's own experience, those that take the visitor from the 'known' to the 'unknown', stories that emphasise people, those that are accessible and fun, those that use all senses, are participatory, and provide a simple and clear direction for the visitor to understand history. By doing so, complications and contradictions that have occurred are removed as visitors need a cognitive map to guide them through the past. Such a map may be based on the provision of a clear timeline, a simple comparison of the past, easily understandable labelling and well-known or iconic landmarks in the past.

Given that interpretation is about communication, it is not surprising that interpretation is heavily embedded in cognitive psychology (Ham, 1983; Hammitt, 1984; Kaplan & Kaplan, 1978), particularly in relation to communication studies (Ajzen, 1992; Borum & Massey, 1990; Lackey & Ham, 2003; Prince, 1981; Roggenbuck, 1992) in an attempt to understand how to convey information. Popular aspects of cognitive psychological theory applied to interpretation in tourist settings include cognitive map theory (Hammitt, 1984; Kaplan & Kaplan, 1978), cognitive dissonance theory (Orams, 1995), the elaboration likelihood model of communication (Lackey, 2002; Petty et al., 1992), the theory of reasoned action (Bright et al., 1993), and the theory of planned behaviour (Ajzen, 1992; Beeton et al., 2005; Hendricks, 2000; Jensen, 2006; Roggenbuck, 1992). Cognitive psychology deals with the way humans obtain, retain and process information. It assumes that individuals act in response to external stimuli but contends that these responses are mediated through mental constructs, representations or belief and value systems, which may be engaged consciously or unconsciously. Clearly, visitors come for a variety of reasons – some for education, some for fun (see Chapters 2 and 6 for a fuller discussion), and it is important that interpretation caters for all these visitor needs. Informal recreational learning or 'edutainment' is now a key principle of the HSLT interpretation communication process.

Interpretation and Edutainment

First coined by the Walt Disney Company in 1948, edutainment has been defined as 'the joining together of educational and cultural activities with the commerce and technology of the entertainment world' (Hannigan, 1998: 98). According to Hertzman (2006), it therefore combines entertainment technologies and historic contents in formats which create interesting, memorable and unique visitor experiences. Moreover, it involves understanding how visitors learn and remember information in a recreational learning environment, where learning occurs voluntarily and gives pleasure. As an objective of interpretation, edutainment is increasingly being embraced by HSLT attractions, including public sector museums, primarily due to technological developments which enable the presentation of content that is inherently educational in an entertaining way. Thus, it is resulting in formerly distinctive venues – most pertinently, public sector museums and private sector heritage tourist attractions – becoming increasingly similar (Ritchie et al., 2003), and this hybridisation is creating new ways in which heritage, screen and literary representations are consumed (Case Study 5.2).

Case Study 5.2 Edutainment and heritage tourist attractions: The case of Storyeum, Vancouver, Canada

Located in the tourist area of Gastown, Vancouver, British Columbia, Storyeum, a private sector edutainment heritage tourist attraction developed by Xperinces Inc., offered a multimedia, multisensory experience during which British Columbia's history was re-created in a 65-minute show set in a unique underground theatre (Plate 5.7). It opened in 2004 and in total there were eight sets, including 360-degree visual demonstrations in the two passenger lifts. The Storyeum experience began in a spacious lobby accessible directly from Gastown's main street. Within the lobby there is an admission desk, a gift shop and a large display of historic photographs of British Columbia which include portraits of prominent people and political figures of the 19th century as well as historic photos of common people, places and life around the province. Visitors then enter a passenger lift and descend below the grounds of Gastown with a tour guide resembling a miner, dressed in a hard hat, khaki trousers and shirt, and carrying a flashlight. Once in the lift, there is an introductory visual presentation about Canada and Vancouver's values and beliefs combined with pivotal moments of Canadian history which represents time travel, taking visitors mentally from the present to the past. Upon exiting the lift, the visitors are guided through six sets

Plate 5.7 Storyeum: Edutainment heritage tourist attraction, Vancouver, Canada
Source: The authors (2017).

that have been transformed into elaborate, immersive environments in which the theatrical vignettes chosen to represent chapters of British Columbia's history are enacted (Hertzman, 2006).

(i) *Ancient trails.* Here, British Columbia's story is retold in a rainforest setting, using real actors/actresses, sets and special effects. Guests experience the retelling of the creation of a man called Takaya, from a wolf, and a woman called Slonite, from sediments found at the bottom of the sea, through the point of view of the British Columbia Tsleil-Waututh, the native people who lived in the region's coastal temperate forests.

(ii) *The big house.* The story of the first man and woman continues with the marriage, life and death of Takaya and Slonite. Black-and-white photographs of native people are projected on a large screen at the back of the set and visitors are able to smell the scent of the cedar beams and planks of the long house as well as see and smell the central fire pit. In the final scene, Takaya lying on his death bed miraculously vanishes during a flash of smoke.

(iii) *New arrivals.* Here, visitors sit on a dock, looking at a ship while it is coming into harbour. It is carrying fur traders and explorers and several historical episodes are presented including the first contact between Europeans and the Indigenous people, the fur trading era, the introduction of smallpox and the decimation of the native population, a biography of James Douglas, the first Governor of the British colonies in British Columbia, and the struggle between Queen Victoria, the British monarch and James Polk, the American President, over the control and boundaries of British Columbia.

(iv) *Gold seekers.* This is set in approximately 1862 and takes place in the town of Barkerville, British Columbia, established by the discovery of gold. The stories represented therefore include the history of the gold rush and the rapid settlement of British Columbia by colonists and immigrants, as well as specific historical events such as the great fire of 1868.

(v) *National dream.* This set is designed to look like a stretch of railway. Visitors experience the unification of Canada by a national rail line spanning the nation from coast to coast. Other issues presented include Women's Suffrage in Canada, the role of the Chinese in building the railway and their sub-standard living and working conditions, and the Chinese Head Tax.

(vi) *Last stop.* The story represented in this last set takes place at Vancouver's first railway station. A replica of its first train engine #375 pulls in and out of the performance area, on a raised platform.

On the platform, a woman waits for her husband to return from WWII in Europe while a man of mixed First Nations and Chinese ancestry waits to depart for the war. The set ends with a grand musical performance with underlying feelings of promoting multi-culturalism and acceptance. This set marks the end of the experi-ence with real actors/actresses, sets and special effects.

The visitor then enters a lift to return to the ground floor. During the ascent, there is a musical and audio montage of historical and contempo-rary photographs and film clips displayed on 360-degree video projection screens, summarising the major historical milestones of British Columbia. It ends with an emotionally charged and multisensory climax of images, music and sound bites of people talking about how much they love and feel proud of British Columbia. The end of this presentation officially marks the end of the Storyeum experience.

Storyeum embodies edutainment by combining characteristics tradi-tionally found in public sector museums with those exhibited by private sector attractions: its name symbolically refers to the idea of a museum; it displays historic photographs and focuses on British Columbia's history. Marketing itself on its official website as 'Vancouver's newest classroom' and stating that 'meaningful learning starts with meaningful experiences', Storyeum aimed to 'combine education and entertainment in a showcase of the culture, people and legends from British Columbia's past; students, teachers and parents alike will enjoy a lesson in history, watching the past come to life around them' (Hertzman, 2006: 11). Moreover, a quote by Marshal McLuhan, one of the first 20th century media theorists to articu-late the interaction of entertainment and education and multimedia com-munication media, is painted on the lobby wall – 'It's misleading to suppose there is any basic difference between education and entertain-ment' – thereby providing a theoretical positioning (Hertzman, 2006).

However, despite being based on state-of-the-art technology, sadly in the wake of diminishing profits and revenue, Storyeum ran its last show on 17 October 2006 and has since ceased daily operations. The City of Vancouver continued as the property landlord and occasionally rents parts of the space for events such as Vancouver Fashion Week, the Juno Awards after-party, Vancouver Film School projects and entertain-ment and cultural celebrations.

However, the appropriateness of combining education and entertain-ment has long been debated, particularly in the context of museums and especially during the period of the great international exhibitions in Europe and America (Greenhalgh, 1988). Hertzman (2006) states that the exhibition planners initially negotiated the combination of academically researched yet popularly appealing displays, installations and amusements. During the early period of the exhibitions between 1851 and 1871 there was recognition that education and entertainment could exist in a synergistic mutually beneficial relationship; the exhibits themselves were seen as amusements because of their entertaining and exotic contents. However, as the exhibition practice became professional within the context of museums, the purpose of the exhibition became more rigidly defined. Exhibitions were to be vehicles of public education and social betterment, particularly for the lower classes. Thus, post-1871 the exhibitions included entertainment but as a separate component from the resources being displayed (Hertzman, 2006). For most museums, this approach characterised interpretation until more recent times, when the need to be commercially viable and competitive in an increasingly saturated marketplace become more pressing (see Chapter 3). Indeed many HSLT attractions have embraced edutainment in order to appeal to a more diverse audience and because their resources may also be considered to be inherently educational (Prentice, 2000). This is not an easy task as meeting the needs of a heterogeneous market itself presents a significant challenge.

The Challenge of Interpretation

Interpretation demands creativity and innovation, not least because it is imperative that it is relevant and comprehensive to all visitors irrespective of age, level of education, existing knowledge and degree of interest in the subject matter. Such a task is onerous since interpretation does not always align with the preferred reading of the resource, site and/or destination, particularly when the content is politically sensitive, contentious or unresolved as in the case of slavery (Buzinde & Santos, 2009) or mass genocide (see Chapter 3 and the politics of HSLT). According to Hall (1980), there are three ways in which a tourist reads or views interpreted messages and stories; they might adopt either a dominant-hegemonic view, a negotiated view or an oppositional view. Thus Hall (1980: 136) states that visitors who take a dominant view accept the meanings provided. In contrast, visitors who adopt a negotiated view, while acknowledging that the dominant view has some legitimacy, also recognise that it contains some substantive contradictions. Meanwhile, visitors who have an oppositional view, despite understanding the preferred message that is being conveyed, reject it in light of alternative frames of reference which they possess.

It is also important to note that tourists are not passive recipients of messages and are integrally involved, whether consciously or subconsciously, in the co-creation of their experience. Indeed, a number of studies have illustrated the active role played by visitors in decoding interpretation. For instance, Bruner's (1993) examination of Abraham Lincoln's re-created home town of New Salem found the existence of a contest between the museum professionals on the one hand who seek historical accuracy and authenticity, and the visitors' own interpretation on the other. According to Bruner (1993: 15), 'despite efforts undertaken by the heritage site managers to craft a pre-ferred reading, tourists ultimately rearticulate it as they see fit'. The active role of tourists in the co-creation of interpretation is also evidenced in Chronis's (2005) study of Gettysburg. It was found that 'tourists utilise their pre-established knowledge, negotiation mechanism, and imagination to engage marketers in the co-construction of meaning' (Chronis, 2005: 286). Tourists therefore draw on their operant resources (Vargo & Lusch, 2008), comprising an array of ideological predispositions, preconceptions and value systems that enable them to make sense of the interpreted resources (Chronis, 2005). Additionally, they are exposed to a range of popular cultural texts such as Hollywood movies, public broadcasting services, documenta-ries and fictional and non-fictional literary works, all of which influence the meaning-making process and ultimately their re-representation of the exist-ing interpretation. Visitors therefore understand HSLT resources, sites and destinations in accordance with their own perceptions and operant resources. As a result and reinforcing the work of Vargo and Lusch (2008), different people attribute different meaning to the same object and use their operant resources to co-create the service experience.

Thus, the numerous ways in which resources, sites and destinations are decoded and co-created pose a challenge for interpreters whose primary aim is to deliver coherent and inclusionary narratives (Buzinde & Santos, 2009). Consequently, it may differ from what tourists may have already gained from being exposed to various sources prior to their visit (Young, 1999), or it may be one-dimensional showing only one narrative (Smith, 1999). These issues are problematic for HSLT. Uzzell (1989) states that interpretation at heritage sites is strongly attached to the past and often ignores current circumstances and the future. In relation to screen and literary tourism, film, TV adapta-tions and fictional and fictitious novels create distorted perceptions of the locations which either directly feature in them or which have been used to portray them, thereby resulting in unrealistic visitor expectations and issues of authenticity (Beeton, 2005, 2015; Bolan et al., 2011; Urry, 1995; see Chapter 7). In fact Young (1999) states that tourists have an enormous amount of stored information or stock of knowledge (Schutz, 1967) from which they build their expectations about a place prior to their visit. Despite the importance of understanding the complexities between interpretation, visitors and place (Poria et al., 2009; Stewart et al., 1998), not enough attention has been paid to the processes by which tourists symbolically interact with a preferred reading of a site to endow it with meaning, and this is particularly neglected in the context of international tourists. Moreover the needs of this cohort and those with special needs also pose a challenge for interpreters.

Cross-cultural and special needs issues

Interpretation may also be influenced by cultural backgrounds (Young, 1999) and nationalities – a fact revealed by Bruner's (1996) study of Elmina Castle, a former slavery trading seaport in Ghana. Examining the manner in which tourists ascribe meaning to the site, he found dissonant interpretations of the same site between African and American tourists; each cohort competed for the construction of relevant meanings that affirmed their sense of being (Buzinde & Santos, 2009). Along with the difficulties of conveying a preferred message to international visitors, making HSLT sites and destinations accessible for all including those with special needs is a basic principle of good interpretation, not least a legal requirement. There are a number of techniques summarised in Text Box 5.2 that can be used to achieve this goal.

Text Box 5.2 Accessible interpretive techniques

- Use large point size text. On graphic panels the text should be at least 18 point with the main introductory text at least 48 point. The minimum text size on publications should be 12 point. There should be a good colour and brightness contrast between the text and the background. The colours red and green should be avoided for the sake of people who are colour blind.
- Pictures with simple captions tell a story to everyone, especially those with learning difficulties.
- Audio facilities can be used in parallel with text, bringing the story more alive for everyone.
- A CD-ROM in a visitor centre can provide a 'virtual tour' to parts of a historic property where universal access is impossible.
- Panels and labels should be fixed at a height, distance and angle to allow people in wheelchairs or using bi-focal glasses to read.
- Avoid reflective surfaces for text and labels and ensure that internal displays are adequately lit.
- Avoid fancy typefaces, extra-bold type and upper case as they are much harder to read.
- Use a text hierarchy, boxes and bullet points.
- Where possible, use symbols and images instead of words.
- Staffed information points should have an induction loop fitted for people with poor hearing.
- Information counters should have a drop-level counter for people in wheelchairs.
- Engage all the senses, for example by using objects and tactile surfaces for people to touch.
- Use Braille or 'talking labels' that read text out loud.

- Websites should contain clear text of at least 12 point. Blind people use audio browsers that translate text into sound, and your website should work with these as well as the usual Internet Explorer and Netscape browsers.
- For the best results, consult with and involve people with disabilities in developing your interpretation.

Source: HDC International (2016b).

Catering for international and special needs visitors is not an easy task as these markets are incredibly diverse and their needs are complex. Along with the characteristics that influence visitor interaction with a place and its meaning previously described, language proficiency is likely to be a major barrier for many international visitors. Moreover, the special needs market is extremely heterogeneous and includes, for example, those who are wheel-chair bound or immobile, blind, partially sighted, deaf, dumb or autistic, and those who have debilitating illnesses or learning difficulties. Additionally, those with less serious or temporary illnesses or impairments, people who are unfit, obese or fatigue easily, parents with prams and pushchairs, and friends, family or carers of disabled people who accompany them also have a variety of needs that need to be taken into account.

Interpretation must therefore convey messages and stories to an extremely varied audience and there are a number of tell-tale signs which may indicate that it might not be meeting its original objectives. These signs encompass: declining or flat-lining visitor numbers; lower visitor numbers compared to those received at other locations in the area; decreasing average length of visit to the site; increasing visitor complaints; visitors leaving confused by the narratives presented; diminishing entrance, retail and catering revenues; low staff morale; high staff turnover; reduced hours of operation due to poor attendance; and poor image or reputation (HDC International, 2016b). Evaluating just how successful the interpretation is on a regular basis is critically important to ensuring visitor satisfaction and remaining competitive and is a key component of the interpretive planning process (Figure 5.1).

Evaluating Interpretation

Guiding any evaluation of the effectiveness of interpretation are the site or destination's objectives. Traditionally, such assessments have tended to focus on the learning impact (be it the acquisition of facts or enhanced understanding) of the site and/or destination on visitors through different media (Prentice *et al.*, 1998a). At its most basic, such assessments may involve assessing the media used such as the clarity of the signs or the legibility of the wall panels. Ryan and Dewar (1995), for example, developed a scale to measure the communication competency of on-site interpreters at Louisburg National Park and related this to retention by visitors. Meanwhile, Light (1995) evaluated three interpretive media at ancient monuments in Wales – exhibitions, outdoor panels and stereo-audio tours – and concluded that interest and attention was greatest for the audio media and less for visual media.

However, Pearce (1984) and Moscardo (1996) argue that evaluating the experience of the learner is also important, a sentiment emphasised by Vargo and Lusch (2008) in their tenth foundational premise which stipulates that value is always judged by the end-user. This is because although only a few detailed facts may be recalled, the experience as a whole may have a significant emotional impact. Indeed, Moscardo (1996) utilises her concept of mindfulness (see Chapter 2 for a fuller discussion), which is stimulated by settings that are interactive, multisensory or dynamic, or by those which include questions and where physical orientation is present, to evaluate the visitor experience. Her approach also takes into consideration the interest of visitors in the content of what is presented and their tiredness when visiting, as both visitors with appropriate characteristics as well as appropriate media need to be included in the study of the effectiveness of interpretation. Other attempts at quantifying the success of interpretation focus on attitudinal changes (Beckmann, 1988; Orams, 1995; Tubb, 2003).

A number of approaches have been developed to measure the comparative effectiveness of various interpretive techniques and include the following.

(i)   *Observations.* This involves examining visitor behaviour, e.g. to determine how long people spend looking at individual exhibits, or how they engage with the provided interpretation.

(ii) *Tracking or behavioural mapping.* This involves following visitors to find out where they go, how they use a space or area, and the amount of time they spend in different places.

(iii) *Questionnaires.* These may be undertaken on a face-to-face or self-complete basis and can contain a mixture of closed and open questions designed to provide insights into visitors' perceptions, feelings and opinions.

(iv) *Interviews.* These usually contain a series of open-ended questions and enable more in-depth information to be gathered regarding visitor perceptions and opinions.

(v)   *Focus groups.* These involve gathering information through semi-structured in-depth interviews with a group of people. The focus group facilitator provides prompts and poses open-ended questions aimed at exploring a topic or issue in some depth.

(vi) *Critical appraisal.* This occurs when an interpretive professional peer-reviews the aims, objectives and effectiveness of the provided interpretation.

Each method has strengths and weaknesses, and usually the employment of a combination of methods produces the best results (Herbert, 1989). Evaluation may begin while the interpretive objectives are being developed and addresses questions such as 'What do the audience already know about this topic?' and 'What are they most interested in?'. By undertaking front-end assessments of this nature, the interpretation may be tailored to the visitors' knowledge and interests (HDC International, 2016b). Formative evaluation can then occur and this tests visitors' reactions to the interpretation. For example, proofs of leaflets and panels can be tested to see if they attract attention and communicate the right messages. Once all the elements in a display are brought together, remedial evaluation can take place to check, for instance, that the lighting is appropriate, that visitor flow patterns are optimised, and that distraction or competition between elements is minimised. Finally, summative evaluation focuses on whether the interpretation is meeting the site or the destination's objectives and is carried out once interpretation has been completed.

Conclusion

The central challenge for managers of HSLT sites, attractions and destinations is to reconstruct real or fictitious events, people and places in the minds of the visitor and to provide a worthwhile and memorable experience while at the same time meeting the objectives of interpretation, whether these are entertainment, education, management or business oriented. Interpretation therefore involves the re-representation and commodification of contingent elements of the natural, built and cultural environment and co-terminality, since the tourist is integral to the value creation of their experience; it is as a result a key component of the HSLT nexus. Value creation can therefore be generated from the interpretation that is provided at and within sites and destinations through co-creation and co-production which enhance the visitor experience (Figure 5.3). This is because, on the one hand, co-creation occurs as a result of interpretation, inducing tourists' involvement and engagement, albeit to varying degrees and depths, with the resource viewed. On the other, it entails co-production, since the interpretation provided may encourage some tourists to actively participate in the creation of the service experience itself. The latter, in turn, highlights the applicability of Vargo and Lusch's (2016) second, third, seventh, eighth, ninth and 11th foundational premises to the study of HSLT (see Table 1.7), all of which relate to aspects of service provision and their role in value co-creation.

However, the extent to which value is co-created is inevitably influenced by the tourist and the nature of their interaction with the resources that are interpreted. In particular, the use of information communication

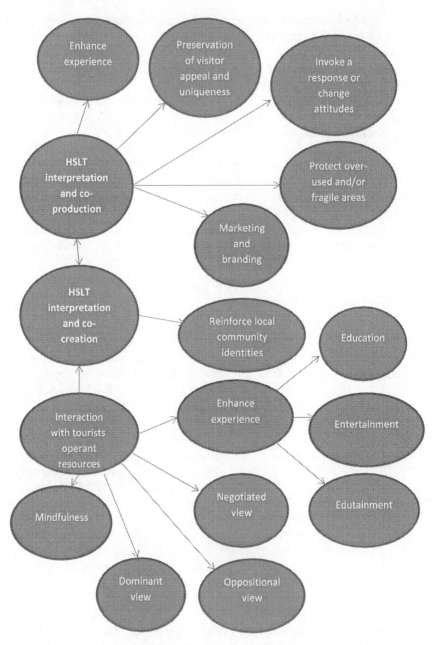

Figure 5.3 Dimensions of heritage, screen and literary tourism interpretation and co-creation
Source: The authors (2017).

technologies such as augmented reality are likely to become more pervasive in value co-creation as they enable the provision of a more connected experience that is personal, richer, meaningful and memorable. Such a view is reinforced by Neuhofer *et al.* (2013), who argue that technology-enhanced experiences will offer consumers a new level of service exchange. But of course tourist interaction with interpretation is fraught with difficulties and indeed the latter part of this chapter highlights some of the challenges which interpreters face when interpreting HSLT resources (see Figure 5.3). Thus, Vargo and Lusch's (2016) first, fourth, sixth and tenth foundational premises (Table 1.7) are all relevant here as they focus on the ways in which consumers use their operant resources to derive and judge value. What becomes clear here is that interpretation is a skill which requires creativity and innovation and must be guided by a planning process that is flexible and iterative. It often provides the fundamental reason why people visit, and thus catering for the visitor and their needs is critically important. Such action demands in-depth understanding of the visitor, and it is this issue that provides the focus for the next chapter.

6 Heritage, Screen and Literary Tourism Consumption

Introduction

With its focus on demand, Chapter 2 discusses the motivations and experiences of heritage, screen and literary tourists and highlights the importance of placing emphasis on their involvement and engagement with the site, object, event or destination visited. Indeed, extant literature is reviewed of the emotional connection and empathetic involvement with the resource that motivates many to engage in these forms of tourism. These studies (e.g. Carl *et al.*, 2007; Kim, 2012; Roesch, 2009) clearly point to the fact that consumption involves co-terminality as it is heavily influenced by tourists' interactions with various contingent elements of such spaces and resources as they co-create their experience. Consumption is thus a key feature of the HSLT nexus as it is shaped and shapes the (re)representation of landscapes associated with people, events and places (see Figure 1.1). This chapter seeks to extend this line of discussion by framing it in the context of S-DL and co-creation. It focuses in the first instance on the factors that influence HSLT consumption, including performance, performativity and cultural competence, and then explores how these translate into touristic practices.

Central to any consideration of consumption is the notion of authenticity and thus the second part of this chapter considers its relevance and importance in the context of HSLT. Popularised by MacCannell (1973, 1976), authenticity has become one of the key themes in the academic literature of tourism, primarily due to the controversy surrounding its usefulness (e.g. Belhassen *et al.*, 2008; Bruner, 1994; Cohen, 1988, 2011; Taylor, 2001; Wang, 1999). The question of authenticity is particularly pertinent to HSLT because objects, places, people and events are of interest to tourists and often feature as a core part of the experience, particularly if they have been subject to meaningful, captivating, engaging and/or creative development (see Chapter 4) and interpretation (see Chapter 5). However, interpreters, filmmakers and novelists are story tellers and, in order to entertain, they present compelling stories and situations. To the audience, these storylines often present a 'promise' (Frost, 2010: 723) of what might occur if they were to travel to consume the object, place or event of interest. Of course, according to Frost (2010), it is not a literal promise but rather a general idea. Nevertheless, it may be highly persuasive, especially if reinforced by repetition in other films, books and media sources. Consequently, perceptions of authenticity or inauthenticity shape consumption and ultimately result in value judgements which impact on visitor satisfaction or dissatisfaction. Thus, issues relating to satisfaction and quality form the focus for the latter part of this chapter.

Heritage, Screen and Literary Tourism Consumption Practices

Many studies suggest that the consumption of HSLT resources and destinations is informed by performance and performativity (Bagnall, 2003; Diekmann & Hannam, 2012; Edensor, 2001; Scarles, 2012). Derived from Austin's (1975: 6) 'performance utterances' or performed and invoked acts, generally speaking, the latter refers to the capacity of speech and communication to act and consummate an action or to construct and perform an identity (Kershaw, 1994). In short, it attempts to explain practices through the act of something being performed (Harwood & El-Manstrly, 2012). Within tourism, performativity has been linked to the commodification, (re)representation and staged nature of tourism experiences (MacCannell, 1973) whereby tourism is a form of embodied performances and practices which comprise the experience (Scarles, 2012). Indeed, according to Crouch (2000: 68), embodiment is 'a process of experiencing, making sense, knowing through practice as a sensual human subject in the world' and, when viewed alongside performativity, denotes a multisensual encounter which results in a change of meaning from that which was initially projected. An increased focus on performativity has thus shifted attention away from what is gazed on and the meanings that are derived from this (Urry, 1990), toward what is done (Valtonen & Viejola, 2011). In fact, Edensor (2001) argues that tourism itself is a range of performances consisting of three dimensions: (i) spatial and temporal which bound the stage on which enactments occur; (ii) the social and spatial regulation of the stage (e.g. how the stage is managed, how movement is choreographed); and (iii) the accomplishment of the performance itself with regard to the desired/expected outcome, from both the perspective of the actors and the intended audience.

In the context of HSLT, performance and performativity is arguably a key component of co-creation, particularly since there are an abundance of opportunities that engage tourists. Vargo and Lusch's (2008) foundational premises one (service is the fundamental basis of exchange), six (the customer is always a co-creator of value), eight (a service-centred view is inherently customer oriented and relational) and 10 (value is always uniquely and phenomenologically determined by the beneficiary) are relevant here as they all focus on the ways in which tourists may interact with the resources consumed to co-create value. Perhaps in its simplest form, the recent practice of 'selfies', where tourists take photographs of themselves consuming a resource, is a good illustration of performance and performativity in value co-creation at work; in the case of one unfortunate tourist, however, who attempted to engage with an object in such a manner, their actions resulted in the knocking over and shattering of a 128-year-old statue of Dom Sebastiao at Rossio train station in Lisbon, Portugal (Payton, 2016).

Edensor (2001) meanwhile identifies four types of opportunities, these being rituals, dramas in theatrical settings, themed tourist spaces and media-tised spaces, each of which are evident within HSLT (Table 6.1). Rituals, or invented traditions as Hobsbawm and Ranger (1983) term them, are often invented ceremonies involving grand traditional rituals and pageantry through which state ideologies are transmitted with eloquent, solemn and precise movements. These are mapped onto symbolic and familiar spaces, thereby forming part of 'social habit memory' (Edensor, 2001: 64), with such performances evoking performativity through the audience's willingness to observe and applaud the ideals being presented. Carnivals are another form of ritual which entail performance and performativity by inscribing and imprinting identity on a site in an emotional, pleasurable and playful manner.

Dramas in theatrical settings are also widely used within HSLT and involve performance and performativity. Many such attractions use the site as a theatrical setting, employing actors to perform to tourists and to cajole tourists into taking on roles and becoming an integral part of the performance. In addition to performances in distinct HSLT settings, performance and performativity occurs within themed, specialised tourist spaces (Gottdiener, 1997) encompassing shopping malls, festival marketplaces, literary quarters and waterfront attractions and extending most notably out into themed pubs and cafés (Edensor, 2001). Each presents soundbites of the past, present and future and uses scenography and stage design (Edensor, 2001: 66) to recreate a simulacrum or pastiche of selected spaces and places (see Case Study 6.1) which mix the everyday with the extraordinary. Through immersion within such environments, and given that 'we are all performers in our own dramas on stages the industry has provided' (Chaney, 1993: 64), tourists are encouraged to play out the theme presented.

Another way in which performance and performativity can occur is with the mediatisation and dramatisation of spaces through literature and screen productions (Edensor, 2001). These media map onto existing landscapes in which they are set and produce, according to Edensor (2001: 68), 'a theatrical signature through which the scenery can be familiarised, associated with characters, episodes and props'. The influence of mediatised spaces in providing opportunities for performance and performativity cannot be underestimated.

Table 6.1 Opportunities for heritage, screen and literary tourism performance and performativity

Opportunity type	Examples
(1) Rituals	
(i) Grand traditional rituals and pageantry	• Trooping the Colour is a ceremony performed by regiments of the British and Commonwealth armies since 1748 to mark the birthday of the British sovereign. It is held annually on a Saturday in June on Horse Guards Parade by St James Park, London.
	• Anzac Day, 25 April is one of Australia's most important national occasions. It marks the anniversary of the first major military action fought by the Australian and New Zealand forces during WWI and involves commemorative services across the nation at dawn – the time of the original landing.
	• Independence Day celebrations around the world within countries celebrating their independence from a former governing country or body. In the USA, it occurs on 4 July, in India on 15 August, in Indonesia on 17 August and in Mexico on 16 September.
	• Oktoberfest held in Munich, Germany since 1810 commemorates Prince Ludwig's wedding.
	• Yi Peng or the Festival of Lights is a religious ceremony held across Thailand to celebrate Buddhism.
(ii) Carnivals	• The Carnival in Rio de Janeiro (Brazil) featuring Samba dancers is considered to be one of the biggest in the world and is held before Lent.
	• The Carnival of Venice (Italy) dates back to 1162, attracting troupes of actors wearing Venetian masks, and takes place the day before Ash Wednesday.
(2) Dramas in theatrical settings	• Universal Studios (Los Angeles, CA) film studio and theme park stages sophisticated dramas to short historical playlets.
	• M/S Maritime Museum (Helsingoer, Denmark) opened in 2013 and traces the seafaring history of the Danes from the Vikings to the Maersk global shipping empire; guided tours are led by costumed actors, and visitors are encouraged to engage in interactive exhibits.
	• The National Wallace Monument (Stirling, Scotland) celebrates the life of Sir William Wallace who fought for Scottish independence during the 13th century. During the summer season, costumed actors regale visitors with tales about the life of this national hero.

(3) Themed tourist spaces	• The Irish Pub Company funded by Guinness manufactures and markets Irish-themed pubs all around the world including: the 'Victorian Dublin' style (in the style of the more lavish Dublin pubs with polished hardwood and etched glass), 'Gaelic style' (designed to demonstrate the merry-making music and craftsmanship of Gaelic people), 'Traditional style' (as in the old corner of the grocery store), 'country cottage style' (to reflect the days when the pub was someone's house) or the 'Brewery' pub (adorned with memorabilia of the brewing process). • The Mara River Safari Lodge (Bali Safari and Marine Park, Bali) reconstructs elements of the African wilderness. It offers a truly unique experience of living in the authenticity of the African wilderness and engaging with endangered exotic animals.
(4) Mediatised spaces	• The fictional novels and TV blockbuster *Game of Thrones* series used several locations in Northern Ireland as scenic backdrops including: Castle Ward, County Down (Winterfell), Ballintoy Harbour, County Antrim (The Iron Islands), Shillanavogy Valley beneath Slemish Mountain, County Antrim (Dothraki grasslands) and Tolleymore Forest Park, County Down (The Haunted Forest). • The fictional novels and Hollywood blockbuster *Star Wars* movies used multiple locations during their production including: Ksar Hadada and Ksar Ouled Soltane, Tunisia (Tatooine Slave Quarters), Onk Jemel, Tunisia (Tatooine desert), Palace of Caserta, Italy (Naboo Royal Palace) and Grindelwad, Switzerland (Alderaan).

Source: Adapted from Edensor (2001: 64–69).

Indeed, Chapter 1 outlines the significance of locations that features within literature and screen productions in stimulating tourist visitation, and Chapter 2 highlights the desire to feel an emotional connection and empathetic engagement and involvement with the resource concerned – a powerful motivator for HSLT (Carl *et al.*, 2007; Kim & Rubin, 1997; Poria *et al.*, 2006; Reijinders, 2010b). Meanwhile, Chapter 4 emphasises the power of literature and screen productions in constructing notions of place which are then re-represented in marketing initiatives designed to attract increased visitation (see Chapter 7).

Case Study 6.1 Performativity, simulacrum and the theming of the Venetian Macao, Macau

The Venetian Macao opened in 2007 and is a luxury Venice-themed hotel and casino resort located on the Cotai Strip in Macau (see Plate 6.1). It stands at 39 storeys and hosts 3000 suites, 110,000 m² of convention space, 150,000 m² of retail, 51,000 m² of casino space and a 15,000-seat arena for entertainment and sports events. The guest suites are

Plate 6.1 The Venetian Macao, Macau
Source: The authors (2017).

Italian themed, with the higher end being luxurious, adorned with marble and gold leaf.

Nestled in the heart of the Venetian Macao is the Grand Canal Shoppes, a luxury shopping mall located on the third floor of the hotel and spanning 22 acres, the design of which has been inspired by the water city of Venice in Italy. The mall is divided into 14 themed areas and reconstructs elements of an imaginary Venice; it has cobblestone walkways centred along a quarter-mile Grand Canal which hosts gondola rides (see Plate 6.2) and the centre features a plaza which is a reproduction of the city's St Mark's Square (see Plate 6.3). An illuminated painted sky hangs over the Grand Canal Shoppes which changes colour as the evening closes in (Plate 6.4), while beautiful reproductions of famous frescos frame the ceilings of the entrance way and lobbies (see Plate 6.5).

In addition to the shops and gondolas, visitors can enjoy live entertainment with characters in period costumes from the 12th to 17th centuries roaming the public areas, opera singing, mime and jesting and, in St Mark's Square, the 'Streetmosphere' performers (street performers) keep visitors entertained. The Grand Canal Shoppes at the Venetian Macao is a simulacrum of the artistic, architectural and commercial centre of Venice in the 16th century. Through this re-representation, as visitors wander through the mall, they are encouraged physically, emotionally and imaginatively to consume the 'real' Venice, and are engaged

Plate 6.2 The Grand Canal, Venetian Macao
Source: The authors (2017).

Plate 6.3 Reproduction of St Mark's Square, Venetian Macao
Source: The authors (2017).

Plate 6.4 Illuminated sky, Venetian Macao
Source: The authors (2017).

Plate 6.5 Replica of fresco, Venetian Macao
Source: The authors (2017).

and involved in such consumption by the shopping experience itself and by the live entertainment provided. Performance and performativity, heavily framed by a heritage pastiche, thus plays a key role in the visitor experience here.

In addition, the many interpretive techniques (see Chapter 5) including guided and self-guided tours, re-enactments of historic events or cinematic and book scenes and the use of live actors, for example, are premised on the fact that tourists become the performers and are integral to the performance with their movements within settings being very much choreographed (Edensor, 2001). As a result, the distance between audiences and performers has diminished: people perform and they see others as performers; they perform for an audience yet they are also members of a range of audiences (Abercrombie & Longhurst, 1998). Moreover, a form of reminiscence is practised, informed by performativity (Kershaw, 1994), as the performance allows the visitor to experience a feeling of connecting or living through the resource being consumed, thereby making it more meaningful. Emotions and the imagination engendered by the physicality of the consumption process are three key dimensions of this activity (Bagnall, 2003; Carl et al., 2007; Roesch, 2009). The physical element of performativity occurs during the tourists' embodiment of resources being consumed. It therefore depends on the capacity of the sites to engage visitors on an emotional level which promotes the process of remembering.

This reminiscing can stimulate the re-awakening of dreams and desires and create a connection between the past and present. These processes allow the tourist to connect to personal emotions and family memories and to memories of scenes and storylines of books and films, of life histories and of personal and family narratives. Such may arise from those employed to perform and stimulate memories and are often used to support and confirm identification with the version of events offered, which in turn enables the visitor to relate the consumptive experience to a range of experienced and imagined worlds (Bagnall, 2003). It is the reality of the emotions felt by the visitors that contributes to their ability to perform at the sites. Thus, the consumption experience is an active rather than a passive process. Such a contention is reiterated by Kim (2012), who in a study of tourist re-enactments and photography of *Winter Sonata* scenes indicates that it is the involvement and participation in re-enacting scenes from the TV series at key sites that lies at the core of the tourist experience. These re-enactments appear to highlight the desire for active involvement stimulated by the emotional connection between the viewer, the scene, the characters and the story (Connell, 2012).

Indeed, Chapter 2 discusses audience involvement and engagement at HSLT sites as visitors physically, emotionally and imaginatively map their consumption. On the one hand, such mapping may evoke a sense of affinity with the resource and how it has been presented. On the other hand, however, some visitors may reject the version of events they are consuming. Thus, as Chapter 5 has described and as Vargo and Lusch (2008) surmise in their fourth (operant resources are the fundamental source of competitive advantage) and sixth (the customer is always a co-creator of value) foundational premises (Table 1.7), the consumption of HSLT is heavily influenced by an individual's operant resources which impact on their preferred reading and interpretation of messages. Competing ideas about what particular sites symbolise may therefore generate contrasting performances (Edensor, 2001). Moreover, different types of audiences may affect the performance of the actors. Hence the idea that visitors simplistically accept a nostalgic re-enactment of the past does not capture the reality of the consumption process. Clearly, the ability to perform is related to the cultural literacy and competency of the visitors.

Visitor cultural literacy and competency

The HSLT consumption process is characterised by complexity and diversity with respect to visitors' faculties (Bagnall, 2003), and the knowledge which is drawn on to make sense of what is being presented, which collectively Vargo and Lusch (2004) term as operant resources. The cultural competence and literacy of visitors may be linked to those interpretations of cultural capital which are person based. This is usually understood to encompass the collection of non-economic forces such as family background, social class and varying investments in and commitment to education and to different resources which influence academic success (Halsey *et al.*, 1980; Hayes, 2006; Savage *et al.*, 2005). But cultural capital in this context need not relate solely to the possession of graduate qualifications. This is because it can be accumulated over time through talent, skills, training and exposure to cultural activity (Matarasso, 2000). Moreover, according to Busby and Meethan (2008), uncertificated education is of equal importance, accumulated via membership of learned societies and other bodies such as the National Trust (of England and Wales). Membership of such bodies provides both contextualised and subliminal learning; and engenders a certain degree of familiarity with a range of heritage.

Typically, HSLT is associated with special interest groups or individuals with increased cultural capital (Busby & Meethan, 2008), perhaps obtained through membership of societies such as the National Trust. This view is supported by Silberberg (1995) and Kerstetter *et al.* (2001), who determine that 'tourists with an interest in visiting heritage or cultural sites tend to stay longer, spend more per trip, are more highly educated, and have a higher average annual income than the general tourists' (Huh *et al.*, 2006: 85). Moreover, a study by Harflett (2015) found that cultural capital provided the key to explaining the predominance of a white, middle-class profile of regular property-based National Trust volunteers. In addition, however, it is important to recognise that while 'credential inflation' (Busby, 2001: 39) axiomatically produces what appears to be better qualified visitors, they may not possess the critical faculties required to appreciate what is in front of them.

In this respect, and as Bourdieu (1984) suggests, it may be more appropriate to interpret cultural capital as the ability of the individual to appreciate or understand what they are looking for, based on the possession of educational credentials, and he identifies three forms of cultural capital, these being: (1) the embodied state; (2) the objectified state; and (3) the institutionalised state. The embodied state is linked directly to and incorporated within the individual and represents what they know and can do; it can therefore be increased by investing time into self-improvement in the form of learning. In contrast, the objectified state of cultural capital is represented by cultural goods, material objects such as books, paintings, instruments and/or music, which can be appropriated both materially with economic capital or symbolically via embodied capital. Cultural capital in its institutionalised state provides academic credentials and qualifications which create 'a certificate of cultural competence which confers on its holder a conventional, constant, legally guaranteed value with respect to power' (Bourdieu, 1984: 248).

Inevitably, cultural capital and literacy has a bearing on the extent to which the experience engenders feelings that are meaningful and real, a response termed by Ang (1985) as emotional realism. Providing 'real' or 'genuine' experiences is often used to sell tourism (Sharpley, 1994) and HSLT is no different in this respect. However, perceptions and expectations of what is and is not genuine and real as opposed to what actually exists, again influenced by cultural capital and literacy, are also relevant here. This point is illustrated by Sharpley (1994: 128), who writes that: 'Visitors to India on a typical Delhi-Jaipur-Agra tour may well believe that they have experienced the "real" India but while there is no doubting the authenticity of individual sights, as collectively they do not represent India. That is, they are a sign of "Indian-ness", a physical manifestation of an image far removed from the realm of modern India.' Another problem to be considered is the extent to which any tourist site or experience may be considered real or genuine once it becomes packaged and sold as part of the overall tourist product. Indeed, according to Carl *et al.* (2007) writing in the context of film tourism, although experiencing the 'authentic' filming location takes many forms, they note that there is a quantum difference between commercialised tour experiences where the experience is formal and structured and the unofficial real place that simply presents itself as a place or space for film tourists. Authenticity, perceptions and expectations of such are thus vital to the HSLT consumptive experience.

Heritage, Screen and Literary Tourism and Authenticity

Ever since MacCannell (1973, 1976) popularised the notion of authenticity, there has been controversy over its usefulness (e.g. Bruner, 1994; Cohen, 1988; Hughes, 1995; Taylor, 2001), not least because it is an extremely ambiguous concept. It was first widely used in a museum context and refers to 'objects which are what they appear to be or are claimed to be' (Trilling, 1972: 93). Museum curators and ethnographers have tended to view the authenticity of primitive and ethnic art in strict terms; to be authentic, things must have been created by traditional craftsmen using traditional materials. In particular, authentic items must have been made for the use of local people rather than for trade or for selling on to strangers. Most importantly, authenticity is a quality that is perceived to be firmly rooted in premodern life, a quality of cultural products produced prior to the penetration of modern Western influences.

In other words, objects can only be authentic if they have been created without the aid of modern materials, tools or machinery; thus anything including society that has been adapted, influenced, altered or contaminated by the modern Western world has lost its authenticity. If the origin of a strictly authentic product lies in pre-modern societies, then by implication modern Western society with all its characteristics of alienation, materialism, mass production and consumption is inauthentic. For the tourist, therefore, authenticity is to be found in pre-modern societies or societies that have yet to become Westernised and developed. According to Sharpley (1994), such an understanding goes some way toward explaining the attraction of the British countryside as a symbol of a pre-industrial, pre-modern era and, more generally, the current fascination with heritage and the past.

Thus an object may be deemed to be authentic because of its intrinsic aesthetic or historical qualities. However, just because an object or an event is not historical, it does not mean to say that it is not authentic. Authenticity as a term has, as a result, been subject to a variety of uses within the tourism literature (Bruner, 1989; Cohen, 1988; Daniel, 1996; Eco, 1986; Hughes, 1995; Reisinger & Steiner, 2006; Selwyn, 1996; see Table 6.2). Cohen (1988), for example, explains how a word that is normally used to describe something that is real or genuine has also become a socially constructed concept whereby the criteria for authenticity are subjective and different for each individual. It therefore varies according to the tourist and their point of view (Cohen, 1988).

Selwyn (1996), in contrast, distinguishes between two interpretations of the term 'authentic', namely 'hot authenticity' and 'cool authenticity'. The former refers to tourism which is based on fiction and myths. This category

Table 6.2 Examples of alternative forms and meanings of authenticity

Alternative forms of authenticity	Meaning
Subjective (Cohen, 1988)	Individuals may differently perceive the authenticity of a place or activity.
Hot authenticity (Selwyn, 1996)	Based on fiction and myths (Cohen, 2011); fake (Cole, 2007a); 'an emotional alienation-smashing' experience (Cohen, 2011: 3). Consists of: (1) myths of the authentic other or the authentically social (Cohen, 2011: 21), in other words the pre-modern; and (2) myths of the authentic self (Cohen, 2011: 24).
Cool authenticity (Selwyn, 1996)	Real, original or genuine (Cole, 2007a); cognitive knowledge about objects or experiences (Cohen, 2011).
Objective (Wang, 1999)	Originality established by predetermined criteria (Wang, 1999).
Constructive/symbolic (Wang, 1999)	Personal perceptions and interpretation of authenticity (Wang, 1999); something that can emerge or acquire social recognition.
Existential (Wang, 1999)	Derived from the experience itself (Wang, 1999); a special state of being in which individuals are true to themselves (Wang, 1999: 56); 'provide tourists with an authentic sense of Being' (Cohen, 2011: 3).

Source: Compiled by the authors (2017).

is subdivided into the more general authenticity of the mythical society which Selwyn (1996: 21) terms 'myths of the authentic other and the authentically social' and the more specific authenticity of the individual tourist within the mythical society, referred to as 'myths of the authentic self' (Selwyn, 1996: 24). According to Selwyn (1996: 23), 'Myths of the authentic other' and the 'authentically social' parallel the notion of the authentic as 'primitive', in that they are based on tourist's search for a pre-modern and pre-commoditised world. Selwyn goes on to suggest that 'what makes a tourist destination attractive is that it is thought to have a special characteristic … which derives from the sociability of its residents' (Selwyn, 1996: 23). Thus the destination is authentically social because it resists the antisocial influences of external forces and has a general sense of a close-knit community. The second form of 'hot authenticity' he labels 'myths of the authentic self' which are based on the more specific sense of the tourist gaining a personal perception that they have proximity to and can identify with the host community in the tourist destination. The more the tourist can identify with members of the host community, including their desire to identify with the perceived tourist, the greater the sense of authenticity. That is the extent to which the individual tourist matches the type of tourist envisaged in the brochure (Cohen, 1996).

Selwyn (1996) also coins the term 'cool authenticity', which refers to the aspects and products of society that can be subject to more stringent, scientifically based investigation. Selwyn argues that the construction of such scientifically based investigation is determined by historical, economic and political forces which influence the knowledge offered to the tourist. In this way, cool authenticity is based on the tourist's search for knowledge and the object will be perceived as authentic if the tourist's hunger for information is satisfied. Cool authenticity is thus achieved if the information offered matches the historical, economic and political beliefs of the tourist. It can be seen therefore that both hot authenticity and cool authenticity hold parallels with Cohen's (1988) negotiated social construct, and are thus specific and unique to the individual. This discussion suggests that the concept of authenticity has often developed into a way of describing the extent to which societies have 'modern' characteristics. If the origin of strictly authentic products lies in pre-modern societies, then by implication modern Western society with all its characteristics of industrialisation is inauthentic (Tetley, 1997).

Wang (1999) also proposes a classification of three different and discrete types of authenticity: (i) object; (ii) constructive; and (iii) existential. Object authenticity refers to the originality of an object such as a site or a specific event which can be measured with predetermined criteria. This interpretation, however, is problematic as it raises authentication issues relating to who has the power to determine what will count as authentic (Appadurai, 1986; Bruner, 1994; Bruner & Kirshenblatt-Gimblett, 1994; Cheong & Miller, 2000;

Taylor, 2001; see Chapter 2). One particular illustration of authentication was observed by Fawcett and Cormack (2001) in a study of three sites relating to L.M. Montgomery, the author of the fictional novel *Anne of Green Gables*, set on Prince Edward Island, Canada. They found that those responsible for managing the sites (L.M. Montgomery's Cavendish Home, Green Gables House and Anne of Green Gables Museum) whom they term as 'site guardians' (Fawcett & Cormack, 2001: 687), provided authentication by making various truth claims based on what they considered to be important about Montgomery and her literary products, and by excluding and suppressing ideas that threatened these truths. Moreover they revealed that the 'site guardians' were committed to directing and influencing touristic constructions as much as possible in the name of good history, family loyalty and local fidelity.

Wang's (1999) constructivist approach meanwhile refers to the heterogeneous ways that tourists perceive authenticity, which can be related to their personal interpretations of the definition of authenticity (Belhassen *et al.*, 2008). In this context, it is emergent in nature and can be attached to places, people, objects and/or events that were initially perceived as inauthentic. In contrast, existential authenticity relates more to the tourist rather than the object in question and equates more to an emotional experience in which contemporary tourists make meaning from their travel experiences (Reisinger & Steiner, 2006). According to Steiner and Reisinger (2006), it draws on a long philosophical tradition concerned with what it means to be oneself and happy (Hegel, 1977; Heidegger, 1996), with authentic individuals taking meaning from the world from their own experiences rather than from what is being portrayed by the state and governing institutions. Given this interpretation, it is not surprising therefore that there is a close relationship between heritage and existential authenticity, since people look to the past to identify and understand themselves (Hewison, 1987; see Chapter 2).

From this discussion it is clear that there are a range of different forms of authenticity, whose meanings, according to Timothy and Boyd (2003), can be conceptualised into three broad but overlapping categories (Table 6.3). In fact, in their study of the authenticity of three literary tourism sites associated with L.M. Montgomery and her fictional work *Anne of Green Gables*, Fawcett and Cormack (2001) observe the overlapping of authenticity meanings by indicating that differing versions of authenticity are manifested in the 'modernist', 'rationalist' and 'eclectic' interpretive forms that are presented (Fawcett & Cormack, 2001: 687). In terms of the 'modernist' interpretation, this was noted at L.M. Montgomery's Cavendish Home and is based on ideas of origin, beginning, truth and un-reproducibility. In this context, Montgomery represents a historical and genealogical anchor with pre-industrial rural Canada, a meaning that is reminiscent of Timothy and Boyd's authentic as primitive category. With respect to what Fawcett and

Table 6.3 Categories and meanings of authenticity

Categories of authenticity	Meanings
Authentic as primitive	Primarily adopted in a museum context to describe ancient objects which are what they appear to be or are claimed to be. This meaning generally tends to refer to objects that are pre-industrial or pre-modern – objects which are not influenced by the modern West.
Authentic as a social construct of modern society	It is a modern value whose emergence is closely related to the impact of modernity on the unity of social existence. An object is only authentic if it is created without the aid of modern tools, materials or machinery. This concept can be stretched to include not just physical objects but also societies, but only if they have not been influenced or altered by the modern Western world.
Authentic as a social or negotiated construct	Its meaning differs between individuals, types of tourists and intellectuals and experts. It is a measure of the tourists' perceptions, as what one tourist may be satisfied with may cause another dissatisfaction or disappointment. Perceptions of authenticity are also dependent on the relationships that tourists have with people in tourist settings (Pearce & Moscardo, 1986). For example, a tourist in an inauthentic environment such as a Western-style hotel may still have an authentic experience through interacting with a local person who works in the hotel.

Source: Adapted from Timothy and Boyd (2003).

Cormack (2001) term the 'rationalist' interpretation presented at Green Gables House, this is similar to Timothy and Boyd's (2003) category of authentic as a social construct of modern society, as tourists are invited to use their imagination to derive meaning from what is presented, but do so within a highly structured framework in which a clear distinction is made between the real and the imaginary.

Regarding the 'eclectic' form of interpretation presented at the Anne of Green Gables Museum, tourists are invited to be creative and playful and to make a story from fictional, fictitious quotes, fragments of information and unexplained objects. Thus, an open, eclectic construction of the past and present is presented and, given this, it is a form of authenticity that is similar to being social or negotiated. This approach is further extended by Wang (2007) in a study of tourists' perceptions of the authenticity of 'Naxi' homestays in Lijiang, a commercialised county located near the Tibetan Plateau in the northwest Yunnan Province in China and a UNESCO World Heritage Site. More specifically, Wang's (2007) study revealed that authenticity was instead 'customised' (Wang, 2007: 797), occurring as a result of co-creation of the experience – through the tourists' search for objective authenticity, through their search for a sense of home and self-orientation, and through the Naxi's framing of this experience through their home making.

As well as the conceptualisation of different forms and meanings of authenticity, there have been a variety of applications of the concept to describe a range of settings. Within the realm of heritage, for example, Bruner established a four-part typology of authenticity. First, there is what may be termed 'authentic reproduction'. This form of authenticity refers to giving the appearance of being original, with most interpreters and managers aiming to make the site and its function credible and convincing. This, Bruner argues, is the primary task of museum professionals – to make a site believable to the visiting public. A good example of this form of authenticity occurs within the Yorvik Viking Centre in York, UK. Everything is based on archaeological facts, from the layout of the houses, the working craftsmen and the language of the gossiping neighbours to the smells of cooking and the cesspit. The second meaning of authenticity is when the site not only resembles the original conditions but is a complete and flawless replication that is historically accurate, as far as accuracy can be guaranteed by scholarly research (see Case Study 6.2).

Case Study 6.2 Authenticity and Lascaux II

Lascaux provides the setting for a complex series of caves in south-west France that are famous for their Paleolithic paintings. They are located near the village of Montignac in the French region of the Dordogne and contain some of the best-known paintings to exist from this era. The paintings are estimated to be between 15,000 and 17,000 years old (Plates 6.6 and 6.7) and generally consist of images of animals, most of which are known to have inhabited the area and which are painted in shades of black, red, brown and yellow. Rooms in the cave include the 'Hall of the Bulls', the 'Passageway', the 'Shaft', the 'Nave', the 'Apse' and the 'Chamber of Felines' (Bahn, 2007).

The caves were discovered on 12 September 1940 by 18-year-old Marcel Ravidat. They were opened to the public in 1948 but by 1955 the carbon dioxide, heat, humidity and other contaminants produced by the 1200 visitors per day who visited the site had visibly damaged the paintings. As a result, the caves were closed to the public in 1963 in order to preserve the art and to restore the paintings to their original state. In 1979 Lascaux obtained UNESCO's World Heritage Site status.

In 1983, Lascaux II – a replica of two of the cave halls, the 'Great Hall of Bulls' and the 'Painted Gallery' – was opened to the public, 200 metres from the original cave complex, so that visitors could view the

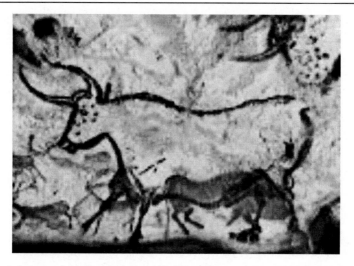

Plate 6.6 Artwork in the 'Hall of the Bulls'
Source: The authors (2017).

artwork without harming the originals. It was the result of 11 years of painstaking work by 20 artists and sculptors using the same methods and materials as the cave painters. Lascaux II is open to the public all year round and offers tours of the cave, lasting around 40 minutes.

Plate 6.7 A decorated cave at Lascaux
Source: The authors (2017).

Since 1998, the original Lascaux cave paintings have been exhibiting signs of damage, most notably the growth of fungus and black mould, thought to be caused by a new air-conditioning system, the use of high-powered lights and over-visitation. Consequently, in January 2008 the French authorities closed the caves for three months, and currently only a few scientific experts are allowed to work inside the cave for a limited amount of time per day. Unfortunately, many of the paintings are now sadly irreparably damaged (Lichfield, 2008).

The third sense of authenticity is labelled 'original instead of copied', and any form of reproduction or alterations renders a site inauthentic. At many historic sites this level of authenticity is difficult to achieve because although some buildings and artefacts are original, in most cases others are brought in to complete the exhibit or are constructed in order to service the needs of tourists. A good example of this is the Bridge over the River Kwai (Plate 6.8). The physical fabric of the bridge has stayed intact but what is important to its authenticity is the landscape setting of the bridge. There is the addition of the new building and much change to the railway station to accommodate many visitors. The most radical impact, however, is the development of a concrete egg carton shop selling souvenirs and housing a restaurant.

The fourth meaning of authenticity implies a sense of authority or legal recognition, although questions do arise as to who has the authority or power to authenticate. In this sense, a site can be authentic because it is duly authorised and it is a representative location of something of historical

Plate 6.8 The Bridge over the River Kwai
Source: The authors (2017).

·importance. However, as Chapter 3 has discussed, authentication is often influenced by the political influences embedded in the presentation of heritage to tourists and, when socially produced, the extent to which it excludes sectional or minority groups is questionable.

Just as authenticity is a negotiated process it can also develop over time (Sharpley, 1994). It is possible for an event that is originally inauthentic to become assimilated into local culture and become authentic. This is because no culture or society is static; new cultural products emerge and therefore authenticity that emerges over time is a valid and realistic process (Cohen, 1988). Overall, authenticity is not just the antithesis of modern life or something that motivates tourists. Just because it is subjective, constructed or consists of a variety of hybrids, as in the case of Wang's (2007) customised authenticity, does not make it a theoretically valid construct. It is unique to each individual tourist, possessing a meaning and importance that can only be assessed alongside an understanding of the various manifestations of heritage, screen and literary tourist experiences (Li, 2000; Steiner & Reisinger, 2006; Wang, 2007).

Heritage, Screen and Literary Tourist Experiences and Authenticity

Authenticity is often used to assess the motivations of tourists (see Chapter 2) and the characteristics of the tourist experience (Tetley, 1997). It is commonly experienced *in situ* or in other words at the actual location or primary site associated with a fictional or fictitious object, person or event, or at museums, memorials and/or visitor centres that have been set up at other locations and referred to as secondary sites. More recently, however, Cohen (2011) found that authenticity may also be experienced *in populo*, a term he uses to describe sites which embody and emphasise the story of a people beset with tragedy which are located at population and/or spiritual centres of the victimised people, but which may be at some geographical distance from the events commemorated.

Consideration of authenticity within the HSLT literature focuses on two key questions which revolve around the extent to which tourists seek out authentic experiences and, if they do, whether they are able to recognise the experience as being so. These questions have caused considerable debate which has become polarised around the thoughts of two academics – Boorstin and MacCannell. Although both take the inauthenticity of modern society as the starting point for their arguments, they reach different conclusions. For Boorstin (1964), modern American society is contrived, illusory and unreal. Tourists are satisfied with inauthentic pseudo-events and the modern mass tourist is satisfied with contrived, meaningless events which can be viewed, preferably, from the comfort and surroundings of the familiar world. The events are supplied by the tourism industry, images of new destinations are contrived by the media, and every effort is made to make the tourist feel at home. As a result, the tourist is increasingly removed from the reality and authenticity of the destination (Sharpley, 1994).

In contrast, MacCannell (1989) argues that tourists from modern Western societies are motivated by the need to experience authenticity. They are able to recognise it and become a kind of secular pilgrim on a quest for authenticity. MacCannell (1973) noted that pilgrims' desire to be in a place associated with religious meanings was comparable to the attraction of tourists to places embedded with social, historical or cultural significance (Belhassen *et al.*, 2008). The modern tourist looks for meaning in the reality of the life of other people and in other places, yet at the same time accepts the inauthentic condition of modernity. Indeed, as if to perpetuate the differentiation between the modern and the pre-modern, modern society collects and preserves the pre-modern in museums and heritage centres, in arts, music, fashion, events and décor, in order to provide havens of reality and authenticity in the turmoil of modern life (Sharpley, 1994). Building on MacCannell's seminal research, Bruner (1991) describes tourists' desire for self-transformation through encounters with authentic cultures, while Galani-Moutafi (2000) examines the tourists' interaction with the Other and the self-discovery process which ensues as a result. Pearce and Moscardo (1986) conclude that tourist satisfaction is linked to a search for authentic experiences.

Regardless of the extent to which heritage, screen and literary tourists are motivated by the desire to experience authenticity, as Chapters 1 and 4 have demonstrated, there is now a demand for products that are the most authentic, and tourism has emerged as a tool for accomplishing this, particularly within the realm of HSLT. But this demand and the marketing of authenticity are not without consequences as it has resulted in commercialisation, a loss of meaning and the staging of authenticity. With respect to the former, the HSLT literature is replete with such examples (e.g. Belhassen *et al.*, 2008; Chhabra *et al.*, 2003). One illustration of the commercialisation of a literary tourist destination has been noted by Squire (1988) in a study of tourism induced by L.M. Montgomery's novels about the fictional 'Anne of Green Gables' on Prince Edward Island, Canada. Based on this case study, it is suggested that historical authenticity is compromised by literary accuracy in order to create a commercial tourist setting, apparent through the site redevelopment. Moreover, the tourism enterprises which surround the area are often guided by details from the fictional novels which may not be historically accurate. Thus, fictional aspects associated with the island are produced specifically for touristic consumption; in other words, they have become commoditised. In terms of the latter – the staging of authenticity – although authenticity can be reaffirmed in the actual consumption of the experience itself, again there are numerous examples of studies that challenge the extent to which HSLT products are staged as opposed to being real and authentic.

Staged Authenticity and Distorted Pasts

Originally conceived by Goffman (1959) and developed by MacCannell (1973, 1989), staged authenticity divides space into front and back regions. The front region is where the social interaction takes place, where hosts meet guests or where servers attend to customers. The back region is the place where members of the host destination retire between performances to relax and to prepare. Performers may appear in both regions, whereas the audience are only allowed into the front region; in other words, the show takes place in the front region but reality exists in the back region (Sharpley, 1994). MacCannell (1989) suggested that this simple front–back dichotomy can be expanded into a continuum comprising six stages which starts at the front and ends at the back, and it is from this that the notion of staged authenticity emerges (see Table 6.4).

According to Timothy and Boyd (2003), the tourist demand for authentic experiences and the resulting staging of cultures, places and events has resulted in several types of distorted pasts which are created by various intentional actions, economic and business processes, political pressures and tourist expectations. Indeed, they identify several types that have occurred as a result of the commodification of HSLT. The first they label as 'invented places' which refer to the creation of replicas of historic sites and objects, non-original renditions of the past, and the development of imaginary, invented and contrived places, people and events which attract tourists in search of the original where it never existed. One example from the US is Liberal, Kansas, the 'real' location of Dorothy's farm in the tale of *The Wizard*

Table 6.4 The staged authenticity continuum

Stage One	This is Goffman's front region, the setting which tourists attempt to penetrate or get behind
Stage Two	Although still a front region, this stage has been given the superficial appearance of the back region
Stage Three	This stage is still firmly embedded in the front region but it is totally organised to resemble a back region
Stage Four	Moving into the back region, tourists are permitted to see this stage
Stage Five	This is the back region to which tourists are occasionally permitted entry
Stage Six	This is Goffman's back region, the ultimate goal of the tourist, but one which is rarely, if ever, reached

Source: Adapted from MacCannell (1989).

of Oz. In truth there is no 'real' farm or land of Oz, but the invented past, created by the medium of film, has constructed such a place in the mind of visitors. This is common within the phenomenon of screen and literary heritage. Places that become real in the children's minds and are remembered over a lifetime are in fact a part of heritage. Thus when tourists visit houses where writers lived and worked and the landscapes that provided the settings for their novels, real-life experiences become blurred with the fictitious, imagined world.

Timothy and Boyd (2003) identify another form of this – 'invented ethnicity' – and cite the example of Leavenworth, WA, a small town that grew during the 19th century as a mining and railroad town. During the Depression the community's economic base began to dwindle, resulting in derelict buildings, high levels of unemployment and outmigration. Tourism was subsequently selected in the 1960s as a means of regenerating the local economy and society, consequently Leavenworth was reinvented as an authentic-looking Bavarian village where tourists, domestic and international, could experience authentic German foods, music, architecture and shopping. However, Leavenworth and its community are not Bavarian, however much they project such an image.

An extension to Timothy and Boyd's (2003) notion of invented places is what is termed here as 'invented architectures'. Bruges, a city in Belgium, is in fact a Victorian pastiche resembling a town that seems much older than it really is (see Plate 6.9). A final example of an invented past occurs with the moving of artefacts from their original location to a different cultural and

Plate 6.9 Bruges: A Victorian pastiche?
Source: The authors (2017).

geographical context. The object may be authentic but the location is not. There are numerous examples of artefacts that have been removed from their original locations and placed elsewhere be it museums or private collections. In addition, examples exist where for a variety of reasons entire structures have been relocated, including the Temples of Abu Simbel in Egypt which were moved to a more elevated location so they would not be destroyed by the creation of Lake Nassar.

The second form of distorted pasts identified by Timothy and Boyd (2003) is what they term 'relative authenticity'. Just as authenticity may be influenced and ultimately defined by cultural and social representations, it is also context and place specific. Ghost towns provide a good example of this as they are different from other types of heritage places. Ghost town authenticity is measured by the degree of decay and tarnish. At most of these types of places, maintenance workers endeavour to carry out a policy of arrested decay or keeping them standing but making them look like they are falling down. Similarly, according to Swarbrooke (1994), part of the authenticity dilemma is whether ancient ruins should be left as ruins or instead reconstructed to look how they would have appeared in their time of operation. Some people feel that ruins should be left alone since reconstruction can detract from the authenticity of the site. This is clearly visible in Arizona where a drive through Navajo Nation Reservation reveals many derelict hogans dotting the landscape. Most have been abandoned since the 1970s and 1980s and do not attract tourists' attention. But abandoned Native American homes and communities from 500 years ago are major attractions and are being conserved by the US National Park Service. Thus the age factor adds value to ruined Indian structures from both touristic and archaeological perspectives.

The third form is termed 'ethnic intruders', where authenticity is diminished in cultural events and ethnic presentations where non-local people play the part of interpreters in a setting that is said to be authentic (Timothy & Boyd, 2003). The fourth is 'sanitised and idealised pasts'. This was born out of the recognition that tourists, while in search of authentic experiences, if faced with truly authentic experiences would cease visiting heritage sites because the 'real' conditions presented would be unimaginable, unbearable and undesirable. In other words, people may prefer to view the past through representations as it is too unpalatable to digest. Historical accuracy consequently is not always compatible with visual and sensory appeal. Thus, heritage and authenticity are said to be sanitised or made attractive to cater to the tastes and desires of tourists.

The fifth form suggested by Timothy and Boyd (2003) is 'unknown past'. It is based on the premise that true authenticity is impossible because people in the modern day cannot precisely understand the lives of people from history or know enough about the details of their everyday lives to make interpretation accurate. Researchers, managers and interpreters lack sufficient knowledge to provide precise depictions of the past. The past is not a known entity: no account can recover the past as it was, because the past is a set of events and situations. Thus, because people view the past from current perspectives and authenticity is socially constructed, all that can be done is to imagine what it was like. Taking all these examples together, there is clearly a range of HSLT settings of staged authenticity which exist and, given their abundance, the extent to which heritage, screen and literary tourists are able to recognise the experience as being so is an issue which has attracted substantive attention.

Tourism Consumption and the Marking of Authenticity

Although the notion of staged authenticity is broadly embraced as one of the best conceptualisations of host–guest interactions and the impact this has on the tourist experience, it has withstood much criticism since it incorrectly suggests that tourists are naïve and ignores their ability to understand and interpret the staged authenticity with which they are presented (Cohen, 1979). Indeed, a raft of HSLT-related studies demonstrate that tourists are not superficial fools satisfied with spuriousness in Boorstin's sense or victims of a falsifying touristic establishment which stages authenticity. Moscardo and Pearce (1986: 471), for example, investigated visitor perceptions of the authenticity of Australian historic theme parks, arguing that since such parks 'preserve or restore some aspects of a nation's heritage' they are almost by definition not authentic in the strict sense used by MacCannell. However, they suggest that visitors generally did perceive these theme parks as being 'authentic' in relation to their being accurate reconstructions of Australia's past rather than their being genuine historical remains. Another illustration is provided by Hills (2002), who points out that some film tourists and particularly real fans of a particular production undertake detailed research to locate precise on-screen locations. As such, it is the authenticity of the actual site that forms the object of consumption.

Cohen (1979) in particular was critical of the suggestion that tourists are unable to distinguish between the real and the falsified, developing the notion of staged authenticity to encompass tourists' impressions of the authentic nature of the setting. Consequently, Cohen proposed a four-cell typology of touristic situations based on two types of settings (real and staged), and on two types of tourists' perceptions of the setting (real and staged) (see Table 6.5). This typology enables the classification and comparison of different kinds of touristic situations. However, just as there are studies which demonstrate the ability of tourists to distinguish between the real and the fake, other investigations reveal that some visitors blur fact and fiction, muddling together the real and the false, and this is particularly

Table 6.5 The four-cell model of tourist situations

Nature of scene	Tourists' impression of scene	
	Real	*Staged*
Real	(A) Authentic and recognised as such	(B) Suspicion of staging and authenticity questioned
Staged	(C) Failure to recognise contrived tourist space	(D) Recognised as contrived tourist space

Source: Adapted from Cohen (1979: 26).

associated with screen and literary tourism. Torchin (2002: 247), for instance, terms it 'authenticity and artificiality' in the film tourism experience, highlighted in the film tour of real locations. Experiencing fictitious locations within or sedimented onto a real environment results in, as Rojeck (1997: 54) argues, a process whereby 'cinematic events are dragged on to the physical landscape and the physical landscape is then reinterpreted in terms of cinematic events'.

In this sense, can literary and screen tourists ever have an authentic experience, especially since films – even documentaries – and literary fiction are understood inherently as representations, simulations, and contrivances? Indeed, Morley and Robins (1995: 90) argue that 'the "memory banks" of our time are in some part built out of the materials supplied by the TV and film industries'. They are emblematic of the proliferation of simulacra and the hyperreal. The creative licence afforded to authors, editorial control, cinematographic skills and technologies, and artistic, entertainment and aesthetic values are all acknowledged to be part of the process of film production (Beeton, 2005, 2015) and indeed literary fiction. As a consequence, there is an uneasy dichotomous relationship between the notion of 'authentic' film and literary experiences and the highly artificial writing and production process. Adding to this complexity is travel to specific destinations which have either been associated with the production of the film or literary work or have been depicted in the screen productions and books, especially if those destinations visited are not actually represented but are a physical substitute for other 'real' places (Buchmann et al., 2010).

Yet authenticity remains relevant for HSLT, not least because tourists attribute high value to their judgements of authenticity. Any such experiences depend on the place as well as on the wider processes in which any interpretations of the experience take place. According to Buchmann et al. (2010: 243) 'such processes amount to something rather more than, for example, individual tourists' expectations or attitudes. They are commitments often but not always of a deep nature. In particular, they are personal commitments to internalised yet broadly operating social processes, values and understandings that have been imbibed through personal experiences, sometimes stretching over a person's entire life. Such processes can facilitate mythological functions which – in properly structured physical settings, places and social situations – deliver to the tourist an experience of considerable significance and particular value'. The tourist experience thus entails place both in its 'real' form, and in its hyper-real form which is constructed through narratives presented in books and film (Buchmann *et al.*, 2010). It therefore appears that there are a range of tourist experiences with the authenticity of each very much influenced by the tourists' ability to distinguish between the real and fake. In addition, however, there are a host of other factors that can influence the authenticity of the experience.

Factors Influencing the Authenticity of the Experience

Early studies revealed that the authenticity of the tourist experience is influenced by the tourists' depth of concern about authenticity (Cohen, 1979; Pearce & Moscardo, 1986); the greater depth of concern for authenticity, the stricter the criteria against which it is evaluated. This argument can be illustrated using Cohen's (1979) five 'modes of touristic experience', which range from the experience of the tourist as a traveller in pursuit of mere pleasure (the 'recreational' tourist) to that of the modern touristic pilgrim in pursuit of discovering and experiencing an alien culture (the 'existential' tourist). The latter wants to experience the real-life nature of the destination and as a result will possess the strictest criteria for authenticity. Hence, there may exist a continuum of evaluations of authenticity among tourists, from complete authenticity, through various stages of partial authenticity, to complete falseness (Tetley, 1997).

Thus, the degree to which a sight or attraction is perceived to be authentic can also depend on the relationship between an individual tourist and that sight or attraction. This relationship in turn depends to a great extent on the attitudes and experience of the tourist but at the same time the significance attached to a particular attraction or sight goes a long way toward determining its authenticity. Authenticity therefore becomes a sign, and tourism rather than a search for authenticity becomes a search for signs. The relationship between a tourist and a sight is not, however, a simple two-way process. The tourist has to know that what is being looked at or experienced is an authentic sign of an attraction that is worth visiting and this is conveyed through markers. A marker informs the tourist that a site is real or that it is worth seeing. If it is not marked then by implication it is not then a notable sight (Culler, 1981). Thus the tourist links the marker with the sight in the process of sightseeing. It is the existence of these markers that confirms a sight or experience as a sign of authenticity.

Cohen (2011) proposes a similar argument, noting that it is the degree of closeness of the destination site to the tourist's spiritual centre which may affect perceptions of authenticity and the meaning of the site. Thus, the same site will be experienced differently depending on the degree to which the tourist is psychologically and emotionally involved with the events memorialised. He draws on the example of heritage associated with death and disaster, stating that the experience will differ for tourists related to the victims, those related to the perpetrators or bystanders, and those who are not directly related to the event (Ashworth & Tunbridge, 1996). Those tourists who have an intimate emotional involvement with the memorialised events may as a result be provided with transient moments of self-actualisation (Maslow, 1971) or flow experiences – recurrent moments of self-actualisation occurring during engagement in an ongoing activity (Cohen, 2008). These experiences are similar to Wang's existential authenticity (Cohen, 2011).

Meanwhile, Pearce and Moscardo (1986) argue that, akin to Selwyn's (1996) notion of 'hot authenticity', it is the tourist's relationship with the host community which can add to the authenticity of tourist experiences. They examine the importance of the tourists' perceptions of experiences with the host community, stating that 'It is the relationship between the tourist and the host which determines authenticity'. That is, all frontstage (inauthentic) actors have a backstage (authentic) region as well, to which certain people are permitted at certain times (Pearce & Moscardo, 1986: 129). In other words, an authentic experience can be achieved through the tourist setting as a whole, i.e. experiencing the tourist 'attraction' and experiencing interaction with the hosts within the setting or through a combination of both elements. As Pearce and Moscardo (1986: 129) conclude, different tourists display different motivations, expectations and experiences and the 'whole issue of whether or not tourists are satisfied with their holiday experience demands a full consideration of the nature of the tourist environment, the tourists' perceptions of that environment and the tourists' need or preference for authenticity'.

Another factor that is emerging from recent HSLT studies which has been found to influence the authenticity of the tourist experience is the degree to which simulation and hyper-real experiences contribute to the tourist experience. One of the earliest studies of this nature was undertaken by Couldry (1998, 2005), who examined visits to the set of the UK soap drama *Coronation Street* at Granada Studios. The studies revealed that the film set was the object of consumption and visitors viewed the set as real because it was where the filming actually took place, thereby providing a sense of social reality. Furthermore, in a study of *The Lord of the Rings* tourists in New Zealand, Carl *et al.* (2007) identified that hyper-real is a prerequisite in ensuring a positive tourist experience, whereby a greater level of involvement and consumption of the film *in situ* generated greater tourist satisfaction. It is important to note, however, that while the physical and social contexts of a site affect tourists' perceptions of its authenticity, simulations or re-enactments at primary sites may create a feeling of inauthenticity (Boorstin, 1964), while memorials located at the site of an atrocity may not enjoy the freedom to provide historical, political and educational contextualisation and interpretation of events. Ultimately, however, as Cohen concludes 'visiting historically authentic sites or viewing authentic relics do not automatically provide tourists with an experience that helps them to understand the events that took place' (2011: 35).

Thus, related to levels of involvement and consumption of HSLT or performativity, as has been discussed earlier in this chapter, is the degree to which co-creation, embodied encounters or, as Wang (1999) states, the activation of the existential state occur, which is another factor influencing the authenticity of experiences. Indeed Buchmann *et al.* (2010) argue that it is the use made out of authenticating resources by tourists that leads them to understand their experiences as more or less authentic. The commodification of the intangible aspects of a book or film allow for the consumption of both objectively and existentially authentic products. The tourist experience, however, is also constructed through action. What tourists do is an integral part of their construction of reality and authenticity. In the case of *The Lord of the Rings*, this is illustrated through the sense of belonging that is created within the group. The group creates a fellowship in which the story can be consumed through activities that take place at locations that have become significant as a consequence of the films. It is through this process that New Zealand is transformed into Middle Earth in the minds of the tourist (Buchmann *et al.*, 2010).

Frost (2010) also highlights the importance of co-creation and embodied encounters in his study of film tourism and the screen portrayal of the Outback in Australia. In films dealing with the Outback, there are strong storylines which essentially take the form of a series of 'promises'. The key promise is that a tourist to this exotic locale will be changed. In many cases, the change presented is a positive one. The tourist is changed from being bored, alienated, frustrated or stagnant to being re-energised, a better person, more tolerant of others, perhaps even spiritually uplifted. The causes of this change are a combination of wilderness, isolation and interaction with people who live a simple life (Frost, 2010). The films are about the perceptions that one's life may be changed by experiences when travelling.

Given the importance of performativity, co-creation and embodied encounters in the authenticity of the tourist experience, Belhassen *et al.* (2008) call for an integrative analysis of authenticity that moves beyond the solely subjective to highlight the intersections of three central factors – place, belief and action – as part of engendering a more in-depth understanding of lived experiences of authenticity. This relationship creates a conceptual framework called 'theoplacity' and demonstrates that authenticity is shaped by the belief underlying the visit, the places visited and their meanings, and the activities undertaken. With respect to HSLT and as illustrated in the HSLT nexus (Chapter 1), experiences largely depend on the tourists' relationships with space, place – that is, the co-contingency of the resources visited – and the (re)representation of such resources, as well as socio-psychological factors, and this combination impacts on service experience, experience quality and satisfaction.

Service Experience, Experience Quality and Satisfaction

Since all three forms of tourism involve experiential consumption, service experience, experience quality and satisfaction are crucially important to the sustainability of HSLT sites and destinations. According to Otto and Richie (2000), service experience is best viewed as the subjective personal reactions and feelings that are felt by consumers when consuming or using a service. It comprises experience quality, which relates to the 'psychological outcome resulting from customer participation in tourism activities' (Chen & Chen, 2010: 30), including interaction with people who contribute to the actual experience, and it has an important influence on tourist evaluations of and satisfaction with a given service or experience. These evaluations in turn impact on value co-creation, as the extent to which it is extracted and exchanged depends, as Vargo and Lusch (2004) suggest in their tenth foundational premise, on the judgements of the end-user.

Simply defined, satisfaction is the result of an experience (Žabkar et al., 2010), and can be considered to be 'the most important judgement that a tourist makes as a consequence of tourist experience' (Bowden & Schouten, 2008: 142). This is due to its significant influence on destination image (Chen & Tsai, 2007; Um et al., 2006; Žabkar et al., 2010; see Chapter 7), tourists' future behavioural intentions, including repeat visitation (Alegre & Garau, 2010; Assaker et al., 2011; Emir & Kozak, 2011; Jang & Feng, 2007; Johnson et al., 2001; Marcussen, 2011; Navrátil et al., 2011) and word-of-mouth recommendations (Bowden & Schouten, 2008; Kao et al., 2008; Prebensen et al., 2010). Satisfaction is considered to have the greatest influence on tourism success, and within HSLT authenticity or at least perceptions of it can lead to quality experiences and satisfaction (Cohen, 1988). Dissatisfaction is caused by differences in tourist expectations compared to their actual experience, which can be greatly influenced by their perceptions of authenticity and by the level of accuracy in presentations of places through film and literature (Frost, 2006b). It can therefore be difficult for sites and destinations to meet tourist expectations which may be unrealistic due to exaggerated or fictional representations found in films and literature.

Research into service experience, experience quality and satisfaction is limited within HSLT. Extant literature has tended to measure satisfaction through tourist evaluations of perceived quality against expectations drawing on confirmation/disconfirmation theories (Caldwell, 2002; de Ruyter *et al.*, 1997; Harrison & Shaw, 2004). For example, Chhabra *et al.* (2003) analysed the relationships between perceived authenticity as a measure of product quality and satisfaction, drawing on the case study of the Flora MacDonald Scottish Highland Games held in North Carolina, USA. The authors revealed that even though this staged event contains elements such as tartan and Scottish dancing which have been modified over time and which in the strictest use of the term are inauthentic, because of their historical roots combined with the fact that they are staged in a similar way across the US they have resulted in perceptions of authenticity and satisfaction; the latter is evidenced by repeat visitation and high spending. Another illustration is a study undertaken by Chen and Chen (2010) who focused on the experience quality of heritage tourism perceived by heritage tourists and explored the relationships between experience quality, perceived value and satisfaction and post-visitation behaviour intentions. They found that enhancing a visitor's experience quality, perceived value and satisfaction is an important management goal of heritage managers.

However, there is also some research which has examined the impact of involvement and emotions experienced by tourists on satisfaction. Hwang *et al.* (2005), in particular, noted an association between involvement and satisfaction in a study of national parks in Taiwan. Indeed, they concluded that increasing the chances for tourists to get involved in tourism activities would increase the level of tourist satisfaction and loyalty. Moreover, in a study of visitors to an interpretation centre, de Rojas and Camarero (2008) found a significant relationship between quality and emotion, with mood state being an important generator of visitor satisfaction. Such studies suggest that value creation produced as an outcome of the co-creation and co-production of the consumptive experience is a crucial determinant of visitor satisfaction and indeed lies at the heart of the HSLT nexus (see Chapter 1).

The upshot of such studies of service quality, experience quality and satisfaction in the context of HSLT is that not every component of the experience need be authentic (or even satisfactory), as long as the combination of elements meets tourists' expectations and generates the required outcome, be it perceptions of authenticity, experience quality or satisfaction (Chhabra *et al.*, 2003). More importantly, perhaps, these studies highlight the fact that staged authenticity does not necessarily equate with artificiality or superficiality; it certainly does not preclude authenticity. Indeed, even in highly staged inauthentic HSLT environments, through the actual experience and consumption process itself, tourists are able to form perceptions of authenticity, best evidenced by repeat visitation and satisfaction. It is also important to remember that different tourists display different motivations, expectations and experiences and the 'whole issue of whether or not tourists are satisfied with their holiday experience demands a full consideration of the nature of the tourist environment, the tourists' perceptions of that environment and the tourists' need or preference for authenticity' (Pearce & Moscardo, 1986: 129).

Conclusion

This chapter has demonstrated that the consumption of HSLT and value co-creation involves all of the components which comprise the nexus (see Chapter 1), these being co-creation, the (re)representation of objects, people, places and events, be they real or imaginary, contingent resources and co-terminality (see Figure 6.1). In the first part of the chapter, consideration is given to the relevance of performance and performativity and it is established that for most tourists, consumption is an active process which requires their involvement in the co-creation of the experience. This discussion highlights the applicability of Vargo and Lusch's (2008) first, sixth and eighth foundational premises (see Table 1.7) to examinations of value co-creation within HSLT consumption. Of course, the role that the tourist plays and their

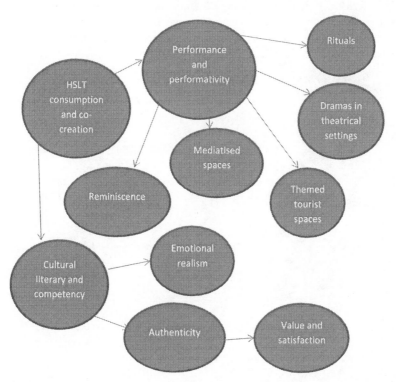

Figure 6.1 Dimensions of heritage, screen and literary tourism consumption and co-creation
Source: The authors (2017).

resulting experience is influenced by their cultural and literacy competence. In addition, however, as discussed, the tourist experience is also shaped by their expectations and perceptions of authenticity. These determinants are again reinforced by Vargo and Lusch's (2008) fourth and tenth foundational premises (see Table 1.7).

Authenticity was thus the focus for consideration in the second part of this chapter in which it is demonstrated that it is a highly contestable concept. This is in part due to its diverse meaning, which as a consequence has resulted in its use to describe a wide range of experiences in various different settings. The discussion establishes the particular importance of authenticity to HSLT, not least because tourist experiences are often complex productions of personal history, knowledge, co-creation, embodiment and the (re)representation of place through heritage interpretation and through screen productions and literature. Even the most staged environments which may be dominated by hyper-reality and simulacra or which may consciously involve the distortion of the past do not necessarily make the experience any less authentic or genuine. Perceptions of authenticity are thus highly subjective and individual with a multitude of factors influencing the outcome, this being service experience, experience quality and satisfaction. The latter were the final issues for consideration in this chapter and their association with the components of the HSLT nexus were outlined.

7 The Heritage, Screen and Literary Tourism Nexus within Tourism Marketing

Introduction

The HSLT nexus as introduced in Chapter 1 is at its most powerful in the production of tourism marketing and branding via the construction of tourism images. Within this context there are complex linkages between the different components of HSLT that either together or individually perform important roles within tourism marketing. These links with tourist image making add to this complexity, as do the ways in which contemporary patterns of consumption are much more than the purchase of a product or service but rather, as Campbell (1987) points out, are concerned with satisfaction from imaginative pleasure seeking or 'imaginative hedonism'. This term describes the importance of not just the purchase of a product but rather the anticipation of the satisfaction from such pleasure seeking (see Chapter 6 for a full discussion).

However, Campbell (1987: 88–95) saw this imaginative pleasure seeking as a relatively autonomous feature of postmodern societies. In this way, he argued, it was somewhat separate from specific institutional aspects, advertising and marketing or indeed forms of social emulation. Urry (2002) has countered these views by agreeing with Selwyn (1996: 14) that it is difficult to view contemporary tourism without understanding how tourist images and activities are 'constructed in our imagination through advertising and the media'. This is supported by Månsson (2011) and Davin (2005), who argue that since the media pervades our society it has a major role to play in tourism, which Månsson terms 'mediatized tourism'. The impact of marketing and branding on tourism is a significant factor in the consumption of HSLT products and such impacts have increased in their intensity as well as their coverage.

The purpose of this chapter is not to explain the nature of tourism marketing as such but rather to explore its growing use and the complexity of its links with the HSLT nexus, drawing on theorisations provided by S-DL and co-creation. We do this by first outlining briefly the growing importance and changing nature of marketing and branding in tourism both for destinations and for specific tourist attractions. This is in part achieved through linking with the ideas of theming the landscape or the use of signs and markers to identify to tourists' significant places (Culler, 1981; Urry, 2002). We then turn to consider the growing linkages between HSLT and the marketing industry and how such linkages have produced an increase in the concepts of branding and the creation and selling of brands based around the HSLT nexus. As we shall see, such developments have implications for these parts of the tourism industry and increasingly seem to shape tourist image making and behaviour. Of equal significance is the globalisation of such trends cutting across very different cultures as the marketing media produces what Urry (2002: 141) calls 'virtual travel through the internet'. He discusses this in terms of 'travel along the infrastructures of the global travel industry'. This idea is further developed by emphasising the global nature of the tourism marketing industry and its strong links with key aspects of the HSLT nexus – in particular, the images produced by films and related images on the internet. It is very often the case that it is the internet and social media which expose consumers to the brand in contemporary patterns of tourist behaviour (Foley et al., 2014: 140), and which provide a range of platforms that provide tourists with the opportunity for ongoing engagement and interaction with businesses and other tourists and stakeholders.

Marketing and Branding Practices

The practices of tourism marketing are being transformed; this is partly in response to the impact of social media on tourists, making them more aware and knowledgeable through 'word of mouth' marketing (Doh & Hwang, 2009; Xiang & Gretzel, 2010). This emphasises a trust in what other tourists say about a hotel, destination or attraction. In this context, as McCabe (2014: 1) points out, 'old certainties are peeling away' and the effectiveness of more traditional marketing practices are often no longer clear. One of the distinctive features of tourism marketing is that it is concerned with a service and more especially an experience, since many aspects of tourism concern its intangibility. While these ideas are important, the one purpose here is to examine how such practices are linked with HSLT. Many of the standard texts on tourism marketing tend to situate their examples around key parts of the tourism system, for example hotels and accommodation units, transport, attractions and of course particular destinations (Fyall & Garrod, 2005; Hudson, 2008; Middleton et al., 2009). In this way the importance of HSLT is rather neglected even though this nexus provides an important marketing strategy.

Marketing is traditionally based on a number of strategic stages shown in Table 7.1. These five main stages are traditionally seen as essential in planning and executing a marketing campaign, although in reality the connection between these stages and how HSLT is used is more complex. First, these components of the nexus exist in different ways. For example, the ideas of literary trails have been widely used to enhance the marketing of particular destinations. In this context, MacLeod *et al.* (2009) developed and partially tested a typology of literary trails that is essentially based on authorship and purpose. In doing so they identified 'biographical trails' mainly developed by literary trusts and societies, 'literary landscape trails' usually developed by a mixed range of stakeholders, and finally 'generic literary trails' produced by local authorities and civic groups.

In terms of marketing, these three different types show variations in the market segments they cover and their means of marketing. For example, 'biographical trails' are aimed at a market with the trail narrative assuming a good level of pre-existing knowledge. Marketing has tended to be relatively low key, as literary societies often have rather limited marketing expertise and budgets. 'Literary landscape trails' are normally developed by civic societies, tourist boards and local authorities, although more often now private sector organisations are involved. These types of trails are marketed increasingly to help develop brand identities for a particular region or for selling holidays. MacLeod *et al.* (2009: 166) give the example of a long-distance route joining together different geographical locations that are mentioned in the best-selling novel *The Da Vinci Code* by Dan Brown (Table 7.2). These trails may be enhanced in popularity by screen tourism, although MacLeod *et al.*

Table 7.1 Key stages in marketing and links with heritage, screen and literary tourism

Stage	Main activities	Implications for HSLT
Market research	Understanding the market (trends and segmentation)	Establish strong links between story, location and characters
Marketing planning	Developing marketing strategies from research stage	Establish different strategies for different phases
Marketing campaign	Integrating elements of the marketing mix into marketing actions (use of media for promotion)	Need to develop marketing partnerships. DMO plus private sector organisations
Evaluation and monitoring	Evaluating the results of marketing campaign	Usually by DMO or consultants

Source: The authors (2017).

Table 7.2 Marketing campaign elements in heritage, screen and literary tourism examples in the UK

Title of novel and author	Story and character driven	Broad appeal	Links to strong brands	Use of historic buildings and dramatic landscapes	Role of 'place' in story	Tourism marketing initiatives and stakeholder
Da Vinci Code (Dan Brown)	✓	✓	✓	✓		Marketing/advertising campaign; events, e.g. 'Join the Quest' Eurostar campaign; 'Seek the Truth'; VisitBritain trail; accommodation tie-ins and deals; VisitScotland itineraries; tie-in film on Rosslyn Chapel (VisitScotland); walking tours; private tours; press coverage; guide books; promotion by individual locations
Harry Potter (J.K. Rowling)	✓	✓	✓	✓	✓	Movie Map (VisitBritain); websites (VisitBritain); video news release; 'behind the scenes' TV programmes; independent private tours; promotion by individual locations; press coverage; development of theme park attractions.
Pride and Prejudice (Jane Austen)	✓	✓	✓	✓		'Pride and Prejudice' country rebranding; DVD insert; Chatsworth premier; websites; itineraries; private tours; press coverage; promotion by individual locations

Source: Modified from Olsberg SPI (2007).

(2009: 166) argue that such screen-based trails 'may have a shorter life span'. Moreover, these trails have wider market appeal as they do not rely on detailed previous knowledge as in the case of 'biographical scales'. In terms of marketing content, they usually have little, most notably in the case of text, but they use a wide range of images – increasingly on social media. The latter is particularly important given the high scope for more personalised marketing strategies. This is explored by Cunningham and Hinze (2013), who argue that in these types of situations digital guides, especially mobile app, offer significant advantages over traditional paper versions. They go on to list a range of generic support for literacy trails, including 'The Southern Literary Trail', which is an app designed to guide users across the Southern USA to key places associated with literary figures, such as Tennessee Williams who was based in New Orleans when he wrote *A Street Car Named Desire* (see Chapter 5 for a fuller discussion of interpretation and augmented reality).

The third type of literacy trail identified by MacLeod *et al.* (2009) is what they termed the 'generic literacy trail', largely developed by local authorities. These are initiated to enhance a place image and as such they are driven mainly by marketing strategies which employ promotional material for a particular destination. As a consequence, narratives such as these are more limited and often less authentic, aimed at a rather undifferentiated market. MacLeod *et al.* (2009) go on to develop ideas presented by Smith (2006), who highlighted the need to develop experiential marketing that would enhance tourist engagement and stimulation. Within the development of literary heritage trails these authors identify the need to develop networks of tourism initiatives with an emphasis on creative interpretation strategies (for example, an increased use of mobile technologies via interactive apps).

Additionally, the latter may be combined with the creation of so-called interpretive highways combining different visitor experiences, including literary trails, interpretive central hubs linking such trails via a hub-and-spoke model. Unfortunately, the few examples that MacLeod *et al.* (2009) provide are rather grounded in more traditional ways of presenting material (see Chapter 5 on interpretive techniques). Their ideas nevertheless point to the importance of increasing design in the development of more experiential marketing for future destination strategies. They very much echo the views presented by Vargo and Lusch (2008) in their foundational premises two (indirect exchange masks the fundamental basis of exchange), three (goods are a distribution mechanism for service provision), eight (a service-centred view is inherently customer oriented and relational) and nine (all social and economic actors are resource integrators). These principles highlight the role of intangible aspects of HSLT in co-creation as well as the empowerment of tourists who now engage with other actors (e.g. tourism businesses, consumer communities and personal networks), who integrate their resources such as information platforms and devices and who participate in the creation of their experiences (Neuhofer, 2016).

In many other instances the location of the novel may be used as a cornerstone by the destination marketing organisation (DMO) or by an individual organisation. In the former case, the British Tourist Authority (which operates in large part as a DMO) published booklets entitled *Literary Tourism*, edited by Liddell and published initially in 1993 and again in 1997. Essentially these acted as locational guides to places related to particular authors or their writings. A comparison even over this short time period of four years illustrates changes in the authors selected, but more importantly, as Robinson and Anderson (2002: 32) point out, it represents a 'more varied view of both the audience for literary tourism and of literary tourism as a tourism product'. Of course such literary guides are not new; the difference in this case was their development and use by a DMO (Robinson & Anderson, 2002). Other organisations have commissioned such guides to literary trails in the past. For example, the National Trust published *Literary Trails: Writers in their Landscapes* (Hardyment, 1999) as part of a broader marketing exercise of the various landscapes and properties associated with famous authors.

These ideas have been brought into a marketing campaign more recently by the DMO VisitEngland, with their launch of so-called 'Literary Inspired Weekends' (VisitEngland, 2016). In this instance we can see the links with a marketing strategy as outlined in Table 7.1. Furthermore, the choice of literary sites is varied, including classic writers (Shakespeare) through to contemporary UK TV detective series (*Midsomer Murders*). More importantly, these weekend breaks are aimed at particular market segments based around lifestyle groups. The online marketing campaign goes further by theming the places and the authors (Table 7.3). The themes of each holiday break are in themselves informative and reflect a range of popular authors, most of whose works have been screened many times. This highlights the strong links between literary and screen tourism in signposting the landscape, or at least how marketers see this process.

Other organisations such as rail companies are also using key literary works to market particular destinations within the UK. For example, in summer 2016 the Great Western Railway launched 'Uncover Britain's World of Literature'. This was based around a range of authors and particular destinations. Once again they show the catholic nature of the literacy types being used to market destinations and related experience. These ranged from a poetry tour of southwest England through exhibitions commemorating the 400th anniversary of Shakespeare's death to the children's author Roald Dahl. Another interesting feature of their promotion is that it was delivered by personal emails to regular customers of the train company, which also launched a related app. Roald Dahl was chosen because of his appeal to children, and as a consequence the marketing campaign was launched at the start of the long summer school holidays, coinciding with a new film release

Table 7.3 Marketing literary-based weekends by VisitEngland

Marketing themes	Author	Location
Readings at Charles Dickens' Birthplace Museum	Charles Dickens	Portsmouth
Retrace the Footsteps of John Keats in Winchester	John Keats	Winchester
Live the Sense and Sensibilities of Jane Austen's Bath	Jane Austen	Bath
Poetry of the Lakes	William Wordsworth	Windermere
Uncover the Mysterious World of Sherlock Holmes	Arthur Conan Doyle	London
A Famous Five Adventure	Enid Blyton	Corfe Castle (Dorset)
Picture Mr Darcy Coming out of the Lake	Jane Austen[a]	Lyme House (Cheshire)

Note: [a]Locational setting of BBC TV *Pride and Prejudice*.
Source: VisitEngland (2016).

based on one of his books, *The BFG*. The campaign also marks 100 years since the birth of the author.

As Watson (2006) has argued, literary tourism in the UK has developed into a strong commercial industry with places associated with novels or authors being used to market a range of destinations. Hoppen *et al.* (2014) point out that an indicator of the importance of literary tourism is that such places have exceptional qualities; these may be a close connection with the writer or the stories and above all an attractive landscape. Herbert (2001) argued that there are exceptional and general aspects of literary places, and clearly it is easier to market and brand the so-called exceptional places. In terms of exceptional places these, according to Herbert (2001), have strong links to the life of the writer, for example, such as Stratford-upon-Avon and William Shakespeare. These may also be places strongly associated with the settings of particular stories – which may be real or imagined in the case of a novel – investing the place with a special meaning, or places connected to some particular dramatic event in the writer's life. Each of these present strong and viable marketing opportunities which can be used as key aspects of experiential marketing strategies that evoke, in some instances, particular memories.

The traditional theming of certain landscapes around particular key authors or even TV series is important but is rarely enough to be sustainable as a destination market strategy given the characteristics and desires of contemporary tourists (see Chapters 2 and 6 for a fuller discussion). Figure 7.1 shows an early and somewhat basic attempt at such literary theming of England, giving or attempting to give a brand image to certain regions. In some instances, academic researchers are involved in initiating literary trials in an

Key:
Authors
Literary and Screen Tourism
Heritage

Catherine Cookson country

Emmerdale country

Haworth
Brontë
country

Robin
Hood
country

Nelson
country

Shakespeare
Country – Stratford-on-
Avon

Constable
Country

Dylan Thomas
country

King
Arthur
country

Sherlock
Holmes

Lorna
Doone
country

Thomas Hardy
country

Poldark
Betjeman country
County

Agatha
Christie

Figure 7.1 Heritage, literary and screen branding in England and Wales
Source: Modified from Travelagewest (2017).

attempt to foster new niche markets. For example, Stiebel (2004: 35) has discussed the development of literary tourism in KwaZulu-Natal in South Africa with the aim of producing a 'literary tourism map of the province'. In one sense this is being developed as an antidote to what Robins (2000) has seen as the commodification of certain city sites within the province. Stiebel (2001) herself sees issues with parts of the province being marketed as the 'Kingdom of the Zulu with nostalgic overtones of a glorious warrior since this has a past familiar to Rider Haggard readers' (Stiebel, 2004: 43). Rider Haggard's best-selling novel *She: A History of Adventure,* first published in 1887, told the story of an adventure to find a lost kingdom in Africa. Given that the story dates from the Imperialist era, it is somewhat controversial within the context of politics in contemporary South Africa (see Chapter 3 for an examination of politics and HSLT). The conclusion is that the development and marketing of literary trails should be done in a sensitive way. Clearly there are issues in this context between the activities of marketing organisations and heritage. Thus the complexities of marketing certain aspects of HSLT are important to note.

In the case of Transylvania in Romania, there are conflicting marketing strategies surrounding heritage sites and in particular the Dracula myth. The character of Dracula was created by Bram Stoker and first published in 1897. Fact and fiction seem to have merged in that Vlad Tepes was a Romanian prince born in the 15th century and renowned for his barbaric punishments (Farson, 1997). Indeed, according to Muresan and Smith (1998: 77), 'There are numerous examples of the fusion between Vlad and Dracula in print and on the screen'. The main issues concern the marketing of the supposed location of Dracula's activities in Transylvania, most notably Bran Castle which is the focus of most tourist visits (Plate 7.1). Today the Romanian Ministry of

Plate 7.1 Bran Castle, near Braşov, Romania
Source: The authors (2017).

Tourism includes the Dracula myth in a limited way as part of its campaigns. As Light (2012) explains, the Transylvanian Society of Dracula entered the promotion of Dracula tourism in 1992, first with a private travel agency and since 1994 via 'its own travel arm – the Company of Mysterious Journeys' (Light, 2012: 125). The references to Dracula were generally fairly limited in campaigns such as 'Holidays in Romania' during the 1990s. Muresan and Smith (1998: 79) argue that Bran Castle is presented as a 'significant national heritage attraction', but that 'tourists arriving at Bran are therefore exposed to two contradictory marketing strategies': the state's factual heritage strategy and the Dracula myth as promoted by private companies.

This raises an important issue in the marking of HSLT concerning the lack of coordination in terms of how destinations and sites are presented. It could potentially result in value co-destruction (Neuhofer, 2016), particularly if the messages visitors leave with are confused or distorted, thereby resulting in dissatisfaction. It also emphasises the need for the collaboration, emphasised by Vargo and Lusch (2016) in their 11th foundational premise between, for example, DMOs and other stakeholders involved in co-creation via marketing.

Trends in the Marketing of the Heritage, Screen and Literary Tourism Nexus

If we take these ideas discussed so far into a more contemporary setting of Pine and Gilmore's (1999) notions of the 'experience economy', a service becomes an experience when a particular theme is used, in this context theming a destination. Mossberg (2007) has explored these ideas in the context of literary tourism using the example of Arn's Footsteps in Arnrike, Sweden. This links together a number of sites in West Sweden via a series of books that connect to aspects of medieval history (Mattson & Praesto, 2005). These experiences may be viewed through the concept of the 'experience-scape' which is a space of pleasure, enjoyment and entertainment as well as a meeting ground (O'Dell, 2005). In essence, the HSLT nexus can form significant parts of such spaces, especially in those exceptional spaces as originally identified by Herbert (2001).

Hoppen et al. (2014: 43) have taken these ideas further and set them within a marketing context. In doing so they draw attention to six 'distinct but interrelated marketing strategies'. These are in fact both opportunities and challenges to the marketing of HSLT in all its combinations. We are not going to go through these in detail but rather explore their challenges to marketing within the broader context of the HSLT nexus. There are three key trends that create both challenges and opportunities in terms of marketing responses. The first relates to the development of experiences and collaborative products, which involves understanding the concepts for the experience economy as linked to the HSLT nexus. Hoppen *et al.* (2014), following Herbert (2001), draw attention to the chemistry that links novels or screen characters with particular places in the minds of visitors. In marketing terms, some argue that the way ahead is through 'experiential marketing' (Pine & Gilmore, 1999; Williams, 2006). This is based on the stronger engagement with potential visitors and as such involves a degree of co-creation with the visitor (see Chapter 9 for a fuller discussion). This engagement is increasingly via social media and builds up trust as well as learning about visitor needs (Schmitt, 1999; Scott *et al.*, 2009).

The concepts underlying experiential marketing all fit with the experiences identified by Herbert (2001) and others regarding aspects of literary tourism, creating an experiential value according to Holbrook (2000). The various scales of measurement proposed to examine aspects of experiential values by Schmitt (1999) and Mathwick *et al.* (2001) have been tested within a tourism context by Wang and Lin (2010). Their case study of a TV drama series called *Black and White* is set in Kaohsiung City in Taiwan. They tested out measures of experiential theory from a sample of viewers of the TV drama. They concluded that experiential marketing of a destination (Kaohsiuing City in this case) featuring a TV drama could create a 'deep impression and can be highly charismatic' in terms of their sense of stimulus (Wang & Lin, 2010: 119). They go on to report from their study that 'In the experiential sense of stimulus it has a multiplying effect on the drama and destination marketing' (Wang & Lin, 2010: 120), a point reinforced by Hoppen *et al.* (2014) who highlight the ideas of experiential development in the context of literary tourism. However, there are also important marketing opportunities in other parts of the HSLT nexus.

A second key trend in aspects of literary tourism is the move from niche to mass markets. Hoppen *et al.* (2014) along with others highlight the rise of literary tourism (Mintel, 2011), pointing out that this has moved from a once rather narrow niche market to one that today has mass appeal. This is due largely to the HSLT nexus and the popularisation of many novels via film, TV and the internet. Added to these are the economic links between literary and screen tourism and the fantasy playgrounds of the global theme parks. Case Study 7.1 and the subsequent discussion of the global popularity of the *Harry Potter* novels is an excellent example of this.

The final key trend relates to the importance of collaboration and co-creation, Vargo and Lusch's (2016) 11th foundational premise, within the complexity of marketing the HSLT nexus. The role of various stakeholders is of increasing note; these range from the private to the public sector as well as across a variety of different tasks that need to be managed. These are discussed later in the context of co-creation around the importance of media coverage surrounding the launch of films based on best-selling novels. This is in terms of both popularising the screen-literacy component and the importance of place marketing via DMOs. There are also other dimensions relating to marketing and destination management. Connell (2005) has drawn attention to these issues in the context of TV-induced tourism, arguing for a clear vision by the management of destinations development. This vision needs to bring together local stakeholders so they are supportive of marketing strategies. In Connell's (2005: 772) words, 'dealing with television-induced tourism is a proactive relationship between destination marketing and destination management'.

So far this chapter has discussed, among other issues, the increased importance of creating an experience for tourists as part of an experiential marketing campaign. The links between literature and screen in terms of both heritage and popular culture are well established (see Chapter 1 for a fuller discussion). The examples of novels such as the *Harry Potter* series and their related films are a strong and important example in the UK. The novels by J.K. Rowling about a young boy with magical powers have been turned into a series of extremely successful films. The first was released in 2001 and made US$975m worldwide; following this success, a further eight films have been made grossing in total US$7.7bn. According to Gunelius (2008, cited in Hoppen *et al.*, 2014: 44), the films of the novels have changed 'the landscape dynamics and marketing and branding potential of literary tourism for destinations around the world'. This somewhat large claim is based on the impact both on particular places within the UK where the films were shot and equally importantly through the development of 'The Wizarding World of Harry Potter' at the Universal theme park in Orlando, FL. In effect, the experience is split between each of Universal's two theme parks in Orlando, such is its importance as an attraction. Interestingly, earlier attempts to develop a themed attraction around the Harry Potter stories on the Gold Coast of Australia by Warner Brothers in their Movie World theme park failed and it was removed after two years to Florida. This was due to a lack of marketing, a relatively weak location and an inadequate product in that it was on too small a scale. The overall theme park continues, however, but without Harry Potter (Case Study 7.1).

Case Study 7.1 From children's fiction to a global phenomenon: The making of the Harry Potter brand

Eighteen years after the publication of the first *Harry Potter* book, the author J.K. Rowling broke new ground by announcing that a Harry Potter stage play was to open in London's West End. This presents a further dimension to the Harry Potter brand which has developed at such a rapid rate and which epitomises the HSLT nexus. It has been seen consistently within the marketing literature as the triumph of marketing and the marketing machine that embraces the books and the films

(Brown, 2005; Brown & Patterson 2010). This machine includes the books, the films, theme parks and the Pottermore website which distributes the Harry Potter ebooks. Of course the support for the brand and its development comes from the interest shown by various DMOs and the placing of the stories at specific locations.

The success of the books and films has been seen to be down to a number of key factors relating to marketing and the actual product. The starting point is the stories and the importance of story telling along with the characters. In this context the books and related films fit the ideas discussed in relation to Figure 7.1. The second area of importance is that of marketing and brand development, with Harry Potter being seen as a 'triumph of marketing'. However, as commentators have argued, 'Harry Potter's essential commitment to story telling provides a catalyst to create a swarm of stories that feed the developing brand story' (Simmons, 2005). The marketing machine built around the Harry Potter stories is what we have described as integrated marketing communications, with a strong emphasis on social media. Much of the early social media came from fan blogs as a means of young fans sharing information about the books. Larger corporations such as Warner Bros have attempted to stop these with limited success in a bid to have a more centralised website.

The marketing success has been both used and enhanced by DMOs in the UK, who have produced a number of film location guides. The major contributor in this context has been VisitBritain who have promoted Harry Potter films repeatedly. Key locations related to such film locations include Alnwick Castle in the North of England which was the film location of the exterior of Hogwarts and saw a 120% increase in visitors generating £9n (Olsberg SPI, 2007). The creation of the global brand of Harry Potter has therefore been the culmination of a range of marketing strategies and product developments. These have included the creation of The Wizarding World of Harry Potter theme park which opened in 2010, as a joint venture between Universal and Warner Bros. Other theme parks under the same brand name have been opened in Osaka, Japan in 2014 and in Universal Studios in Hollywood in 2016. These capture the essence of the stories, films and the places in a hyper-reality world which, together with the various related computer games, sustain and enlarge the brand.

In summary, the place marketing by DMOs has in some way contributed to the marketing of Harry Potter, but has in turn benefited much more by the creation of a global brand. This is now sustained by a complex marketing machine that uses every possible means of sustaining the brand.

Increasingly, place marketing strategies within the UK are being designed to widen the appeal and reach of the films, helping to create a mass appeal but more importantly to brand certain destinations. This shows clearly how various stakeholders help co-create a marketing strategy to enable this branding. As Case Study 7.2 shows, there were a number of such stakeholders involved including the South West Film Commission who gave assistance in the development of film locations, as did the London Film Commission, while the British Tourist Authority (which became VisitBritain in 2003) launched an international tourism campaign jointly with Warner Bros. This was under the brand 'Discovering the Magic of Britain' which highlighted 32 Harry Potter locations and linked sites on a Movie Map, both in hard copy and on a website (Olsberg SPI, 2007). In addition, Warner Brothers have established their own tours of their London studios, marketed through their website. Moreover, there was a high degree of PR via the media and press coverage both online and offline.

While the growth and dynamics of Harry Potter is in some ways exceptional, the marketing strategies discussed above and within the case study are now a blueprint for many other campaigns. The HSLT nexus exerts a strong power over destination marketing in a number of complex interactions. Table 7.2 shows examples of these marketing strategies along with some of the key elements that have made these particular cases successful. As can be seen, these are a range of different elements of the HSLT nexus. For example, there is a mixture of film and TV, along with the basis of literary underpinnings both from predominantly contemporary writers such as J.K. Rowling (*Harry Potter*) and Dan Brown (*The Da Vinci Code*) and the classic novel *Pride and Prejudice* written by Jane Austen. In the case of the latter this was an example of rebranding and, as discussed, in a slightly different context of the same general destination. O'Connor *et al.* (2010) have explored the notion of developing a re-imaging management strategy based on screen tourism (Case Study 7.2).

There are also significant stages in the marketing strategies of screen tourism as identified in an empirical study by Hudson and Ritchie (2006a). They uncovered two main stages in the destination marketing model of screen tourism. Stage 1 concerns the period before the film or TV series is released. At this time some DMOs such as VisitBritain, which actively engage with the film companies, start promoting the destination actually during the making of the film. Canada and the Bahamas have also identified screen tourism as a major marketing opportunity, and in doing so employ global public relations companies to get maximum exposure for their destinations. Typical of the film location promotion companies that aid DMOs is Pegasus, based in Iceland, helping to make the country a major location for screen tourism. This has been boosted by parts of *Game of Thrones*, HBO's popular series filmed partly in Iceland; the past decade has seen a rapid growth of screen tourism. The Icelandic government has, since 1999, offered major financial inducements in the form of a reimbursement of 20%. The country is now a major global player with a range of film locations that have formed part of a new screen tourism product (Amey, 2015). DMOs sometimes develop marketing material in advance of the release of the film – increasingly using websites and social media. This is typical of the activities of VisitBritain as a DMO who tend to use multimedia outlets to promote screen tourism, with increased press coverage and via the use of their own website.

Case Study 7.2 Rebranding using Jane Austen's *Pride and Prejudice*

Jane Austen's most popular novel published in 1813 was made into a new film in 2005 with the actress Keira Knightley taking the lead female role in this romantic film. The film's directors deliberately decided to present an earlier view of the period rather than a perfectly sanitised one of Regency England. This contrasted with previous film versions and was directed in large part at a younger market segment. It attempted to create a more realistic view of the period, making it more commercial than previous versions (Cartmell, 2013).

The locations used for the film ranged over parts of the East Midlands (Lincolnshire, Derbyshire including the Peak District). Co-creation took place between EM-Media working with the film company Universal Films, East Midland Tourism (DMO), VisitLincolnshire (DMO) and Derbyshire (DMex) and the Peak Destination Management Partnerships. All of these organisations worked together to produce the destination marketing campaign. This was focused on a rebranding exercise with the areas involved being rebranded as 'Pride and Prejudice Country'. This was also supported by VisitBritain (DMO). The rebranding was linked to the creation of short break promotions to see 'in the real life the movie set'; these were linked to the official Pride and Prejudice website. Other organisations also marketed the rebrand via its website and promoted the various film locations (Plate 7.2).

The website has the facility to download the movie map of the film locations. According to O'Connor and Pratt (2008: 6), 'the movie map provides a tangible marketing tool that potential visitors can use to plan their trip itinerary'. Other related marketing activities including independent tour companies starting Pride and Prejudice tours, while the National Trust have highlighted their properties used in the film. Finally, there are literary walks developed, for example, by Kent Libraries and Archives entitled 'Jane Austen and Tonbridge'. O'Connor and Pratt

Plate 7.2 Chatsworth House, Derbyshire, UK. This was used as both exterior and interior locations of Pemberley for the 2005 film, *Pride and Prejudice*
Source: The authors (2017).

(2008) detail the survey work undertaken to explore the value of the marketing efforts of various DMOs. The survey of 1500 respondents examined the reaction and decision making of potential visitors. Table 7.4 shows those stating possible intentions to visit the film location destinations in terms of the influence of the marketing formats.

One of the significant findings surrounding this case study is the survey work undertaken by a consortium of DMOs (Lincolnshire Tourism, Visit Peak District and Derbyshire), all of whom had film locations used in the making of the 2005 film. These DMOs developed a marketing campaign across both domestic and international markets which was financed by East Midland Tourism. This was a multifaceted campaign involving TV features on the locational settings of the film plus press and radio coverage, all at different stages, i.e. before, during

Table 7.4 The potential influence of differing marketing components on visitor intentions

Respondents' intentions to visit	Film	Movie map	Website	Press, TV, radio
Definitely	51.9	38.0	25.7	8.5
Probably	15.0	31.3	28.3	26.2
Possibly	23.8	23.3	25.7	34.0
Not at all	8.8	4.3	17.7	23.4
Don't know	0.5	3.1	2.6	7.8
	100.0	100.0	100.0	100.0

Source: Modified from O'Connor and Pratt (2008).

and after the film. Some 90 journalists from the UK and abroad visited the various film locations, all adding to the publicity (O'Connor & Pratt, 2008). The DMOs rebranded around the film and a new website www. prideandprejudice.com was established, providing a means of online booking and short break packages.

Of course in many cases the influence of the marketing components is cumulative in that, having seen the film, people went on to visit the website and download the movie map. However, the survey suggests the large influence of the movie map in that 83% of the visitors influenced by the movie map went on to visit one of the film locations compared with 53% of those not influenced by the movie map.

There was clearly a commonality of marketing initiatives, including a high degree of joint marketing with the public sector – usually DMOs such as regional and national tourist organisations. The development of guides, movie maps and the very strong use of online activities via websites, along with the increased use of social media were employed to rebrand the destination. In addition, there was a big push to generate substantial PR through all kinds of media after the release of the film.

During the second phase after the release of a film, DMOs again play a significant role in that they usually step up their promotional activities. In the case of the Harry Potter movies, VisitBritain collaborated on producing movie maps (Case Study 7.1). Grihault (2003) has examined a number of such DMO activities, including the Tourism Authority of Thailand which promoted related destinations and attractions during the release of *The Beach*, and included joint marketing activities with 20th Century Fox to promote Thai beaches. The DMO also paid for UK travel writers and travel agents to embark on familiarisation trips, along with awareness campaigns. Increasingly, the internet and social media are being used as major marketing tools for screen tourism by DMOs given their global reach. The study by Hudson and Ritchie (2006a) showed that the most significant successful activity in the first phase is proactively targeting filmmakers, usually by employing a global PR firm to promote destinations to the film companies. Within the second stage, joint promotional activities is the key activity, producing interest in the destination that links with the film.

The changing relationships between DMOs and screen tourism obviously vary across the different stages of the production cycle. As Figure 7.2 shows, there are three areas of interlinking activities, namely the creative and financing aspects starting with the idea/creative input and secondly the physical development process including the selection of screen locations. The third area concerns collaboration between the film and activities of key DMOs, as

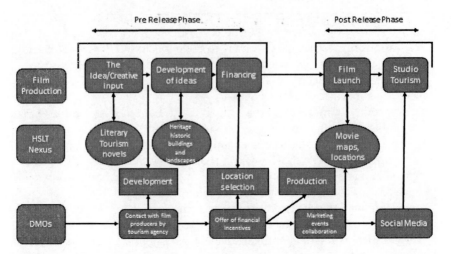

Figure 7.2 Phases in the creation and marketing of the heritage, screen and literary tourism nexus
Source: The authors (2017).

has just been discussed. All of these may be viewed in terms of production and marketing issues either in pre- or post-release, as examined by Hudson and Ritchie (2006a). Furthermore, in terms of the HSLT nexus itself, linkages extend to literary inputs in the creative/ideas stage and also via heritage aspects, depending on the storyline, to historic sites and landscapes. Again in the marketing stage these become more significant for the DMO.

The increasing synergy between screen and place marketing has led the UK Screen Tourism Strategy Group to recommend the development of a toolkit for intervention in order to give advice on how to maximise 'the tourism benefit of a film or television programme' (Olsberg SPI, 2007: 38). This in part follows the establishment by the UK Film Council of a Research and Statistics Unit (Steele, 2004). In addition, the report produced for the UK Film Council by Olsberg SPI from which these ideas are drawn has made a range of recommendations that are aimed at improving best practice relating to tourism marketing, which embraces many aspects of HSLT (Table 7.5).

Table 7.5 Key marketing aspects relating to screen tourism and destinations

---
- Identifying specific markets for screen tourism marketing campaigns
- Creating national screen tourism campaigns
- Organising events on screen tourism to raise awareness and help develop co-creation with stakeholders' public-private sector efforts
- Identifying the most effective screen products
- Creating a regular series of events to maximise PR

Source: Modified from Olsberg SPI (2007).

The Role of Co-creation in the Heritage, Screen and Literary Tourism Nexus and Marketing Process

One of the critical lessons relating to the marketing around HSLT is the important role of co-creation between various stakeholders. This is due to the need to create substantial media coverage as well as to use some stakeholders to direct marketing messages to potential visitors. In many destinations where there is a large screen industry such as New York State, there is strong evidence of a clustering effect of organisations producing the films and TV programmes and tourism industries (Camoin Associates, 2015; Mitchell & Stewart, 2012). A good example of joint marketing around both a novel and related film is that based on Tolkien's book *The Hobbit*. In this case Tourism New Zealand, a DMO, and Air New Zealand signed an agreement in 2014 to undertake joint marketing activity for one year to promote holiday travel in key international markets with each partner investing $10m. They have agreed to extend the partnership to market to Singapore to support New Zealand's alliance with Singapore Airlines. The exercise has produced a rise in visitor numbers, creating a successful marketing campaign. As Chris Luxon, Air New Zealand CEO claimed, 'Working together to capitalise on this momentum is a natural progression that will positively impact on New Zealand's tourism industry and is a wonderful example of collaboration' (Marketing, Advertising & Media Intelligence, 2016: 1).

The marketing of the HSLT nexus needs therefore a strong degree of co-creation with a series of particular elements that help link together the key elements of literary and screen tourism. These include a strong narrative from a novel that is story and character driven. In the three examples shown in Table 7.2 this is obviously the case. As argued elsewhere, aspects of heritage and notions of authenticity are more fluid, following the ideas highlighted by Wang (1999), who identified three types of authenticity (see Chapter 6). Within the marketing context these issues are overcome by the development of a high-visibility brand and the role of place within the story which in turn is highlighted by the film locations. Hoppen *et al.* (2014: 45) extend this further in terms of destination branding by arguing that generating an interest and consequently leading to the decision to visit requires a 'more embedded approach with longer term benefits to be derived from deeper and experiential engagement'. In the next section, the increased use of social media and its contribution to this experiential push is considered. A final important element in the context of literary and screen tourism marketing is the addition of relevant locations. These are often historic buildings and historic settings in the case of Harry Potter and *Pride and Prejudice*, often connected by beautiful landscapes. Finally, these literary and film elements have scenes, either real or fictional, with 'place' playing a key role. In experiential terms the lead characters are set within such places and have varying experiences that capture the viewer's interests.

Integrated marketing communications and the heritage, screen and literary tourism nexus in the era of social media

The experiential nature of tourism has been increasingly encouraged and supported by social media. This has been a major turning point for many DMOs and their marketing campaigns, including the way in which the HSLT nexus is being marketed. In specific terms, DMOs are turning to the use of integrated marketing communications (IMC) using social media, leading to what Mangold and Faulds (2009: 357) term a 'new hybrid element of the promotion mix'. In essence, this approach attempts to coordinate the components of the promotional mix in order to develop a unified customer-focused message. IMC in a practical sense uses a range of communication tools including the use of social media and electronic word-of-mouth (eWOM) to achieve its goals (Pike, 2004). Wang *et al.* (2010) have applied IMC to heritage tourism in Taiwan and concluded that the approach was able to create strong brand awareness and 'sharpen the image of heritage destinations' (Wang *et al.*, 2010: 228).

The significance of the promotional mix is made more telling in the marketing of the HSLT nexus through both the importance of social media and the role played by DMOs in the process. In terms of the former, the 'leverage of eWOM is critical to understand what motivates travellers to participate in online communities' (Lange-Faria & Elliot, 2012: 199). User-generated content (UGC) is also at the heart of such information sharing and is becoming the primary vehicle for visitors from the point of view of tourism products and destinations (Gretzel *et al.*, 2008). Of course, the use of social media and eWOM are both significant and varied. These include Facebook, Twitter, Flickr, MySpace, Instagram and blogs, for example. The complexity and interconnectivity of different social media places new pressures on the management of DMOs and those marketing HSLT tourism products. In this context, marketing organisations face a continuous stream of new challenges, as identified by Felix *et al.* (2016) in their study of 43 social media marketing organisations, only two of which involved tourism, however.

Evidence suggests that currently blogs are one of the most frequently used forms of UGC as utilised by DMOs (Kaplan & Haenlein, 2010; Lange-Faria & Elliot, 2012). Blogs can be viewed as important in marketing the HSLT nexus in a number of ways: first, as a way of helping to market and brand a destination, since they act as a means of telling a story. In this context Tussyadiah and Fensenmaier (2008) report on the activities of the Pennsylvania Tourist Office website and its blog section entitled 'Roadtrippers'. The DMO offers visitors the opportunity to share their experiences of the state on what appears to be an open platform. However, in reality it is carefully managed by the tourist office which selects and moderates stories. This highlights some key marketing aspects that are relevant to destination marketing as shown in Table 7.6. The importance of travel blogs is therefore a significant marketing tool, particularly given the evidence of digital story telling in

Table 7.6 Key marketing elements relating to destination marketing organisation blogs

Development of tourist identities through different travel genres: A type of customisation of eWOM where the different blog narratives are delivered to different market segments. This is achieved by using blogs created by different types of visitors. In this way the reader of the blog is led into believing they may experience the same experience as the person who narrated the blog.
Introduce an interesting narrative by presenting multiple characters: Developing an interesting narrative in that containing different characters helps create a sense of realness and can lead to some degree of empathy. This in turn may strengthen the desire to visit the area, which Escalas and Stern (2003) term the 'ad attitude'.
Encourage the discussion of travel/movement as a product characterisation: The trips highlighted in the blog narratives are used to place emphasis on movements and visitor activities. This is done to help strengthen the blog's power to communicate the sense of travel

Source: Modified from Tussyadiah and Fesenmaier (2008)

tourist blogs, since they offer the potential visitor an opportunity to 'immerse themselves in the writer's experience' (Pudliner, 2007: 57). Volo (2010) goes much further in examining the ways in which blogs influence decision making and visitor intentions. Increasingly, DMOs are fostering travel blogs in an attempt to strengthen and in one sense manage the flow of eWOM information, as the case of Pennsylvania demonstrates.

A second way in which blogs are important in destination marketing is in the role they play in destination branding (Woodside *et al.*, 2007). According to a number of authors, 'one of the most important roles of brand image is its impact on the tourism decision-making process' (O'Connor *et al.*, 2010: 62; Woodside & Lysonski, 1989). Others go further, stating that 'The tourist has taken the driving seat in brand identity' (Oliveira & Panyik, 2015: 54), given the increased significance of social media platforms in spreading narratives and experiences about a particular destination. If we add to this the power of the HSLT nexus to help brand and rebrand destinations, then this provides a new dimension. For example, travel blogs can be used to highlight the links with a particular film location or a particular author. This is clearly evident in the marketing and branding activities by the Shakespeare Birthplace Trust between 2011 and 2015 in collaboration with a range of other key partners as shown in Case Study 7.3, which highlights the increasing importance of social media.

The rising trend of social media usage is highlighted by the fact that there were almost 2.8 billion social media accounts globally in 2015, of which at least 1.7 billion were active (European Digital Landscape, 2014, cited in Oliveira & Panyik, 2015), with Facebook dominating and Instagram growing rapidly. The importance of various social media appears to vary at different

Table 7.7 Social media platforms and holiday decision processes for international visitors to the UK

Social media	Deciding to visit UK (%)	Planning what to do (%)	Choosing what to do on the trip (%)	Sharing holiday experiences on return home (%)
Facebook	44	43	40	41
YouTube	34	35	23	18
Twitter	15	18	21	16
Instagram	12	15	10	13
Google+	19	21	17	16

Source: VisitBritain (2015: 4).

stages of the holiday decision-making process. While Facebook is the most significant across a range of different stages as shown in Table 7.7, beyond this Twitter seems to be more influential for suggestions/advice when visitors are actually on holiday. The other interesting aspect is that respondents within this particular study all indicated that they had used social media at every stage of their holiday. However, the early planning phase – which in marketing terms is 'inspirational' in the key decision to visit a particular destination, in this case the UK – is notably significant. Furthermore, it is equally important in, for example, visiting a DMO-based heritage tourism product. Thus the complexity of social media impacts on the branding strategies of DMOs with a number of key ones such as those for Tourism Australia and VisitSweden adopting new approaches. The latter, as Christensen (2013) points out, developed an innovative Twitter campaign aimed at improving its brand. This was achieved by the use of a different person every week to Tweet their feelings about various activities. There is increasing evidence that many DMOs are starting to make use of professional bloggers in their attempts to use social media to help in their branding exercise. The continual rise of Instagram is also being used with so-called professional 'influencers'. In this approach DMOs recruit and pay for these people and in many instances use them to blog their activities within the destination to would-be visitors.

Case Study 7.3 Social media and the marketing of Shakespeare's birthplace: Literary place marketing

Stratford-upon-Avon, Shakespeare's birthplace, is an international literary place which receives around 5 million visitors annually. The Shakespeare Birthplace Trust which runs the paid visitor centre has a development plan that sees visitor numbers reaching 1 million by 2018 (McGuckin, 2015). Paid visitor numbers recorded in 2014, however, show just under 403,000 visitors (VisitEngland, 2015). A larger group of attractions make up the key literary and heritage product, namely: Shakespeare's House and Gardens which the figure from VisitEngland refers to, Education and Learning, Collections, and Campaigns and Outreach. The major changes involve the development of a specific DMO as 'Shakespeare's England'. This is a collaboration between public and private sector partners and is visualised in the Warwickshire Visitor Economy Framework 2013–2018 (Warwickshire Tourism, 2012) as the main marketing organisation. This is detailed in a later destination management plan for the region (Shakespeare's England, 2015).

As part of this new strategy and the new DMO, there is increased recognition of the role played by digital marketing and social media. There are a number of strands to this, including an integrated digital 'content ecosystem' involving 'The Shakespeare Blog' (Plate 7.3). The Shakespeare Trust is currently taking the lead in terms of digital media operating via Facebook, Twitter, YouTube and Flickr, the latter currently

The Shakespeare blog

Shakespeare's Stratford-upon-Avon app

A new walking guide to Stratford-upon Avon for smartphones has just been launched by the author of The Shakespeare blog.

Shakespeare's Stratford-upon-Avon has been developed in collaboration with the Hungarian company Pocket Guide which creates walking guide apps for cities around the world.

By linking stories about real people and places with quotations from the plays it shows how Shakespeare brought his memories of the town and the Warwickshire countryside into his work. It also shows how he is commemorated in Stratford.

Once you've downloaded the app you make your way to the start of the walk and my voice guides you round the town.

It's a really convenient way of finding out about Shakespeare's Stratford for those who don't have time for a town tour, or indeed for people who can't visit the town at all but are interested in its Shakespeare connections. The app uses the phone's GPS system so you don't have to keep stopping to read a guide book or consult a map, though the onscreen map always shows you where you are, and the commentary can also be

Subscribe to the blog
Enter your email address and get the blog sent to you

Subscribe Delivered by Feed-Burner

Search the site

Search

Latest posts
- Finding Shakespeare in the tropics
- Welcome to Shakespeare Conferences 2016
- Shakespeare memories from the Bush
- Shakespeare in Miniature
- Shakespeare in Sydney 2

Categories
- Legacy (341)
- Plays and Poems (164)
- Shakespeare on Stage (248)
- Shakespeare's World (283)
- Sources (76)
- Stratford-upon-Avon (249)
- Uncategorized (16)

Recent comments
- C L Couch on Shakespeare in Sydney 2
- Jan on Shakespeare in Sydney 2
- Ann McDermott on Shakespeare

Plate 7.3 The Shakespeare blog advertising the new pocket guide and the related app

having only a limited number of followers. The Trust developed its first iPhone app in 2012 called 'Eye Shakespeare'. There is also a further pocket guide app – 'Shakespeare's Stratford-upon-Avon' developed as a walking guide in collaboration with a Hungarian publishing company.

The new DMO, Shakespeare's England, is tasked with drawing together the activities of the Shakespeare Company and other DMOs within the region to develop a coordinated tourism marketing campaign around literary and heritage products (Plate 7.4). In doing so, there is recognition of the importance of increasing the skillset in digital marketing aimed at businesses within the region to help create an online presence. This is designed to improve the total marketing of the literary place and its various tourism assets.

Plate 7.4 The organisations collaborating in the new marketing strategy and destination management plan for Stratford-upon-Avon

The complexity of digital marketing has led many DMOs to use a variety of eWOM strategies to attract the attention of potential visitors. These so-called 'content ecosystems' involve linking together a range of 'influencers' via Instagram, together with blog sites and YouTube pages, along with Twitter (see, for example, Mistilis *et al.*, 2014). More specifically, Buhalis and Amaranggana (2014) examine these ideas within the context of 'smart tourism destinations', involving interconnecting stakeholders via a digital platform with multiple touch points accessed 'through a variety of end-user devices' (Buhalis & Amaranggana, 2014: 557). These end-users are also connected to a range of different digital contents promoting the destination. The use of such 'content ecosystems' within destination marketing has been examined by Oliveira and Panyik (2015) in the context of Portugal, where they examined the contents of 20 digital articles. These involved a range of different contents including some relating to aspects of heritage, namely a UNESCO rock art World Heritage Site in Porto, which was using Twitter and Instagram, and built heritage sites (palaces and cathedrals) based on blogs that were open to comments. In a more detailed study of Florence, Bellini and Pasquinelli (2015: 13) demonstrate the importance of selling a cultural heritage experience based on what they call an 'urban value ecosystem'. Here the emphasis is on fashion brands, as for example in the history of high-end fashion heritage at the Gucci Museum.

For the blog to be effective as a marketing tool for destination branding around the HSLT nexus it needs to have novelty of content, reliability and understandability and to be of interest (Chen *et al.*, 2014). From the perspective of the DMO, in addition to those elements noted in Table 7.8, there is a need to identify the most influential bloggers with an ability to reach a wide audience, along with those who can target specific market segments (Prats & Marin, 2012).

Within the overall context of marketing the HSLT nexus either via DMOs or more specifically as individual tourism products by private sector businesses, social media marketing provides a range of opportunities. These

Table 7.8 Advantages of social media as a marketing tool

- Allows one-to-one contact
- Supports personal virtual interactions between visitor and the DMO
- Is accessible 24:7 as a virtual source
- Is dynamic as changes to information can be made quickly
- Can provide access to multimedia documents
- Provides potential to reduce marketing costs
- Provides considerable information for potential data mining and analysis on market trends and personal opinion

---

Source: Adapted from Olsberg SPI (2007).

include those of building relationships with customers, communities and various stakeholders, which Felix *et al.* (2016) see as 'explorer' organisations. Alternatively, those organisations which merely use social media as just another communication channel with which to provide information to potential customers are viewed as so-called 'defender' organisations. In the latter case, these 'defender' types fail to build strong relationships with customers and as such do not develop any meaningful strategies of relationship marketing (Payne & Frow, 2005).

The concept of relationship marketing (RM) was introduced by Berry (1983: 25), and defined as 'attracting, maintaining, and in multiservice organisations – enhancing customer relationships'. Early use of RM within tourism came with simple loyalty schemes initially used by airlines and slightly later by hotels in an attempt to build basic relationships with customers (Gummesson, 1994). In a broader context, Fyall *et al.* (2005) argued that RM remained a somewhat untested concept in terms of destination marketing. However, they do identify both the need and the difficulties of deploying an RM strategy by DMOs.

This complexity is also relevant in part to the marketing of HSLT with its strong ties with place marketing. There are a number of key aspects that make RM a potentially important concept in the HSLT nexus. These include the increasing importance of eWOM on visitor decision making and therefore its influence on marketers. For example, PhoCusWright (2010, cited in Lexhagen *et al.*, 2013) claimed 'travellers' reviews, photos, trip planning and sharing and blogging' all influence how visitors make decisions. Others go much further and see social media as empowering consumers, leading to a further stage of customer RM which they term consumer-centric marketing (Niininen *et al.*, 2007). This has led to an increased use of blogs, etc. by DMOs, as has already been discussed. At the heart of these ideas is the notion of building strong relationships and getting the potential visitor to identify with the destination. From this point of view, there is also increasing emphasis being placed on co-creating an experience via the HSLT nexus. This goes beyond RM and into the theory developed by Vargo and Lusch (2006) of service-dominant logic. As Li and Petrick (2008) explain, this concept builds on ideas of customer-centric marketing by essentially co-creating products and experiences with consumers. Increasingly it is social media that is acting as a touch point for co-creating experiences.

This section of the chapter has highlighted the key aspects of social media impacting on DMOs and the HSLT nexus. The first aspect we examined was the role blogs are helping to play in marketing a destination, the second being the role they play in aspects of branding. A third key aspect must also be considered, as identified by Lange-Faria and Elliot (2012), which concerns the usefulness of social media in monitoring visitor attitudes as a means of informing DMOs and their links with the HSLT nexus on their marketing strategies. Given the emotional links with, say, literary and screen tourism, social media can provide good intelligence on the meaning various places hold for certain visitors. As we have seen, stories and travel blogs 'have the unique ability to show how visitors live out the stories that the destinations evoke for them' (Lange-Faria & Elliot, 2012: 200). However, such sources also provide considerable amounts of information in the form of UGC to marketers, prompting the increased use of web data analysis tools and the use of data mining. Olmeda and Sheldon (2002) stress the importance of such data mining techniques and point to the basic advantages of the internet over traditional marketing media as shown in Table 7.7. Finally, as we have seen in this chapter, the marketing of the HSLT nexus is a critical area for many DMOs but as well as being an area providing many marketing opportunities it is also one full of challenges.

Conclusion

This chapter has explored the marketing of the HSLT nexus, drawing on the frameworks of S-DL and co-creation. It discusses the significant links between the components of the HSLT nexus, experiential marketing and the theming, branding and place marketing of sites and destinations. In this context, Figure 7.2 attempts to show the phases along with the relationships between film production and other aspects of the HSLT nexus. In addition, it highlights the changing nature of the HSLT market alongside the growing importance of the so-called integrated marketing systems that have developed in response to the need to accommodate co-creation.

In essence, co-creation has converted the market into a forum in which the design of experiences and value co-creation occurs through dialogue among consumers, businesses, consumer communities and networks of businesses (Prahalad & Ramaswamy, 2004). Tourists now regularly use social media and other networking applications to connect and share experiences and to engage and co-create experiences with an array of actors (Kim & Tussyadiah, 2013; McCabe et al., 2012). Within the context of HSLT and marketing, sites and destinations must be customer centric and interactional, as Vargo and Lusch (2008) contend in their eighth foundational premise. More importantly, however, what this chapter has demonstrated, as Vargo and Lusch (2016) suggest in their ninth and 11th foundational premises (Table 1.7), is the need for marketing to be undertaken by networks of organisations and businesses who must all collaborate and coordinate their activities if a strong, clear brand and/or theme is be projected (see Figure 7.3).

HSLT marketing activities are now increasingly led by DMOs, particularly across the screen and literary tourism divide. The significance of HSLT has been a factor in the way that destinations position and market themselves. Furthermore, the importance of eWOM marketing via blogs, Twitter and Instagram has taken on a central role in the activities of DMOs – a trend

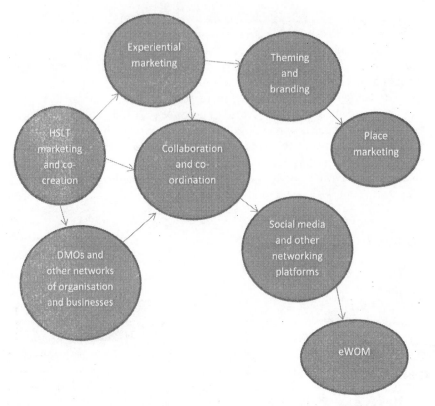

Figure 7.3 Dimensions of heritage, screen and literary tourism marketing and co-creation
Source: The authors (2017).

which serves to reinforce Neuhofer's (2016: 6) view that, in the age of co-creation, technology must be 'considered as an operant resource that needs to be contextually meaningful to provide consumers with tools to integrate and co-create their own value in context and use'.

However, the use and monitoring of UGC has brought extra pressures on many DMOs, which have had to change their marketing strategies. Those that have been innovative in the use of social media have made greater impact and better use of the marketing of HSLT products. Collaboration, coordination, the careful story telling by some DMOs and the management of blogs has been a significant strategy so as to avoid the projection of confused, erroneous or distorted messages that may result in visitor dissatisfaction or value co-destruction. Ensuring that resources create instead of destroy value is a theme that forms a large part of the next chapter which focuses on the management of HSLT sites and destinations, especially those that are susceptible to over-consumption.

8 Visitor Management for Heritage, Screen and Literary Tourism

Introduction

The popularity of HSLT has been discussed in Chapters 1 and 2 and, like other destinations and market segments, these environments experience positive and negative economic, sociocultural and environmental impacts which need to be managed (see Chapter 4). Thus, value co-creation and value co-destruction may occur in the tourist experience. Visitation in particular can bring unbearable pressure on a destination and its community, and given that the appreciation and enjoyment of such places is the outcome of the value that is created and extracted, minimising any negative effects is a major management issue. However, visitor management is much more than ameliorating the negative impacts of visitor pressure. This is because the provision of a high-quality experience can encourage visitors to be more respectful. Indeed, Timothy and Boyd (2003) go as far as to contend that high-quality experiences which satisfy visitor expectations, motivations and needs encourage more responsible and sensitive behaviour, thereby enabling the resources visited to be conserved and/or preserved.

Consequently, by far the biggest challenge for those HSLT sites and/or destinations which are fortunate enough to experience an excess of demand is to ensure that all visitors have a high-quality experience and leave the destination unimpaired for others. This requires the promulgation of sustainable forms of tourism which in turn is contingent on effective visitor management. This chapter therefore, within the contexts of the S-DL and co-creation frameworks, discusses the meaning and importance of visitor management and examines the utility of existing visitor management procedures and frameworks. Specific management tools and techniques are detailed and in particular the challenges facing World Heritage Sites (WHSs) are considered. The chapter ends with a summary and some concluding statements.

Visitor Management

Visitor management may be defined as an administrative management action, oriented toward maximising the quality of the visitor experience while also assisting with the achievement of the site's overall objectives, most notably the maintenance of the quality of its resources (Candrea & Ispas, 2009; Hall & McArthur, 1998). Initially developed in the context of national parks and protected areas, it is a concept that focused solely on the resource to counter overuse by growing numbers of tourists. More recently, however, a key part of visitor management involves ensuring the provision of quality experiences. This development is perhaps an indication of increasing awareness of the benefits that tourism brings to many HSLT sites and destinations (see Chapter 4), particularly for conservation, along with a recognition that tourists engage in value creation during their visits which subsequently results in varying degrees of satisfaction.

Given this dual role, visitor management requires detailed quantitative and qualitative knowledge of visitor numbers and activities undertaken at a site and/or destination as well as accurate information on visitors' needs and wishes. Several direct and indirect methods may be used to gather visitor number data. Directly, simply keeping a count of the number of visitors at a site at predetermined points during the day is the most effective method. This may be done manually or electronically with digital or video cameras, but is dependent on the site being relatively self-contained and having a limited number of entry points. In situations where visitor numbers are less easily able to be monitored, indirect methods may be more appropriate. While such methods do not provide accurate figures, they do provide a crude indication of visitor numbers. These may include the use of self-registration documents such as guest books, fishing licences, permits or the number of vehicles in car parks. Observation is another method that may be used involving the identification of signs of use and/or wear and tear. With regard to visitors' needs and wishes, while being time consuming and costly, the best way to collect this information is through face-to-face interviews or questionnaires.

The diversity of HSLT sites and destinations means that visitor management is highly dependent on the context in which it occurs, as this can affect levels of demand. Those that are close to major cities or neighbour to a well-developed tourism destination are naturally going to attract more visitors. Context can also influence the manifestation of visitor pressure and value co-creation or co-destruction, particularly where there is a certain degree of specialisation, a contention encompassed in Vargo and Lusch's (2008) fifth foundational premise (all economies are service economies). In tourist historic cities for example, the main consideration is concentration of visitors in specific areas at certain times or, in other words, their carrying capacity. This is captured by Orbasli (2000: 164), who states that 'while a narrow medieval street may have the physical capacity to accommodate a given number of persons, the valued image and context of a medieval quarter are lost once it is overcrowded'. In contrast, a natural area might have the physical space to accommodate large numbers of visitors, but due to its ecological fragility even visitation by a small number of tourists may result in environmental degradation. Clearly, visitor management is not a straightforward task, made even more difficult by a number of challenges which arise within HSLT destinations.

Challenges of Visitor Management

The twin demands of balancing conservation and commercial success and ensuring value creation as opposed to value destruction with visitor and community needs is one particular challenge which many HSLT sites and destinations experience (see Chapter 4; Case Study 8.1). While resources must be protected and conserved, the livelihoods of those who depend on tourism must not be compromised. This specific management dilemma is complicated by the added difficulty of channelling tourism income into visitor management and conservation as well as coordinating tourism promotion which is often undertaken as a separate activity (Timothy & Boyd, 2003). Moreover, while visitor data are critical to effective management decision making, they are often not collected as it is costly and time consuming to do so.

Additionally, managing the complex array of demands posed by different user groups, be they residents, businesses or tourists, is extremely problematic. Inevitably there are conflicts of interest, especially as not everyone gains equally from tourism, combined with the fact that there are often present a diverse range of organisations with an interest in and responsibility for the operation of a site or destination. These might include local and central government departments and agencies, commercial interest groups such as hotelier associations, retailer groups, chambers of commerce, public-private organisations, voluntary sector organisations such as civic societies, resident associations and environmental groups, with each having different remits and operating on a separate basis. Given the involvement of these multiple parties, and in order to ensure that a balance of all needs including those of the tourist and the resource is achieved, as Vargo and Lusch (2008) suggest in their ninth (all social and economic actors are resource integrators) and 11th (collaboration and coordination) foundational premises, co-creation requires the participation, collaboration and coordination of networks of organisations and businesses constituting the service exchange. It is with this in mind that a number of visitor management processes and frameworks have been developed.

Case Study 8.1 Visitor management in Venice, Italy

Venice is a city located on a group of 118 small islands linked by canals and bridges on the Venetian Lagoon in northeast Italy. It is a UNESCO World Heritage Site and is renowned for its beautiful cityscape, architecture and rich musical and artistic heritage, with tourists in particular coming to see St Mark's Basilica, St Mark's Square and the Grand Canal. More recently, it has become a major centre for international conferences and festivals, notably the prestigious Venice Film Festival which attracts visitors from all over the world (UNESCO, 2012). On average, 60,000 tourists visit Venice each day, more than the entire population of the city, and in 2015 it was ranked 29th in the world's most popular city destinations with 5159.6 million international arrivals in 2013 (Euromonitor International, 2015). The city also relies heavily on the cruise business. Over the past 15 years there has been a 439% increase in cruise dockings. The Cruise Venice Committee has estimated that cruise ship passengers spend more than €150m (US$193m) annually in the city (Mack, 2012).

However, Venice's popularity as a major worldwide tourist destination is under threat due the devastating negative impacts of mass tourism which are being experienced, including pollution, gentrification, congestion and overcrowding (UNESCO, 2012). The immense visitor pressure which the city is subject to is perhaps the most notable unsustainable problem facilitated by the availability of low-cost flights and a range of hotel options. Moreover, literacy and cultural awareness are growing, as is the US population and incomes in India, China and Eastern Europe. As a result, the number of people who want to see Venice and can afford to do so might expand significantly over the next few decades. Consequently, overcrowding is a regular occurrence and the city is sinking due to the sheer weight of tourists, making it more vulnerable than ever to climate change induced flooding (see Plates 8.1 and 8.2).

During ten days of the year, over 100,000 visitors converge on the city daily (UNESCO, 2012), impairing the quality of the experience for both residents and tourists alike, with a peak of 200,000 daily visitors on special occasions. Many are low-spend, low-yield day visitors who come to soak up the city's cultural beauty and atmosphere (UNESCO, 2012), and only a small fraction of whom visit one or more cultural attractions such as museums or art exhibitions. According to UNESCO (2012), for two-thirds of the year the number of visitors easily surpasses the social-economic carrying capacity of the city.

Venice is clearly in need of a management strategy which addresses visitor pressure so that as many visitors as possible are able to construct

Plate 8.1 A flooded St Mark's Square, Venice
Source: The authors (2017).

Plate 8.2 Flooding in St Mark's Square, Venice
Source: The authors (2017).

their own personal experience (Kay, 2009), and which also considers the wellbeing of the local community. Day visitors, who constitute the vast majority of total visitors to Venice, pose a particular problem because they do not use any central services and consequently bring little benefit to the city. Furthermore, their arrival is not predictable and is therefore very difficult to manage. To address this issue, the new Special Law for Venice (under preparation) introduces a new tax for visitors. Authorities are considering a new tax for each night visitors spend in a hotel. Such a tax system, however, may prove to be counterproductive as it would discourage visitors from staying in Venice and exploring the city over several days.

A particular issue in managing visitor pressure is accommodating the seasonal nature of visitor flows to Venice. Currently attempts are underway to make Venice more attractive during non-peak seasons, for example, with special offers and lower prices. Additionally, a Venice Card has been launched, the aim being to make people stay in Venice and book visits to the city in advance. Visitors are invited to book their visit to Venice and receive in exchange a card that offers them a series of special advantages and possibilities not accessible to visitors who do not book. The number of cards issued equals the most restrictive carrying capacity defined for Venice (socio-economic in this case). Residential tourists automatically receive a card when reserving hotel accommodation. In order for such a system to work, however, a high amount of cooperation is necessary between the different users of the system.

Moreover, the municipality is trying to attract tourists from different regions and emerging countries and to encourage them to consider travel in off-peak seasons. The Chamber of Commerce also seeks to encourage tourists to explore the mainland, as implied in their campaign, 'Venice is not an Island'. This initiative is in line with the hoped-for reduction of one-day 'touch-and-go' tourism. By bringing tourists into closer contact with local communities and enterprises, the Chamber of Commerce seeks a deeper interaction between tourists and visitors and the city, and works toward ensuring that their activities are much more sustainable (UNESCO, 2012).

Visitor Management Concepts and Frameworks

Perhaps the most well-known concept underpinning all visitor management is carrying capacity. It relates to use levels and involves the establishment of a ceiling level for tourist destinations which if exceeded will result in impacts that are deemed to be negative by evaluative standards (Shelby &

Heberlain, 1986; Wight, 1998). Despite being a useful concept, its practical application is problematic for a variety of reasons. First, the notion of a capacity implies a fixed limit but this is difficult to determine as sites and/or destinations are comprised of a number of physical, economic, social, perceptual, environmental and infrastructural components, each with varying capacities and limits to accommodate tourists. Carrying capacity is also not reached at a particular point in time, when a specific number of tourists are present, at a certain place. Rather, the process of tourism-related damage is likely to be progressive and management decisions are unable to take into account the uniqueness of place, be it natural, built or cultural, which inevitably affects the rate of resource replenishment or recovery and/or levels of tolerance, all of which are difficult to establish. Moreover, capacity management goes beyond visitor pressure as a town or city's tourism function and related shops, accommodation and services can completely overwhelm the need to cater for local residents by becoming 'living museums', particularly in the core visited areas.

In an attempt to overcome the problems associated with the carrying capacity concept, several visitor management frameworks have been developed which, while incorporating the notion of capacity limits, emphasise instead preferred resource conditions, the quality of experience and the quality of the environment (Timothy & Boyd, 2003). These frameworks include the recreation opportunity spectrum (ROS), visitor experience and resource protection (VERP), visitor impact management (VIM), visitor activity management process (VAMP) and limits of acceptable change (LAC). Overall, these management frameworks follow a sequential process of assessing and managing visitor impacts and have a number of strengths and weaknesses (Table 8.1). Clark and Stankey (1979) offered the first framework, the ROS, which was developed for the US Forest Service and Bureau of Land Management in response to concerns about growing recreational demands and conflict over the use of scarce resource (Eagles et al., 2002). It employs six specific attributes – access, users, acceptability of impacts from visitor user and acceptable levels of control – to define the nature of opportunities for recreation which are deemed possible across a spectrum of recreational settings that vary from pristine wilderness to high-density urban areas. In doing so, it integrates the setting, activities, user expectations and the role of management and enables sensitive sites to be identified and protected while at the same time highlighting others which are capable of withstanding higher visitor pressure (Timothy & Boyd, 2003).

The ROS concept underpins several other visitor management frameworks which have been advanced, including VERP, VIM, VAMP and LAC. In terms of VERP (National Park Service, 1997), this was created by the US National Park Service to protect the quality of the resources visited and the visitor experience. It compares desired conditions to existing conditions and defines what levels of use are appropriate, where, when and why, through

Table 8.1 Process, strengths and weaknesses of visitor management frameworks

Visitor management framework	Process	Strengths	Weaknesses
ROS	Define the recreation opportunity classes; estimate the demand for opportunities along the ROS for the area(s) of interest; assess potential recreation capabilities of the area(s) to provide for different recreation opportunities; identify current patterns of recreation provision and use along the ROS in the area(s); determine where and how different opportunities should be provided; identify conflicts and recommend mitigation; schedule; design; implement and monitor.	Enables the resource to be protected while at the same time providing a range of recreation opportunities to the public. Provides a wealth of information which can be used for management planning.	Information gathering is critical to this framework which is time consuming and costly. Application is dependent on management acceptance of the ROS.
VERP	Assemble an interdisciplinary team; develop a public involvement strategy; set preliminary objectives; compile inventory of park resources and existing use; analyse; describe a potential range of visitor experiences and resource conditions; allocate the potential zones to specific locations in the park; select indicators and specify standards for each zone; monitor; review; adjust plans in light of implementation.	Requires managers to understand the significance and importance of the resources they manage. Allows managers to determine specific threats to resources and the current status of the resource. Management actions can be tailored for the specific problems that exist within each park. Frequent monitoring is required.	Focuses on the impact of visitors on environmental resources and is therefore difficult to apply outside National Parks.

	Stages/steps	Strengths	Weaknesses
VIM	Review and identify issues; review management objectives; select key indicators; compile resources inventory; select standards for key impact indicators; compare standards and existing conditions; identify probable causes of impacts; identify management strategies; implement.	Process combines scientific and judgemental considerations. Identifies unacceptable impacts, determines potential causal factors affecting the occurrence and severity of unacceptable impacts and enables the selection of potential management strategies to address the unacceptable conditions.	Does not differentiate between different types and intensities of use. Addresses impacts that are occurring and potential impacts are unassessed. Based on managers' perceptions rather than stakeholder views.
VAMP	Terms of reference and objective setting; database development and data analysis; development of alternative visitor activity concepts; documentation of plan; implementation.	Most usefully applied to a single site.	Based on managers' perceptions rather than stakeholder views.
LAC	Identify area concerns and issues; select indicators of resource and social conditions; assess existing resource and social conditions; evaluate and select preferred alternatives; implement actions and monitor conditions.	Based less on subjection, as criteria for determining change are predetermined and are based on detailed sociocultural information.	Requires the collection of detailed information for each site; otherwise the criteria or standards that are adopted will be arbitrary. Open to manipulation as lower standards may be chosen than are necessary to maintain the long-term environmental and cultural integrity of an area. Does not consider the cumulative effects of tourism activities in surrounding areas. Assumes tourism is the most appropriate form of economic activity.

Source: Adapted from Clark and Stankey (1979), Eagles et al. (2002), Environment Canada and Park Service (1991), Graefe et al. (1990), Stankey et al. (1985), Timothy and Boyd (2003), and Valliere and Manning (2002).

public involvement. VIM was developed by Graefe *et al.* (1990), working for the US National Park Service and Conservation Association; it focuses on the impacts of visitors and their causes, and can be applied in a wide variety of settings including HSLT sites and destinations. Meanwhile, VAMP (Environment Canada & Park Service, 1991) focuses on managing visitors through their activities, whereas LAC, the most recently developed visitor management framework, addresses issues of managing impact and ensures quality touristic experiences. Unlike capacity management which focuses on visitor numbers, LAC is a planning process designed to identify preferred and acceptable resource and social and environmental conditions in a destination and to guide the development of a set of management actions needed to protect or achieve those conditions. In determining the level of change that is acceptable to host communities, public involvement is a key component of LAC (Stankey *et al.*, 1985).

These frameworks work on the premise that every visitor use problem can be solved through design and/or management. However, a number of challenges arise when such all-encompassing approaches are adopted. All are extremely labour and time intensive and very costly to operationalise. Where there are gaps in scientific knowledge about visitor impacts, judgements have to be made subjectively or on the basis of limited information. Additionally, the management action called for is not always taken, even when limits are far exceeded, because of lack of staff resources or because management is unwilling to face up to hard choices. It is not surprising, therefore, that their application to HSLT destinations is virtually non-existent. Visitor management consequently is more likely to involve the implementation of specific management tools and techniques designed for addressing particular problems caused by visitor pressure.

Specific management tools and techniques

In addition to these management frameworks, a range of specific techniques and tools are at the disposal of managers of HSLT sites and destinations. These relate broadly to four strategic approaches which entail the regulation of access directly and indirectly in order to enhance the visitor experience and to secure a high-quality environment for tourists and residents to enjoy (Timothy & Boyd, 2003). Such approaches include: (i) managing the supply of tourism or visitor opportunities; (ii) managing the demand for visitation; (iii) managing the destination's capabilities; and (iv) managing the impacts of use. These and their associated techniques are summarised in Table 8.2. Often they co-exist at sites and destinations as the amelioration of visitor pressure is tackled in a variety of ways. Of course, at each site and/or destination, the scope of visitor management and the selection of approaches and techniques are determined by relevant legislation, by the objectives and goals of the management strategy and by resourcing implications.

Table 8.2 Summary of approaches and associated visitor management tools and techniques

Strategic approach to visitor management	Associated tools and techniques
Managing the supply of tourism or visitor opportunities	• Increasing or decreasing the space available • Increasing or decreasing the time available to accommodate more or less use (e.g. seasonal closures) • De-marketing
Managing the demand for visitation	• Restrictions on length of stay • Limiting numbers • Limiting type of use • Tourist taxes and fees • Off-season marketing
Managing the destination's capabilities	• Hardening • Zoning • Developing specific facilities
Managing the impact of use	• Area protection • Modifying the type of use • Dispersing and concentrating use • Traffic management • Tourist education • Codes of conduct • Interpretation

Source: Adapted from Eagles *et al.* (2002).

With respect to managing the supply of tourism or visitor opportunities, specific techniques might entail increasing or decreasing the space or time available within which visitation can occur. Extending or limiting opening times, for example, or opening on more days of the year or imposing a seasonal closure are strategies which may be adopted. De-marketing is a particular technique that can be used to discourage rather than attract tourists to sites and/or destinations that are over-visited and usually involves simply reducing or ceasing altogether the amount of promotion and advertising. For many years, the historic cities of Cambridge and Oxford in the UK, for example, stopped printing tourism brochures. The effectiveness of such a strategy is limited, however, since many tourists become aware of destinations from other sources. Certainly this might be the case for Cambridge and Oxford, both of which are internationally renowned university cities whose top-class educational facilities are marketed to international audiences. An alternative approach therefore might involve raising the cost of the visit so as to discourage demand or by allowing a certain number of people per day through a ticket system (Case Study 8.2), although Timothy and Boyd (2003) state that this should be a last-resort solution to overcrowding as it can impact on revenue generation. Another de-marketing technique might focus on the attraction of 'quality' tourists, or in other words those that are low in volume and high in yield.

Managing visitor demand is another approach that may be used to manage visitor pressure. Specific techniques include restricting the length of stay or the size of groups at certain times of the day or week, although these measures are less than satisfactory as they again are likely to result in a loss of revenue. Advance bookings or timed visits are another tool for managing demand, as is limiting the type of use. Levying tourist taxes (Case Study 8.2), implementing visitor payback schemes that encourage the donation of monies and charging for admission/entrance are other ways of managing demand. The funds generated may be used to help pay for the maintenance and development of local infrastructure. In Belize, for example, a US$3.75 departure tax goes directly to conserving the barrier reef and rainforest (UNEP, 2015), whereas in Kruger National Park, South Africa every tourist pays a conservation fee for each day of their visit. Meanwhile, despite controversy, many HSLT sites use entrance or admission fees to manage visitation (see Chapter 4). For example, the Colosseum, Roman Forum and Palatine Hill in Rome, Italy are covered by an admission charge. Moreover, the charging of fees can be used to decrease overcrowding at peak times of the day, week or year. Off-season marketing is also a particularly useful technique, especially when it is not the total volume of visitors that a site/destination receives that is the problem but the seasonal peaks in visitation. The challenge here is to develop new products and/or offer existing products at reduced prices so as to tempt people to visit at quieter times of the year instead.

Case Study 8.2 Visitor pressure and *The Beach*, Koh Phi Phi, Thailand

Situated about 45 km east of Phuket, Thailand in the Andaman Sea, Koh Phi Phi comprises four main islands, the largest and most developed being Koh Phi Phi Don. This small archipelago in Krabi Province marks the boundary between the Pacific and Indian Oceans, and includes extensive coral reefs and mangrove forests which are home to a wide variety of marine and terrestrial animals and plants. The islands are of great environmental significance and thus became part of the Hat Nopparat Thara-Ko Phi Phi Marine National Park in 1983. Tourists have been attracted to the islands for many decades due to their inherent beauty, clear tropical waters and exquisite sandy beaches. However, in 2000 the islands received global attention with the release of the movie *The Beach*, starring Leonardo DiCaprio. Today, in addition to tourists visiting Maya Bay, one of the movie sets (Plate 8.3), Koh Phi Phi offers tourists a wealth of recreational activities including scuba diving, snorkelling and kayaking.

Not surprisingly, over the past few years the islands have grown into one of the busiest tourist destinations in Thailand. In 1998 over 150,000 tourists visited the islands, 85% of whom were from overseas (Phuket Gazette, 2010). Currently more than 1000 visitors arrive on Koh Phi Phi Don daily; however, the total number is likely to be much larger as it excludes those who arrive directly onto the beaches by way of the hundreds of privately operated speedboats and yachts. As a result, Koh Phi Phi is under an enormous amount of visitor pressure and, despite its National Marine Park status, its reefs are being degraded and unplanned development is occurring (Seenprachawong, 2001). This has prompted Dr Thon Thamrongnawasawat – an environmental activist and member of Thailand's National Reform Council – to label the islands a slum (Sidasathian & Morison, 2015). Litter is also a notable problem. Koh Phi Phi produces an average of 25 tonnes of rubbish a day, with this amount rising to 40 tonnes during the high season. Moreover, raw sewage is pumped into the sea and the water purification plant which recycles water has never been used (Phuket Gazette, 2010).

According to Dr Thon, 'Fifteen years ago, Koh Phi Phi were among the great natural destinations. It cost 2000 baht to visit the islands. These days, a trip to Phi Phi costs less than 1000 baht. In five years, it will cost

Plate 8.3 Maya Bay, Koh Phi Phi, Thailand
Source: The authors (2017).

less than 500 baht. Goodbye, Phi Phi.' The environmental damage to the islands has not gone unnoticed by tourists either. For example, one concerned visitor wrote to the Gazette saying that 'Year after year, Phi Phi Island is losing its beauty. Without more responsible and strict management of the environment, Thailand will lose one of its most beautiful places.' According to Dr Thon Thamrongnawasawat, 'Phuket and the Andaman have the choice between the mass market and the jet-skis mentality or putting a limit on the number of visitors, preserving nature – and controlling those visitor numbers carefully' (Phuket Gazette, 2010).

In an attempt to manage visitor pressure, a number of management strategies have been implemented recently. In 2010, a 20 baht visitor fee has been introduced at the main pier on Koh Phi Phi Do. Up to 20,000 baht is collected daily (Phuket Gazette, 2010). This money is then used to pay a private company to haul the rubbish from the island to mainland Krabi to be disposed of. In addition, tourists are being educated not to leave rubbish on the island and to take it with them when they leave. Koh Phi Phi is also being redeveloped as a luxury tourist destination. The Thai Government's vision of a sustainable future for Koh Phi Phi focuses on fewer, high-spending tourists in all-inclusive resorts backed by big business from outside (Phuket Gazette, 2010).

Managing the destination's capabilities is an approach that may also be used to address the negative impacts of visitor pressure. Specific techniques that are used are often referred to as hard and soft measures. An example of a hard measure is the surfacing of access routes and walkways (Hall & McArthur, 1998), but care must be taken not to comprise the authenticity of the site (see Chapter 7). Examples of soft measures include zoning and the roping off or shielding of sensitive areas or resources. In terms of the former, prohibiting traffic and pedestrianising the central areas of historic cities is common. This technique is used to reduce the impacts of traffic on significant buildings and areas within historic cities and to provide a safer and more enjoyable tourist environment (Timothy & Boyd, 2003).

With reference to the latter, this may be achieved by limiting physical contact between HSLT sites and tourists and can be seen in practice at Stonehenge in the UK and at Chichen Itza, Mexico, for example, while fragile heritage, screen and literary related artefacts can be found housed in glass casing at all sites. Another technique is to develop specific facilities such as visitor centres or visitor interpretive centres at sites that are particularly sensitive to damage from visitor traffic. They either act as a substitute to the resource itself or serve to capture the bulk of visitors, thereby sparing the resources from over-visitation. An example of the use of visitor centres in this way occurs at Lidice, a small village near Prague, whose residents were murdered by the Nazis on 10 June 1942 in retaliation for the assassination of Reinhard Heydrich, the acting Reichsprotekor of Bohemia and Moravia. A museum and visitor centre is located near the car park, some 200 km away from the memorial garden and approximately 500 km from the graves of the victims; together they serve to deter and distract tourists from visiting the latter areas which are subject to the most visitor pressure.

Over-visitation may also be addressed by managing the impact of use. Perhaps the most obvious technique in achieving this is by area protection, be it National Park, Wildlife Reserve, Biosphere Reserve, Site of Special Scientific Interest or Area of Outstanding Natural Beauty designation. Modifying the type of use is another technique and is most often used to protect environmental resources that are being degraded by high-impact hobbies such as horse riding and off-road biking. Instead, lower impact activities like birdwatching and walking are encouraged. Dispersing and concentrating use is a tool that is employed to manage the impact of use. In relation to the latter, such a technique might be used if sites have already been irreparably damaged or if they are more robust and resilient to intense pressure. In terms of the former, this technique helps to alleviate some of the physical pressures by dispersing the concentration of tourists at one specific site, with the added benefit of spreading the economic benefits of tourism across a wider area.

This approach can also be applied to resolving traffic congestion and there are various examples of traffic management initiatives around the world which encourage tourists to leave their cars at home and either walk or use public transport instead. For instance, traffic congestion in central urban areas, most notably historic cities such as Bruges (Belgium), Prague (Czech Republic), Stockholm (Sweden), Copenhagen (Denmark) and Nuremberg (Germany) is reduced by directing vehicles along routes which avoid their centres. Lower speed limits can calm the traffic situation, as can establishing park-and-ride programmes and facilities at the edges of historic cities, and creating efficient and user-friendly urban transport systems (Timothy & Boyd, 2003). It is not just the built environment which suffers from this particular problem; traffic congestion has become a real issue in many US National Parks (e.g. Yosemite, Arches and Canyonlands) as visitor numbers have quadrupled, 80% of whom arrive by car. Currently, visitation exceeds the parks' car parking capacity and cars parked poorly on roadside verges and traffic congestion are degrading the visitor experience and negatively impacting upon the fragile ecosystems. At present, a range of integrated shuttle transport systems are being investigated in an attempt to reduce the number of cars within the parks.

Managing the impact of use may also be attempted through tourist education, which endeavours to influence tourist attitudes and modify behaviour by combining knowledge with the emotional experience of visitation. Traditionally, it has been used extensively within protected natural areas such as national parks to heighten tourist awareness of tourism's impacts and the benefits of adopting responsible behaviour. Increasingly, however, within some destinations, it is being applied to a social context to increase cultural awareness and to encourage sensitive behaviour. One notable example of the use of tourist education to manage the impact of use occurs in Ladakh, a mountainous trans-Himalayan region in India which has experienced rapid tourism development since the mid-1970s and which is causing cultural disharmony between the area's residents and tourists. In an attempt to resolve such discordance and to foster greater understanding, the Mindful Travel/ Tourist Education Program was launched in 2006 by Local Futures, an international non-profit organisation dedicated to the revitalisation of cultural and biological diversity and the strengthening of local communities and economies worldwide (Local Futures, 2015). Its objectives are to provide tourists with knowledge of Ladakh's history, to sensitise them to the impact of their stay and to provide guidelines for responsible behaviour. Tourist education activities are provided daily with the exception of Sundays and the workshops attract more than 4000 participants each year (Local Futures, 2015).

The effectiveness of tourist education, however, is debatable. While some research, most notably undertaken by Orams (1996, 1997, 1998), found that it not only increased enjoyment and understanding but also promoted more environmentally responsible behaviour, there is little compelling evidence to suggest that it is successful in the longer term. This is perhaps not surprising given that evidence from other well-meaning education campaigns such as those relating to sex, drugs and teenage pregnancies appears to show that their impact is severely limited and dependent on the intended audience's willingness to hear and act upon the message.

A similar tool which may be used is the dissemination of a tourist code of conduct at sites and destinations. One of the first to be developed and promoted in Britain in the 1980s was the Countryside Commission's *Country Code* (1987) and this is still in use today. The aims of tourist codes of conduct are to reduce negative impacts by raising tourist awareness, educating visitors about the fragility of the site or destination visited and providing guidelines on appropriate behaviour and the importance of being a responsible tourist. Similarly to the value of tourist education, the effectiveness of tourist codes of conduct has been questioned (Cole, 2007b). This is because modifying behaviour and attitudes is extremely difficult to achieve, particularly as it more than likely involves making some kind of sacrifice on the part of the tourist. In any event, attempting to influence the well-established behaviour of millions of people is an expensive activity that takes a long time to take effect.

Interpretation is another valuable tool for managing the impact of tourist use and, as Chapter 5 has discussed, it is a means of communication which builds awareness and educates in order to develop appropriate attitudes and behaviour. In doing so, interpretation facilitates the way in which tourists interact and engage with the places visited. Moreover, interpretative techniques such as the use of guided or self-guided walks and tours can be used to steer people away from over-visited or sensitive areas and redirect them toward more robust areas or places which are able to accommodate more visitors. Furthermore, it can be used effectively to manage the spatial and temporal distribution of visitors or, in other words, visitor flows within a particular attraction or site. The availability of information at HSLT sites and destinations is very important, the benefits of which include the provision of facts, advice and guidelines which help inform and educate the visitor, resulting in more visitors adopting appropriate behaviours that will reduce impacts and provide the visitors with a more satisfying visit.

Overall, it is evident that there are many approaches and techniques of visitor management which focus primarily on the reduction of the negative impacts caused by visitor pressure. Increasingly, however, experience-centred service organisations such as HSLT attractions and destinations recognise that the physical environment in which the experience takes place – or the servicescape, as it has been termed (Bitner, 1992) – drives customers' perceptions of value and ultimately their experience and satisfaction (Ferndandez & Neves, 2014). Indeed, servicescapes not only influence the customers' value creation, but also have an impact on their repatronage (Pareigis *et al.*, 2012). According to a study by Fyall and Garrod (1998), heritage tourists identified a number of environmental items that contributed to an enjoyable and satisfying visit to an attraction. These include: value for money, cost, user friendly, physically and intellectually accessible to as many different visitor groups as possible, and authentic.

Consequently, visitor management arguably now involves a fifth approach, this being to manage the visitor experience in order to stimulate value co-creation. Since the place of consumption often has the strongest impact on customer perceptions of the service experience (Ferdandez & Neves, 2014), creating value-in-context through the management of a site or a destination's environmental dimensions is critical. Knowing what visitors remember most from their visits is essential to understanding how best to create pleasant experiences for them (Timothy & Boyd, 2003). Moreover, recognising the role that the servicescape plays in the delivery of the experience may provide HSLT sites and destinations with a sustainable competitive advantage in a cut-throat global marketplace.

Most HSLT sites and destinations implement a range of approaches and techniques in order to manage visitor pressure (Case Study 8.3), with their success ultimately influenced by the degree of management and/or government support to enforce sanctions against perpetrators. While they primarily seek to effect positive change, in some instances such practices may result in unintended negative consequences. For example, if a site is well known to tourists, improved interpretation of other less well-known sites could simply increase overall demand and result in new pressures being placed on previously little-used sites as well as continuing pressures on already popular sites. Another illustration is that the spreading of the tourist load could lead to dispersing the negative impacts of tourism across a wider area. Often, however, the lure of the economic benefits that can accrue is too great and the problems of those sites that are over-visited are sometimes overlooked as a result. This is a particular problem for WHSs.

World Heritage Sites and Visitor Management

WHSs are unique and diverse, encompassing a vast array of places, including towns and cities, cathedrals and monuments that are listed by the United Nations Educational, Scientific and Cultural Organization (UNESCO) as being of special cultural or physical significance. The list is maintained by the international World Heritage Programme administered by the UNESCO World Heritage Committee, composed of 21 UNESCO member states who are elected by the General Assembly. The programme, established by an international treaty called the Convention Concerning the Protection of the World's Cultural and Natural Heritage and adopted by the General Conference of UNESCO in 1972, catalogues, names and conserves sites of outstanding cultural or natural importance to the common heritage of humanity. As of May 2015, 1007 sites are listed: 779 cultural, 197 natural and 31 mixed properties, in 161 state parties. While each WHS remains part of the legal territory of the state where the site is located, UNESCO considers it in the interest of the international community to preserve each site.

Given that tourism is highly developed in Europe and North America and both regions possess rich cultural and historical attractions, it is perhaps not surprising that WHSs are mainly concentrated in these regions, accounting for 48% of the total in 2015. Asia and the Pacific have 23% of the total, Latin America and the Caribbean 13%, Africa 9% and the Arab States 8% (World Heritage Centre, 2015a). Italy has 50 sites and possesses the greatest number, followed by China (47), Spain (44), France (39), Germany (39), Mexico (32) and India (32) (UNESCO, 2015). Some countries possess only cultural sites, such as Iran and the Czech Republic, each of which has 12, while others such as the USA and Australia are endowed with more natural sites. Since the adoption of the Convention Concerning the Protection of World Natural and Cultural Heritage in 1972, the total number of WHSs has risen steadily from 12 in 1978, 468 in 1995, 788 in 2004, 936 in 2011 to 1007 in 2015 (World Heritage Centre, 2015a).

The World Heritage Convention is based on the premise that WHSs belong to everyone and should be preserved for future generations (Pedersen, 2002) by raising awareness and mobilising resources for their long-term conservation (World Heritage Centre, 2015b). The public should therefore be encouraged rather than prevented from visiting, and in doing so international and national heritage identities are strengthened among tourists and residents alike (Drost, 1996). Despite the fact that at the heart of WHS designation is protection, conservation and preservation, given the purpose of designation, it is of no surprise that in most cases it has resulted in an increase in international tourist arrivals and visitation (Su & Lin, 2014; Tucker & Emge, 2010; Yang et al., 2010). This is because, on the one hand, designation acts as a signal for the importance and objective authenticity of the displayed heritage and is thus used to promote tourism through branding (Timothy, 2011) or labelling (Yang et al., 2010) among tourist-generating destinations as the status increases the global visibility of the host country (Drost, 1996; Su & Lin, 2014). Indeed, studies of the impact of WHSs on tourism demand reveal its positive effect on the promotion of domestic and foreign tourism in countries such as England (Herbert, 2001; McIntosh & Prentice, 1999), China (Li et al., 2008; Yang et al., 2010), and Germany, Hungary and Romania (Light, 2000). On the other hand, according to Su and Lin (2014), UNESCO financially assists developing countries which lack the resources or ability to repair and maintain their WHSs, and if used wisely such aid can help to develop the necessary infra- and superstructure required for tourism to grow.

As a consequence, in reality WHS designation is another example of the tension which exists between the tourism development and conservation outlined in Chapter 4 and which may result in value co-destruction. Tourism's ability to generate revenue and create employment makes it attractive to local governments and communities, particularly of developing countries, where WHSs are situated (Li et al., 2008). Conservation, however, in this context, is often 'the last line item to be included in national budgets and the first line item to be cut' (ICOMOS, 1993: vii) and as a result increased visitation is challenging their sustainability (Li et al., 2008; Pedersen, 2002; see Case Study 8.3). Indeed, Hall and Piggin (2001) drew attention to significant visitor management issues at WHSs including lack of funding, congestion, overcrowding and site degradation, while Su and Lin (2014) state that the situation is particularly serious in developing highly populated countries like China, where the carrying capacities of WHSs are pronounced. China, in particular, has attracted much attention since it has the largest population in the world. This is exemplified by Li et al.'s (2008) study which revealed that, based on the 2002 World Heritage list, the 28 sites inscribed in China serve an average of more than 45.6 million people. The situation is exacerbated by China's economic policies which identify tourism as a key growth sector. Thus, not unexpectedly, population pressure (Liu & Yang, 1999; Tao, 2001; Zhang & Kong, 2006), the development policies of local governments (Yan, 2006; Zhang, 2003; Zhang & Kong, 2006) and lack of financial support (Liang, 2005; Zhu, 2004) are three problems which are negatively impacting on WHSs.

Around the world, much effort has been made to balance the needs of conservation and tourism development at WHSs through more effective visitor management by raising admission prices and restricting the number of visitors. In China, for example, Li *et al.* (2008) state that real-time monitoring with remote-sensing technologies and high-definition satellite pictures takes place twice a year to oversee patterns of use. Moreover, central governmental inspectors monitor local governments' management and use of sites. Additionally, specific management measures have been implemented at individual sites. For instance, the Mogao Cave in Dunhuang has introduced virtual tours in order to reduce overcrowding while the Jiuzhaigou Valley Scenic and Historic Interest Area has built trails and introduced environmentally friendly transportation to minimise destruction from visitor flow (Li *et al.*, 2008). However, despite these efforts, Wei *et al.* (2002, cited in Li *et al.*, 2008) state that population pressure still constitutes a major threat.

Case Study 8.3 Managing visitor pressure at a World Heritage Site: The case of the Galápagos Islands

The Galápagos are a volcanic archipelago of 19 islands, situated in the Pacific Ocean approximately 906 km off the coast of Ecuador, South America, which comprise a national park and unique biological marine reserve or living museum. Located at the convergence of three ocean currents, the Galápagos are a 'melting pot' of marine species (World Heritage Centre, 2015b). The extreme isolation of the islands has contributed to the development of unique fauna and flora such as the marine iguana which is the only lizard to swim in the ocean, and a giant Pinta tortoise, which unfortunately died in 2012, and inspired Charles Darwin's theory of evolution by natural selection following his visit in 1835. The islands were among the first inscribed natural WHSs in 1978 but despite this, due to the impact of tourism, most notably increased visitor pressure, they were included in the list of World Heritage in Danger in 2007 (World Heritage Centre, 2015b).

Tourism to the islands has grown considerably in recent years, facilitated by increased accessibility particularly by air. Since 1991 tourist numbers have soared from 41,000 to more than 160,000 annually, while the local population has grown by 4% every year to reach more than 40,000 (Gray, 2009), leading to a multitude of issues threatening sustainability. Due to the range of tour options and activities offered by numerous tour operators (Plate 8.4) there are few areas on the islands that visitors are unable to access. In addition, hotel development and related infrastructure is transforming large areas of the islands and such growth in tourism has contributed to substantial migration from Ecuador for jobs. This in turn has resulted in rapid, unplanned urbanisation. According to the World Heritage Centre (2015b), the local flora and fauna of such a fragile ecosystem is now under threat due to the introduction of invasive species, increased and poor waste management, pollution and changes to many of the intangible attributes of the remote site.

Plate 8.4 Tourist diving with a turtle at the Galápagos Islands
Source: The authors (2017).

As more sites are likely to be given World Heritage status in the future, it remains to be seen whether WHSs continue to act as tourism magnets and, like many tourism destinations, become victims of their own success. Increased inscription may serve to water down the significance of the designation, while continued overcrowding may mean that the visitor experience is compromised and value co-destruction occurs, particularly if they are more interested in authentic site experiences as opposed to the objective authenticity of the displayed heritage (see Chapters 2 and 6). Indeed, a study undertaken by Poria *et al.* (2013) of visitors' perceptions of WHSs reveals some potentially worryingly signs that WHSs may be experiencing the impact of over-consumption and exploitation. Specifically, the authors found that selected visitors did not view some of the current sites to be worthy of the designation and that they were perceived to be more crowded and expensive than other historic sites. As the growth of tourism is forecast to continue, visitor management is likely to remain a key challenge at WHSs in the future.

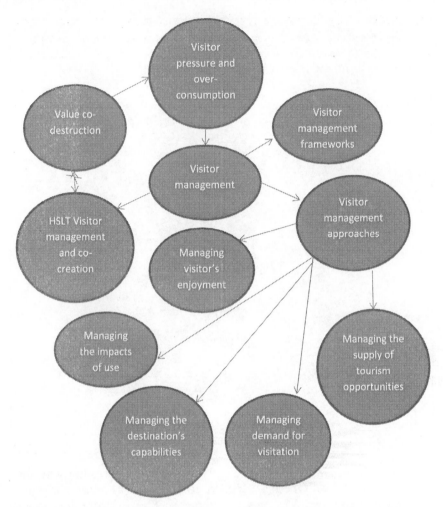

Figure 8.1 Dimensions of heritage, screen and literary tourism visitor management and co-creation
Source: The authors (2017).

Conclusion

This chapter focuses on visitor management and has discussed its relevance to HSLT sites and destinations, focusing in particular on issues relating to overconsumption and on the potential for value co-destruction (see Figure 8.1). It first establishes the nature of visitor management and highlights the relevance of Vargo and Lusch's (2016) ninth and 11th foundational premises which entail collaborative and cooperative working between networks of institutions, organisations and businesses. Then the chapter moves on to consider some of the challenges encountered. This is followed by an examination of visitor management processes and frameworks and by consideration of four established approaches and their associated tools and techniques. Here it is suggested that an additional fifth approach which focuses on the management of visitor enjoyment as opposed to managing the impacts of visitor pressure is now a priority for many sites and destinations, given the importance of the servicescape on influencing and shaping visitor experiences and satisfaction.

The chapter ends with an examination of WHSs, in which some of the problems currently being experienced as a result of their designation are highlighted. From this discussion, it is evident that visitor management is important to HSLT sites and destinations in helping to ensure that the negative impacts of visitor pressure are ameliorated and that the very resources that tourists come to see are conserved and preserved for future generations. It is therefore integral to the HSLT nexus as it influences the extent to which value is created and extracted or destroyed. In addition to working toward securing sustainable futures for many HSLT sites and destinations, it plays a vital educational role and has been used around the world to raise tourists' awareness and knowledge of their impacts but also of the significance and fragility of the resources visited in the hope that more responsible behaviour will be adopted. With global tourism forecast to grow well into the foreseeable future, visitor management will become a necessary requirement, providing the framework and protocols to guide future planning and management decisions.

9 Conclusion

Reading a book is like re-writing it for yourself. You bring to a novel,
anything you read, all your experience of the world. You bring
your history and you read it in your own terms.

Angela Carter

Just as Angela Carter, UK novelist, reportedly stated, consumer engagement
with novels and indeed with movie and TV productions is personal and
idiosyncratic, and it is this interaction which inevitably co-creates the resulting experience. Value is now focused on experiences, and HSLT destinations
and/or sites can no longer act autonomously in designing products and marketing messages and in orchestrating the experience. Indeed, according to
Prahalad and Ramaswamy (2004: 6) 'consumers can choose the firms they
want to have a relationship with based on their own views of how value
should be created for them'. Such a view is re-affirmed by Neuhofer (2016: 3),
who states that 'Tourists have become empowered actors who (a) engage
with other actors (e.g. tourism businesses, consumer communities, personal
networks and wider stakeholders), (b) integrate their resources (e.g. information platforms and devices) and (c) participate in the design and creation of
their experiences'. Thus, because it is impossible to predict the experience
that a consumer will have at any one point in time, a central challenge for
HSLT providers is to create innovative and robust 'experience environments'
(Prahalad & Ramswamy, 2004: 6) so as to differentiate one from another.

In order to capture the changing nature of market relationships and interactions between tourists and HSLT destinations and/or sites, this book inno-
vatively applies the framework provided by service-dominant logic (S-DL)
and co-creation to examine the demand, consumption, development, marketing, interpretation and management of the global phenomena of HSLT.
The adoption of such a perspective originates from the recognition that there
has been a failure within tourism to embrace the contributions of S-DL and
co-creation (Shaw *et al.*, 2011), and enables for the very first time a multidimensional nexus to be conceptualised which binds these three forms of tourism together. This original nexus identified in Chapter 1 (p. 2; Figure 1.1)
comprises four key elements, namely co-creation, (re)representation and
commodification, contingency and co-terminality. The role played by, and

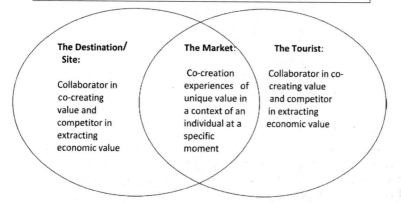

HSLT Destinations/Sites and Tourists' Interaction

(i)   Interaction is the locus of co-creation of value and economic value extraction by the consumer and the firm

(ii)   Co-creation experiences are the basis of value

The Destination/ Site:

Collaborator in co-creating value and competitor in extracting economic value

The Market:

Co-creation experiences of unique value in a context of an individual at a specific moment

The Tourist:

Collaborator in co-creating value and competitor in extracting economic value

Figure 9.1 Co-creation and new tendencies in the heritage, screen and literary tourism market

Source: The authors (2017). Adapted from Prahalad and Ramaswamy (2004).

the implications of each for the demand (Chapter 2), development (Chapters 3 and 4), interpretation (Chapter 5), consumption (Chapter 6), marketing (Chapter 7) and management (Chapter 8) of HSLT sites and destinations are examined.

Additionally, and again for the first time in this context, the applicability of the 11 foundational premises of S-DL proposed by Vargo and Lusch (2016) to HSLT is highlighted throughout this book. Examples of the applicability of such premises to value co-creation in HSLT are summarised in Table 9.1. Clearly, a new practice for experience creation is evident within HSLT which is reshaping understanding of how current interactions, experiences and value are constructed. Underpinning these new tendencies is the convergence of the roles of destinations and/or sites and of tourists. As a consequence and in accordance with Prahalad and Ramaswamy (2004: 11), both producers and consumers should be more appropriately viewed as 'collaborators and competitors; collaborators in value creation and competitors for the extraction of economic value' (Figure 9.1). Co-creation is not about HSLT providers pampering tourists with lavish customer service (Prahalad & Ramaswamy, 2004), but instead is best understood as 'any act of collective creativity that is experienced jointly by two or more people. It is a special case of collaboration, where the intent is to create something that is not known in advance' (Sanders & Simons, 2009: 1).

Table 9.1 Examples of the applicability of service-dominant logic foundational premises to heritage, screen and literary tourism

Premise number	Foundational premise	Examples of value co-creation within HSLT	Examples of value co-destruction
FP1	Service is the fundamental basis of exchange	• Current demand for heritage, literary and screen experience environments. • Tourists' anticipation of participation in the experience prior to consumption acts as a powerful motivator to engage in HSLT. • Tourists' motivations to visit and their subsequent experiences are influenced by their prior knowledge, values and ideology.	• Historical distortion and the blurring of fact and fiction may result from the exchange. • Over-consumption and associated negative environmental and sociocultural impacts may occur as a result of service provision in some environments.
FP2	Indirect exchange masks the fundamental basis of exchange	• Emotions generated indirectly prior to HSLT consumption at a site or destination as a result of reading or watching books and screen productions about the resource to be consumed are just as important to service exchange as the actual visit.	
FP3	Goods are a distribution mechanism for service provision	• Suppressed or unrecognised motivations represent an intangible good which contributes to the service experience but which may not always be apparent. • The interpretation of HSLT resources is crucial to co-creation.	
FP4	Operant resources are the fundamental source of competitive advantage	• Demand is influenced by the ability of tourists to use their operant resources to co-create the experience. • HSLT tourists are notoriously rich in cultural capital. • Experience at HSLT sites and destinations is unique and personal, based on the tourist's own emotions, imagination, interpretation and memory.	• The extent to which historical distortion and the blurring of fact and fiction affect the quality of the service experience depends on the operant resources that are available and which enable the tourist to identify untruths, re-inventions and the manipulation of pasts.

FP5	All economies are service economies	• The size and significance of HSLT in most economies globally. • Creation of specialised HSLT destinations such as book towns and bookstore tourism and sites including clusters and trials.	• Over-consumption in historic cities and honeypot sites are evidence of over-specialisation and over-consumption.
FP6	The customer is always a co-creator of value	• Demand generally and motivations specifically are stimulated by the tourist who is always the co-creator of value. • Tourists employ different processes to obtain value from an experience. • The re-enactment of actions and scenes from screen productions and books. • Tourists desire to be engaged and involved at HSLT sites and destinations.	• HSLT tourists are not always passive audiences and some are able to identify historical distortion and the blurring of fact and fiction. • Tourists interpret information in different ways and may adopt a dominant, oppositional or negotiated view of the resource that is subject to interpretation, based on their prior knowledge and experience.
FP7	The enterprise cannot deliver value but only offer value propositions	• Networks of state-related institutions and organisations can create and affirm national identities but it is up to the tourist to derive and extract value.	• Networks of state-related institutions and organisations can present historically distorted versions of the past but it is up to the individual as to whether or not the presented version is accepted.
FP8	A service-centred view is inherently customer oriented and relational	• Interpretation at HSLT sites and destinations is driven by the characteristics of the visitors and their needs. • The engagement of some tourists with social media prior to, during and after their visit.	• Tourists' reading of interpretation at HSLT sites and destinations does not necessarily equate to the interpreters' preferred readings and may result in negotiated or oppositional views being formed.

Table 9.1 (Continued)

FP9	All social and economic actors are resource integrators	• Networks of state-related institutions and organisations can create and reaffirm national identities. • Networks of state-related institutions and organisations can produce collective myths that encourage the diaspora to return to their homeland.	• Networks of state-related institutions and organisations can present historically distorted versions of the past. • Networks of state-related institutions and organisations can use HSLT resources to politically legitimise oppressive or undemocratically elected regimes.
FP10	Value is always uniquely and phenomenologically determined by the beneficiary	• The meaning and value tourists attach to HSLT resources inspires actual visits. • Visitation is influenced by perceptions of the value extracted from the visit. • Satisfaction is linked to the value that is created and extracted by the tourist.	• The extent to which historical distortion and the blurring of fact and fiction negatively impact on the perceived quality of the experience is determined by the tourist.
FP11	Value co-creation is coordinated through actor-generated institutions and institutional arrangements	• The linking of products with marketing through theming and branding. • Visitor management requires the collaboration and coordination of a range of public and private sector institutions, organisations and businesses.	• Failure to collaborate and coordinate the marketing activities of DMOs and individual operators within a destination may result in a distorted, erroneous or confused message being portrayed to tourists which in turn may reduce satisfaction.

Source: The authors (2017). Adapted from Vargo and Lusch (2008, 2016).

However, this exploration of HSLT within the theoretical propositions provided by S-DL and co-creation also highlights the fact that value creation might not always be positive. Instead, value within a tourist experience may be negative and result in what Chathoth *et al.* (2013: 100) term 'value co-destruction'. According to Neuhofer (2016: 4), this concept acknowledges that 'value might not be created but destroyed by the actors (e.g. the tourist) or the resources that are integrated into the process', thereby resulting in a diminished experience and value. Certainly, as Table 9.1 demonstrates, there are numerous examples of some resources within HSLT not value adding but instead value destroying. This is particularly the case with selected modes of interpretation that employ ICT, for example, or which do not take the tourists' needs into consideration (see Chapters 5 and 6) or with destinations and sites that have become over-commercialised or which seek to entertain as opposed to educate (see Chapters 3, 4 and 8).

Taking these original contributions together, this book draws attention to a number of key themes which cross-cut all three forms of tourism along a co-creation and co-destruction dichotomy, and which pose varying degrees of challenges to its future development and management. These themes include value co-creation at one end of the co-creation–co-destruction spectrum, and historical distortion and over-consumption at the other. Furthermore, it demonstrates that the HSLT market is heavily influenced by a variety of interrelated demand-led (Chapters 1, 2 and 6) and supply-led (Chapters 4 and 7) drivers. Many may be broadly related to a range of socio-economic macro trends, and these and others are likely to have an impact on HSLT's future prospects. Thus, this final chapter reviews the key themes which have emerged, and discusses their implications for site and destination management within the context of HSLT. It begins by focusing on value-co-creation. Next it moves on to consider aspects relating to value co-destruction, namely historical distortion and over-consumption. Following this, the chapter shifts focus to examine key economic, demographic, consumer behaviour and technological drivers and trends which are likely to influence the consumption and production of HSLT in the future. Some final concluding remarks are then provided.

Key Themes and Management Implications

Value co-creation

Value co-creation is arguably the most important issue and outcome of the HSLT nexus to emerge from this analysis. Its relevance is proposed in Chapter 1, while Chapter 2 explores the ways in which it may occur. This theme is further considered in Chapter 6, in which HSLT experiences are examined. The extent to which tourists feel emotionally connected and involved with the resources consumed influences the creation of value. Thus it is a negotiated construct which is created on an individual basis and which is made up of pleasure, imagination and fulfilment. The determinants of experience are multidimensional in quality, as the same product can be experienced in many different ways. Of course, value creation is not only influenced by tourists' interaction with resources and places, as the ways in which the latter are constructed and communicated is also critical. Such a contention is analysed in Chapter 4 particularly in the context of notions of place and the development of clusters, trails, festivals and book towns, in Chapter 5 through interpretive techniques which engage the audience, and in Chapter 7 in relation to place-branding strategies.

Viewing HSLT within the context of S-DL and value creation is valuable as it theoretically and practically enhances knowledge and understanding of these three forms of tourism. In terms of the latter, it highlights the fact that competitive advantage may be gained in a variety of ways because S-DL views 'the customer as an operant resource ...' capable of acting on other resources, a collaborative partner who co-creates value with the firm' (Lusch et al., 2007: 6). Thus, in response to learning about tourists' interactions and experiences, the quality of service delivery may be enhanced accordingly and existing products may be tweaked so that they more closely match their needs. Moreover, such information informs product innovation which can be tested and developed further by involving tourists in the process. The adoption of such an approach is vital as in today's tourism market the product is experience itself (Nurick, 2000). But of course it is not as straightforward as it might first appear, since the extent of the tourists' role in co-creation is uneven and is dependent on their levels of experience and expertise, the availability of time and the perceived economic and experiential benefits which may be gained (Shaw et al., 2011). Furthermore, S-DL and value creation have practical implications for the HSLT industry as they highlight the fact that their management should go beyond the mere presence of tourists and their associated impacts. Instead they should also take into consideration the actual relationship and interaction between the space concerned, the resource visited and the individual.

With respect to the former, S-DL and value creation highlight the importance of the consumer in the co-creation and co-production of the HSLT experience, thereby providing researchers with a highly relevant and robust theoretical framework within which to examine its implications for their development, marketing, interpretation, planning and management. However, in addition it draws attention to the fact that although the tourist plays a central role in the co-creation process, there are also some important management implications relating to the facilitation of the process in the first instance and thereafter. Most notable is the way in which businesses engage with tourists and how they manage the process, particularly given that tourists' involvement in co-creation is highly selective (Shaw et al.,

2011). Additionally, as has been demonstrated throughout this text, value co-creation can be negative and result in value co-destruction.

Value co-destruction

Given that the main role of HSLT is to provide commercially viable, memorable and worthwhile experiences while at the same time entertaining, educating and/or managing visitors, historical distortion and the blurring of fact and fiction and over-consumption also cross-cut these three forms of tourism. Thus they are key themes to emerge from this analysis, impacting on the development, interpretation, marketing, consumption and management of HSLT. In relation to the former, Chapters 1 and 3 contend that historical distortion and the blurring of fact and fiction is inherent in definitions of HSLT. The recognition, value assigned and display of heritage inevitably involves selectivity as choices are made in terms of what to inherit and pass on and which resources to display. Chapter 3 most notably discusses in some considerable depth the sanitisation of heritage and the portrayal of a nostalgic version of the past at many sites which are seeking to edutain their visitors. This is because, for most, the ways in which the past is remembered is often more palatable than what it was like in reality.

The historical distortion of the past and blurring of fact and fiction is also discussed most notably in Chapter 3 in the contexts of screen and literary tourism. Historical dramas including TV and film productions and novels, whether fictional or non-fictional, shape the viewing of the past and the understanding of the versions of events that are presented. Novelists and the makers of screen productions can reveal great truths, while writers of fiction use fact to make their work believable. As the past can never be accurately recaptured, through research pseudo-authentic settings are created which encourage the visitor to see and believe what is being presented. Together with heritage tourism, Chapter 3 moves on to demonstrate that these three forms of tourism are truly powerful political weapons, capable of manipulating and re-inventing the past in order to create and affirm national identities and/or diaspora, and to politically legitimise a ruling body especially in contexts where there is contested or dissonant heritage. Moreover, they may also be used for collective amnesia and sometimes for more sinister purposes, notably in the case of ethnic cleansing and/or heritage genocide.

In particular, it is the power of the narrative or the story presented, as Chapters 3, 4, 5 and 6 demonstrate, which facilitate the colliding of the imaginary and real worlds. Through development, interpretation and marketing, the visitor is emotionally and cognitively connected to the resource. Notably, Chapter 3 considers how some HSLT developments draw on hyper-reality and simulacra to bring fantasies and fictional worlds to life. Meanwhile, Chapter 4 provides an array of different types of development including book towns, trails, clusters and festivals to demonstrate just how destinations are transforming the links associated with the past or with real or fictional events, people and places into symbolic capital which, in turn, is being used to create new attractions, events and spectacles. Interpretation and marketing are used to convey the theme of these developments through a variety of narratives as Chapters 5 and 6 discuss. It is the projection of such stories which may lead to historical distortion and the blurring of fact and fiction, not least because of an inability to faithfully recreate the past, but also because its portrayal is usually from an individual or collective perspective, thereby representing one version of events. Whose story is being presented, why this version has been selected and what the effects are of tourist engagement with such distortions are pertinent questions which should be at the forefront of all destinations' and attractions' interpretive and marketing strategies, particularly if a more balanced view is to be presented.

Historical distortion and the blurring of fact and fiction, however, is not an outcome whereby heritage, screen and literary tourists are passive victims of half-truths and myths. It is in this context, particularly in relation to screen and literary tourists, that this market is notably distinctive. As Chapters 2 and 6 demonstrate, heritage, screen and literary tourists are not solely attracted to destinations and attractions in order to experience the reality of the place. Instead, a key expressed motivation is to consume the story presented, a contention that is reinforced by Pine and Gilmore (1999) who argue that consumers are no longer interested in tangible goods but rather in memories, stories and experiences. Consequently, HSLT specifically involves the selling of dreams and fantasies and this colliding of the imaginary world with reality results from the interaction between tourists, the place visited, the event experienced and/or the object viewed. Moreover, the tourists themselves contribute to the distortion of the narrative presented as outlined in Chapters 2, 5 and 6 in several ways. Indeed an integral part of the tourist experience is their engagement of emotions and immersion within the narrative, irrespective of how representative of the truth this is. In addition, the consumption of HSLT varies greatly from one individual to another, as differing levels of knowledge, awareness and skills, as well as existing biases and opinions, may taint the narrative presented. HSLT clearly involves the consumption of acquired meanings. Given this, can historical distortion and the blurring of fact and fiction ever be avoided and if the tourist is unaware of it does it always lead to value co-destruction?

Over-consumption is another issue which emerges from the HSLT nexus. Chapter 1 outlined the growth and significance of HSLT and its impact on destinations, particularly in terms of attracting increasing numbers of tourists to specific locations. These considerations were further elaborated on in Chapter 2 in which the nature of demand was discussed in more depth. Like other forms of tourism, in some locations HSLT has become a victim of its own success as its rapid development over the last three decades has led to a number of management challenges, one of which is over-consumption.

The environmental pressures, notably damage to resources and over-visitation, which are subsequently being experienced at sites and destinations, are detailed in Chapters 4 and 8, while ways of alleviating these pressures through the use of interpretation and marketing are described in Chapters 5 and 7, respectively. Here it is demonstrated that interpretation may be used as a soft and hard management tool in helping to ameliorate over-consumption, because as well as educating tourists to be more respectful and sensitive to the fragility of the resources visited, it may be used to zone off or steer tourists away from vulnerable areas through the use of guided and un-guided walks and trails. Moreover, marketing generally but specifically de-marketing may be used as a strategy to reduce the number of tourists to particular sites and destinations.

Clearly then, S-DL and value co-creation and value co-destruction are valuable concepts for both tourists and HSLT attraction and destination managers alike, as they demonstrate how value can be created and destroyed; the outcome is contextual and is dependent entirely on the tourists' interactions with the resource consumed. Together with a host of macro socio-economic trends, they should be used to shape the future of this industry.

Future Trends in Heritage, Screen and Literary Tourism

In order to ensure that HSLT is capable of meeting consumer expectations and retaining viable and successful market segments in the future, understanding what consumers want is really important, as is knowledge of key economic, demographic, consumer and technological drivers which might influence their future travel behaviour and their propensity to participate in HSLT.

Economic drivers

Perhaps the most influential macro-economic driver to influence HSLT is the rebalancing of economic power (Future Foundation, 2015) due to the relative liquidity of the BRICS (Brazil, Russia, India, China and South Africa) countries and other emerging economies such as Indonesia and Malaysia. These are the world's developing major economies, home to 42% of the earth's population and responsible for approximately 20% of the world's GDP (IMF, 2015). This driver is creating a new, wealthy segment of the world's population, enabling many more people to participate in tourism and accounts for a wealth of positive economic forecasts concerning the growth of the industry. Indeed in 2014 1.1 billion tourists travelled and it is projected that this figure will double between 2013 and 2035 (UNTWO, 2015). China is the leading tourist-generating country with more than 100 million travellers spending approximately US$129bn on international tourism in 2013 (UNTWO, 2013). Clearly, the emergence of these markets has implications for domestic and international HSLT, with the ability of sites and destinations to tap into this growth strongly impacting on their competitiveness. Of course, these forecasts are largely dependent on the continued growth of these emerging economies in light of some early signs of an economic slowdown in some countries, most notably China (BBC News, 2015).

Moreover, global projections of the growth of tourism are based on an assumption that there will not be a scarcity of oil or an impending energy crisis which some commentators predict (Becken, 2011). Global consumption of oil products in 2004 amounted to about 30 billion barrels, and demand is predicted to continue to rise by at least 50% by 2030, with more than 85% of the increase in consumption occurring among developing nations (Becken & Lennox, 2012). Although new oil reserves are being discovered at a greater rate than consumption, new oil fields are declining and their average total yield is diminishing (Hirsch, 2008). Furthermore, the development and adoption of alternative energies has been extremely slow in the developed Western world, so much so that renewable energy is not expected to be a significant source within the next 25 years. The immediate impact of escalating oil prices in the wake of oil depletion is the reduction of tourism demand globally due to a rise in the overall cost of short- and long-haul air travel. Thus those HSLT destinations which are dependent on overseas markets are most vulnerable and all are likely to be reliant on domestic tourism which will be expected to compensate for reduced outbound international travel. Even if alternative fuels become commercially available for airlines, they are still likely to be more expensive than present aviation fuel, thereby causing most tourists to shift from more distant to closer destinations. Additionally, an energy crisis has implications for HSLT sites as the costs of higher energy prices equate to higher operating costs. In a price-sensitive and highly competitive environment, profit margins are likely to be affected. It is likely that biofuel mixes will increasingly be used but their adoption will inevitably carry a cost which requires substantial financial investment, often out of reach of small and medium-size enterprises.

Demographic drivers

The world's population continues to grow unabated and by 2030 it is estimated that there will be an extra 1 billion people in the world, of which 20% will be travelling. The population is forecast to reach 9.6 billion by 2050 according to the UN Department of Economic and Social Affairs (2013), with much of it concentrated in a small group of developing countries. Indeed, Europe's population is forecast to decrease by 14% by 2050 and fertility rates in the large developing countries such as China, India, Brazil, South Africa and Iran are in fact falling rapidly. While much has been written about limits to growth and the perils this poses to the survival of humanity, if such growth were to be accompanied by family planning, state welfare, increased affluence and standards of living and resulting population decline as has been the case across the developed world, a stable global tourism market may well be created. However, the composition of the global travel market is likely to change profoundly in the future with increases in ageing societies becoming more prolific (Future Foundation, 2015). According to the UN Department of Economic and Social Affairs (2013), globally the population of older persons is growing by 2% each year, considerably faster than the population as a whole. The world population of 65+ year olds will rise from 600 million in 2015 to more than 1 billion in 2030 (UN Department of Economic and Social Affairs, 2013).

Clearly, a major part of today's global tourism market is composed of retired people. In the USA, for example, people aged 50 and over now represent nearly a quarter of the total adult US population. Indeed, seniors in the USA have become the fastest growing segment of the population and have become one of the most viable segments of the tourism industry consumer market (Resonance Consultancy, 2015a). In Europe, meanwhile, according to the UN Department of Economic and Social Affairs (2013), there are currently more elderly people than children living in the EU, as its young population has decreased by 21% – or 23 million – in 25 years. In fact, only 16.2% of today's EU population is under 14 years old, while one-sixth (16.6%) is 65 years old or more. In addition, one out of every 25 EU citizens is over 80 years old. The globally ageing population presents a number of opportunities to HSLT as it has led to a growth in the senior travel market, many of whom will visit such sites and destinations. The quantitative impact of this particular demographic driver is already evident within the developed world. In the UK, for example, according to VisitBritain (2006), one in every five people is over 65 and on average takes 1.5 overnight domestic holiday trips. Of course, the number of visits made specifically to HSLT-related sites and destinations is debatable, and much depends on the quality of experience such places can offer. What is unequivocal, however, is that retirees are an attractive and potentially highly lucrative market since they are generally associated with having enhanced purchasing powers and are unconstrained by time, thereby having the ability to take long holidays outside the peak season. Given their importance, adapting and catering for the needs, demands and expectations of the senior travel market is crucial to ensuring the continued viability of HSLT.

Consumer drivers

Consumer behaviour has a significant influence on tourism demand, and is underpinned by a number of drivers which are likely to impact upon HSLT in the future. Perhaps the most important is co-creation of the tourist experience. While tourists are already sophisticated and expect high quality, it is likely that they will become even more demanding. In a quest to create real value, they will seek a greater degree of engagement with, and transparency from, HSLT sites and/or destinations. Such actions are particularly relevant to attractions and areas whose heritage is contested or dissonant, as Chapter 3 has discussed. However, due to the growing cultural complexity of communities, the presentation of a single story about a particular heritage is no longer sufficient. Multiple narratives will need to be conveyed and tourists will also want to make their own creative interpretations of those stories that relate to their own history and identity.

Moreover, in light of the increasing pervasiveness of the knowledge economy, consumers are making greater use of available digital media for information gathering, booking and cultural consumption. In an effort to manage the avalanche of available information, the breadth of expertise provided online by their networks of family, friends and other consumers through reviews, blogs and social media posts will become the preferred advisory sources. In 2017 more than 3 billion people will have mobile internet access (PwC, 2015). In particular, travel reviews have a significant influence on the travel decisions of millennials (18–34), as almost 80% said that their travel decisions were influenced by reviews either 'often' or 'sometimes' (WYSE Travel Confederation, 2015); 57% of US millennials travellers take and post pictures on social media networks hourly and daily while on vacation versus 29% of all US travellers (Resonance Consultancy, 2015b). Consequently user-generated content will surpass branded content in influencing decisions and subsequent behaviour in the future, thereby necessitating content co-creation between tourists and HSLT sites and destinations (Future Foundation, 2015).

Social and environmental concerns are another consumer driver that is expected to become more influential in the future in tourists' purchasing decisions. As a consequence, corporate social responsibility will become a prerequisite for all HSLT attractions and destinations which will have to explicitly demonstrate to tourists that their business operations and practices throughout the whole of their supply chain are of a high ethical and sustainable standard. According to Future Foundation (2015), such eco-ethical concerns will inspire micro-concessions being awarded to less wasteful and unsustainable behaviour. Micro-sanctions might also occur, with tourists avoiding businesses and areas that undermine the wellbeing of local residents and the environment, and the rewarding of those that achieve high levels of environmental performance.

Technological drivers

There is little doubt that technology will radically shape the demand and supply of HSLT in the future. Inevitably, the growth of these forms of tourism is closely aligned with their ability to adapt their online presence to fast-moving change which is occurring around the use of the internet. Around 40% of the world's population spread across the developed and developing worlds have internet access, representing approximately 3.2 billion people (Internet Livestat, 2015). By 2030 it is likely that only the world's poorest will not be connected. Consequently, in addition to the continued opportunities which online platforms such as Facebook, Flickr, Instagram and Twitter afford for the promotion and marketing of HSLT sites and destinations, further technological developments may redefine what constitutes travel (Brewer & Nakamura, 1984), resulting in more widespread participation in virtual tourism by tourists and destinations (Mascho & Singh, 2014). At present, opportunities for virtual tourism are in their infancy, with arguably the best known example being Second Life (SL). This platform combines a computer game with a chatroom where 3D virtual worlds are created. It is a social world that promotes interaction and socialisation over mission-oriented narratives and goals. Launched in 2003, the total number of SL members has reached 25 million, of which there are an average 900,000 active users (Weinberger, 2015), to whom it provides a growing range of holiday experiences (Mascho & Singh, 2014). For example, the city of Amsterdam (The Netherlands) has been recreated within SL. It offers a wide array of products such as flower stands, coffee shops, bicycles, boat rides, shops and information booths, provides a map for visitors, and links to travel deals, the Amsterdam tourism board and real-life shops who market and sell their products to this set of online consumers (Mascho & Singh, 2014).

For virtual tourism to become more attractive in the future, the environment provided by companies such as SL needs to be physically immersive and have a psychological presence so that users really believe that they are within the environment experienced (Guttentag, 2010). Indeed, SL is developing a second-generation 3D platform drawing on the latest technologies in anticipation that 3D virtual worlds are likely to increase in popularity (Weinberger, 2015). Of course, some commentators doubt its ability to provide tourists with anything other than technology-enhanced experiences, since physical contact is the most desired aspect of travel (Neuhofer et al., 2014; Richards, 2014). However, such a proposition is perhaps not too far-fetched, given that tourists routinely actively engage with hyper-reality and simulacra (see Chapter 2) through the consumption of artificial, man-made realities, pseudo-events and staged authenticity (Holmes, 2001). Moreover, the act of travelling itself is becoming instantaneous, leading Hall (1997) to contend that virtual and embodied travel appear to be collapsing onto one another, since virtual travellers expect more realism while actual tourists visit non-places.

Moreover, if the adoption of visual technology such as Google Glasses becomes widespread (see Chapter 5 for fuller discussion of virtual and augmented reality), it means that tourists are better able to co-create and individualise the experience by taking pictures of whatever they see, whenever they like. Consequently, according to Richards (2014: 9), 'different tourists may access different content, not only in terms of different languages, but also different viewpoint supplied by different intermediaries'. Tourism will thus be shaped by the devices tourists carry (Hui, 2013), and the future of all HSLT sites and destinations will inevitably be determined by investment in digital marketing strategies, and by which content providers gain the most access to the new platforms providing tourism information (Richards, 2014). The replication of virtual worlds presents a variety of interesting marketing (Huang *et al.*, 2013), development and management possibilities to HSLT, not least to those sites and destinations which are experiencing varying degrees of environmental degradation and over-visitation (see Chapter 8), and to those segments of the population such as Muslim women whose travel opportunities are limited or non-existent (Tavakoli & Mura, 2015). In the future, the conscious exploitation of technology in the quest to provide even greater levels of escapism is likely to shape the consumption and production of HSLT.

Environmental drivers

There is no doubt that the climate is changing and while this change is in part due to natural occurrences, it has been accelerated by human action (IPCC, 2013). Given that the impacts of global warming are already being felt most notably through the increased incidence of extreme weather events, climate change is probably the most important driver which is likely to affect HSLT in the future. There is much evidence of its occurrence around the world and of the challenges it poses for HSLT sites and destinations. For instance, in 2011 the USA experienced an unprecedented 14 disastrous weather events resulting in an estimated US$53bn in damage, while in 2012 drought affected more than two-thirds of the country with the months of January–July being the hottest ever recorded. In 2013 there was large-scale flooding across central and eastern Europe affecting Germany, Prague and Hungary, while in the UK heavy rains combined with strong winds and high waves led to widespread flooding and coastal damage causing significant disruption to individuals, businesses and infrastructure. Moreover, Australia recently banned tourists from the Outback due to heatwaves, the new Maldives president has bought up land in India for relocation due to rising sea levels, and in Venice, hit by floods during the winter of 2014, the mayor has called on tourists not to come to the city. Additionally, in a report written by Churchill Insurance with the help of the Centre for Future Studies (2006) entitled 'The Future of World Travel', by 2020 many significant heritage sites will be irreparably damaged and many coastal and marine environments will become seriously overcrowded. It predicted that in a little more than a decade global warming will heat up many Mediterranean destinations. Tuscany and the Amalfi Coast in Italy and the Island of Crete, for example, will experience more heatwaves with an increase in dry days and a greater risk of fire. Southern Spain may become a suitable habitat for malaria-bearing mosquitoes.

Climate change is unequivocal and, as opposed to considering whether it is occurring or not, scientific debate now focuses on the pace of such change (IPCC, 2013). Consequently, HSLT businesses and destinations across the world need to recognise the risks imposed, particularly by extreme weather, and proactively adapt to its impacts. However, KPMG (2009) claims that tourism is among the industries least prepared and most vulnerable to climate change, both physically and in terms of its image. Heatwaves, droughts and rising sea levels are some factors that will directly impact on many HSLT destinations in the short term. In the longer term, water shortages and scarcer resources may lead to social conflict, which could adversely affect the stability of the tourism sector. Indeed, controversially, Kelley *et al.* (2015) argue that there is evidence that the 2007–2010 drought experienced in Syria has contributed to conflict and to the refugee crisis, impacting on most countries across Europe. The lack of industry preparedness is reinforced by Becken (2013), who states that there is poor integration of climate change adaptation into tourism policy, evidence that tourism stakeholders do not consider climate change to be a problem and insufficient communication among government departments. Despite global efforts to tackle global warming, climate change will continue to pose key challenges for the tourist industry generally and HSLT specifically, not only in relation to infrastructure and day-to-day operations, but also in terms of economic viability, competitiveness and sustainability through destination health, choice, visitor experience and tourist spending.

Conclusion

This chapter has revisited the applicability of S-DL and co-creation as concepts within which to couch an investigation of contemporary developments within HSLT. It posits the importance of the HSLT nexus and of value co-creation in constructing quality tourist experiences, while at the same time drawing attention to the fact that value co-creation is not always positive as it can also result in value co-destruction. It is within the context of the value co-creation and value co-destruction spectrum that this text reviews the key themes and issues that have arisen from this in-depth analysis, these being value creation and historical distortion and over-consumption. In addition, this chapter highlights a range of economic, demographic, consumer, technological and environmental drivers which are likely to affect the future of HSLT. It is extremely difficult to predict which, if any, are going to impact the most, whether positively or negatively. Thus it is imperative that, together, these issues and trends are considered in any future developments.

References

Abercrombie, N. and Longhurst, B. (1998) *Audiences*. London: Sage.

Abeyraine, R.I. (1995) Proposals and guidelines for the carriage of elderly and disabled persons by air. *Journal of Travel Research* 33 (3), 52–59.

Agnew, J.A. and Duncan, J.S. (1989) *The Power of Place*. London: Unwin Hyman.

Ajzen, I. (1992) Persuasive communication theory in social psychology: A historical perspective. In M. Manfredo (ed.) *Influencing Human Behaviour: Theory and Applications in Recreation, Tourism and Natural Resources Management* (pp. 1–27). Champaign, IL: Sagamore.

Alderson, W.T. and Low, S.P. (1976) *Interpretation of Historic Sites*. Nashville, TN: American Association for State and Local History.

Alegre, J. and Garau, J. (2010) Tourist satisfaction and dissatisfaction. *Annals of Tourism Research* 37 (1), 52–73.

Aluza, A., O'Leary, J. and Morrison, A. (1998) Cultural and heritage tourism: Identifying niches for international travellers. *Journal of Tourism Studies* 9 (2), 2–13.

ALVA (Association of Leading Visitor Attractions) (2015) *Latest Visitor Figures*. See www.alva.org.uk/details.cfm?p = 423 (accessed 28 July 2015).

Amey, K. (2015) From Game of Thrones to Thor: Iceland sees tourism boom as a favourite filming spot for hit TV shows and Hollywood blockbusters. *Mail Online*, 6 April. See http://www.dailymail.co.uk/travel/travel_news/article-3019329/Iceland-sees-tourism-boom-thanks-filming-locations-used-Game-Thrones.html (accessed 7 July 2015).

Amrhein, S. (2014) 'Bollywood Oscars' IIFA in Florida for US Debut. *Reuters Entertainment News*, 26 April. See http://in.reuters.com/article/2014/04/25/us-film-usa-bollywood-idINKBN0DB15T20140425 (accessed 30 July 2015).

Andersen, H.C. and Robinson, M. (eds) (2002) *Literature and Tourism: Reading and Writing Tourism Texts*. London: Continuum.

Anderson, D., Horlock, N. and Jackson, T. (2000) *Testing the Water: Young People and Galleries*. Liverpool: Liverpool University Press.

Andoni, B. (2013) Albania struggles to protect its vandalised heritage. *BalkanInsight*, 18 February. See www.balkaninsight.com/en/article/albania-struggles-to-protect-its-vandalized-heritage (accessed 30 June 2016).

Andrades, L. and Dimanche, F. (2014) Co-creation of experience value: A tourist behaviour approach. In M. Chen and J. Uysal (eds) *Creating Experience Value in Tourism* (pp. 95–112). London: CABI.

Ang, I. (1985) *Watching Dallas: Soap Opera and the Melodramatic Imagination*. London: Metheun.

Angkawi Insight (2016) *Langkawi International Book Village*. See https://www.langkawi-insight.com/langkawi_0000a9.htm (accessed 30 June 2016).

Anglesey Tourism (2016) *Anglesey: A Bridge Through Time*. See http://www.angleseyheritage.com/ (accessed 1 July 2016).

Anne Frank House (2015) *From Hiding Place to Museum*. See http://www.annefrank.org/en/Museum/From-hiding-place-to-museum/ (accessed 9 June 2016).

Apostolakis, A. (2003) The convergence process in heritage tourism. *Annals of Tourism Research* 30 (4), 795–812.

Appadurai, A. (1981) The past as a scarce resource. *Man, New Series* 16, 201–219.

Appadurai, A. (1986) (ed.) *The Social Life of Things*. Cambridge: Cambridge University Press.

Ashworth, G. (1990) *Selling the City*. London: Belhaven Press.

Ashworth, G. (1994) From history to heritage – from heritage to identity. In search of concepts and models. In G.J. Ashworth and P.J. Larkham (eds) *Building a New Heritage Tourism, Culture and Identity in the New Europe* (pp. 13–30). London: Routledge.

Ashworth, G. (1995) Heritage, tourism and Europe: A European future for a European Past. In D. Herbert (ed.) *Heritage Tourism and Society* (pp. 68–84). London: Mansell.

Ashworth, G. (1998) Heritage, identity and interpreting a European sense of place. In D. Uzzell and R. Ballantyne (eds) *Contemporary Issues in Heritage and Environmental Interpretation* (pp. 112–132). London: Stationary Office.

Ashworth, G.J. and Larkham, P.J. (1994) *Building a New Heritage: Tourism, Culture and Identity in the New Europe*. London: Routledge.

Ashworth, G. and Tunbridge, J. (1996) *Dissonant Heritage. The Resource in Conflict*. New York: Wiley.

Assaker, G., Vinzi, V. and O'Connor, P. (2011) Examining the effect of novelty seeking, satisfaction, and destination image on tourists' return pattern: A two factor, non-linear latent growth model. *Tourism Management* 32 (4), 890–901.

Austin, J.L. (1975) *How to Do Things With Words*. Oxford: Oxford University Press.

Axtell, N. (2012) Record-breaking crowds continue at DuPont. *Blueridgenow.com*, 29 November. See www.blueridgenow.com/article/20121129/ARTICLES/121129785 (accessed 29 July 2015).

Azevedo, A. (2009) Designing unique and memorable experiences: Co-creation and the 'surprise' factor. Paper presented at the *III Congresso Internacional de Turismo de Leiria e Oeste – 2009*, Leiria, Portugal.

Bagnall, G. (2003) Performance and performativity at heritage sites. *Museum & Society* 1 (2), 87–103.

Bahn, P. (2007) *Cave Art: A Guide to the Decorated Ice Age Caves of Europe*. London: Frances Lincoln.

Baker, V. (2014) Hay-on-Wye: Beyond the festival. *Guardian Online*, 17 May. See http://www.theguardian.com/travel/2014/may/17/hay-on-wye-beyond-the-festival (accessed 27 June 2016).

Bal, M. (1997) *Narratology: Introduction to the Theory of Narrative*. Toronto: University of Toronto Press.

Ballantyne, R. and Uzzell, D. (1998) *Contemporary Issues in Heritage and Environmental Interpretation: Problems and Prospects*. London: Stationery Office.

Ballantyne, D. and Varey, R.J. (2008) The service-dominant logic and the future of marketing. *Journal of the Academy of Marketing Science* 36 (1), 11–14.

Bandyopadhyay, R., Morais, D.B. and Chick, G. (2008) Religion and identity in India's heritage tourism. *Annals of Tourism Research* 35 (3), 790–780.

Bartlett, A. and Kelly, L. (2000) *Youth Audiences: Research Summary*. Sydney: Australian Museum.

Basu, P. (2007) *Highland Homecomings: Genealogy and Heritage Tourism in the Scottish Diaspora*. London: Routledge.

Baum, T. (1995) Ireland – the peace divided. *Insights* July, A9–A14.

Baurillard, J. (1983) *Simulations*. New York: Semiotext(e).

BBC (2005) *Gloucestershire: Harry Potter's County*. See http://www.bbc.co.uk/gloucester-shire/content/articles/2005/04/21/harry_potters_county_feature.shtml (accessed 7 June 2010).

BBC News (2015) China economy: New signs of economic growth slowing. *BBC News,* 13 September. See http://www.bbc.co.uk/news/business-34237939 (accessed 9 October 2015).

Becken, S. (2011) A critical review of tourism and oil. *Annals of Tourism Research* 38 (2), 359–379.

Becken, S. (2013) A review of tourism and climate change as an evolving knowledge domain. *Tourism Management Perspectives* 6, 53–62.

Becken, S. and Lennox, J. (2012) Implications of a long-term increase in oil prices for tourism. *Tourism Management* 33 (1), 133–142.

Beckmann, E.A. (1988) Interpretation in Australia: Some examples outside national parks. *Australian Parks and Recreation* 24 (3), 8–12.

Beeho, A., Davies, A. and Prentice, R. (1997) Seeking generic motivations for visiting and not visiting museums and like cultural attractions. *Museum Management and Curatorship* 16, 45–70.

Beeton, S. (2001) Smiling for the camera: The influence of film audiences on a budget tourism destination. *Tourism, Culture & Communication* 3 (1), 15–25.

Beeton, S. (2005) *Film-Induced Tourism*. Bristol: Channel View Publications.

Beeton, S. (2010) The advance of film tourism. *Tourism, Hospitality Planning & Development* 7 (1), 1–6.

Beeton, S. (2015) *Travel, Tourism and the Moving Image*. Bristol: Channel View Publications.

Beeton, S. (2016) *Film-Induced Tourism* (2nd edn). Bristol: Channel View Publications.

Beeton, S., Weiler, B. and Ham, S. (2005) *Contextual Analysis for Applying Persuasive Communication Theory to Managing Visitor Behaviour: A Scoping Study of Port Campbell National Park*. Gold Coast: Cooperative Research Centre for Sustainable Tourism.

Belfast City Council (2015) *Literary Belfast*. See http://www.belfastcity.gov.uk/tourism-venues/tourism/literarybelfast.aspx (accessed 29 July 2014).

Belhassen, Y., Caton, K. and Stewart, W.P. (2008) The search for authenticity in the pilgrim experience. *Annals of Tourism Research* 35 (3), 668–689.

Bellini, N. and Pasquinelli, C. (2015) Urban brandscape as value ecosystem: The cultural destination strategy of fashion brands. *Place Branding and Public Diplomacy* 12 (1), 5–16.

Berry, L.L (1983) Relationship marketing. In L. Berry, G.L. Shostack and G.D. Upah (eds) *Emerging Perspectives on Services Marketing* (pp. 25–28). Chicago, IL: American Marketing Association.

Bertella, G. (2014) The co-creation of animal-based tourism experience. *Tourism Recreation Research* 39 (1), 115–125.

Bessière, J. (1998) Local development and heritage: Traditional food and cuisine as tourist attractions in rural areas. *Sociologia Ruralis* 38 (1), 21–34.

Binkhorst, E. (2005) *The Co-creation Tourism Experience*. Sitges: Whitepaper Co-creations.

Binkhorst, E. and Den Dekker, T. (2009) Agenda for co-creation tourism experience research. *Journal of Hospitality Marketing & Management* 18 (2), 311–327.

Biran, A., Poria, Y. and Oren, G. (2011) Sought experiences at (dark) heritage sites. *Annals of Tourism Research* 38, 820–841.

Bitner, M. (1992) Servicescapes: The impact of physical surroundings on customers and employees. *Journal of Marketing* 56, 57–71.

Blakely, R. (2009) Slum tours get Slumdog Millionaire boost. *Times Online*, 21 January. See http://www.timesonline.co.uk/tol/news/world/asia/article5555635.ece (accessed 23 September 2010).

Bolan, P. and Williams, L. (2008) The role of image in service promotion: Focusing on the influence of film on consumer choice within tourism. *International Journal of Consumer Studies* 32, 382–309.

Bolan, P., Boy, S. and Bell, J. (2011) We've seen it in the movies, let's see if it's true: Authenticity and displacement in film-induced tourism. *Worldwide Hospitality and Tourism Themes* 3, 102–116.

Boorstin, D.J. (1964) *The Image: A Guide to Pseudo Events in America*. New York: Harper.

Bordwell, D. and Thompson, K. (1993) *Film Art: An Introduction*. New York: McGraw-Hill.

Borum, M. and Massey, C. (1990) Cognitive science research and science museum exhibits. In S. Bitgood, A. Benefield and U. Patterson (eds) *Visitor Studies: Theory, Research and Practice* (pp. 231–236). Jacksonville, AL: Centre for Social Design.

Bossen, C. (2000) Festival mania, tourism and nation building in Fiji: The case of the Hibiscus Festival, 1956–1970. *Contemporary Pacific* 12 (1), 123–154.

Bourdieu, P. (1984) *Distinction: A Social Critique of the Judgement of Taste*. London: Routledge.

Bowden, D. and Schouten, A.F. (2008) Tourist satisfaction and beyond: Tourist migrants in Mallorca. *International Journal of Tourism Research* 10 (1), 141–153.

Boyd, S.W. (2000) Heritage tourism in Northern Ireland: Opportunity under peace. *Current Issues in Tourism* 3 (3), 150–174.

Bradburne, J. (1998) Dinosaurs and white elephants: The science centre in the 21st century. *Museum Management and Curatorship* 17, 119–137.

Bradley, D., Bradley, J., Coombes, M., Grove, L., Thomas, S. and Young, C. (2012) *The Extent of Crime and Anti-Social Behaviour Facing Designated Heritage Assets. Final Report*. London: English Heritage.

Braid, D. (1996) Personal narrative and experiential meaning. *Journal of American Folklore* 109, 5–30.

Bredevoort (2016) *Bredevoort*. See http://www.bredevoort.nu/english.php (accessed 27 June 2016).

Brewer W.F. and Nakamura, G.V. (1984) The nature and functions of schema. In R.S. Wyer and T.K. Srull (eds) *The Handbook of Social Cognition* (Vol. 1, pp. 119–160). Hillsdale, NJ: Lawrence Erlbaum.

Bright, A., Manfredo, M., Fishbein, M. and Bath, A. (1993) Application of the theory of reasoned action to the National Park Service's controlled burn policy. *Journal of Leisure Research* 25 (3), 263–280.

Britton, S. (1991) Tourism, capital and place: Towards a critical geography of tourism. *Environment and Planning D: Society and Space* 9, 451–478.

Brodie, I. (2003) *The Lord of the Rings Location Guidebook*. New Zealand: Harper Collins.

Brooker, W. (2005) The blade runner experience: Pilgrimage and liminal space. In W. Brooker (ed.) *The Blade Runner Experience* (pp. 11–30). London: Wallflower.

Brooker, W. (2007) Everywhere and nowhere: Vancouver, fan pilgrimage and the urban imaginary. *International Journal of Cultural Studies* 10 (4), 434–444.

Brown, S. (2005) *Wizard!: Harry Potter's Brand Magic*. London: Cyan Books.

Brown, S. and Patterson, A. (2010) Selling stories: Harry Potter and the marketing plot. *Psychology and Marketing* 27 (6), 541–556.

Bruner, E.M. (1989) Tourism, creativity and authenticity. *Studies in Symbolic Interaction* 10, 109–114.

Bruner, E.M. (1991) Transformation of self in tourism. *Annals of Tourism Research* 18 (2), 238–250.

Bruner, E. (1993) Lincoln's New Salem as a contested site. *Museum Anthropology* 17 (3), 14–25.

Bruner, E.M. (1994) Abraham Lincoln as authentic reproduction: A critique of post-modernism. *American Anthropologist* 96 (2), 397–415.

Bruner, E. (1996) Tourism in Ghana: The representation of slavery and the return of the Black Diaspora. *American Anthropologist* 98 (3), 291–304.

Bruner, E.M. and Kirshenblatt-Gimblett, B. (1994) Masai on the lawn: Tourist realism in East Africa. *Cultural Anthropology* 9 (4), 435–470.

BTA/ETB (1996) *Overseas Visitor Survey 1996*. London: British Tourist Authority/English Tourist Board Research Services.

BTA/ETB (1998) *Visits to Tourist Attractions 1998*. London: British Tourist Authority/ English Tourist Board Research Services.

Buchmann, A. (2010) Planning and development in film tourism: Insights into the experience of Lord of the Rings film guides. *Tourism and Hospitality Planning & Development* 7 (1), 77–84.

Buchmann, A., Moore, K. and Fisher, D. (2010) Experiencing film tourism. Authenticity and fellowship. *Annals of Tourism Research* 37 (1), 229–248.

Buckley, P.J. and Klemm, M. (1993) The decline of tourism in Northern Ireland. *Tourism Management* 14 (3), 184–194.

Büecherstadt Tourismus (2016) *Book and Bunker Town Wünsdorf*. See http://www.buecherstadt.com/en/ (accessed 30 June 2016).

Buhalis, D. and Amaranggana, A. (2014) Smart tourism destinations. In Z. Xiang and I. Tussyadiah (eds) *Information and Communication Technologies in Tourism 2014* (pp. 553–564). Vienna: Springer.

Burgess, J. (1990) The production and consumption of environmental meanings in the mass media: A research agenda for the 1990s. *Transactions of the Institute of British Geographers* 15 (2), 139–161.

Busby, G. (2001) Vocationalism in higher level tourism courses: The British perspective. *Journal of Further and Higher Education* 25 (1), 29–43.

Busby, G. and Devereux, H. (2015) Dark tourism in context: The Diary of Anne Frank. *European Journal of Tourism, Hospitality and Recreation* 6 (1), 27–38.

Busby, G. and George, J. (2004) *The Tailor of Gloucester: Potter Meets Potter – Literary Tourism in a Cathedral City. Conference Proceedings: Tourism & Literature*, Harrogate, 22–26 July.

Busby, G. and Haines, C. (2013) Doc Martin and film tourism: The creation of destination image. *Tourism* 61, 105–120.

Busby, G. and Hambly, Z. (2000) Literary tourism and the Daphne Du Maurier Festival. In P. Payton (ed.) *Cornish Studies* (Vol. 8, pp. 197–212). Exeter: Exeter University Press.

Busby, G. and Klug, J. (2001) Movie-induced tourism: The challenge of measurement and other issues. *Journal of Vacation Marketing* 7 (4), 316–332.

Busby, G. and Meethan, K. (2008) Cultural capital in Cornwall: Heritage and the visitor. In P. Payton (ed.) *Cornish Studies Sixteen* (pp. 146–166). Exeter: University of Exeter Press.

Busby, G. and O'Neill, K. (2006) Cephallonia and Captain Corelli's Mandolin: The influence of literature and film on British visitors. *Acta Turistica* 18 (1), 30–51.

Butler, D. (2001) Whitewashing plantations: The commodification of a slave-free antebellum South. In G. Dann and A. Seaton (eds) *Slavery Contested Heritage and Thanatourism* (163–176). Binghamton, NY: Haworth Hospitality Press.

Butler, R. (1986) Literature as an influence in shaping the image of tourist destinations: A review and case study. In J. Marsh (ed.) *Canadian Studies of Parks, Recreation and Foreign Lands* (pp. 111–132). Occasional paper no. 11, Peterborough: Department of Geography, Trent University.

Butler, R.W. (1996) The influence of the media in shaping international tourist patterns. *Tourism Recreation Research* 15 (2), 46–53.

Butler, R. (2011) It's only make believe: The implications of fictional and authentic locations in films. *Worldwide Hospitality and Tourism Themes* 3 (2), 91–101.

Buzinde, C. (2007) Representational politics of plantation heritage: The contemporary plantation as a social imaginary. In C. McCarthy, A. Durham, L. Engel, A. Filmer, M. Giardina and M. Malagreca (eds) *Globalizing Cultural Studies: Ethnographic Interventions in Theory Method and Policy* (pp. 229–252). New York: Peter Lang.

Buzinde, C. and Osagie, I.F. (2011) Slavery, heritage representations, cultural citizenship and judicial politics in America. *Historical Geography* 39, 41–64.

Buzinde, C. and Santos, C.A. (2008) Representations of slavery. *Annals of Tourism Research* 35 (2), 469–488.

Buzinde, C.N. and Santos, C.A. (2009) Interpreting slavery tourism. *Annals of Tourism Research* 36 (3), 439–458.

Byrne, D. (1991) Western hegemony in archaeological management. *History and Anthropology* 5 (2), 269–276.

Cadw (2012) *The Story So Far ... An Overview of the Pan-Wales Heritage Interpretation Plan.* Wales: Cadw.

Caldwell, N. (2002) (Rethinking) the measurement of service quality in museums and galleries. *International Journal of Non-Profit and Voluntary Sector Marketing* 7 (2), 161–171.

Camoin Associates (2015) *Economic Impact of the Film Industry in New York State.* Saratuga Springs, NY: Camoin Associates.

Campbell, C. (1987) *The Romantic Ethic and the Spirit of Modern Consumerism.* Oxford: Blackwell.

Campos, A.C., Mendes, J., Oom do Valle, P. and Scott, N. (2015) Co-creation of tourist experiences: A literature review. *Current Issues in Tourism*; http://dx.doi.org/10.1080/1 3683500.2015.1081158.

Candrea, A.N. and Ispas, A. (2009) Visitor management, a tool for sustainable tourism development in protected areas. *Bulletin of the Transylvania University of Brasov Economic Sciences Series* 5 (2), 131–136.

Carl, D., Kindon, S. and Smith, K. (2007) Tourists' experiences of film locations: New Zealand as 'Middle-Earth'. *Tourism Geographies* 9 (1), 49–63.

Carnegie, E. and McCabe, S. (2008) Re-enactment events and tourism: Meaning authenticity and identity. *Current Issues in Tourism* 11 (4), 349–368.

Cartmell, D. (2013) Becoming Jane in screen adaptations of Austen's fiction. In J. Buchanan (ed.) *The Writer on Film: Screening Literary Authorships* (pp. 151–163). Basingstoke: Palgrave.

Cavinato, J.L. and Cuckovich, M.L. (1992) Transportation and tourism for the disabled: An assessment. *Transportation Journal* 31 (3), 46–53.

Cesaroni, F. and Duque, L.C. (2013) Open innovation and service dominant logic: Application of foundational premises to innovative firms. *Harvard Deusto Business Research* 2 (1), 17–34.

Chan, B. (2007) Film-induced tourism in Asia: A case study of Korean TV drama and female viewers' motivation to visit Korea. *Tourism, Culture & Communication* 7 (3), 207–224.

Chan, J.K.L. (2009) The consumption of museum service experiences: Benefits and value of museum experiences. *Journal of Hospitality Marketing & Management* 18, 173–196.

Chaney, D. (1993) *Fictions of Collective Life.* London: Routledge.

Chathoth, P., Altinay, L., Harrington, R.J., Okumus, F. and Chan, E.S. (2013) Co-production versus co-creation: A process based continuum in the hotel service context. *International Journal of Hospitality Management* 32, 11–20.

Chen, C.-F. and Chen F.-S. (2010) Experience quality, perceived value, satisfaction and behavioural intentions for heritage tourists. *Tourism Management* 31 (1), 29–35.

Chen, C.-F. and Tsai, D. (2007) How destination image and evaluative factors affect behavioural intentions? *Tourism Management* 28 (4), 1115–1122.

Chen, Y.C., Shang, R.A. and Li, M.J. (2014) The effects of perceived relevance of travel blogs' content on the behavioural intention to visit a tourist destination. *Computers in Human Behaviour* 30, 787–799.

Cheong, S. and Miller, M. (2000) Power and tourism: A Foucauldian observation. *Annals of Tourism Research* 27 (2), 371–390.

Chhabra, D., Healy, R. and Sills, E. (2003) Staged authenticity and heritage tourism. *Annals of Tourism Research* 30 (3), 702–719.

China Daily (2013) *A Rewarding Tourist Experience.* See https://www.pressreader.com/china/china-daily-usa/20130222/281913065519986 (accessed 15 June 2017).

China Highlights (2015) *The Top Movie (and TV) Destinations in China.* See http://www.chinahighlights.com/travelguide/article-top-movie-destinations-in-china.htm (accessed 28 July 2015).

China Highlights (2016) *China's Classic Novels.* See http://www.chinahighlights.com/travelguide/culture/china-classic-novels.htm (accessed 9 June 2016).

Chistensen, C. (2013) @Sweden: Curating a nation on Twitter. *Popular Communication: International Journal of Media and Culture* 11 (1), 30–46.

Chronis, A. (2005) Co-constructing heritage at the Gettysburg storyscape. *Annals of Tourism Research* 32 (2), 386–406.

Churchill Travel Insurance (2006) *The Future of Travel: The 'Disappearing Destinations' of 2020.* Report prepared on behalf of Churchill Travel Insurance by the Centre of Future Studies. Leeds: Churchill Travel Insurance.

CIA (2016) *The World Factbook.* Washington, DC: Central Intelligence Agency. See https://www.cia.gov/library/publications/the-world-factbook/ (accessed 16 June 2016).

Clark, R. and Stankey, G. (1979) *The Recreation Opportunity Spectrum: A Framework for Planning, Management and Research.* Washington, DC: US Government Printing Office.

Cohen, D. (1994) *The Combining of History.* Chicago, IL: University of Chicago Press.

Cohen, E. (1979) Rethinking the sociology of tourism. *Annals of Tourism Research* 6 (1), 18–35.

Cohen, E. (1988) Authenticity and commoditization in tourism. *Annals of Tourism Research* 15 (3), 371–386.

Cohen, E. (1996) The sociology of tourism: Approaches, issues and findings. In Y. Apostolopoulos, S. Leivadi and A. Yiannakis (eds) *The Sociology of Tourism: Theoretical and Empirical Investigations* (pp. 51–74). London: Routledge.

Cohen, E. (2008) Know thyself? Assimilating the classical leisure ideal, self-actualisation, flow experience and existential authenticity. In P. Gilchrist and B. Wheaton (eds) *Whatever Happened to the Leisure Society? Theory, Debate and Policy* (pp. 165–180). Eastbourne: Leisure Studies Association.

Cohen, E. (2011) Educational dark tourism at an 'in populo' site. The Holocaust Museum in Jerusalem. *Annals of Tourism Research* 38 (1), 193–209.

Cole, S. (2007a) Beyond authenticity and commodification. *Annals of Tourism Research* 34 (4), 943–960.

Cole, S. (2007b) Implementing and evaluating a code of conduct for visitors. *Tourism Management* 28 (2), 443–451.

Connell, J. (2005) Toddlers, tourism and Tobermory: Destinations marketing issues and TV-induced tourism. *Tourism Management* 26 (5), 749–755.

Connell, J. (2012) Film tourism – evolution, progress and prospects. *Tourism Management* 33 (5), 1007–1029.

Connell, J. and Meyer, D. (2009) Balamory revisited: An evaluation of the screen tourism destination–tourist nexus. *Tourism Management* 30 (2), 194–207.

Couldry, N. (1998) The view from inside the 'simulacrum': Visitors' tales from the set of Coronation Street. *Leisure Studies* 17 (2), 94–107.

Couldry, N. (2005) On the actual street. In D. Crouch, R. Jackson and F. Thompson (eds) *The Media and the Tourist Imagination: Converging Cultures* (pp. 60–75). London: Routledge.

Cresswell, T. and Dixon, D. (eds) (2002) *Engaging Film: Geographies of Mobility and Identity.* Lanham, MD: Rowman & Littlefield.

Cronon, W. (1992) A place for stories: Nature, history and narrative. *Journal of American History* 78, 1347–1376.

Crouch, D. (2000) Places around us: Embodied lay geographies in leisure and tourism. *Leisure Studies* 19 (1), 63–76.

Croy, W.G. and Heitmann, S. (2011) Tourism and film. In P. Robinson, S. Heitmann and P. Dieke (eds) *Research Themes in Tourism* (pp. 188–204). Wallingford: CABI.

Culler, J. (1981) Semiotics of tourism. *American Journal of Semiotics* 1 (1–2), 127–140.

Cunningham, S.J. and Hinze, A. (2013) Supporting the reader in the wild: Identifying design features for a literary tourism application. *Proceedings of the 14th Annual Conference of the New Zealand Chapter of the ACM's Special Interest Group on Human–Computer Interaction (CHINZ '13).* Christchurch, NZ: Association for Computing Machinery.

Dahles, H. (1998) Redefining Amsterdam as a touristic destination. *Annals of Tourism Research* 25 (1), 55–69.

Daniel, Y. (1996) Tourism dance performances: Authenticity and creativity. *Annals of Tourism Research* 23 (4), 780–797.

Daniels, B. (2015) Alnwick Castle takes on record staff as it expects bumper season. *ChronicleLive*, 3 April. See http://www.chroniclelive.co.uk/lifestyle/travel/alnwick-castle-takes-record-staff-8973475 (accessed 30 July 2015).

Dann, G. and Potter, R. (2001) Supplanting the planters: Hawking heritage in Barbados. In G. Dann and A. Seaton (eds) *Slavery, Contested Heritage and Thanatourism* (pp. 51–84). Binghamton, NY: Haworth Hospitality Press.

Dann, G. and Seaton, A. (eds) (2001) *Slavery, Contested Heritage and Thanotourism.* Binghamton, NY: Haworth Hospitality Press.

Darcy, S. (2012) (Dis)embodied air travel experiences: Disability, discrimination and the effect of a discontinuous air travel chain. *Journal of Hospitality and Tourism Management* 19 (1), 91–101.

Daruwalla, P. and Darcy, S. (2005) Personal and societal attitudes to disability. *Annals of Tourism Research* 32 (3), 549–570.

Davies, A. and Prentice, R. (1995) Conceptualising the latent visitor to heritage attractions. *Tourism Management* 16, 491–500.

Davin, S. (2005) Tourists and television viewers: Some similarities. In D. Crouch, R. Jackson and F. Thompson (eds) *The Media and the Tourist Imagination: Converging Cultures* (pp. 170–182). London: Routledge.

Den Norske Bokbyen (2016) *About the Book Town.* See http://bokbyen.no/en/start-page/ (accessed 30 June 2016).

Department of Enterprise, Trade and Investment (2010) *A Draft Tourism Strategy for Northern Ireland to 2020.* Belfast: Department of Enterprise, Trade and Investment.

Department of Tourism (2011) *National Tourism Sector Strategy.* Pretoria: Department of Tourism, Republic of South Africa.

de Rojas, C. and Camarero, C. (2008) Visitors' experience, mood and satisfaction in a heritage context: Evidence from an interpretation centre. *Tourism Management* 29 (3), 525–537.

de Ruyter, K., Wetzels, M., Lemmink, J. and Mattsson, J. (1997) The dynamics of the service delivery process: A value-based approach. *International Journal of Research in Marketing* 14 (3), 231–243.

Diekmann, A. and Hannam, K. (2012) Touristic mobilities in India's slum spaces. *Annals of Tourism Research* 39 (3), 1315–1336.

Digital Tourism Think Tank (2015) *Insights: Augmented Reality in Tourism*. See http://thinkdigital.travel/all-insights/augmented-reality-in-tourism/ (accessed 1 July 2016).

Doh, S.J. and Hwang, J.S. (2009) How consumers evaluate eWOM messages. *Cyber Psychology and Behaviour* 12 (2), 193–197.

Drost, A. (1996) Developing sustainable tourism for World Heritage sites. *Annals of Tourism Research* 23 (2), 479–492.

Durham, C. (2008) Finding France on film: Chocolat, Amélie and Le Divorce. *French Cultural Studies* 19 (2), 173–197.

Eagles, P.F., McCool, S.F. and Haynes, C. (2002) *Sustainable Tourism in Protected Areas: Guidelines for Planning and Management*. Glad and Cambridge: International Union for Conservation of Nature (IUCN).

Earl, B. (2008) Literary tourism: Constructions of value, celebrity and distinction. *International Journal of Cultural Studies* 11 (4), 401–417.

Eco, U. (1975) *Travels in Hyperreality*. New York: Harcourt Brace Jovanovich.

Eco, U. (1986) *Travels in Hyperreality* (2nd edn). San Diego, CA: Harcourt Brace Jovanovich.

Edensor, T. (2001) Performing tourism, staging tourism: (Re)producing tourist space and practice. *Tourist Studies* 1 (1), 59–81.

Edensor, T. (2005) Mediating William Wallace: Audio-visual technologies in tourism. In D. Crouch, R. Jackson and F. Thompson (eds) *The Media and the Tourist Imagination: Converging Cultures* (pp. 105–118). London: Routledge.

Ek, R., Larsen, J. and Hornskov, S.B. (2012) A dynamic framework of tourist experiences: Space–time and performances in the experience economy. *Scandinavian Journal of Hospitality and Tourism* November, 37–41.

Emir, O. and Kozak, M. (2011) Perceived importance of attributes on hotel guests' repeat visit intentions. *Tourism* 59 (2), 131–143.

Environment Canada and Park Service (1991) *Selected Readings on the Visitor Activity Management Process*. Ottawa: Environment Canada.

Ernst & Young (2009) *Economic and Fiscal Impacts of the New Mexico Film Production Tax Credit*. Prepared for the New Mexico State Film Office and State Investment Council. London: Ernst & Young.

Escalas, J.E. and Stern, B.B. (2003) Sympathy and empathy: Emotional responses to advertising drama. *Journal of Consumer Research* 29, 566–578.

Escher, A. and Zimmerman, S. (2001) Geography meets Hollywood: The role of landscape in feature films. *Geographische Zeitschrift* 89 (4), 227–236.

ETurboNews (2009) *Mexico City Expects Tourist Numbers to Increase 35% in 2010*. See http://www.eturbonews.com/13578/mexico-city-expects-tourist-numbers-increase-35-2010 (accessed 15 June 2017).

Euromonitor International (2015) Top 100 city destinations ranking. *Euromonitor International*, 27 January. See blog.euromonitor.com/2015/01/top-100-city-destinations-ranking.html (accessed 10 July 2015).

Eurostar (2006) *Eurostar to spearhead the Da Vinci Code tourism campaign as it becomes film's global partner*. See http://www.eurostar.com/uk-en/about-eurostar/press-office/press-releases/2006/eurostar-spearhead-the-da-vinci-code-tourism (accessed 15 June 2017).

Evaluate Communicate Evolve (2010) *Sapphire Coast Heritage Tourism Strategy (2011–2015)*. See http://www.sapphirecoast.com.au/wp-content/uploads/2013/06/Sapphire-Coast-Heritage-Tourism-Strategy-Final-Updated-9-June.pdf (accessed 20 June 2016).

Evans, M. (1997) Plugging into TV tourism. *Insights* D35–D38.

Falk, J.H. and Dierking, L.D. (2012) *The Museum Experience Revisited*. Washington, DC: Whalesback.

Farson, D. (1997) *The Man Who Wrote Dracula: A Biography of Bram Stoker*. London: Michael Joseph.

Faust, C.G. (2009) 'Angels and Demons' tour illuminates the charms of Rome. *USA Today*. See www.usatoday.com/travel/destinations/2009-05-14-rome-angels-and-demons-tour_N.htm (accessed 15 October 2010).

Fawcett, C. and Cormack, P. (2001) Guarding authenticity at literary tourism sites. *Annals of Tourism Research* 28 (3), 686–704.

Fayos-Sola, E. (1996) Tourism policy: A midsummer night's dream? *Tourism Management* 17 (6), 405–412.

Felix, R., Rauschnabel, P.A. and Hinsch, C. (2016) Elements of strategic social media marketing: A holistic framework. *Journal of Business Research*; doi:10.1016/j.jbusres.2016.05.001.

Fernandez, T. and Neves, S. (2014) The role of Servicescape as a driver of customer value in experience-centric service organisations: The Dragon Football Stadium case. *Journal of Strategic Marketing* 22 (6), 548–560.

Fleming, D. (1999) A question of perception. *Museums Journal* 2, 29–35.

Foley, A., Fahy, J. and Ivers, A.-M. (2014) Brand experience in tourism in the internet age. In S. McCabe (ed.) *The Routledge Handbook of Tourism Marketing* (pp. 140–150). London: Routledge.

Foreign and Commonwealth Office (2016) *Foreign Travel Advice*. See https://www.gov.uk/foreign-travel-advice (accessed 7 June 2017).

Fraser, G.M. (1988) *The Hollywood History of the World*. Michael Joseph: London.

Frost, W. (2006a) Braveheart-ed Ned Kelly: Historic films, heritage tourism and destination image. *Tourism Management* 27 (2), 247–254.

Frost, W. (2006b) *Cultural Heritage and Tourism in Australia. Concepts and Issues*. Working Paper 35/06. Australia: Department of Management, Monash University.

Frost, W. (2010) Life changing experiences: Film and tourists in the Australian outback. *Annals of Tourism Research* 37 (3), 707–726.

Furness, H. (2014) Wolf Hall sets ready for tourist invasion. *Telegraph Online*, 14 December. See www.telegraph.co.uk/culture/tvandradio/bbc/11292423/Wolf-Hall-sets-ready-for-tourist-invasion.html (accessed 30 July 2015).

Future Foundation (2015) *Future Traveller Tribes 2030: Understanding Tomorrow's Traveller*. London: Future Foundation.

Fyall, A. and Garrod, B. (1998) Heritage tourism: At what price? *Managing Leisure: An International Journal* 3 (4), 213–228.

Fyall, A. and Garrod, B. (2005) *Tourism Marketing: A Collaborative Approach*. Clevedon: Channel View Publications.

Fyall, A., Callod, C. and Edwards, B. (2005) Relationship marketing: The challenge for destinations. *Annals of Tourism Research* 30 (3), 644–659.

Galani-Moutafi, V. (2000) The self and the other: Traveller, ethnographer, tourist. *Annals of Tourism Research* 27 (1), 203–224.

Garrod, B. and Fyall, A. (2000) Managing heritage tourism. *Annals of Tourism Research* 27, 682–708.

Garrod, B. and Fyall, A. (2001) Heritage tourism: A question of definition. *Annals of Tourism Research* 28 (4), 1049–1052.

Gergen, K. and Gergen, M. (1988) Narrative and the self as relationship. *Advances in Experimental Social Psychology* 21, 17–56.

GfK Public Affairs and Corporate Communications (2015) *The Anholt-GfK Roper Nation Brands Index*. New York: GfK Public Affairs and Corporate Communications.

Gibson, S. (2006) A seat with a view: Tourism, (im)mobility and the cinematic-travel glance. *Tourist Studies* 6 (2), 157–178.

Gilmore, J.H. and Pine, B.J. (2002) *The Experience is the Marketing*. Aurora, OH: Strategic Horizons.

Gilsdorf, E. (2006) Cities both big and small are offering tours to film locations. *USA Today*, 9 November. See www.usatoday.com/travel/destinations/2006-11-09-movie-tourism_x.htm (accessed 3 October 2010).

Global Heritage Fund (2012) *Asia's Heritage in Peril: Saving Our Vanishing Heritage*. Palo Alto, CA: Global Heritage Fund.

Goffmann, E. (1959) *The Presentation of Self in Everyday Life*. Garden City, NY: Doubleday.

Goh, E. (2010) Understanding the heritage tourist market segment. *International Journal of Leisure and Tourism Marketing* 1 (3), 257–270.

Goldhill, O. (2014) Thrifty aristocrat tips: 'My house has 61 rooms but I get pens free from hotels'. *Telegraph Online*, 6 June. See http://www.telegraph.co.uk/finance/personalfinance/money-saving-tips/10880791/Thrifty-aristocrat-tips-My-house-has-61-rooms-but-I-get-my-pens-free-from-hotels.html (accessed 30 June 2016).

Goodall, B. (1993) Industrial heritage and tourism. *Built Environment* 19 (2), 93–104.

Goodman, D. (1998) Eureka stockade. In G. Davison, J. Hirst and S. MacIntrye (eds) *The Oxford Companion to Australian History* (pp. 227–228). Melbourne: Oxford University Press.

Gordon, S. (2009) Harry Potter and Angels & Demons cause tourism boom. *Mail Online*, 6 May. See www.dailymail.co.uk/travel/article-1187809/Harry-Potter-Angels—Demons-cause-soaring-tourism-films-locations.html (accessed 10 October 2015).

Gottdiener, M. (1997) *The Theming of America*. Oxford: Westview Press.

Goulding (1999) Interpretation and presentation. In A. Leask and I. Yeoman (eds) *Heritage Visitor Attractions: An Operation Management Perspective* (pp. 54–67). London: Cassell.

Goulding, C. and Domic, D. (2009) Heritage, identity and ideological manipulation: The case of Croatia. *Annals of Tourism Research* 36 (1), 85–102.

Graburn, N. (1997) Tourism and cultural development in East Asia. In S. Yamashita, K. Din and J. Eades (eds) *Tourism and Cultural Development in Asia and Oceania* (pp. 194–213). Selangor: Penerbit Universiti Kebangsaan.

Graefe A.R., Kuss, F.R. and Vaske, J.J. (1990) *Visitor Impact Management: The Planning Framework*. Washington, DC: National Parks and Conservation Association.

Gray, L. (2009) Darwin's Galapagos Islands under threat from tourism, warns Andrew Marr. *Telegraph Online*, 12 February. See www.telegraph.co.uk/news/earth/earthnews/4592437/Darwins-Galapagos-islands-under-threat-from-tourism-warns-Andrew-Marr.html (accessed 26 June 2015).

Greenhalgh, P. (1988) *Ephemeral Vistas: The Expositions Universelles, Great Exhibitions and World Fairs, 1851–1939*. New York: Manchester University Press.

Gretzel, U., Kang, M. and Yoo, K.H. (2008) Differences in consumer-generated media adoption and use: A cross-national perspective. *Journal of Hospitality Marketing & Management* 17 (1), 99–120.

Grihault, N. (2003) Film tourism – international. *Travel and Tourism Analyst* 5, 1–22.

Grimm, S. (2010) *Germany's Post-1945 and Post-1989 Education Systems*. World Development Report Background Papers. Washington, DC: World Bank.

Gubrium, J. and Holstein, J. (1998) Narrative practice and the coherence of personal stories. *Sociological Quarterly* 39, 163–187.

Gummesson, E. (1994) Making relationship marketing operational. *International Journal of Service Industry Management* 5 (5), 5–20.

Gunelius, S. (2008) *Harry Potter: The Story of a Global Business Phenomenon*. Basingstoke: Palgrave McMillan.

Guttentag, D. (2010) Virtual reality: Applications and implications for tourism. *Tourism Management* 31 (5), 637–651.

Hailey, A.J. (1999) Residents' opinions of tourism development in the historic city of York, England. *Tourism Management* 20 (5), 595–603.

Hailey, A.J., Snaith, T. and Miller, G. (2005) The social impacts of tourism: A case study of Bath, UK. *Annals of Tourism Research* 32 (3), 647–668.

Hall, C.M. (1997) Geography, marketing and the selling of places. *Journal of Travel and Tourism* 6 (3–4), 61–88.

Hall, C.M. and McArthur, S. (1998) *Integrated Heritage Management*. London: Stationery Office.

Hall, C.M. and Williams A.M. (2008) *Tourism and Innovation*. London: Routledge.

Hall, C.M., Hall, M.C. and Williams, A.M. (2008) *Tourism and Innovation*. London: Routledge.

Hall M.C. and Piggin, R. (2001) Tourism and World Heritage in OECD countries. *Tourism Recreation Research* 26 (1), 103–105.

Hall, S. (1980) Encoding and decoding. In S. Hall, D. Hobson, A. Lowe and P. Willis (eds) *Culture, Media, Language* (pp. 117–127). Thousand Oaks, CA: Sage.

Halsey, A.H., Heath, A. and Ridge, J. (1980) *Origins and Destinations*. Oxford: Oxford University Press.

Ham, S. (1983) Cognitive psychology and interpretation: Synthesis and application. *Journal of Interpretation* 8 (1), 11–28.

Hammitt, W.E. (1984) Cognitive processes involved in environmental interpretation. *Journal of Environmental Education* 15 (4), 11–15.

Hampton, M.P. (2005) Heritage, local communities and economic development. *Annals of Tourism Research* 32 (3), 735–759.

Han, D., Jung, T. and Gibson, A. (2014) Dublin AR: Implementing augmented reality (AR) in tourism. In Z. Xiang and I. Tussyadiah (eds) *Information and Communication Technologies in Tourism* (pp. 511–523). New York: Springer International.

Handler, R. and Gabler, E. (1997) *The New History in an Old Museum: Creating the Past at Colonial Williamsburg*. Durham, NC: Duke University Press.

Hannigan, J. (1998) *Fantasy City: Pleasure and Profit in a Post-Modern Metropolis*. London: Routledge.

Hardyment, C. (1999) *Literary Trails: Writers in their Landscapes*. London: National Trust.

Harflett, N. (2015) 'Bringing them with personal interests': The role of cultural capital in explaining who volunteers. *Voluntary Sector Review* 6 (1), 3–19.

Harrison, D. (2004) Levuka, Fiji: Contested heritage. *Current Issues in Tourism* 7 (4 & 5), 346–369.

Harrison, P. and Shaw, R. (2004) Consumer satisfaction and post-purchase intentions: An exploratory study of museum visitors. *International Journal of Arts Management* 6 (2), 23–33.

Harvey, D. (1989) *The Condition of Post-Modernity*. Oxford: Blackwell.

Harwood, S. and El-Manstrly, D. (2012) The performativity turn in tourism. University of Edinburgh Business School Working Paper No. 12/05. University of Edinburgh.

Hayes, D. (2006) 'Take those old records off the shelf': Youth and music consumption in the postmodern age. *Popular Music and Society* 29 (1), 51–65.

Hay Festival (2016) *Hay Festival. Imagine the World*. See https://www.hayfestival.com/portal/index.aspx?skinid = 1&localesetting = en-GB (accessed 30 June 2016).

HDC International (2016a) *Developing Tourism Partnerships*. See http://www.heritagedestination.com/guide-to-partnerships.aspx (accessed 30 June 2016).

HDC International (2016b) *Heritage Interpretation Editing and Copy Writing*. See http://www.heritagedestination.com/copy-writing.aspx (accessed 01 July 2016).

Hegel, G. (1977) *Phenomenology of Spirit*. Oxford: Clarendon Press.

Heidegger, M. (1996) *Being and Time*. Albany, NY: State University of New York Press.

Hendricks, W. (2000) Attitudes toward roles in a wilderness education program. In D. Cole, S. McCool, W. Borrie and J. O'Loughlin (eds) *Forest Service Proceedings* (Vol. 4, pp. 203–220). Fort Collins, CO: Rocky Mountain Research Station, Department of Agriculture and Forest Service.

Herbert, D. (1989) Does interpretation help? In D.T. Herbert, R. Prentice and C.J. Thomas (eds) *Heritage Sites: Strategies for Marketing and Development* (pp. 191–230). Aldershot: Avebury.

Herbert, D. (1995) (ed.) *Heritage, Tourism and Society*. London: Pinter.

Herbert, D. (1996) Artistic and literary places in France as tourist attractions. *Tourism Management* 17 (2), 77–85.

Herbert, D. (2001) Literary places, tourism and the heritage experience. *Annals of Tourism Research* 28 (2), 312–333.

HLF (Heritage Lottery Fund) (2016a) *Our Grant Programmes*. See www.hlf.org.uk/looking-funding/our-grant-programmes (accessed 17 June 2016).

HLF (Heritage Lottery Fund) (2016b) *Our Strategic Framework*. See https://www.hlf.org.uk/about-us/our-strategy (accessed 30 June 2016).

Hertzman, E. (2006) Visitors' evaluations of the historic content at Storyeum: An edutainment heritage tourism attraction. MA thesis, Faculty of Graduate Studies (Anthropology), University of British Columbia.

Hewison, R. (1987) *The Heritage Industry: Britain in a Climate of Decline*. London: Methuen.

Hills, M. (2002) *Fan Cultures*. London: Routledge.

Hirsch, R.L. (2008) Mitigation of maximum world oil production: Shortage scenarios. *Energy Policy* 36, 881–889.

Historic Houses Association (2016) *Giving a Gift in Your Will*. London: Historic Houses Association.

Hobsbawn, E. and Ranger, T. (1983) (eds) *The Invention of Tradition*. Cambridge: Cambridge University Press.

Holbrook, M.B. (2000) The millennial consumer in the texts of our times: Experience and entertainment. *Journal of Macro Marketing* 20 (2), 178–192.

Holbrook, M.B. (2006) Consumption experience, customer value, and subjective personal introspection: An illustrative photographic essay. *Journal of Business Research* 59, 714–725.

Holmes, D. (2001) (ed.) *Virtual Globalisation: Virtual Spaces/Tourist Places*. London: Routledge.

Hong Kong Tourism Board (2016) *Lung Yeuk Tau Heritage Trail*. See http://www.discover-hongkong.com/uk/see-do/culture-heritage/historical-sites/chinese/lung-yeuk-tau-heritage-trail.jsp (accessed 30 June 2016).

Hooper, J. and Weiss, K. (1991) Interpretation as a management tool: A national study of interpretive professional views. *Legacy* 2, 10–16.

Hoppen, A., Brown, L. and Fyall, A. (2014) Literary tourism: Opportunities and challenges for the marketing and branding of destinations? *Journal of Destination Marketing and Management* 3 (1), 37–47.

Horton, D. and Wohl, R. (1956) Mass communication and parasocial interaction. *Psychiatry* 19, 215–229.

Housham, J. (2007) Long ago, far away and worth millions. *Guardian Online*, 3 November. See www.guardian.co.uk/books/2007/nov/03/featuresreviews.guardianreview22 (accessed 15 June 2016).

Howard, P. (2003) *Heritage: Management, Interpretation, Identity*. London: Continuum.

Huang, Y.-C., Backman, S., Mcguire, F., Backman, K. and Chang, L.-L. (2013) Second-life: The potential of 3D virtual worlds in travel and tourism industry. *Tourism Analysis* 18 (4), 471–477.

Hudson, S. (2008) *Tourism and Hospitality Marketing: A Global Perspective*. London: Sage.

Hudson, S. and Ritchie, J.R.B. (2006a) Promoting destinations via film tourism: An empirical identification of supporting marketing initiatives. *Journal of Travel Research* 44 (3), 387–396.

Hudson, S. and Ritchie, J.R.B. (2006b) Film tourism and destination marketing: The case of Captain Corelli's Mandolin. *Journal of Vacation Marketing* 12 (3), 256–268.

Hughes, G. (1995) Authenticity in tourism. *Annals of Tourism Research* 22 (4), 781–803.

Huh, J., Uysal, M. and McCleary, K. (2006) Cultural/heritage destinations: Tourist satisfaction and market segmentation. *Journal of Hospitality and Leisure Marketing* 14 (3), 81–99.

Hui, A. (2013) Moving with practices: The discontinuous, rhythmic and material mobilities of leisure. *Social and Cultural Geography* 14 (8), 888–908.

Hwang, S.-N., Lee, C. and Chen, H.-J. (2005) The relationship among tourists' involvement, place attachment and interpretation satisfaction in Taiwan's national parks. *Tourism Management* 26 (2), 143–156.

ICOMOS (1993) *Tourism at World Heritage Cultural Sites: The Site Manager's Handbook* (2nd edn). Madrid: World Tourism Organisation.

Im, H. and Chon, K. (2008) An exploratory study of movie-induced tourism: A case of the movie *The Sound of Music* and its locations in Salzburg, Austria. *Journal of Travel and Tourism Marketing* 24 (2–3), 229–238.

IMF (International Monetary Fund) (2015) *World Economic Outlook*. See www.imf.org/external/pubs/ft/weo/2015/01/ (accessed 12 October 2015).

Internet Livestat (2015) *Internet Users*. See www.internetlivestats.com/internet-users/ (accessed 8 July 2016).

Ioannides, D. and Debbage, K. (1997) Post Fordism and flexibility: The travel industry polyglot. *Tourism Management* 18 (4), 229–241.

IOB (International Organisation of Book Towns) (2016) *Our History*. See http://www.booktown.net/history.html (accessed 27 June 2016).

IPCC (Intergovernmental Panel on Climate Change) (2013) *Climate Change 2013. The Physical Science Basis*. Working Group I Contribution to the Fifth Assessment Report of the Intergovernmental Panel on Climate Change. Cambridge: Cambridge University Press.

Israeli, A. (2002) A preliminary investigation of the importance of site accessibility factors for disabled tourists. *Journal of Travel Research* 41 (1), 101–104.

Iwashita, C. (2006) Media representation of the UK as a destination for Japanese tourists. *Tourist Studies* 6 (1), 59–77.

Jameson, F. (1985) Postmodernism and consumer society. In H. Forster (ed.) *Postmodern Culture* (pp. 111–125). London: Pluto Press.

Jang, S. and Feng, R. (2007) Temporal destination revisit intention: The effects of novelty seeking and satisfaction. *Tourism Management* 28 (1), 580–590.

Jensen, K. (2006) Effects of the artistic design of interpretive signage on attracting power, holding time and memory recall. Master's thesis, Humboldt State University.

Johnson, M.D., Gustafsson, A., Andreassen, T., Lervik, L. and Cha, J. (2001) The evolution and future of national customer satisfaction index models. *Journal of Economic Psychology* 22 (2), 217–245.

Johnson, N. (1995) Cast in stone: Monuments, geography and nationalism. *Environment and Planning D: Society and Space* 13, 51–65.

Johnson, R. (1986) What is cultural studies anyway? *Social Text* 16, 38–80.

Jolliffe, L. and Smith, R. (2001) Heritage tourism and museums. The case of the North Atlantic Islands of Skye, Scotland and Prince Edward Island, Canada. *International Journal of Heritage Studies* 7 (2), 149–172.

Jones, C.M. (2015) Indian movie filming in Jacksonville sign of increased activity – and $1 million economic impact. *Jacksonville Business Journal*, 22 June. See http://www.bizjournals.com/jacksonville/news/2015/06/22/indian-movie-filming-in-jacksonville-sign-of.html (accessed 30 July 2015).

Jones, T., Hughes, M., Peel, V., Wood, D. and Frost, W. (2007) *Assisting Local Communities to Develop Heritage Tourism Opportunities*. Queensland: Cooperative Research Centre for Sustainable Tourism.

Jowell, T. (2006) From consultation to conservation: The challenge of better places to live. In K. Clark (ed.) *Capturing the Public Value of Heritage*. Proceedings of the London Conference, 25–26 January (pp. 7–13). Swindon: English Heritage.

Kao, Y.-F., Huang, L.-S. and Wu, C.-H. (2008) Effects of theatrical elements on experiential quality and loyalty intentions for theme parks. *Asia Pacific Journal of Tourism Research* 13 (2), 163–174.

Kaplan, A. and Haenlein, M. (2010) Users of the world, unite! The challenges and opportunities of social media. *Business Horizons* 53 (1), 59–68.

Kaplan, S. and Kaplan, R. (1978) *Humanscape: Environments for People*. Belmont, CA: Duxbury Press.

Karakurum, D. (2006) Cracking the Da Vinci Code: An analysis of the Da Vinci Code phenomenon. Unpublished doctoral dissertation, NHTV Breda University.

Kay, J. (2009) *Venice in Peril. Venice is a Management Challenge*. See http://www.venicein-peril.org/newsroom/news/venice-management-challenge (accessed 22 July 2015).

Keeble, J. (1999) Picture perfect: Film locations. *Telegraph Online*, 20 March. See http://www.telegraph.co.uk/travel/destinations/europe/france/normandyandbrittany/721603/Picture-Perfect-Film-locations.html (accessed 15 June 2017).

Kelley, C.P., Mohtadi, S., Crane, M., Seager, R. and Kushnir, Y. (2015) Climate change in the fertile crescent and implications of the recent Syrian drought. *Proceedings of the National Academy of Sciences of the USA* 112 (1), 3241–3246.

Kelly, G., Mulgan, G. and Muers, S. (2002) *Creating Public Value: An Analytical Framework for Public Service Reform*. London: Strategy Unit, Cabinet Office.

Kelly, L. and Bartlett, A. (2009) *Young People and Museums*. Report produced for the Australian Museum Audience Research Department. See https://www.australian-museum.net.au/young-people-and-museums (accessed 20 October 2014).

Kelly, L., Bartlett, A. and Gordon, P. (2002) *Indigenous Youth and Museums*. Sydney: Australian Museum.

Kershaw, B. (1994) Framing the audience for theatre. In R. Keat, N. Whitely and N. Abercrombie (eds) *The Authority of the Consumer* (pp. 166–186). London and New York: Routledge.

Kerstetter, D., Confer, J. and Bricker, J. (2001) Industrial heritage attractions: Types and tourists. *Journal of Travel and Tourism Marketing* 7 (2), 91–104.

Kim, H. and Richardson, S. (2003) Motion picture impacts on destination images. *Annals of Tourism Research* 30 (1), 216–237.

Kim, J.-H. (2010) Determining the factors affecting the memorable nature of travel experiences. *Journal of Travel and Tourism Marketing* 27 (8), 780–796.

Kim, S. (2010) Extraordinary experience: Re-enacting and photographing at screen tourism locations. *Tourism and Hospitality Planning & Development* 7 (1), 59–75.

Kim, S. (2012) Audience involvement and film tourism experiences: Emotional places, emotional experiences. *Tourism Management* 33, 387–396.

Kim, S. and Rubin, A.M. (1997) The variable influence of audience activity on media effects. *Communication Research* 24 (2), 107–135.

Kim, J. and Tussyadiah, I.P. (2013) Social Networking and Social Support in Tourism Experience: The Moderating Role of Online Self-Presentation Strategies. *Journal of Travel & Tourism Marketing* 30 (1-2), 78–92.

Kim, S., Wong, K. and Cho, M. (2007a) Assessing the economic value of a World Heritage site and willingness-to-pay determinants: A case study of Changdeok Palace. *Tourism Management* 28 (1), 317–322.

Kim, S., Agrusa, H., Lee, H. and Chon, K. (2007b) Effects of Korean TV dramas on the flow of Japanese tourists. *Tourism Management* 28 (5), 1340–1353.

Kim, S., Long, P. and Robinson, M. (2009) Small screen, big tourism: The role of popular Korean television dramas in South Korean tourism. *Tourism Geographies* 11 (3), 308–333.

Kong, L., Yeoh, B. and Teo, P. (1997) The experience of place in old age: A case study of Singapore. *Geographical Review* 86 (4), 529–549.

Korea Tourism Organisation (2016) *Filming Location Tours*. See https://english.visitkorea.or.kr/enu/ATR/SI_ENG_6_4.jsp (accessed 15 June 2017).

Korn, R. (2008) *Audience Research: Young Adult Study*. Boston, MA: Randi & Korn.

KPMG (2009) *World Business Summit on Climate Change, Copenhagen 24–26 May*. See www.kpmg.com/CN/en/IssuesAndInsights/ArticlesPublications/Documents/World-business-summit-200905-o.pdf (accessed 8 July 2016).

Lackey, B. (2002) Empirical and theoretical analysis of communication focused on human–black bear conflicts in Yosemite National Park. PhD thesis, University of Idaho.

Lackey, B. and Ham, S. (2003) Assessment of communication focused on human–black bear conflict at Yosemite National Park. *Journal of Interpretation Research* 8 (1), 25–40.

Laffont, G.H. and Prigent, L. (2011) Paris transformed into an urban set: Dangerous liaisons between tourism and cinema. *Teoros, Revue de Recherche en Tourisme* 30 (1), 108–118.

Laing, J., Wheeler, F., Reeves, K. and Frost, W. (2014) Assessing the experiential value of heritage assets: A case study of a Chinese heritage precinct, Bendigo, Australia. *Tourism Management* 40, 180–192.

Lander, S. (2009) Switzerland to woo India with Bollywood film locations tourism campaign. *Mail Online*, 4 March. See www.dailymail.co.uk/travel/article-1255400/Switzerland-woo-India-Bollywood-film-locations-tourism-campaign.html (accessed 29 September 2010).

Lange-Faria, W. and Elliot, S. (2012) Understanding the role of social media in destination marketing. *Tourismos: An International Multidisciplinary Journal of Tourism* 7 (1), 193–211.

Larry Portzline (2016) *Bookstore Tourism*. See http://www.larryportzline.com/bt.html (accessed 30 June 2016).

Leask, A. and Yeoman, I. (1999) *Heritage Visitor Attractions: An Operations Management Perspective*. London: Thomson.

Lee, B.K., Agarwal, S. and Kim, H.Y. (2012) Influences of travel constrained on the people with disabilities' intention to travel: An application of Seligman's helplessness theory. *Tourism Management* 33, 569–579.

Leinhardt, G., Martin, L. and Schauble, L. (1998) A framework for organising a cumulative research agenda in informal learning contexts. *Journal of Museum Education* 22, 3–8.

Levy, D. and Sznaider, N. (2002) Memory unbound: The Holocaust and the formation of cosmopolitan memory. *European Journal of Social Theory* 5, 87–106.

Lexhagen, M., Larson, M. and Lundberg, C. (2013) The virtual fan (G) community: Social media and pop culture tourism. *Tourism Social Media: Transformations in Identity, Community and Culture* 18, 133–157.

Li, M., Wu, B. and Cai, L. (2008) Tourism development at World Heritage sites in China: A geographic perspective. *Tourism Management* 29, 308–319.

Li, X. and Petrick, J. (2008) Tourism marketing in an era of paradigm shift. *Journal of Travel Research* 46, 235–244.

Li, Y. (2000) Geographical consciousness and tourism experience. *Annals of Tourism Research* 27 (4), 863–883.

Liang, D. (2005) Applying the stock cooperation system to running the World Heritage resources in ancient villages in southern Anhui. *China Population, Resources and Environment* 15 (4), 123–126.

Lichfield, J. (2008) Six months to save Lascaux. *The Independent*, 11 July. See http://www.independent.co.uk/news/world/europe/six-months-to-save-lascaux-865819.html (accessed 25 May 2016).

Liddell, R. (1993) *Literary Tourism*. London: British Tourist Authority.

Liddell, R. (1997) *Literary Tourism* (2nd edn). London: British Tourist Authority.

Light, D. (1995) Visitors' use of interpretive media at heritage sites. *Leisure Studies* 14, 132–149.

Light, D. (2000) Gazing on Communism: Heritage tourism and post-Communist identities in Germany, Hungary and Romania. *Tourism Geographies* 2 (2), 157–176.

Light, D. (2001) 'Facing the future': Tourism and identity-building in post-Socialist Romania. *Political Geography* 20, 1053–1074.

Light, D. (2012) *The Dracula Dilemma: Tourism, Identity and the State of Romania*. Farnham: Ashgate.

Liu, Q. and Yang, S. (1999) Protection of mountain resort and its outlying temples in Chengde. *Chinese Landscape Architecture* 13 (3), 35–36.

Local Futures (2015) *Mindful Travel and Tourist Education Program*. See http://www.local-futures.org/ladakh-project/mindful-travel-a-tourist-education/ (accessed 22 July 2015).

Lowenthal, D. (1985) *The Past is a Foreign Country*. Cambridge: Cambridge University Press.

Lukinbeal, C. and Zimmermann, S. (2006) Film geography: A new subfield (Film-geographie: Ein neues Teilgebiet). *Erdkunde* 60 (4), 315–325.

Lumley, R. (1987) Museums in a post-modern world. *Museums Journal* 87 (2), 81–83.

Lumley, R. (1988) *The Museum Time-Machine: Putting Cultures on Display*. London: Routledge.

Lumley, R. (1994) The debate on heritage reviewed. In R. Miles and L. Zavala (eds) *Towards the Museums of the Future. New European Perspectives*. London: Routledge.

Lusch, R.F. and Vargo, S.L. (2014) *Service-Dominant Logic: Premises, Perspectives, Possibilities*. Cambridge: Cambridge University Press.

Lusch, R.F., Vargo, S.L. and O'Brien, M. (2007) Competing through service: Insights from service-dominant logic. *Journal of Retailing* 83 (1), 5–18.

Ma, M., Weng, J. and Yu, L. (2015) Market scale, scale economies and tourism market structure: A case of historic water town tourism in China. *Tourism Management* 49, 119–137.

MacCannell, D. (1973) Staged authenticity: Arrangements of social space in tourist settings. *American Journal of Sociology* 79 (3), 589–603.

MacCannell, D. (1976) *The Tourist: A New Theory of the Leisure Class*. London: MacMillan.

MacCannell, D. (1989) *The Tourist. A New Theory of the Leisure Class* (2nd edn). New York: Random House.

MacCannell, D. (1992) *Empty Meeting Grounds: The Tourist Papers*. London: Routledge.

Macionis, N. (2004) Understanding the film-induced tourist. In W. Frost, W.G. Croy and S. Beeton (eds) *Proceedings of the International Tourism and Media Conference* (pp. 86–97). Melbourne: Tourism Research Unit, Monash University.

Macionis, N. and Sparks, B. (2009) Film-induced tourism: An incidental experience. *Tourism Review International* 13 (2), 93–101.

Mack, B. (2012) Tourism overwhelms vanishing Venice. *Deutsche Welle*, 9 November. See www.dw.com/en/tourism-overwhelms-vanishing-venice/a-16364608 (accessed 10 July 2015).

MacKenzie, R. and Stone, P. (1990) (eds) *The Excluded Past: Archaeology in Education*. London: Unwin Hyman.

MacLeod, N., Hayes, D. and Slater, A. (2009) Reading the landscape: The development of a typology of literary trails that incorporate an experiential design perspective. *Journal of Hospitality Marketing & Management* 18 (2–3), 154–172.

Mangold, W.G. and Faulds, D.J. (2009) Social media: The new hybrid element of the promotion mix. *Business Horizons* 52 (4), 357–365.

Mansfield, C. (2015) *Researching Literary Tourism.* Plymouth: TKT.

Månsson, M. (2011) Mediatised tourism. *Annals of Tourism Research* 58 (4), 1634–1652.

Månsson, M. and Eskilsson, L. (2013) *The Attraction of Screen Destinations: Baseline Report Assessing Best Practice.* Sędziszów, Poland: Pracownia Pomysłów.

Marcussen, C.H. (2011) Determinants of tourist satisfaction and intention to return. *Tourism* 59 (2), 203–221.

Marketing, Advertising and Media Intelligence (2016) *The Hobbit Connection Proves Its Worth as Tourism New Zealand and Air New Zealand Renew Their Marketing Vows.* See http://stoppress.co.nz/news/hobbit-connection-proves-its-worth-tourism-new-zealand-and-air-new-zealand-renew-their-marketing-vows?page = 5 (accessed 18 April 2016).

Martin-Jones, D. (2014) Film tourism as heritage tourism: Scotland, diaspora and the Da Vinci Code (2006). *New Review of Film and Television Studies* 12 (2), 156–177.

Masberg, B.A. and Silverman, L.H. (1996) Visitor experiences at heritage sites: A phenomenological approach. *Journal of Travel Research* 34 (4), 20–25.

Mascho, E. and Singh, N. (2014) Virtual tourism: Use of 'second life' for destination marketing. *Anatolia: An International Journal of Tourism and Hospitality Research* 25, 140–143.

Maslow, A. (1971) *The Farther Reaches of Human Nature.* Harmondsworth: Penguin.

Matarasso, F. (2000) Developing understanding of the social impact of the arts. *Culturelink* 51–58.

Mathwick, C., Malhotra, N. and Rigdon, E. (2001) Experiential value: Conceptualization, measurement and application in the catalog and internet shopping. *Journal of Retailing* 77 (1), 39–56.

Mattson, J. and Praesto, A. (2005) The creation of a Swedish heritage destination: An insider's view of entrepreneurial marketing. *Scandinavian Journal of Hospitality and Tourism* 5 (2), 152–166.

McCabe, S. (2014) Introduction. In S. McCabe (ed.) *The Routledge Handbook of Tourism Marketing* (pp. 1–12). London: Routledge.

McCabe, S., Sharples, M. and Foster, C. (2012) Stakeholder engagement in the design of scenarios of technology-enhanced tourism. *Tourism Management Perspectives* 4, 36–44.

McCain, G. and Ray, N. (2003) Legacy tourism: The search for personal meaning in heritage travel. *Tourism Management* 11 (6), 1859–1863.

McCarthy, C. and Mason, D. (2008) The feeling of exclusion: Young people's perceptions of art galleries. *Museum Management and Curatorship* 2, 1–19.

McGuckin, M. (2015) Literary tourism and Yeats' legacy: What can we learn from Shakespeare's birthplace? Paper presented at the *11th Annual Tourism and Hospitality Research in Ireland Conference (THRIC 2015),* 11–12 June.

McIntosh, A.J. (2009) Religious and spiritual tourism: Co-creating meaningful experiences through tourism. In *Tourism, Religion and Culture: Regional Development through Meaningful Tourism Experience Conference,* University of Salento, Leece, Italy.

McIntosh, A. and Prentice, R. (1999) Affirming authenticity: Consuming cultural heritage. *Annals of Tourism Research* 26, 589–612.

McVeigh, T. (2015) The stunning locations cashing in on Britain's film and TV fame. *Guardian Online,* 8 March. See http://www.theguardian.com/tv-and-radio/2015/mar/08/locations-cashing-in-britain-film-tv-fame (accessed 30 July 2015).

Merrill, S. (2011) Grafitti at heritage places: Vandalism as cultural significance or conservation sacrilege? *Time and Mind* 4 (1), 59–75.

Middleton, V., Fyall, A., Morgan, M. and Ranchod, A. (2009) *Marketing in Travel and Tourism* (4th edn). London: Elsevier.

Minkiewicz, J., Evans, J. and Bridson, K. (2009) Co-creation in the heritage sector, In *ANZMAC 2009: Sustainable Management and Marketing Conference* (pp. 1–10). Melbourne, Victoria: ANZMAC.

Mintel (2011) *Literary Tourism – International – September.* London: Mintel International.

Mistilis, N., Buhalis, D. and Gretzel, U. (2014) Future eDestination marketing: Perspective of an Australian tourism stakeholder network. *Journal of Travel Research* 53 (6), 778–790.

Mitchell, H. and Stewart, M.F. (2012) Movies and holidays: The empirical relationship between movies and tourism. *Applied Economic Letters* 19, 1437–1440.

Mohktar, M.F. and Kasim, A. (2012) Motivations for visiting and not visiting museums among young adults: A case study on Uum students. *Journal of Global Management* 3 (1), 43–58.

Moran, A. (2006) Migrancy, tourism, settlement and rural cinema. In C. Fowler and G. Helfield (eds) *Representing the Rural: Scene, Place and Identity in Films about the Land* (pp. 225–239). Detroit, MI: Wayne State University.

Morley, D. and Robins, K. (1995) *Spaces of Identity.* London: Routledge.

Moscardo, G. (1996) Mindful visitors: Heritage and tourism. *Annals of Tourism Research* 23 (2), 376–397.

Moscardo, G. (2001) Cultural and heritage tourism: The great debates. In B. Faulkner, G. Moscardo and E. Laws (eds) *Tourism in the 21st Century* (pp. 3–17). London: Continuum.

Moscardo, G. and Ballantyne, R. (2008) Interpretation and attractions. In A. Fyall, B. Garrod, A. Leask and S. Wanhill (eds) *Managing Visitor Attractions: New Directions* (pp. 237–252). Oxford: Elsevier.

Moscardo, G.M. and Pearce, P.L. (1986) Historic theme parks: An Australian experience in authenticity. *Annals of Tourism Research* 13, 467–479.

Mossberg, L. (2007) A marketing approach to the tourist experience. *Scandinavian Journal of Hospitality and Tourism* 7 (1), 59–74.

Mosse, K. (2008) *Sepulchre Tour.* See https://www.katemosse.co.uk/wp-content/uploads/2011/09/Sepulchre-tour.pdf (accessed 07 June 2017).

Muresan, A. and Smith, K.A. (1998) Dracula's castle in Transylvania: Conflicting heritage marketing strategies. *International Journal of Heritage Studies* 4 (2), 73–85.

Nash, E. and O'Connor, N. (2015) To investigate the economic impact of the Irish film industry with particular emphasis on the tourism sector. Paper presented at the *11th Annual Tourism and Hospitality Research in Ireland Conference (THRIC 2015)*, 11–12 June.

National Geographic (2015) *Top 10 Literary Cities.* See http://travel.nationalgeographic.com/travel/top-10/literary-cities/#page = 1 (accessed 30 July 2016).

National Great Blacks in Wax Museum (2016) *Then and Now.* See http://www.greatblacksinwax.org/expansion_plans.htm (accessed 16 June 2016).

National Park Service (1997) *VERP: The Visitor Experience and Resource Protections (VERP) Framework – A Handbook for Planners and Managers.* Denver, CO: Denver Service Centre.

Navrátil, J., Pícha, K. and Navrátilová, J. (2011) Impact of visit on visitors' perceptions of the environments of nature-based tourism sites. *Tourism* 59 (1), 7–23.

Neuhofer, B. (2016) Value co-creation and co-destruction in connected tourist experiences. In A. Inversini and R. Schegg (eds) *Information and Communication Technologies in Tourism 2016.* Cham: Springer.

Neuhofer, B., Buhalis, D. and Ladkin, A. (2013) Experiences, co-creation and technology: A conceptual approach to enhance tourism experiences. In J. Fountain and K. Moore (eds) *Conference Proceedings 2013: Tourism and Global Change CAUTHE* (pp. 546–555). Christchurch: Lincoln University.

Neuhofer, B., Buhalis, D. and Ladkin, A. (2014) A typology of technology enhanced experiences. *International Journal of Tourism Research* 16, 340–350.

Newby, P. (1981) Literature and the fashioning of tourist taste. In D. Pocock (ed.) *Humanistic Geography and Literature: Essays on the Experience of Place* (pp. 130–141). London: Croom Helm.

New Zealand Tourism Guide (2017) *Lord of the Rings – New Zealand*. See http://www.tourism.net.nz/lord-of-the-rings.html (accessed 03 June 2017).

Niininen, O., Buhalis, C. and March, R. (2007) Customer empowerment in tourism through consumer centric marketing (CCM). *Qualitative Market Research* 10 (3), 265–282.

Northern Ireland Audit Office (2011) *Northern Ireland Tourist Board – Review of the Signature Projects*. Belfast: Northern Ireland Audit Office.

Northern Ireland Tourist Board (2004) *Tourism in Northern Ireland. A Strategic Framework for Action (2004–2007)*. Belfast: Northern Ireland Tourist Board.

Novinite.com (2015) Bollywood star to participate in video advertising Bulgaria as a tourist destination. *Novinite.com*, 13 June. See http://www.novinite.com/articles/169200/Bollywood+Star+to+Participate+in+Video+Advertising+Bulgaria+as+Tourist+Destination (accessed 30 July 2015).

Nurick, J. (2000) Heritage and tourism. *Locum Destination Review* 2, 35–38.

Nuryanti, W. (1996) Heritage and postmodern tourism. *Annals of Tourism Research* 23 (2), 249–260.

O'Connor, B. (1993) Myths and mirrors: Tourist images and national identity. In B. O'Connor and M. Cronin (eds) *Tourism in Ireland: A Critical Analysis* (pp. 68–85). Cork: Cork University Press.

O'Connor, N. and Kim, S. (2013) Pictures and prose: Exploring the impact of literary and film tourism. *Journal of Tourism and Cultural Change* 12 (1), 1–17.

O'Connor, N. and Pratt, S. (2008) Using movie maps to leverage a tourism destination – Pride and Prejudice (2005), The 4th Tourism & Hospitality Research Conference – Reflection: Irish Tourism & Hospitality – A Success Story. Tralee Institute of Technology Conference, Tralee, Co. Kerry, 10–11 June.

O'Connor, N., Flanagan, S. and Gilbert, D. (2010) The use of film in re-imaging a tourist destination. A case study of Yorkshire, UK. *Journal of Vacation Marketing* 16 (1), 61–74.

O'Dell, T. (2005) Experiencescapes: Blurring borders and testing connections. In T. O'Dell and P. Billing (eds) *Experiencescapes – Tourism, Culture and Economy*. Copenhagen: Business Press.

Oliveira, E. and Panyik, E. (2015) Content, context and co-creation: Digital challenges in destination branding with references to Portugal as a tourist destination. *Journal of Vacation Marketing* 21 (1), 53–74.

Olmeda, I. and Sheldon, P.J. (2002) Data mining techniques and applications for tourism internet marketing. *Journal of Travel and Tourism Marketing* 11 (2–3), 1–20.

Olsberg SPI (2007) *Stately Attraction: How Film and TV Programmes Promote Tourism in the UK*. London: Film Council.

Olsen, K. (2000) Ethnicity and representation in a 'local' museum. In P. Anttonen, A.L. Siikkala, S.R. Mathisen and L. Magnusson (eds) *Folklore, Heritage, Politics and Ethnic Diversity: A Festschrift for Barbro Klein*. Botkyrka: Multicultural Center.

Olson, D. (1990) Thinking about narrative. In B. Britton and A. Pelligrini (eds) *Narrative Thought and Narrative Language* (pp. 99–112). Hillsdale, NJ: Lawrence Erlbaum.

O'Neill, K., Butts, S. and Busby, G. (2005) The Corellification of Cephallonian tourism. *Anatolia* 16 (2), 207–226.

Ontario Ministry of Culture (2006) *Heritage Conservation Districts. A Guide to District Designation under the Ontario Heritage Act*. Ontario: Queen's Printer.

Ontario Ministry of Tourism, Culture and Sport (2016) *Heritage Conservation Districts*. See http://www.mtc.gov.on.ca/en/heritage/heritage_conserving_districts.shtml (accessed 30 June 2016).

Orams, M.B. (1995) Using interpretation to manage nature-based tourism. *Journal of Sustainable Tourism* 4 (2), 81–94.

Orams, M. (1996) A conceptual model of tourist–wildlife interaction: The case for education as a management strategy. *Australian Geographer* 27 (1), 39–51.

Orams, M. (1997) The effectiveness of environmental education: Can we turn tourists into 'greenies'? *Progress in Tourism and Hospitality Research* 3 (4), 295–306.

Orams, M. (1998) Controlling the ecotourist in a wild dolphin feeding program: Is education the answer? *Journal of Environmental Education* 29 (3), 33–38.

Orbasli, A. (2000) *Tourists in Historic Towns. Urban Conservation and Heritage Management.* London: E. & F.N. Spon.

Oswell, P. (2007) Finding your way around Bollywood UK. *Mail Online*, 30 May. See www.dailymail.co.uk/travel/article-595825/Finding-way-Bollywood-UK.html (accessed 29 September 2010).

Otto, J.E. and Ritchie, J.R.B. (2000) The service experience in tourism. *Tourism Management* 17 (3), 165–174.

Ousby, I. (1990) *The Englishman's England.* Cambridge: Cambridge University Press.

Oxford Economic Forecasting (2012) *The Economic Contribution of the UK Film Industry.* Oxford: Oxford Economic Forecasting.

Palmer, C. (1998) From theory to practice: Experiencing the nation in everyday life. *Journal of Material Culture* 3 (2), 175–199.

Palmer, C. (1999) Tourism and the symbols of identity. *Tourism Management* 20 (3), 313–322.

Palmer, C. (2005) An ethnography of Englishness: Experiencing identity through tourism. *Annals of Tourism Research* 32, 7–27.

Pan, S. and Ryan, C. (2013) Film-induced heritage site conservation: The case of 'Echoes of the Rainbow'. *Journal of Hospitality and Tourism Research* 37 (1), 125–150.

Pareigis, J., Echeverri, P. and Edvardsson, B. (2012) Exploring internal mechanisms forming customer servicescape experiences. *Journal of Service Management* 23, 677–695.

Park, H.Y. (2010) Heritage tourism. Emotional journeys into nationhood. *Annals of Tourism Research* 37 (1), 116–135.

Payne, A. and Frow, P. (2005) A strategic framework for customer relationship management. *Journal of Marketing* 69 (4), 167–176.

Payton, M. (2016) Tourist knocks over 126-year-old Portuguese statue after trying to take a selfie with it. *The Independent*, 8 May. See http://www.independent.co.uk/news/world/europe/tourist-knocks-over-126-year-old-portugese-statue-after-trying-to-take-a-selfie-with-it-lisbon-a7019456.html (accessed 7 June 2016).

Pearce, D.G. and Tan, R. (2004) Distribution channels for heritage and cultural tourism in New Zealand. *Asia Pacific Journal of Tourism Research* 9 (3), 225–237.

Pearce, P.L. (1984) Tourist–guide interaction. *Annals of Tourism Research* 11, 129–146.

Pearce, P.L. and Moscardo, G. (1986) The concept of authenticity in tourist experiences. *Australian and New Zealand Journal of Sociology* 22 (1), 121–132.

Pedersen, A. (2002) *Managing Tourism at World Heritage Sites: A Practical Manual for World Heritage Site Managers.* World Heritage Manuals. Paris: UNESCO World Heritage Centre.

Peleggi, M. (1996) National heritage and global tourism in Thailand. *Annals of Tourism Research* 23 (2), 432–448.

Perse, E.M. (1990) Media involvement and local news effects. *Journal of Broadcasting and Electronic Media* 34 (1), 17–36.

Petersen, K. (1994) The heritage resource as seen by the tourist: The heritage connection. In J. Van Harssel (ed.) *Tourism: An Exploration.* Englewood Cliffs, NJ: Prentice Hall.

Petty, R., McMichael, S. and Brennon, L. (1992) The elaboration likelihood model of persuasion: Applications in recreation and tourism. In M. Manfredo (ed.) *Influencing Human Behaviour: Theory and Applications in Recreation, Tourism and Natural Resources Management* (pp. 77–101). Champaign, IL: Sagamore.

Phuket Gazette (2010) Special report: Phi Phi cries for help. *Phuket Gazette*, 25 October. See www.phuketgazette.net/phuket-news/Special-Report-Phi-Phi-cries-help/38250#ad-image-0 (accessed 7 July 2015).

Pike, S. (2004) *Destination Marketing Organisations*. Oxford: Elsevier.

Pine, B.J. and Gilmore, J.H. (1999) *The Experience Economy: Work is Theatre and Every Business a Stage*. Boston, MA: Harvard Business School Press.

Planet Bollywood (2010) *Switzerland Tourism to Capitalise on Bollywood Obsession*. See www.planetbollywood.com/displayArticle.php?id = n071810100940 (accessed 29 October 2010).

Pocock, D.C.D. (1981) *Humanistic Geography and Literature*. London: Croom Helm.

Pocock, D.C.D. (1982) Writers who knew their places. *Geographical Magazine* 54 (1), 40–43.

Pocock, D.C.D. (1992) Catherine Cookson Country: Tourist Expectation and Experience. *Geography* 77, 236–243.

Poon, A. (1993) *Tourism, Technology and Competitive Strategies*. Oxford: CABI.

Poria, Y. and Ashworth, G. (2009) Heritage tourism: Current resource for conflict. *Annals of Tourism Research* 36 (3), 522–525.

Poria, Y., Butler, R. and Airey, D. (2001) Clarifying heritage tourism. *Annals of Tourism Research* 28 (4), 1047–1049.

Poria, Y., Butler, R. and Airey, D. (2003) The core of heritage tourism. *Annals of Tourism Research* 30 (1), 238–254.

Poria, Y., Reichel, A. and Biran, A. (2006) Heritage site management: Motivations and expectations. *Annals of Tourism Research* 33 (1), 162–178.

Poria, Y., Biran, A. and Reichel, A. (2009) Visitors' preferences for interpretation at heritage sites. *Journal of Travel Research* 33 (1), 162–178.

Poria, Y., Reichel, A. and Brandt, Y. (2010) The flight experiences of people with disabilities: An exploratory study. *Journal of Travel Research* 49 (2), 216–227.

Poria, Y., Reichel, A. and Cohen, R. (2013) World Heritage site – is it an effective brand name? A case study of a religious heritage site. *Journal of Travel Research* 50 (5), 482–485.

Prahalad, C.K. and Ramaswamy, V. (2000) Co-opting customer competence. *Harvard Business Review* 78 (1), 79–87.

Prahalad, C.K. and Ramaswamy, V. (2001) The value creation dilemma: New building blocks for co-creating experience. *Harvard Business Review* 18 (3), 5–14.

Prahalad, C.K. and Ramaswamy, V. (2004) Co-creation experiences: The next practice in value creation. *Journal of Interactive Marketing* 18 (3), 5–14.

Prats, L. and Marin, J. (2012) BlogTrip in Costa Brava or the use of bloggers as destination image ambassadors. In *Actes del Congrés OCITUR 2012*. Spain: Escola Universitària del Maresme.

Prebensen, N., Skallerud, K. and Chen, J. (2010) Tourist motivation with sun and sand destinations: Satisfaction and the WOM-effect. *Journal of Travel and Tourism Marketing* 27 (8), 858–873.

Prebensen, N.K., Vitterso, J. and Dahl, T.I. (2013) Value co-creation significance of tourist resources. *Annals of Tourism Research* 42, 240–261.

Pred, A. (1984) Place as historically contingent processes: Structuration and the time-geography of becoming places. *Annals of the Association of American Geographers* 74, 279–297.

Prentice, R. (1993) *Tourism and Heritage Attractions*. London: Routledge.

Prentice, R. (2000) The economic perspectives: Creating strategic positions for future success in cultural management. *Tourist Review* 55 (4), 4–8.

Prentice, R. (2001) Experiential cultural tourism: Museums and the marketing of the New Romanticism of evoked authenticity. *Museum Management and Curatorship* 19 (1), 5–26.

Prentice, R. and Andersen, V. (2007) Interpreting heritage essentialisms: Familiarity and felt history. *Tourism Management* 28, 661–676.

Prentice, R., Witt, S. and Hamer, C. (1993) The experience of industrial heritage: Market overview and the case of Black gold. *Built Environment* 25, 1–24.

Prentice, R., Witt, S. and Hamer, C. (1996) Tourism as experience: The case of heritage parks. *Annals of Tourism Research* 25, 1–24.

Prentice, R., Guerin, S. and McGugan, S. (1998a) Visitor learning at a heritage attraction: A case study of *Discovery* as a media product. *Tourism Management* 19 (1), 5–23.

Prentice, R., Witt, S. and Hamer, C. (1998b) Tourism as experience: The case of Heritage Parks. *Annals of Tourism Research* 25 (1), 1–24.

Pretes, M. (1995) Postmodern tourism: The Santa Claus industry. *Annals of Tourism Research* 22 (1), 1–24.

Pretes, M. (2003) Tourism and nationalism. *Annals of Tourism Research* 30 (1), 125–142.

Prince, D. (1981) Evaluating interpretation: A discussion. Occasional Paper No. 1, Centre for Environmental Interpretation, Manchester University.

Pudliner, B.A. (2007) Alternative literature and tourist experience: Travel and tourist web blogs. *Journal of Tourism and Cultural Change* 5 (1), 46–59.

PwC (2015) *Global Entertainment and Media Outlook 2015–2019: Customers*. See http://www.pwc.com/gx/en/issues/customers.html (accessed 12 October 2015).

Rains, S. (2003) Home from home: Diasporic images of Ireland in film and tourism. In M. Cronin and B. O'Connor (eds) *Irish Tourism Image, Culture and Identity* (pp. 196–214). Clevedon: Channel View Publications.

Redu Village du Livre (2013) *Redu. The Book Village*. See http://www.redu-villagedulivre.be/ (accessed 30 June 2016).

Reijnders, S. (2009) Watching the detectives. Inside the guilty landscapes of Inspector Morse, Bantjer and Wallander. *European Journal of Communication* 24 (2), 165–181.

Reijnders, S. (2010a) On the trail of 007. Media pilgrimages into the world of James Bond. *Area* 42 (2), 369–377.

Reijnders, S. (2010b) Places of the imagination: An ethnography of the TV detective tour. *Cultural Geographies* 17 (1), 37–52.

Reijnders, S. (2011a) *Places of the Imagination: Media, Tourism and Culture*. Farnham: Ashgate.

Reijnders, S. (2011b) Stalking the count. Dracula, fandom and tourism. *Annals of Tourism Research* 38 (1), 231–248.

Reisinger, Y. and Steiner, C. (2006) Reconceptualising object authenticity. *Annals of Tourism Research* 33 (1), 65–86.

Relph, E. (1976) *Place and Placelessness*. London: Pion.

Research Resolutions and Consulting (2003) *Canada's Heritage Tourism Enthusiasts*. Vancouver: Canada Tourism Commission.

Resonance Consultancy (2015a) *Portrait of the US Senior Traveler*. New York: Resonance Consultancy.

Resonance Consultancy (2015b) *Portrait of the US Millennial Traveler*. New York: Resonance Consultancy.

Richards, G. (1996) Production and consumption of European cultural tourism. *Annals of Tourism Research* 23 (2), 261–283.

Richards, G. (2002) Tourism attraction systems: Exploring cultural behaviour. *Annals of Tourism Research* 29, 1048–1064.

Richards, G. (2013) Creativity and tourism in the city. *Current Issues in Tourism* 17 (2), 119–144.

Richards, G. (2014) *Tourism Trends: The Convergence of Culture and Tourism*. See www.academia.edu/9491857/Tourism_trends_The_convergence_of_culture_and_tourism (accessed 26 July 2015).

Rihova, I., Buhalis, D., Moital, M. and Gouthro, M.B. (2013) Social layers of customer-to-customer value co-creation. *Journal of Service Management* 24 (5), 553–566.

Riley, R. (1994) Movie induced tourism. In A.V. Seaton, C.L. Jenkins, R.C. Wood, P. Diele, M. Bonneett, L.R. MacLellan and R. Smith (eds) *Tourism: The State of the Art* (pp. 453–458). Chichester: John Wiley.

Riley, R. and Van Doren, C. (1992) Movies as tourism promotion: A 'pull' factor in a 'push' location. *Tourism Management* 13 (3), 267–274.

Riley, R., Baker, D. and Van Doren, C. (1998) Movie induced tourism. *Annals of Tourism Research* 25 (4), 919–935.

Ritchie, B.W., Carr, N. and Cooper, C. (2003) *Managing Educational Tourism*. Buffalo, NY: Channel View Publications.

Robins, S. (2000) City sites. In S. Nuttall and C.A. Michael (eds) *Senses of Culture: South African Culture Studies* (pp. 408–425). Oxford: Oxford University Press.

Robinson, J. (1981) Personal narratives reconsidered. *Journal of American Folklore* 94, 58–85.

Robinson, M. and Andersen, H.C. (2002) (eds) *Literature and Tourism*. London: Thomson.

Roesch, S. (2009) *The Experiences of Film Location Tourists*. Bristol: Channel View Publications.

Roggenbuck, J. (1992) Use of persuasion to reduce resource impacts and visitor conflicts. In M. Manfredo (ed.) *Influencing Human Behaviour*. Champaign, IL: Sagamore.

Rojeck, C. (1997) Indexing, dragging and the social construction of tourist sights. In C. Rojeck and J. Urry (eds) *Touring Cultures: Transformations of Travel and Theory* (pp. 52–74). London: Routledge.

Rosenstone, R.A. (1995) *Visions of the Past: The Challenge of Film to our Idea of History*. Cambridge, MA: Harvard University Press.

Rosslyn Chapel Trust (2014) *Scaffolding Coming Down Helps Visitor Numbers Go Up*. See www.rosslynchapel.com/news/scaffolding-coming-down-helps-visitor-numbers-go-up/ (accessed 29 July 2015).

Roushanzamir, E. and Kershel, P. (2001) Gloria and Anthony visit a plantation: History into heritage at Laura Plantation, a Creole plantation. *International Journal of Hospitality and Tourism Administration* 2 (3–4), 177–200.

Rubin, A. and Perse, E.M. (1987) Audience activity and soap opera involvement: A uses and effects investigation. *Human Communication Research* 14, 246–268.

Ruiz Ballesteros, E. and Hernández Ramirez, M. (2007) Identity and community: Reflections on the development of mining heritage tourism in southern Spain. *Tourism Management* 28 (3), 677–687.

Ryan, C. and Dewar, K. (1995) Evaluating the communication process between interpreter and visitor. *Tourism Management* 16 (4), 295–303.

Saenz, A. (2009) Augmented reality does time travel tourism. *Singularity Hub*, 19 November. See http://singularityhub.com/2009/11/19/augmented-reality-does-time-travel-tourism/ (accessed 1 July 2016).

Sakellari, M. (2014) Film tourism and ecotourism: Mutually exclusive or incompatible? *International Journal of Culture, Tourism and Hospitality Research* 8 (2), 194–202.

Sanders, L. and Simons, G. (2009) A social vision for value co-creation in design. *Open Source Business Resource* December.

Sands, C. (2014) *Cultural Heritage Ethics: Between Theory and Practice*. Cambridge: Open Book Publishers.

Savage, M. Gayo-Cal, M., Warde, A. and Tampubolon, G. (2005) Cultural capital in the UK: A preliminary report using correspondence analysis. CRESC Working Paper No. 4, Centre for Research on Sociocultural Change, University of Manchester.

Scarles, C. (2012) The photographed other: Interplays of agency in tourist photography in Cusco, Peru. *Annals of Tourism Research* 39 (2), 928–950.

Schellhase, J. (2016) *This Small Village in Spain is Home to More Books than People*. See http://all-that-is-interesting.com/uruena-spain (accessed 30 June 2016).

Schmitt, B.H. (1999) Experiential marketing. *Journal of Marketing Management* 15 (1), 53–67.

Schofield, P. (1996) Cinematographic images of a city. *Tourism Management* 17 (5), 333–340.

Schutz, A. (1967) *The Phenomenology of the Social World*. Evanston, Ill: Northwestern University Press.

Scott, N., Laws, E. and Boksberger, P. (2009) The marketing of hospitality and leisure experiences. *Journal of Hospitality Marketing & Management* 18 (2–3), 99–110.

Seaton, A.V. (1996) Hay-on-Wye, the mouse that roared: Book towns and rural tourism. *Tourism Management* 17 (5), 379–385.

Secretaría De Turismo (2010) *Cultural Tourism in Mexico*. See www.sectur.gob.mx/en/securing/cultural_tourism (accessed 18 October 2010).

Secretaría De Turismo (2015) *Pueblos Magicos*. See www.sectur.gob.mx/pueblos-magicos/ (accessed 28 July 2015).

Sedbergh Book Town Literary Trust (2016) *Sedbergh Book Town*. See http://sedberghbook-town.co.uk/ (accessed 27 June 2016).

Sedbergh Information Centre (2016) *Book Town*. See http://www.sedbergh.org.uk/shops-businesses/book-town/ (accessed 30 June 2016).

Seenprachawong, U. (2001) *Putting a Price on Paradise: Economic Policies to Preserve Thailand's Coral Reefs*. See https://idl-bnc-idrc.dspacedirect.org/bitstream/handle/10625/28308/117866.pdf?sequence=5&isAllowed=y (accessed 15 June 2017).

Selwyn, T. (1996) *The Tourist Image: Myths and Myth Making in Tourism*. Chichester: Wiley.

Shackley, M. (2001) *Managing Sacred Sites*. London: Continuum.

Shakespeare's England (2015) *A Destination Management Plan for Shakespeare's England Region 2015–2025*. See https://www.stratford.gov.uk/files/seealsodocs/170581/final%2Ddmp%2Ddestination%2Dmanagement%2Dplan%2Dmay%2D2015%2Dfinal.pdf (accessed 10 July 2016).

Sharpley R. (1994) *Tourism, Tourists and Society*. Huntingdon: Elm Publications.

Shaw, G. and Williams, A.M. (1994) *Critical Issues in Tourism: A Geographical Perspective*. Oxford: Blackwell.

Shaw, G., Bailey, A. and Williams, A. (2011) Aspects of service-dominant logic and its implications for tourism management: Examples from the hotel industry. *Tourism Management* 32 (2), 207–214.

Shelby, B. and Heberlein, T. (1986) *Carrying Capacity in Recreation Settings*. Corvalis, OR: Oregon State University Press.

Shiel, M. (2001) Cinema and the city in history and theory. In M. Shiel and T. Fitzmaurice (eds) *Cinema and the City: Film and Urban Societies in an Urban Context* (pp. 1–18). Oxford: Blackwell.

Shrapnel, E. (2012) Engaging young adults in museums: An audience research study. Unpublished MSc thesis, Museum Studies, Australian Museum, Sydney.

Sidasathian, C. and Morison, A. (2015) Mass tourism makes 'a slum' of Phi Phi. *Phuket Wan Tourism News*, 21 March. See http://phuketwan.com/tourism/phi-phi-slum-mass-tourism-destroys-thailands-natural-heritage-22092/ (accessed 7 July 2015).

Silberberg, T. (1995) Cultural tourism and business opportunities for museums and heritage sites. *Tourism Management* 16 (5), 361–365.

Simmons, J. (2005) Harry Potter, marketing magician. Business. *The Observer*, 26 June. See https://www.theguardian.com/business/2005/jun/26/media.books (accessed 10 June 2017).

Simpson, F. (1999) Tourism impact in the historic centre of Prague: Resident and visitor perceptions of the historic built environment. *Geographical Journal* 165 (2), 173–183.

Singh, K. and Best, G. (2004) Film-induced tourism: Motivations of visitors to the Hobbiton movie set as featured in the Lord of the Rings. In W. Frost, G. Croy and S. Beeton (eds) *Proceedings of the International Tourism and Media Conference, Melbourne, Australia* (pp. 98–111). Melbourne: Tourism Research Unit, Monash University.

Siyabona Africa (2016) *Wildlife Conservation: National Parks of Botswana.* See http://www.botswana.co.za/Wildlife_Conservation-travel/botswana-national-parks.html (accessed 27 June 2016).

Smith, J.G. (1999) Learning from popular culture: Interpretation, visitors and critique. *International Journal of Heritage Studies* 5, 135–148.

Smith, K.A. (2003) Literary enthusiasts as visitors and volunteers. *International Journal of Tourism Research* 5 (2), 83–95.

Smith, L. (1998) War and tourism. *Annals of Tourism Research* 25 (1), 202–227.

Smith, R.W. (1987) Leisure of disabled tourists: Barriers to participation. *Annals of Tourism Research* 14, 376–389.

Smith, W. (2006) Experiential tourism around the world and at home: Definitions and standards. *International Journal of Services and Standards* 2 (1), 1–14.

Sood, S. (2002) Audience involvement and entertainment-education. *Communication Theory* 12 (2), 153–172.

Southern Literary Trail (2016) *Trail Towns, Writers & Houses.* See http://www.southernliterarytrail.org/trail.html (accessed 30 June 2016).

Squire, S.J. (1988) Wordsworth and Lake District tourism: Romantic reshaping of landscape. *Canadian Geographer* 32 (3), 237–247.

Squire, S.J. (1994) Gender and tourist experiences: Assessing women's shared meanings for Beatrix Potter. *Leisure Studies* 13 (3), 195–209.

Squire, S.J. (1996) Literary tourism and sustainable tourism: Promoting 'Anne of Green Gables' in Prince Edward Island. *Journal of Sustainable Tourism* 4 (3), 119–129.

Stankey, G., Cole, D., Lucas, R., Peterson, M., Frissell, S. and Washburne, R. (1985) *The Limits of Acceptable Change (LAC) System for Wilderness Planning.* USDA Forest Service General Technical Report INT-176. Ogden, UT: USDA Forest Service Intermountain Forest and Range Experiment Station.

Statistics New Zealand (2016) *International Visitor Arrivals to New Zealand.* See www.stats.govt.nz/browse_for_stats/population/Migration/international-visitor-arrivals-apr-16.aspx (accessed 9 June 2016).

Steele, D. (2004) Developing the evidence base for UK film strategy: The research process at the UK Film Council. *Cultural Trends* 13 (4), 5–21.

Steiner, C. and Reisinger, Y. (2006) Understanding existential authenticity. *Annals of Tourism Research* 33 (2), 299–318.

Stewart, E.J., Hayward, B.M., Devlin, P.J. and Kirby, V.G. (1998) The 'place' of interpretation: A new approach to the evaluation of interpretation. *Tourism Management* 19 (2), 257–264.

Stiebel, L. (2001) *Imaging Africa: Landscapes in H. Rider Haggard's Africa Romances.* Westport, CT: Greenwood Press.

Stiebel, L. (2004) Hitting the hotspots: Literary tourism as a research field with particular reference to KwaZulu-Natal, South Africa. *Critical Arts: South-North Cultural and Media Studies* 18 (2), 31–44.

Stoker, B. (1897) *Dracula.* London: Archibald Constable.

Stratford-Upon-Avon District Council (2013) *Summary for the 2013 Tourism Economic Impact Assessments.* Stratford-Upon-Avon: Stratford-Upon-Avon District Council.

Su, Y.-W. and Lin, H.-L. (2014) An analysis of international tourist arrivals worldwide: The role of World Heritage sites. *Tourism Management* 40 (1), 46–58.

Swarbrooke, J. (1994) The future of the past: Heritage tourism in the 21st century. In A.V. Seaton (ed.) *Tourism: The State of the Art* (pp. 222–229). Chichester: John Wiley.

Tahana, N. and Oppermann, M. (1998) Maori cultural performances and tourism. *Tourism Recreation Research* 23 (1), 23–30.

Taiwan Today (2010) 'Monga' success feeds local tourism. *Taiwan Today*, 10 February. See http://taiwantoday.tw/ct.asp?xItem=94152&ctNode=454&mp=9 (accessed 1 August 2015).

Talley, M.K. (1995) The old road and the mind's internal heaven: Preservation of the cultural heritage in times of armed conflict. *Museum Management and Curatorship* 14 (1), 57–64.

Tan, S.-K., Kung, S.-F. and Luh, D.-B. (2013) A model of 'creative experience' in creative tourism. *Annals of Tourism Research* 41, 153–174.

Tao, W. (2001) *Study on Sustainable Tourism Development in World Heritage Sites in China*. Beijing: China Travel and Tourism Press.

Tavakoli, R. and Mura, P. (2015) Journeys in Second life: Iranian Muslim women's behaviour in virtual tourist destinations. *Tourism Management* 46, 398–407.

Taylor, J.P. (2001) Authenticity and sincerity in tourism. *Annals of Tourism Research* 28 (1), 7–26.

Teo, P. and Yeoh, B. (1997) Remaking local heritage for tourism: Haw Par Villa in Singapore. *Annals of Tourism Research* 24 (1), 192–213.

Teo, C., Khan, N. and Rahim, F. (2014) Understanding cultural heritage visitor behaviour: The case of Melaka as world heritage city. *Procedia – Social and Behaviour Sciences* 130, 1–10.

Tetley, S. (1997) Visitor attitudes to authenticity at literary and television-related destinations. Unpublished PhD thesis, Sheffield Hallam University.

Texas Historical Commission (2016) *Texas Heritage Trails*. See http://www.thc.state.tx.us/preserve/projects-and-programs/texas-heritage-trails (accessed 30 June 2016).

The Age (2010) *Australia film helps keep tourism steady*. See www.theage.com.au (accessed 3 October 2010).

The Examiner (2009) *National Trust Picks its Tasmanian Icons*. See http://www.examiner.com.au/story/487660/national-trust-picks-its-tasmanian-icons/ (accessed 15 June 2017).

The Guardian (2015) Armenia is wiping out Azerbaijani cultural heritage. *Guardian Online*, 2 September. See www.theguardian.com/world/2015/sep/02/armenia-is-wiping-out-azerbaijani-cultural-heritage (accessed 17 June 2016).

Thompson, K. (2004) Post-colonial politics and resurgent heritage: The development of Kyrgystan's heritage tourism product. *Current Issues in Tourism* 7 (4), 370–382.

Thrift, N. (1989) Images of social change. In C. Hamnett, L. McDowell and P. Sarre (eds) *The Changing Social Structure* (pp. 12–42). London: Sage.

Tilden, F. (1957) *Interpreting Our Heritage* (1st edn). Chapel Hill, NC: University of North Carolina Press.

Tilden, F. (1977) *Interpreting Our Heritage* (3rd edn). Chapel Hill, NC: University of North Carolina Press.

Timothy, D. and Boyd, S. (2003) *Heritage Tourism*. Harlow: Prentice Hall.

Timothy, D.J. (2011) *Cultural Heritage and Tourism: An Introduction*. Bristol: Channel View.

Titanic Belfast (2015) *Three Years On and Still Making History!* See http://titanicbelfast.com/Blog/October-2015/Titanic-Belfast-%E2%80%93-Three-Years-On-and-Still-Making/ (accessed 20 June 2016).

Tooke, N. and Baker, M. (1996) Seeing is believing: The effect of film on visitor numbers to screened locations. *Tourism Management* 17 (2), 87–94.

Torchin, L. (2002) Location, location, location: The destination of the Manhattan TV tour. *Tourist Studies* 2 (3), 247–266.

Touchstone Heritage Management Consultants, Red Kite Environment and Creu-Ad (2011) *Cadw: Pan Wales Heritage Interpretation Plan. Celtic Saints, Spiritual Places and Pilgrimage*. Wales: Cadw.

Tourism-Review.com (2017) *Mexico City Expects 29.6 Million Tourists in 2016.* See http://www.tourism-review.com/mexico-city-tourism-board-expects-increased-tourism-numbers-news4867 (accessed 16 June 2017).

Tourism and Transport Forum (2016) *Cultural and Heritage Tourism in Australia.* See http://www.ttf.org.au/wp-content/uploads/2016/06/TTF-Cultural-Tourism-2016.pdf (accessed 03 June 2017)

Towner, J. (1996) *An Historical Geography of Recreation and Tourism in the Western World 1540–1940.* Chichester: Wiley.

Travelagewest (2017) *Literary UK and Ireland. A Bibliophile's Guides.* http://www.travelagewest.com/uploadedImages/All_Gateways/Europe/Features/Literary%20Travel%20in%20the%20U.K.%20and%20Ireland.jpg (accessed 10 June 2017).

Trilling, L. (1972) *Sincerity and Authenticity.* London: Oxford University Press.

TripAdvisor (2013a) Review of the Little Mermaid. See http://www.tripadvisor.co.uk/ShowUserReviews-g189541-d245024-r174993332-The_Little_Mermaid_Den_Lille_Havfrue-Copenhagen_Zealand.html (accessed 4 August 2015).

TripAdvisor (2013b) Review of Hans Christian Andersen Museum. See http://www.tripadvisor.co.uk/ShowUserReviews-g189524-d243797-r160149762-Hans_Christian_Andersen_Museum-Odense_Funen_and_Islands.html (accessed 4 August 2015).

TripAdvisor (2014a) Review of Hans Christian Andersen Museum. See www.tripadvisor.co.uk/ShowUserReviews-g33103-d3813102-r197026024-Hans_Christian_Andersen_Museum-Solvang_California.html (accessed 4 August 2015).

TripAdvisor (2014b) Flat Earth New Zealand Experiences. See www.tripadvisor.co.uk/Attraction_Review-g255115-d1236103-Reviews-Flat_Earth_New_Zealand_Experiences-Wellington_Greater_Wellington_North_ Island.html (accessed 20 October 2014).

TripAdvisor (2015) Review of Hans Christian Andersen Museum. See www.tripadvisor.co.uk/Attraction_Review-g189541-d2626671-Reviews-Hans_Christian_Andersen_Place-Copenhagen_Zealand.html (accessed 4 August 2015).

Tuan, Y.-F. (1974) *Topophilia: A Study of Environmental Perception, Attitudes and Values.* Englewood Cliffs, NJ: Prentice Hall.

Tuan, Y.-F. (1991) Space and place: Humanistic perspective. *Progress in Geography* 6, 211–252.

Tubb, K.N. (2003) An evaluation of the effectiveness of interpretation within Dartmoor National Park in reaching the goals of sustainable development. *Journal of Sustainable Tourism* 11 (6), 476–498.

Tucker, H. and Emge, A. (2010) Managing a World Heritage site: The case of Cappadocia. *Anatolia* 21 (1), 41–54.

Tunbridge, I. and Ashworth, G. (1996) *Dissonant Heritage.* Chichester: Wiley.

Tunbridge, I. and Ashworth, G. (2017) Is all tourism dark? In G. Hooper and J. Lennon (eds) *Dark Tourism. Practice and Interpretation* (pp. 12-25). London: Routledge.

Tussyadiah, I.P. and Fesenmaier, D.R. (2008) Marketing places through first-person stories: An analysis of Pennsylvania road tripper blog. *Journal of Travel and Tourism Marketing* 25 (3–4), 299–311.

Tzanelli, R. (2004) Constructing the 'cinematic tourist': The 'sign' industry of the *Lord of the Rings. Tourist Studies* 4 (1), 21–42.

Tzanelli, R. (2007) *The Cinematic Tourist. Explorations in Globalisation, Culture and Resistance.* London: Routledge.

Um, S., Choy, K. and Ro, Y. (2006) Antecedents of revisit intention. *Annals of Tourism Research* 33 (4), 1141–1158.

UN Department of Economic and Social Affairs (2013) *World Population Prospects.* See http://esa.un.org/unpd/wpp/Publications/Files/Key_Findings_WPP_2015.pdf (accessed 12 October 2015).

UNESCO (2012) *Technical Report 20: The Impact of Tourism and Visitors Flow Management in Aix-en-Provence, Amsterdam, Bruges, Florence, Oxford, Salzburg and Venice.* Paris: UNESCO.

UNESCO (2015) *World Heritage List Statistics.* See http://whc.unesco.org/en/list/stat#d1 (accessed 22 July 2015).

UNESCO (2016) *List of World Heritage in Danger.* See whc.unesco.org/en/danger (accessed 16 June 2016).

UNTWO (2004) *Tourism Market Trends.* Madrid: World Tourism Organisation.

UNTWO (2013) *Tourism Highlights.* Madrid: World Tourism Organisation.

UNTWO (2014a) *Tourism Highlights.* Madrid: World Tourism Organisation.

UNTWO (2014b) *World Tourism Barometer.* Madrid: World Tourism Organisation.

UNTWO (2015) *World Tourism Barometer.* Madrid: World Tourism Organisation.

Urry, J. (1990) *The Tourist Gaze.* London: Sage.

Urry, J. (1995) *Consuming Places.* London: Routledge.

Urry, J. (2002) *The Tourist Gaze* (2nd edn). London: Sage.

Uzzell, D. (1989) Introduction: The visitor experience. In D. Uzzell (ed.) *Heritage Interpretation. Vol. 2* (pp. 1–15). London: Belhaven.

Uzzell, D. (1996) Creating place identity through heritage interpretation. *International Journal of Heritage Studies* 1, 219–228.

Valliere, W. and Manning, R. (2002) Applying the Visitor Experience and Resource Protection (VERP) framework to cultural resources in the national parks. In *North-eastern Recreation Research Symposium. Proceedings of the 2002 North-eastern Recreation Research Symposium,* 13–16 April, The Sagamore on Lake George on Bolton Landing, New York.

Valtonen, A. and Viejola, S. (2011) Sleep in tourism. *Annals of Tourism Research* 38 (1), 175–192.

Vargo, S.L. and Lusch, R.F. (2004) Evolving to a new dominant logic for marketing. *Journal of Marketing* 68 (1), 1–17.

Vargo, S.L. and Lusch, R.F. (2006) *The Service Dominant Logic of Marketing: Dialog, Debate and Directions.* Armonk, NY: M.E. Sharpe.

Vargo, S.L. and Lusch, R.F. (2008) Service-dominant logic: Continuing the evolution. *Journal of the Academy of Marketing Science* 36 (1), 1–10.

Vargo, S.L. and Lusch, R.F. (2016) Institutions and axioms: An extension and update of Service-dominant logic. *Journal of the Academy of Marketing Science* 44 (1), 5–23.

VisitBritain (2006) *The Short Break Market: An Analysis.* London: VisitBritain.

VisitBritain (2010) *Culture and Heritage Topic Profile.* See https://www.visitbritain.org/sites/default/files/vb-corporate/Documents-Library/documents/Culture_and_Heritage_Topic_Profile_Full.pdf (accessed 18 October 2010).

VisitBritain (2012) *Delivering a Golden Legacy: A Growth Strategy for Inbound Tourism to Britain from 2012 to 2020.* London: VisitBritain.

VisitBritain (2014) Leveraging Britain's culture and heritage. *Foresight* 134.

VisitBritain (2015) *Activities Undertaken in Britain.* See www.visitbritain.org/activities-undertaken-britain (accessed 28 July 2015).

VisitEngland (2015) *Visitor Attraction Trends in England 2014.* See https://www.visiteng-land.com/sites/default/files/va_2015_trends_in_england-full_report_version_for_publication_v3.pdf (accessed 16 May 2017).

VisitEngland (2016) *Literary Inspired Weekends.* See https://www.visitengland.com/things-to-do/literary-inspired-weekend (accessed 7 July 2016).

VisitNorway (2016) *The Book Town at the Skagerrak Strait.* See https://www.visitnorway.com/places-to-go/southern-norway/arendal/tvedestrand/ (accessed 30 June 2016).

Visit Peak District & Derbyshire (2014) Peak District plays host to national film and TV makers. *News release,* 27 March. See http://mediafiles.thedms.co.uk/Publication/DS/cms/pdf/PR14_Creative_England.pdf (accessed 9 June 2016).

VisitScotland (2015) *Hooray for Bollywood!* http://mediacentre.visitscotland.org/pressre-leases/hooray-for-bollywood-1107408 (accessed 31 July 2015).

VisitWales (2016) *Welsh Food and Drink Festivals Get Boost from Welsh Assembly Government.* See http://www.traveltrade.visitwales.com/en/content/cms/news/welsh-food-drink-f/ (accessed 27 June 2016).

Voase, R. (2003) Rediscovering the imagination: Meeting the needs of the 'new' visitor. In A. Fyall, B. Garrod and A. Leask (eds) *Managing Visitor Attractions* (pp. 255–269). Oxford: Butterworth-Heinemann.

Volo, S. (2009) Conceptualizing experience: A tourist based approach. *Journal of Hospitality Marketing & Management* 18 (2–3), 111–126.

Volo, S. (2010) Bloggers' reported tourist experiences: Their utility as a tourism data source and their effect on prospective tourists. *Journal of Vacation Marketing* 16 (4), 297–311.

Wager, J. (1995) Developing a strategy for the Angkor World Heritage site. *Tourism Management* 16 (7), 515–523.

Wall, G. (1996) Terrorism and tourism: An overview of an Irish example. In A. Pizam and Y. Mansfeld (eds) *Tourism, Crime and International Security Issues* (pp. 143–158). Chichester: John Wiley.

Walsh, K. (1990) *The Post-Modern Threat to the Past.* In I. Bapty and T. Yates (eds) *Archaeology after Structuralism: Post-structuralism and the Practice of Archaeology* (pp. 278–292). London: Routledge.

Walsh-Heron, J. and Stevens, T. (1990) *The Management of Visitor Attractions and Events.* Englewood Cliffs, NJ: Prentice Hall.

Wandering Italy (2016) *Montereggio – A Book Town in Italy.* See http://www.wanderingit-aly.com/blog/article/548/montereggio-a-booktown-in-italy (accessed 30 June 2016).

Wang, C.Y. and Lin, C.H. (2010) A study of the effect of TV drama on relationships among tourists' experiential marketing, experiential value and satisfaction. *International Journal of Organizational Innovation* 2 (3), 107–123.

Wang, N. (1999) Rethinking authenticity in tourism experience. *Annals of Tourism Research* 26 (2), 349–370.

Wang, Y. (2007) Customised authenticity begins at home. *Annals of Tourism Research* 34 (3), 789–804.

Wang, Y.-J., Wu, C. and Yuan, J. (2010) Exploring visitors' experiences and intention to revisit a heritage destination: The case for Lukang, Taiwan. *Journal of Quality Assurance in Hospitality and Tourism* 11 (3), 162–178.

Warwickshire Tourism (2012) Appendix I. Warwickshire Visitor Economies Framework 2013–2018. *Warwickshire Tourism Policy Framework (May 2015).* See www.team-tour-ism.com (accessed May 2016).

Watson, N.J. (2006) *The Literary Tourist.* Basingstoke: Belgrave Macmillan.

Weinberger, M. (2015) This company was 13 years early to virtual reality – and it's getting ready to try again. *Business Insider,* 29 March. See http://uk.businessinsider.com/second-life-is-still-around-and-getting-ready-to-conquer-virtual-reality-2015-3?r=US&IR=T (accessed 12 October 2015).

Wight, P.A. (1998) Tools for sustainability analysis in planning and managing tourism and recreation in the destination. In C.M. Halland and A.A. Lew (eds) *Sustainable Tourism: A Geographic Perspective* (pp. 75–91). Harlow: Addison Wesley Longman.

Wigtown Festival Company (2016) *Wigtown: Scotland's National Book Town.* See http://www.wigtown-booktown.co.uk/ (accessed 27 June 2016).

Williams, A. (2006) Tourism and hospitality marketing: Fantasy, feeling and fun. *International Journal of Contemporary Hospitality Management* 18 (6), 482–495.

Wobst, H.M. (2010) Diaspora and heritage: A perennial source of conflict. *Museum International* 62 (1–2), 100–103.

Woodside, A.G. and Lysonski, S. (1989) A general mode of traveller destination choice. *Journal of Travel Research* 27 (2), 8–14.

Woodside, J.A., Cruickshank, F.B. and Dehuang, N. (2007) Stories visitors tell about Italian cities as destination icons. *Tourism Management* 28 (1), 162–174.

World Heritage Centre (2015a) *World Heritage List.* See http://whc.unesco.org/en/list/&order=year (accessed 22 July 2015).

World Heritage Centre (2015b) *World Heritage.* See http://whc.unesco.org/en/about/ (accessed 22 July 2015).

Wreyford, P. (1996) *A Literacy Tour of Devon.* Chudleigh: Orchard Publications.

Wright, P. (1985) *On Living in an Old Country: The National Past in Contemporary Britain.* Oxford: Oxford University Press.

WYSE Travel Confederation (2015) *Millennial Traveller Report.* Amsterdam: World Youth Student and Education Travel Confederation.

Xiang, Z. and Gretzel, U. (2010) Role of social media in online travel information search. *Tourism Management* 31 (2), 179–188.

Xie, C., Bagozzi, R.P. and Troye, S.V. (2008) Trying to prosume: Toward a theory of consumers as co-creators of value. *Journal of the Academy of Marketing Science* 36, 109–122.

Yale, P. (1991) *From Tourist Attractions to Heritage Tourism.* Huntingdon: Elm Publications.

Yan, G., So, S.-I., Morrison, A. and Sun, Y.-H. (2007) Activity segmentation of the international heritage tourism market to Taiwan. *Asia Pacific Journal of Tourism Research* 12 (4), 333–347.

Yan, W. (2006) A comparative study of the management pattern between World Heritage sites and protected areas. *Urban Problem* 79–81.

Yang, C.-H., Lin, H.-L. and Han, C.-C. (2010) Analysis of international tourist arrivals in China: The role of World Heritage sites. *Tourism Management* 31, 827–837.

Yankholmes, A. and McKercher, B. (2015) Understanding visitors to slavery heritage sites in Ghana. *Tourism Management* 51, 22–32.

Yau, M.K.-S., McKercher, B. and Packer, T. (2004) Travelling with a disability: More than an access issue. *Annals of Tourism Research* 31 (4), 946–960.

Yeoman, I. and Drummond, S. (2001) *Quality Issues in Heritage Visitor Attractions.* Oxford: Butterworth-Heinemann.

Yost, J. (2014) *Building a Heritage Tourism Strategy to Increase Economic Vitality in Red Cloud.* See www.willacather.org/sites/default/files/files/5/2014_heritage_tourism_study_summary_for_red_cloud_may_2014.pdf (accessed 20 June 2016).

Young, A. and Young, R. (2008) Measuring the effects of film and television on tourism to screen locations: A theoretical and empirical perspective. *Journal of Travel and Tourism Marketing* 24 (2–3), 195–212.

Young, M. (1999) The social construction of tourist places. *Australian Geographer* 30, 373–389.

Yue, A. (2009) Film-induced domestic tourism in Singapore: The case of Krrish. In S. Singh (ed.) *Domestic Tourism in Asia: Diversity and Divergence.* London: Earthscan.

Žabkar, V., Brenčič, M. and Dmitrović, T. (2010) Modelling perceived quality, visitor satisfaction and behavioural intentions at the destination level. *Tourism Management* 31 (4), 537–546.

Zhang, Q. (2003) A study of tourism development and protection of World Heritage sites in China. *Human Social Science* 1, 182–183.

Zhang, Y. and Kong, L.D. (2006) The protection of China's world cultural heritage and tourism development: A case study of the Mogao Caves. *Thinking* 2 (32), 123–128.

Zhu, J.A. (2004) Market process and regulating: A possible approach to reform the existing World Heritage management system. *China Soft Science* 12–17.

Index